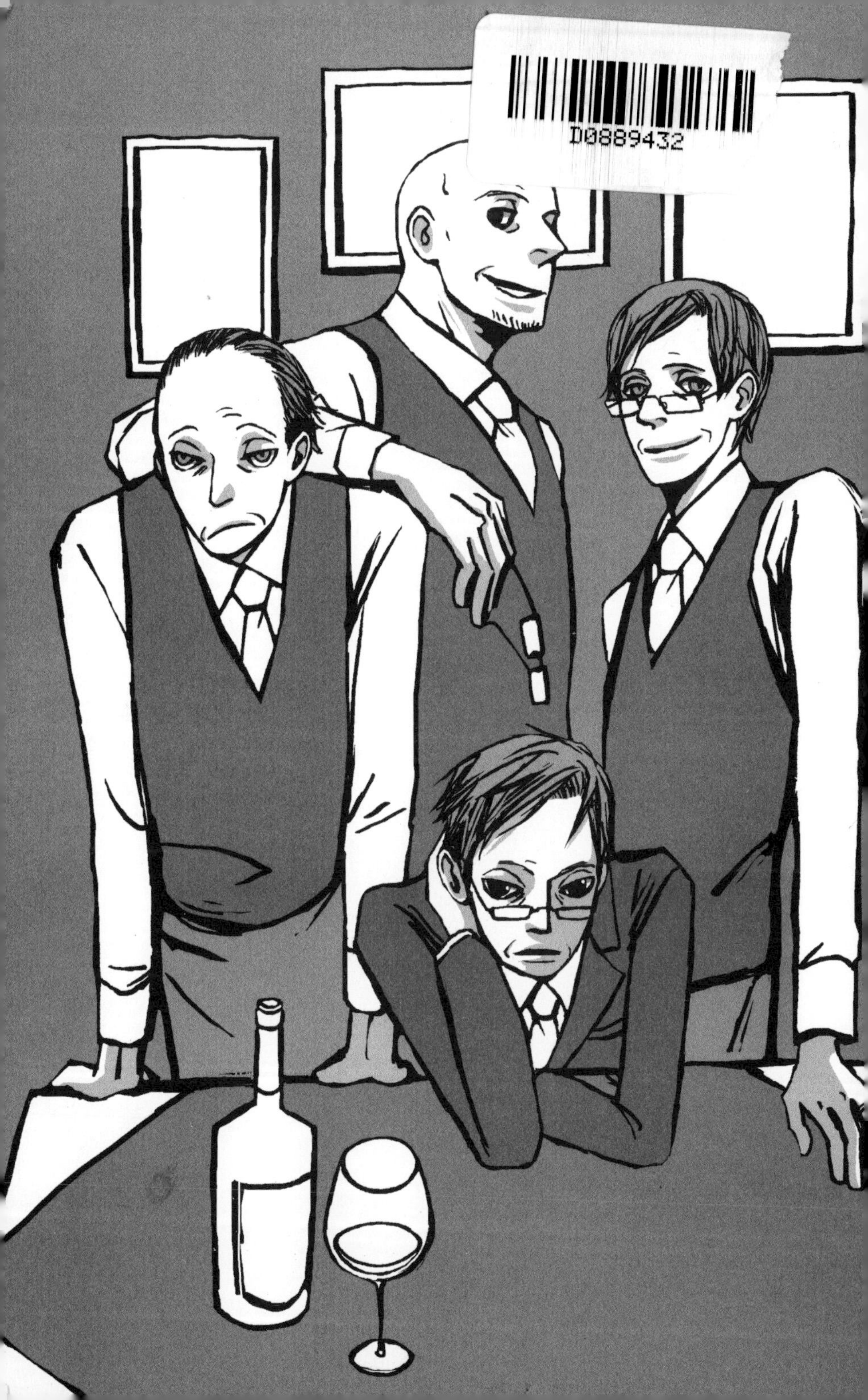

THE CHARACTERS

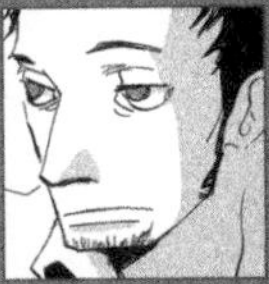

Teo

· CHEF ·

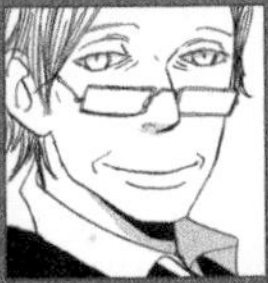

Claudio

· CAPO CAMERIERE ·

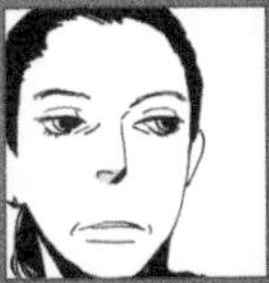

Vanna

· CHEF ·

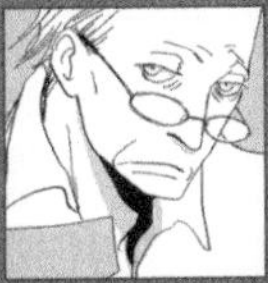

Luciano

· CAMERIERE ·

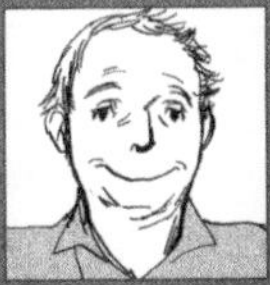

Marzio

· KITCHEN STAFF ·

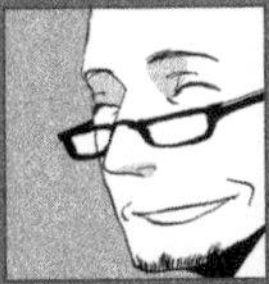

Vito

· CAMERIERE ·

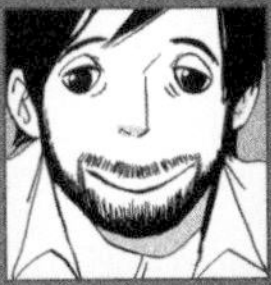

Lorenzo

· OWNER ·

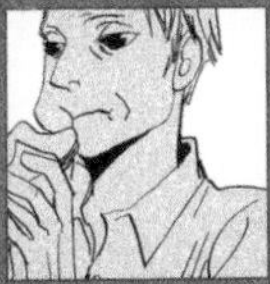

Gigi

· SOMMELIER ·

GENTE

THE PEOPLE OF RISTORANTE PARADISO

①

Natsume Ono

THE CONTENTS

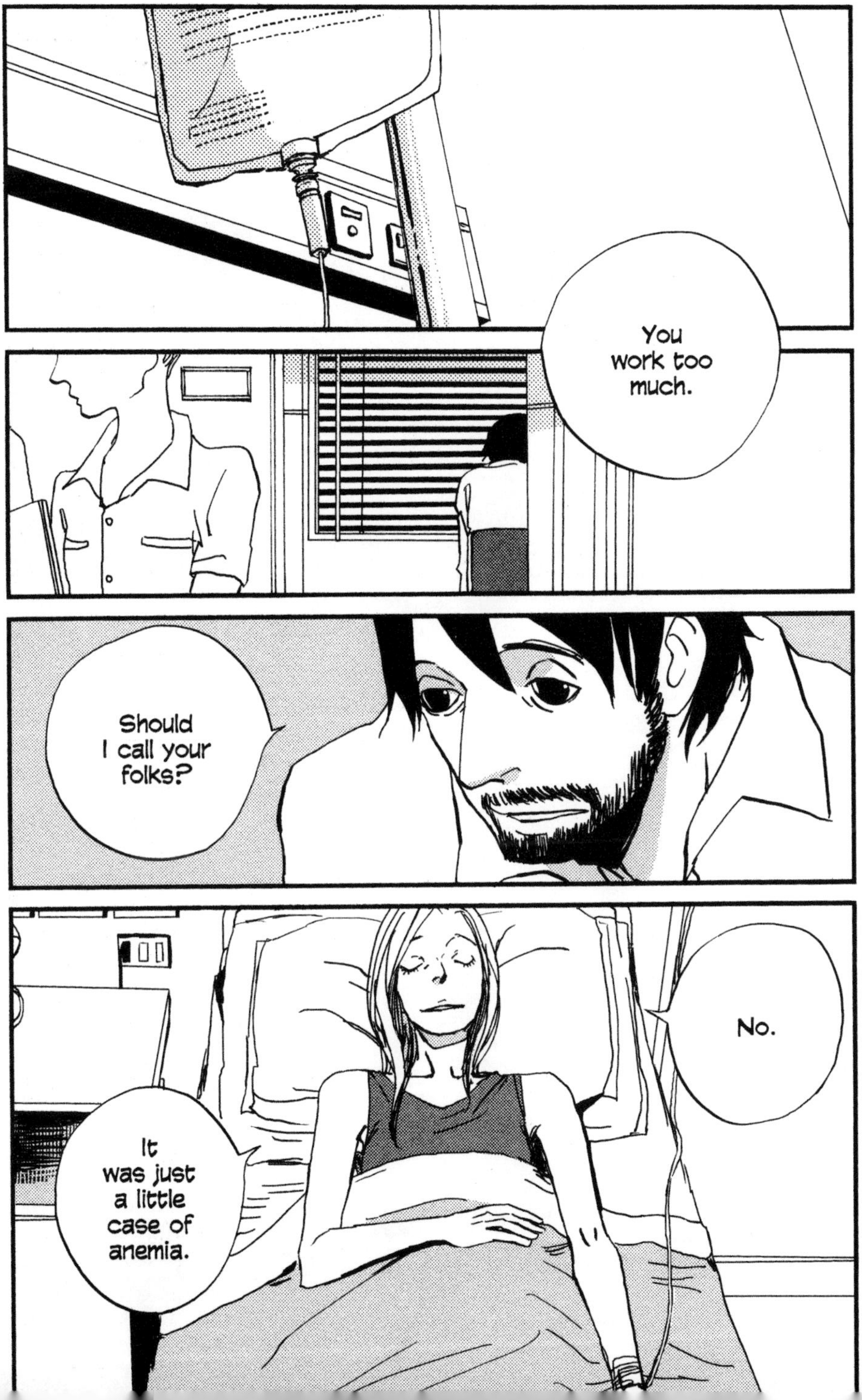

You work too much.
Should I call your folks?
No.
It was just a little case of anemia.

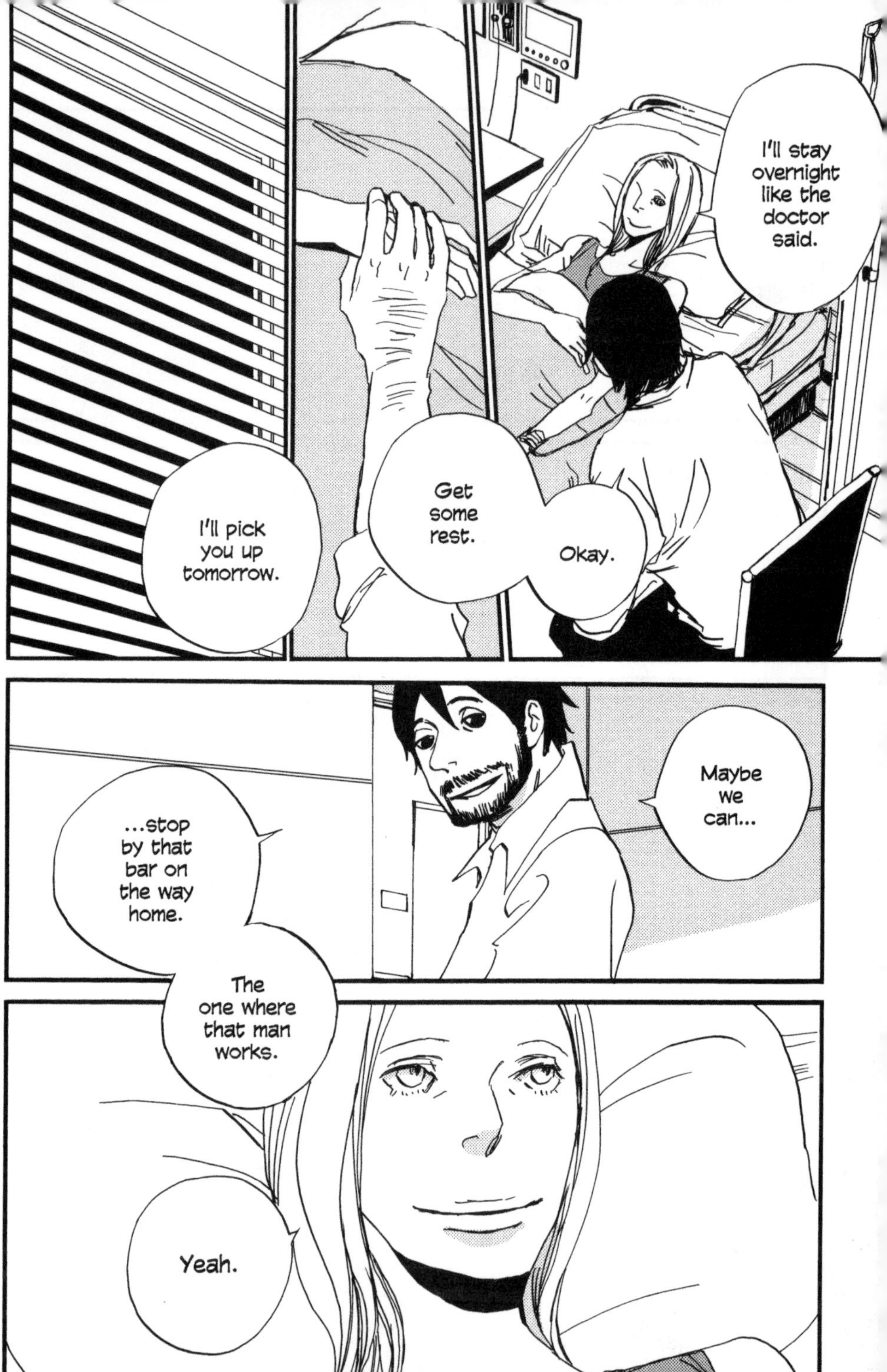
I'll stay overnight like the doctor said.
Get some rest.
Okay.
I'll pick you up tomorrow.
Maybe we can...
...stop by that bar on the way home.
The one where that man works.
Yeah.

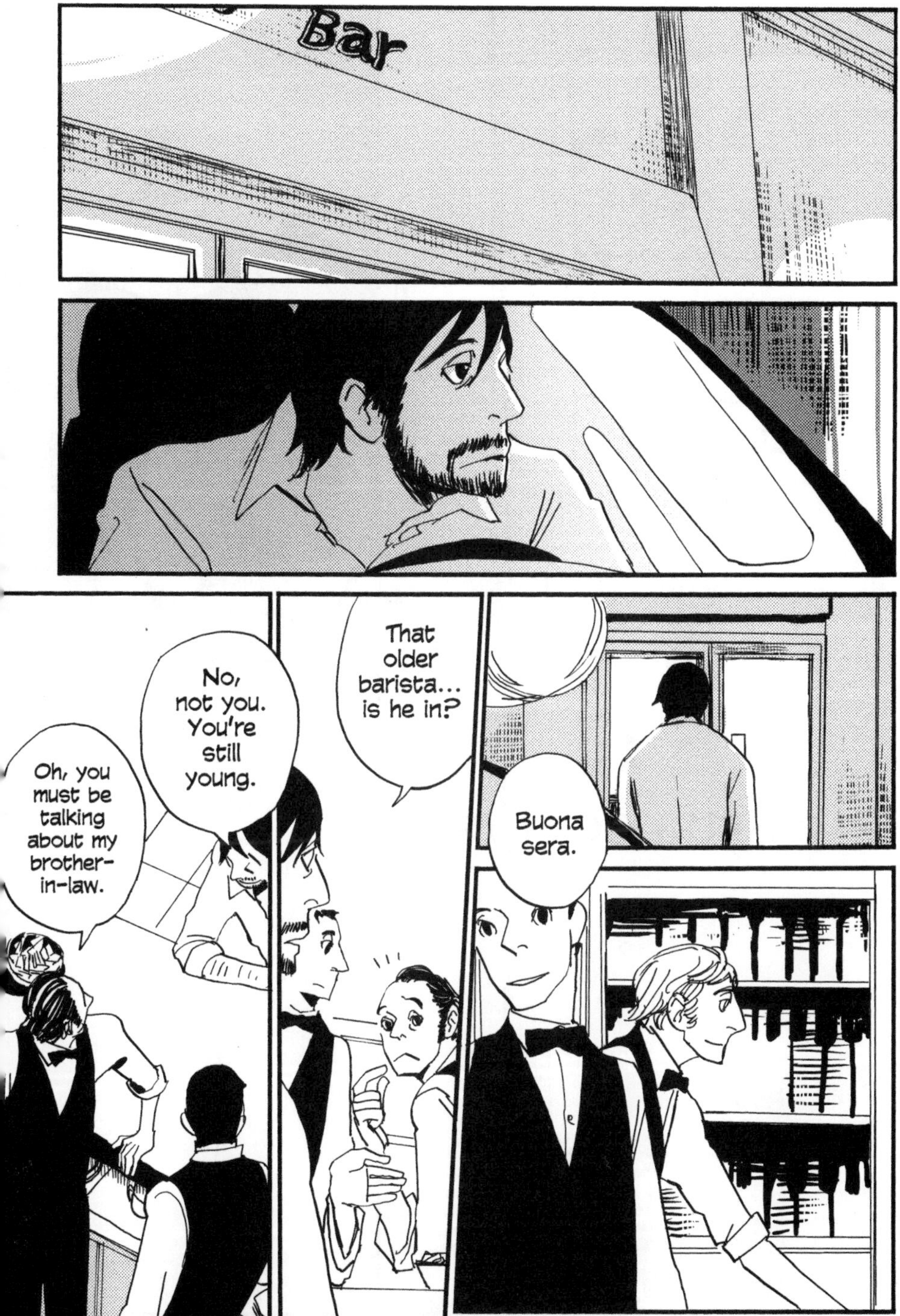
Bar
Buona sera.
That older barista... is he in?
No, not you. You're still young.
Oh, you must be talking about my brother-in-law.

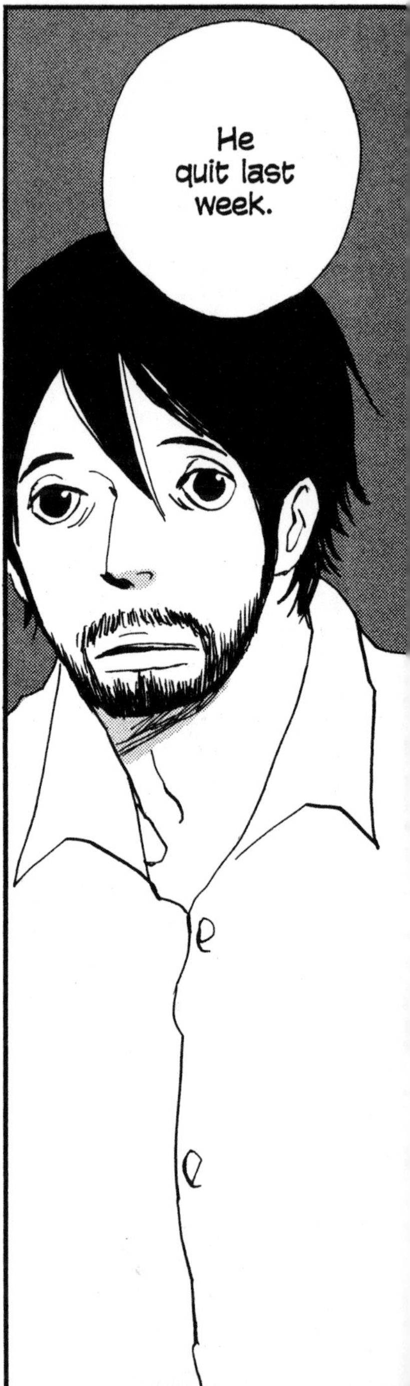
He quit last week.

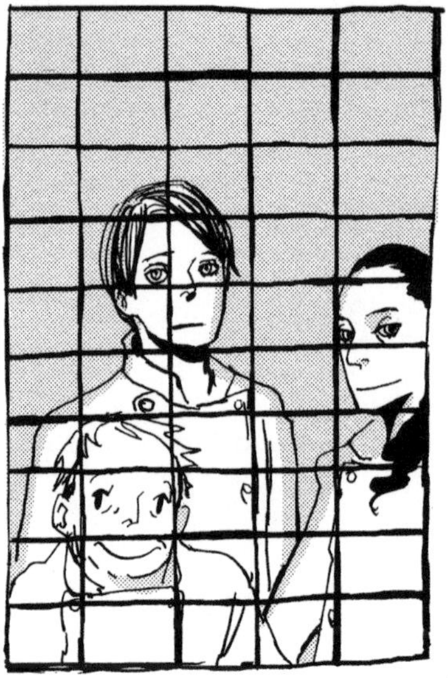

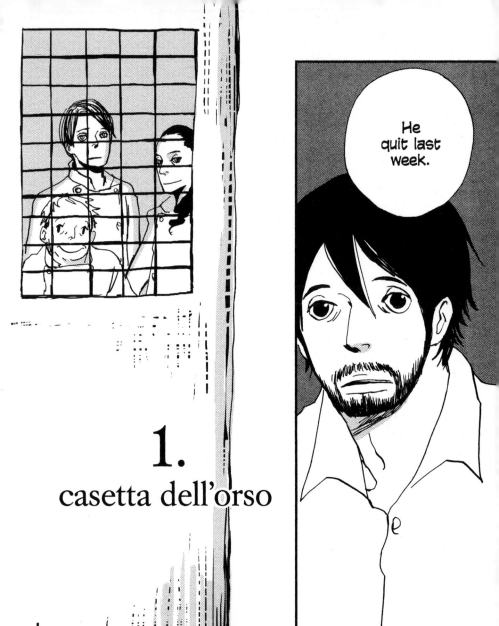

1.
casetta dell'orso

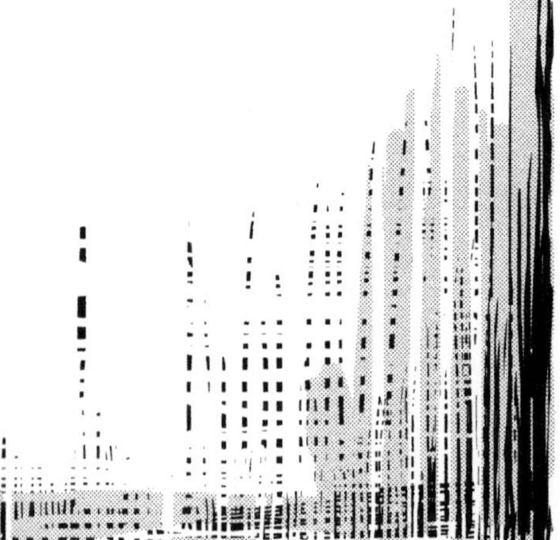

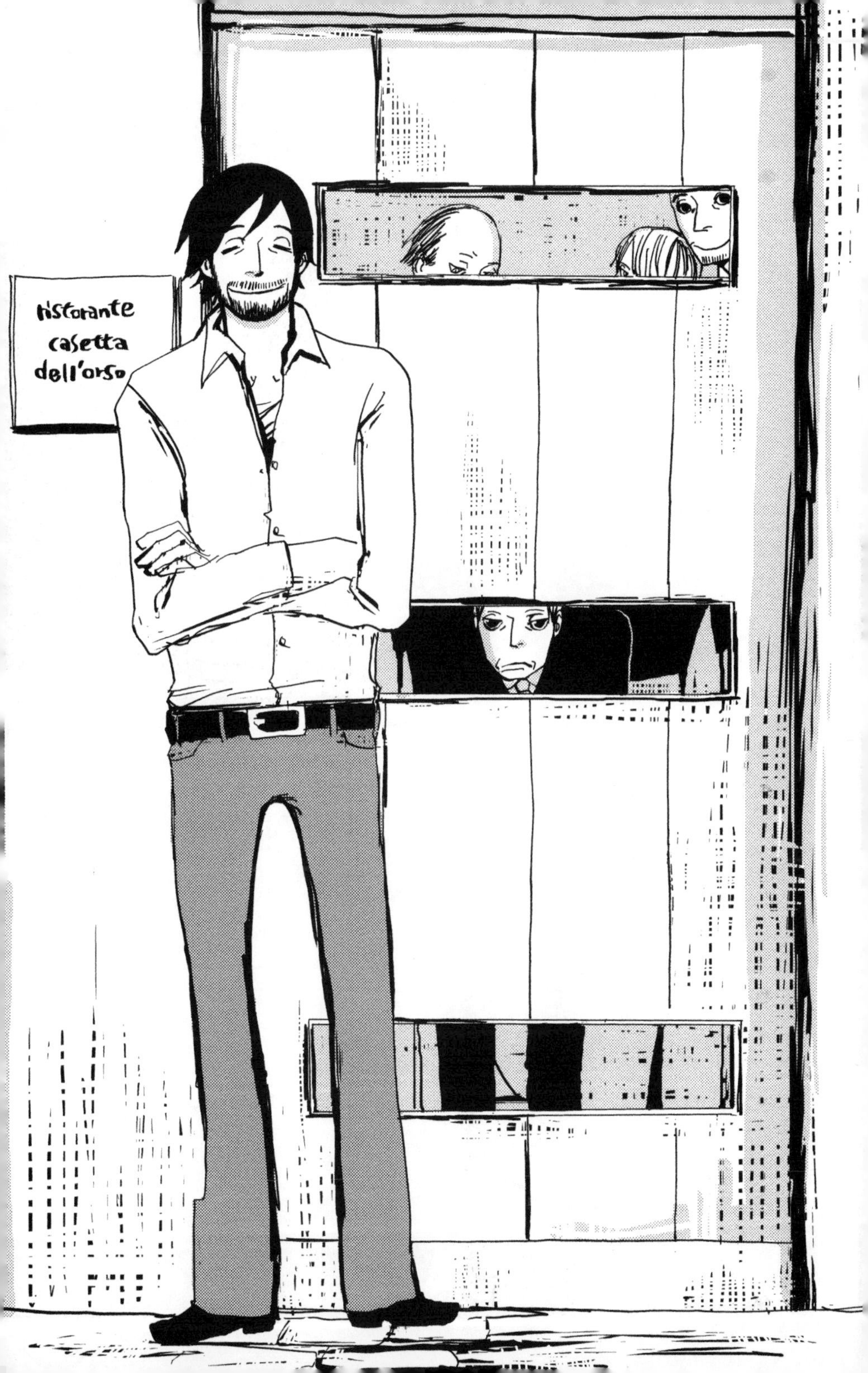
ristorante casetta dell'orso

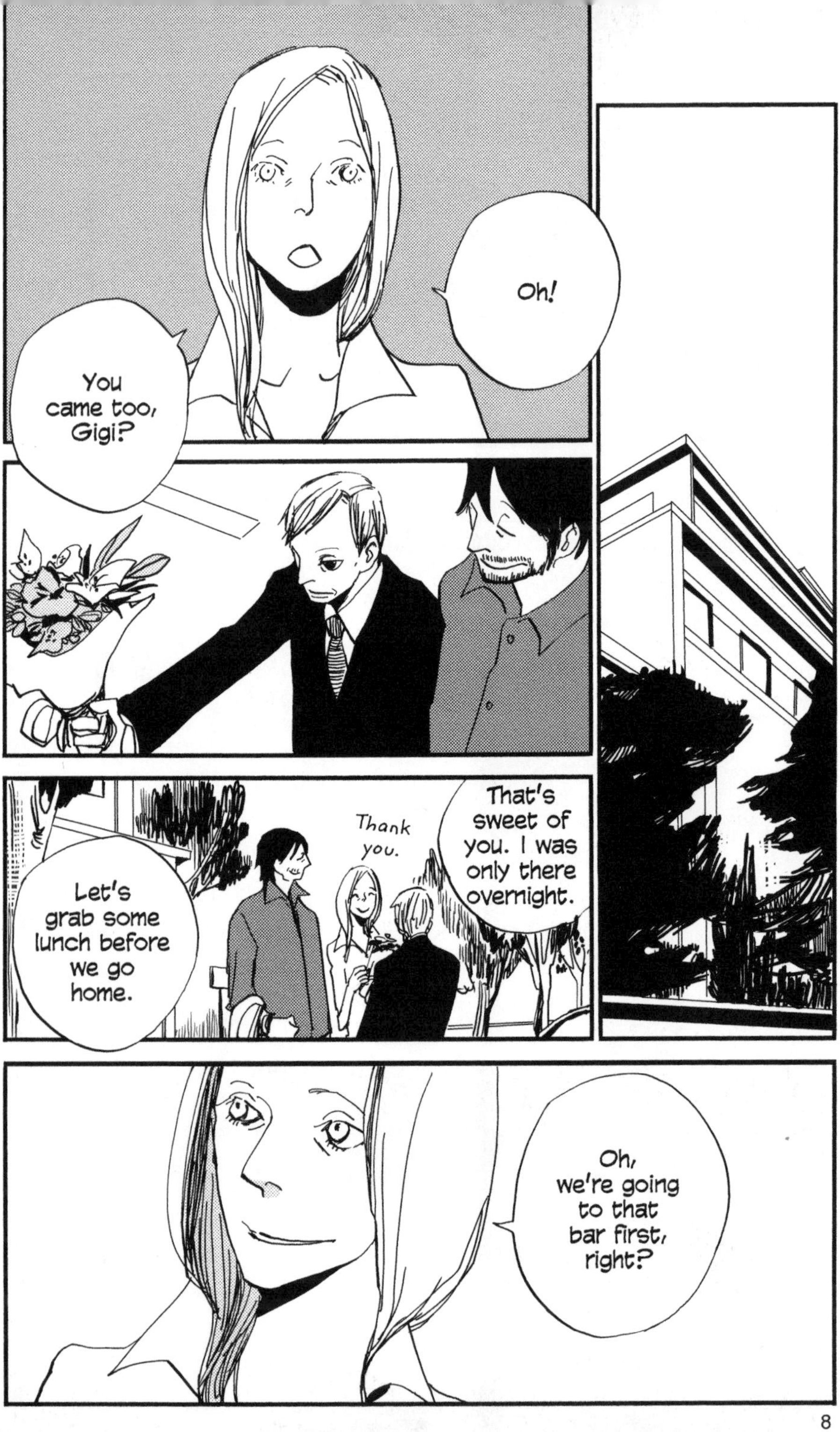
Oh!
You came too, Gigi?
That's sweet of you. I was only there overnight.
Thank you.
Let's grab some lunch before we go home.
Oh, we're going to that bar first, right?

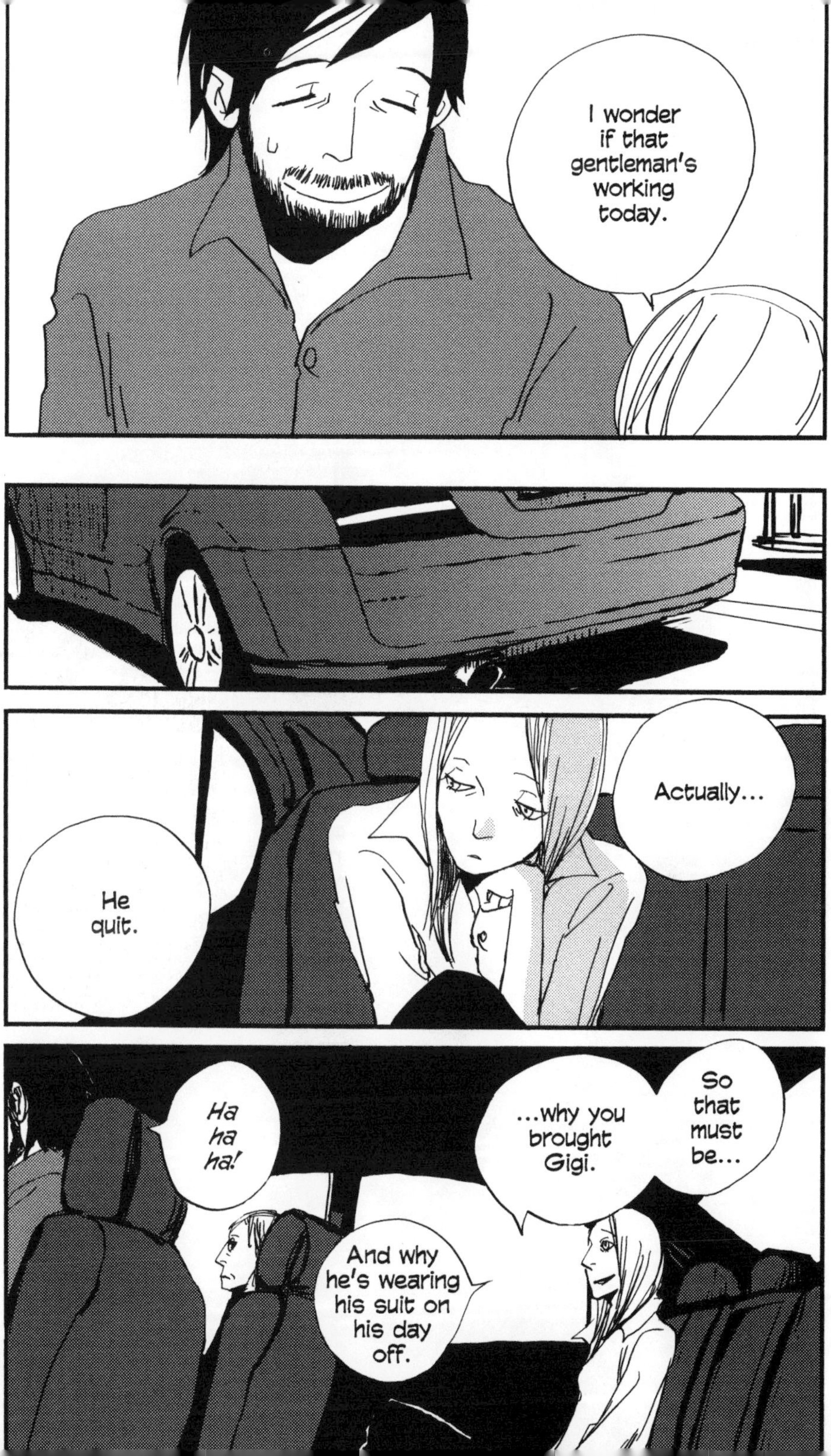
I wonder if that gentleman's working today.
Actually...
He quit.
So that must be...
...why you brought Gigi.
And why he's wearing his suit on his day off.
Ha ha ha!

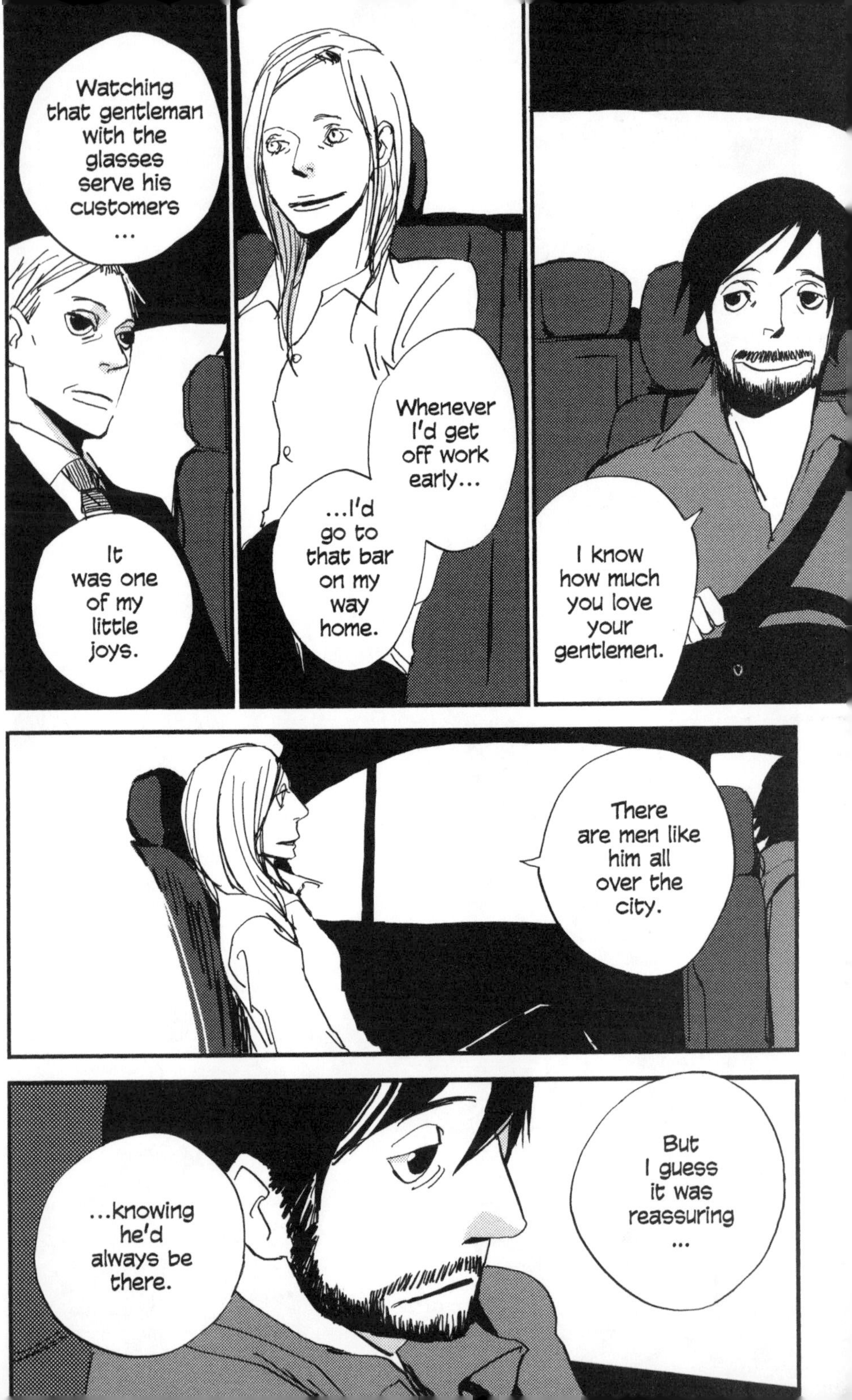
I know how much you love your gentlemen.
Whenever I'd get off work early...
...I'd go to that bar on my way home.
Watching that gentleman with the glasses serve his customers ...
It was one of my little joys.
There are men like him all over the city.
But I guess it was reassuring ...
...knowing he'd always be there.

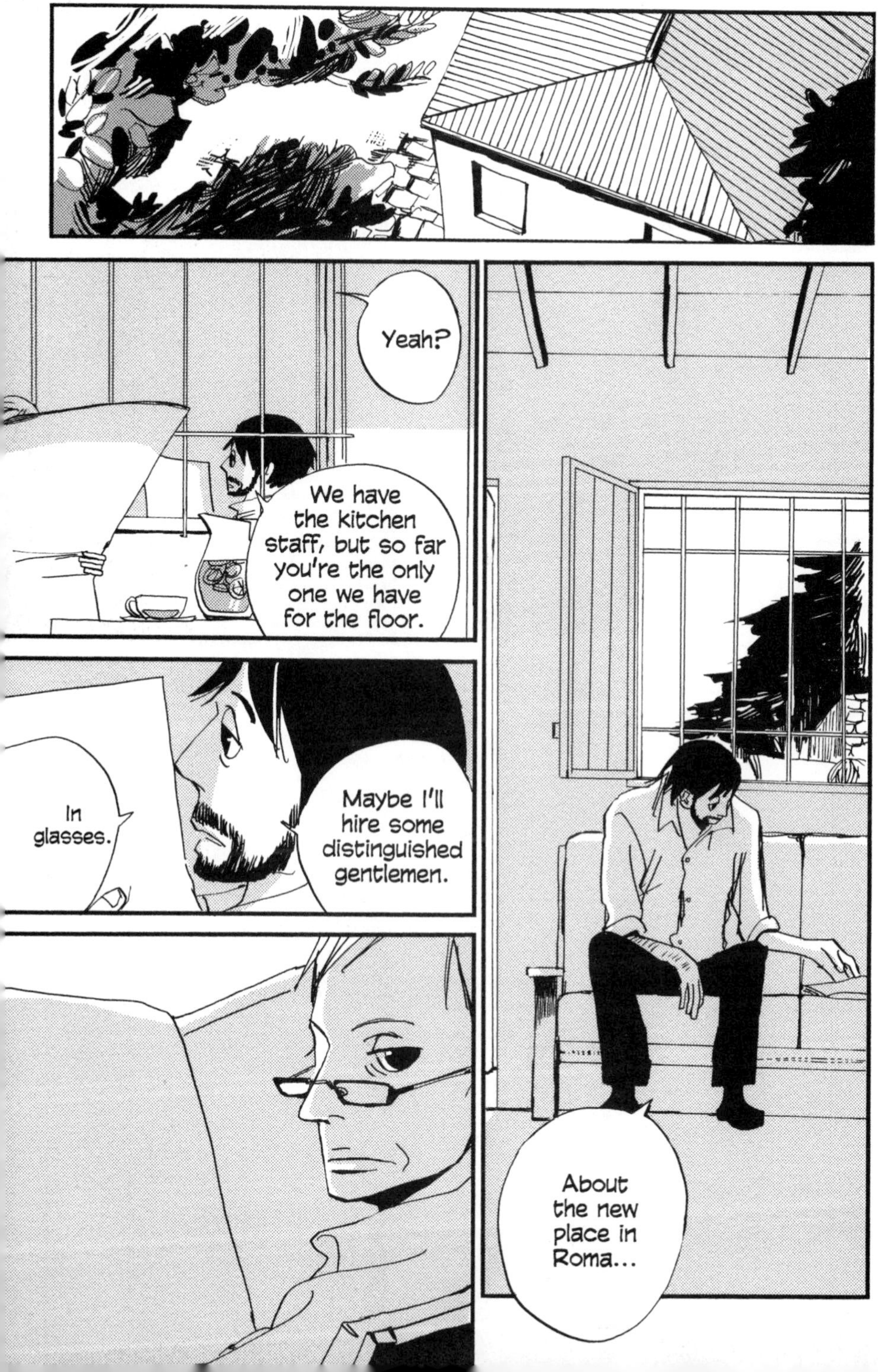
About the new place in Roma...
Yeah?
We have the kitchen staff, but so far you're the only one we have for the floor.
Maybe I'll hire some distinguished gentlemen.
In glasses.

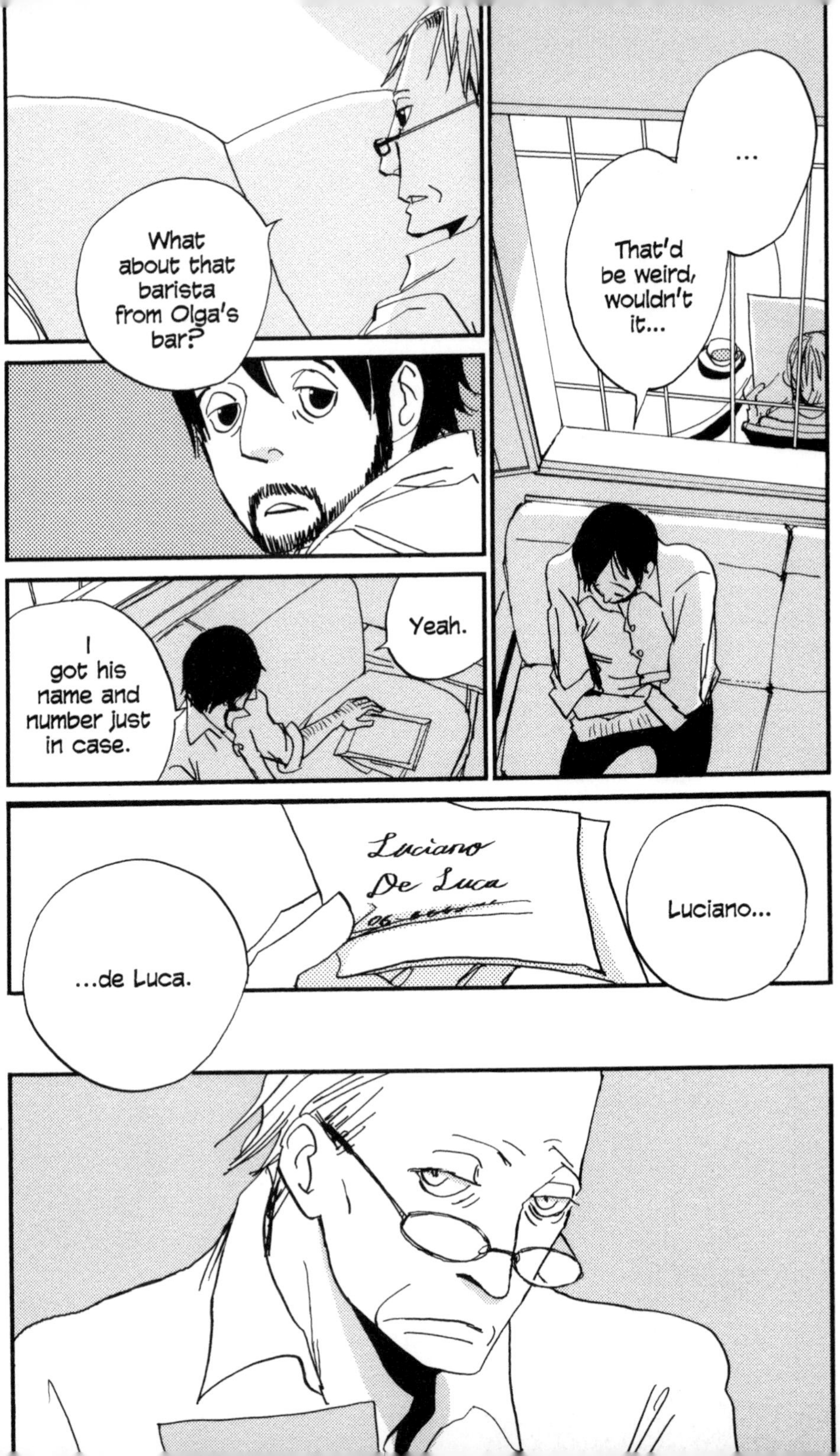
...
That'd be weird, wouldn't it...
What about that barista from Olga's bar?
Yeah.
I got his name and number just in case.
Luciano...
Luciano De Luca
...de Luca.

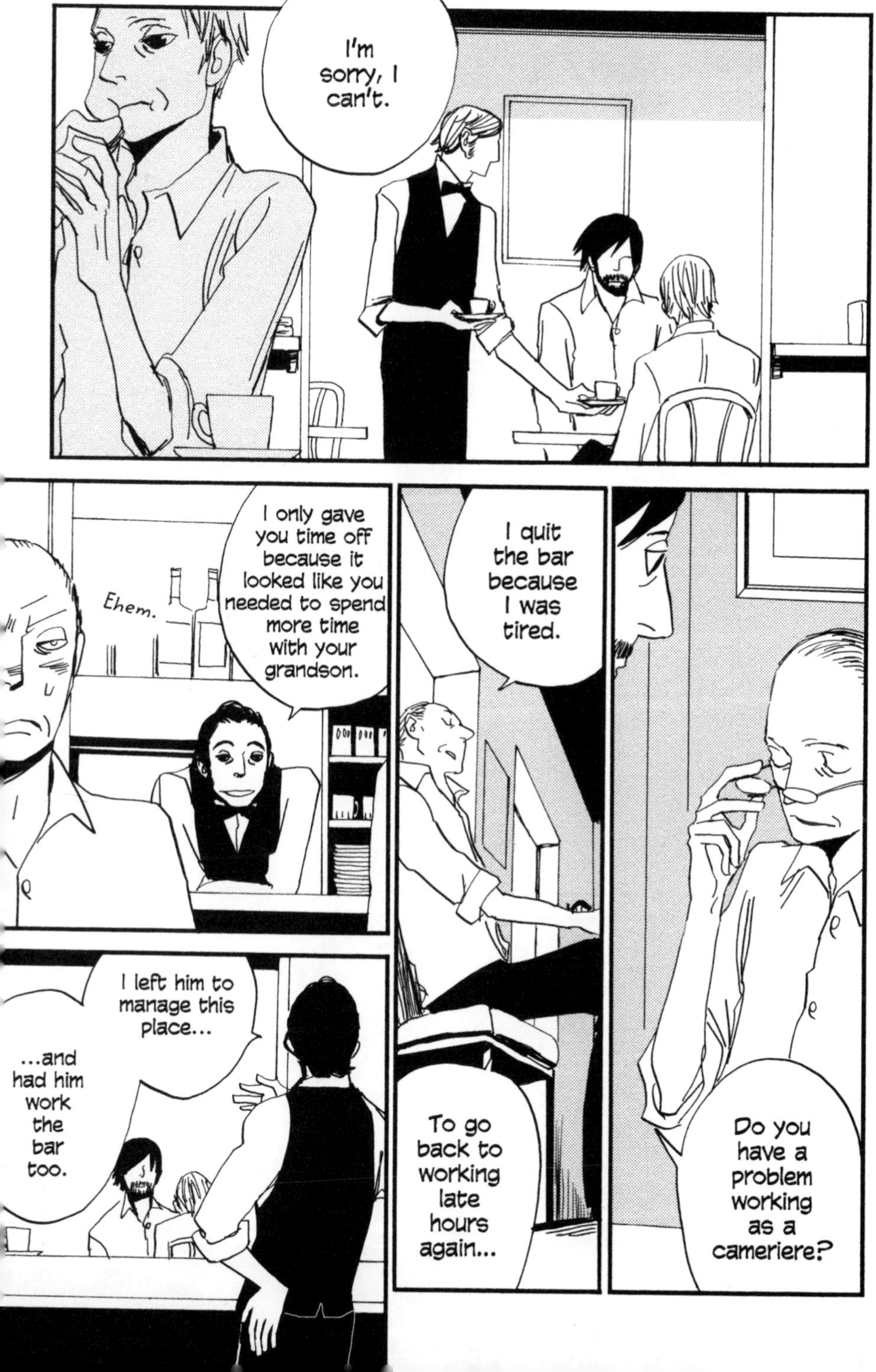

I'm sorry, I can't.
Do you have a problem working as a cameriere?
I quit the bar because I was tired.
To go back to working late hours again...
I only gave you time off because it looked like you needed to spend more time with your grandson.
Ehem.
I left him to manage this place...
...and had him work the bar too.

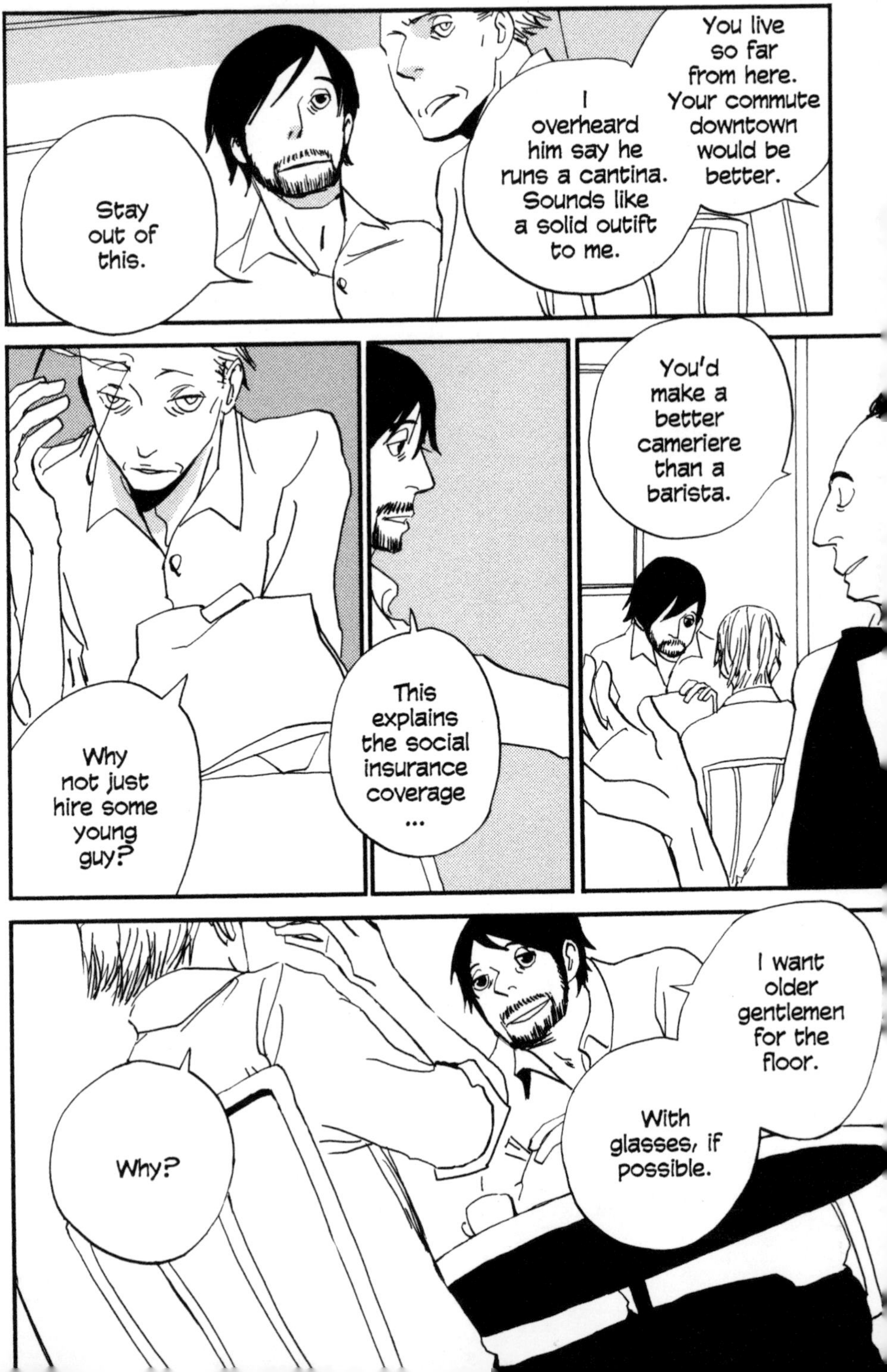
You live so far from here. Your commute downtown would be better.
I overheard him say he runs a cantina. Sounds like a solid outift to me.
Stay out of this.
You'd make a better cameriere than a barista.
This explains the social insurance coverage ...
Why not just hire some young guy?
I want older gentlemen for the floor.
With glasses, if possible.
Why?

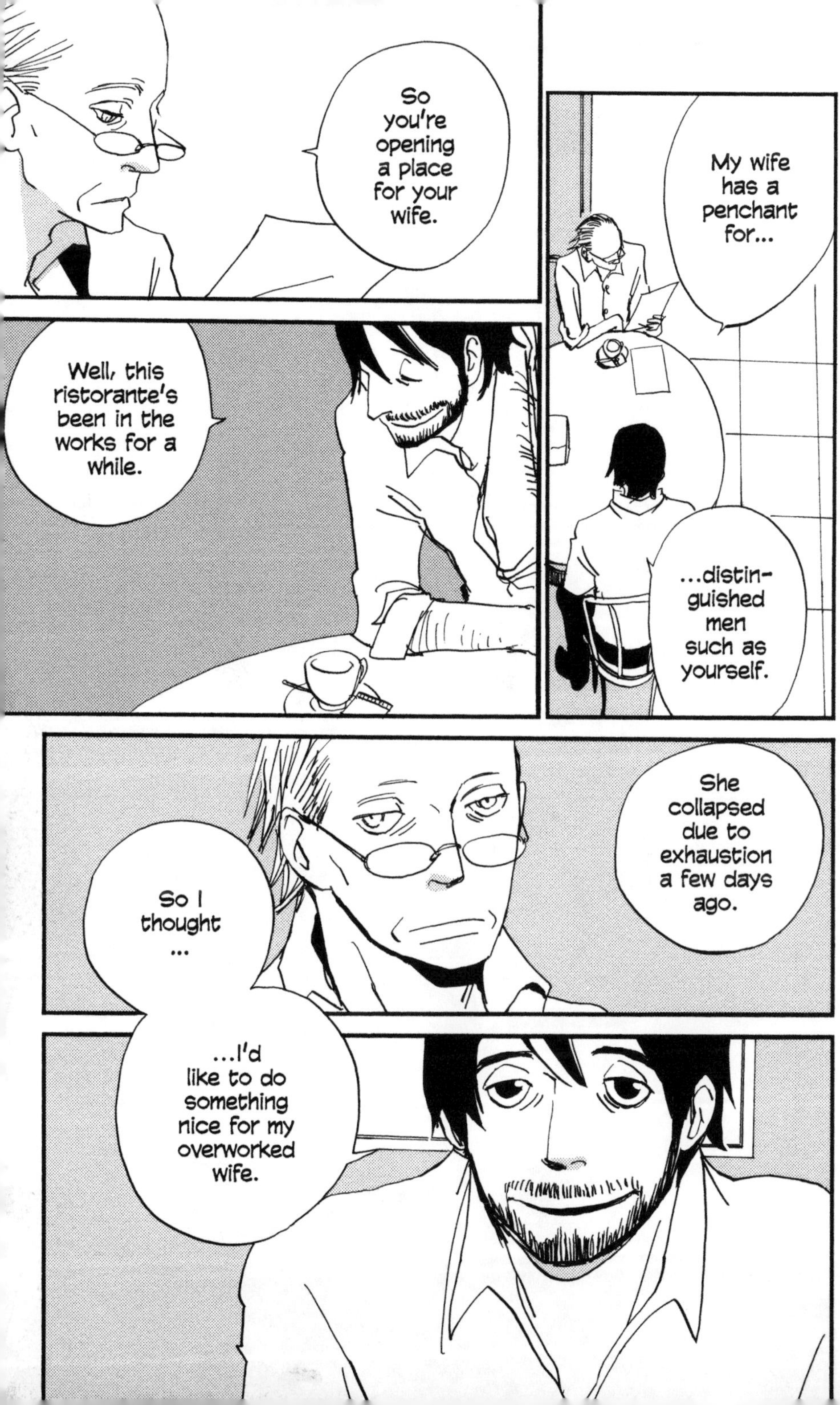
My wife has a penchant for...
...distin-guished men such as yourself.
So you're opening a place for your wife.
Well, this ristorante's been in the works for a while.
She collapsed due to exhaustion a few days ago.
So I thought...
...I'd like to do something nice for my overworked wife.

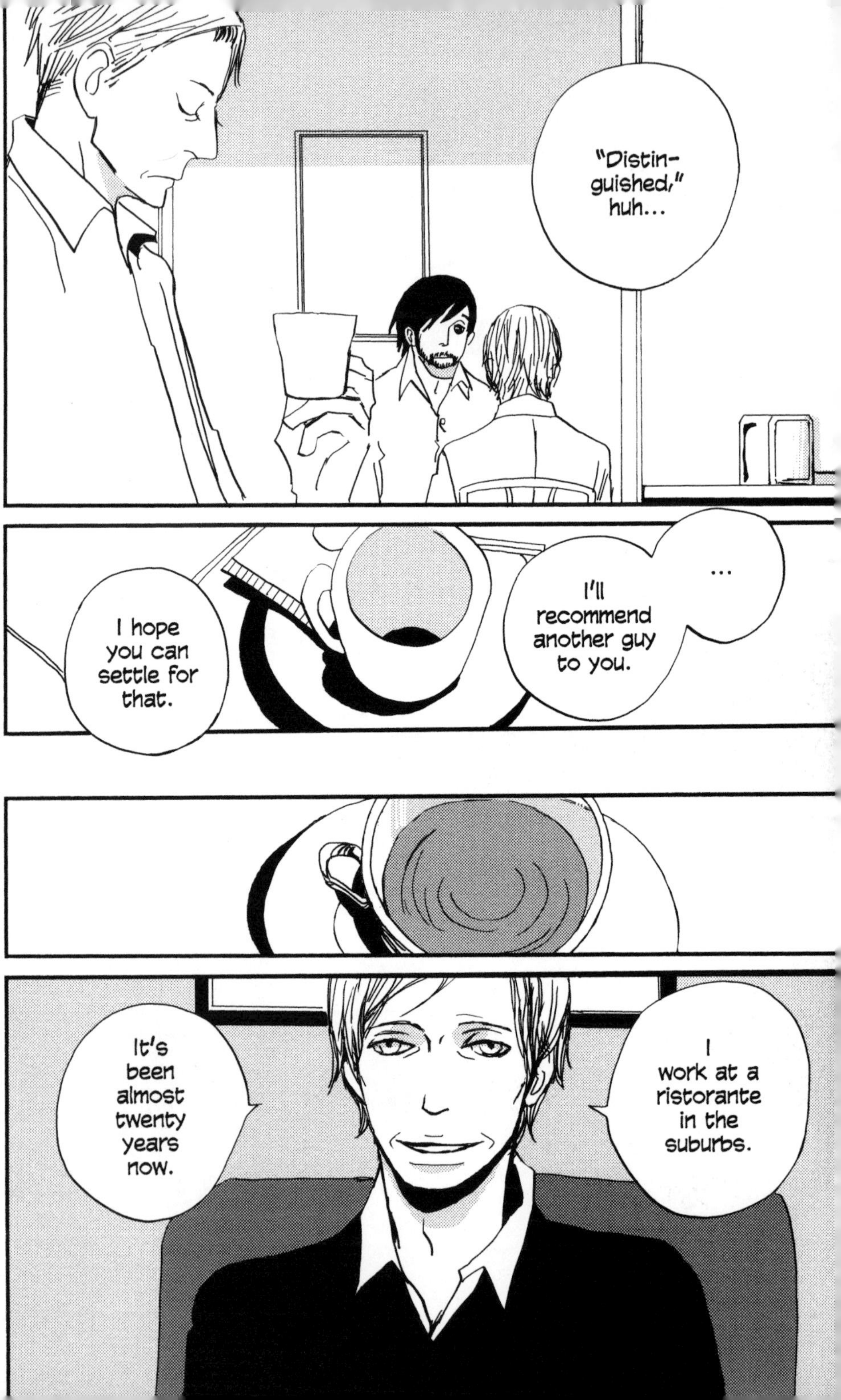
"Distin-guished," huh...
...
I'll recommend another guy to you.
I hope you can settle for that.
I work at a ristorante in the suburbs.
It's been almost twenty years now.

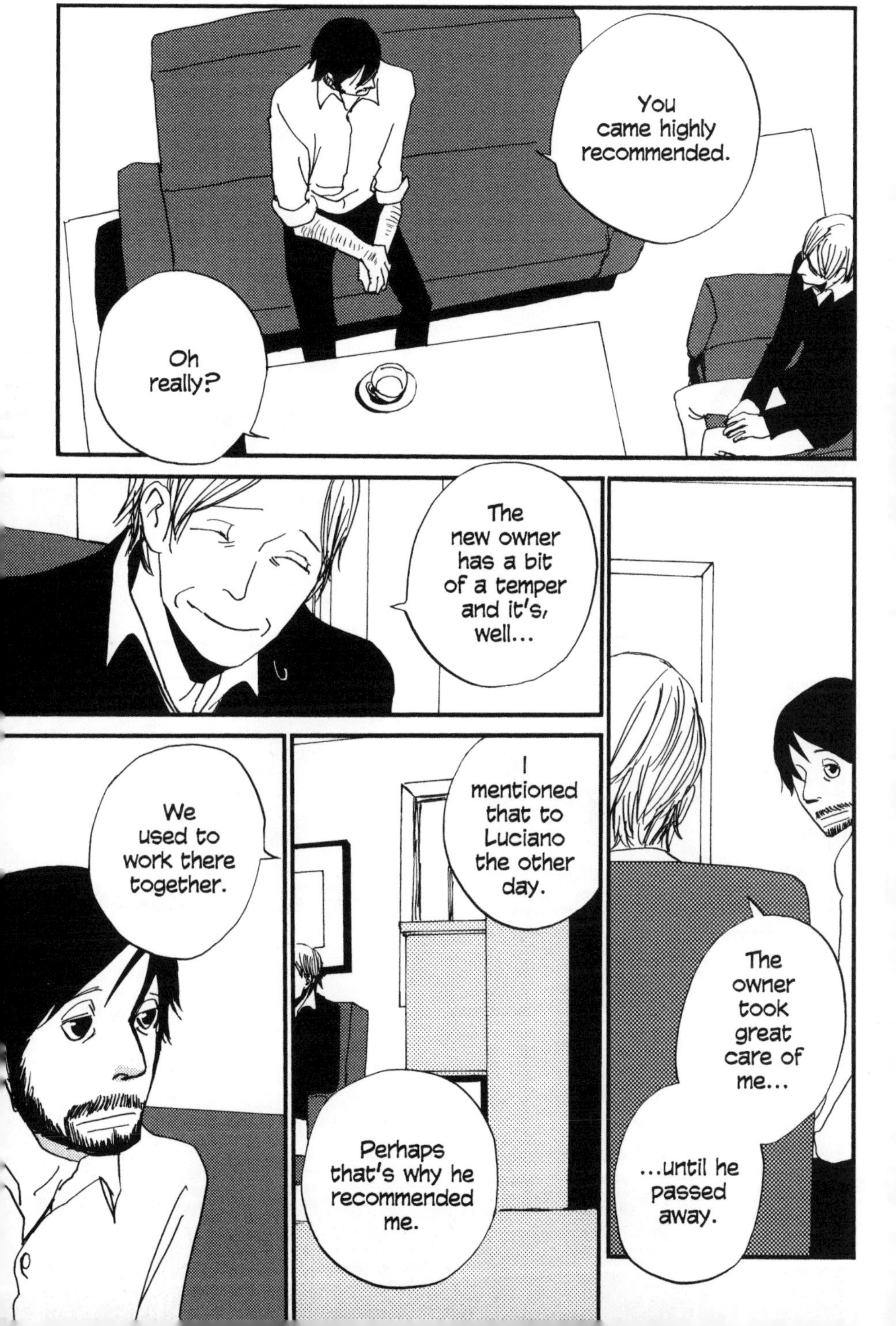
You came highly recommended.
Oh really?
The owner took great care of me...
...until he passed away.
The new owner has a bit of a temper and it's, well...
I mentioned that to Luciano the other day.
Perhaps that's why he recommended me.
We used to work there together.

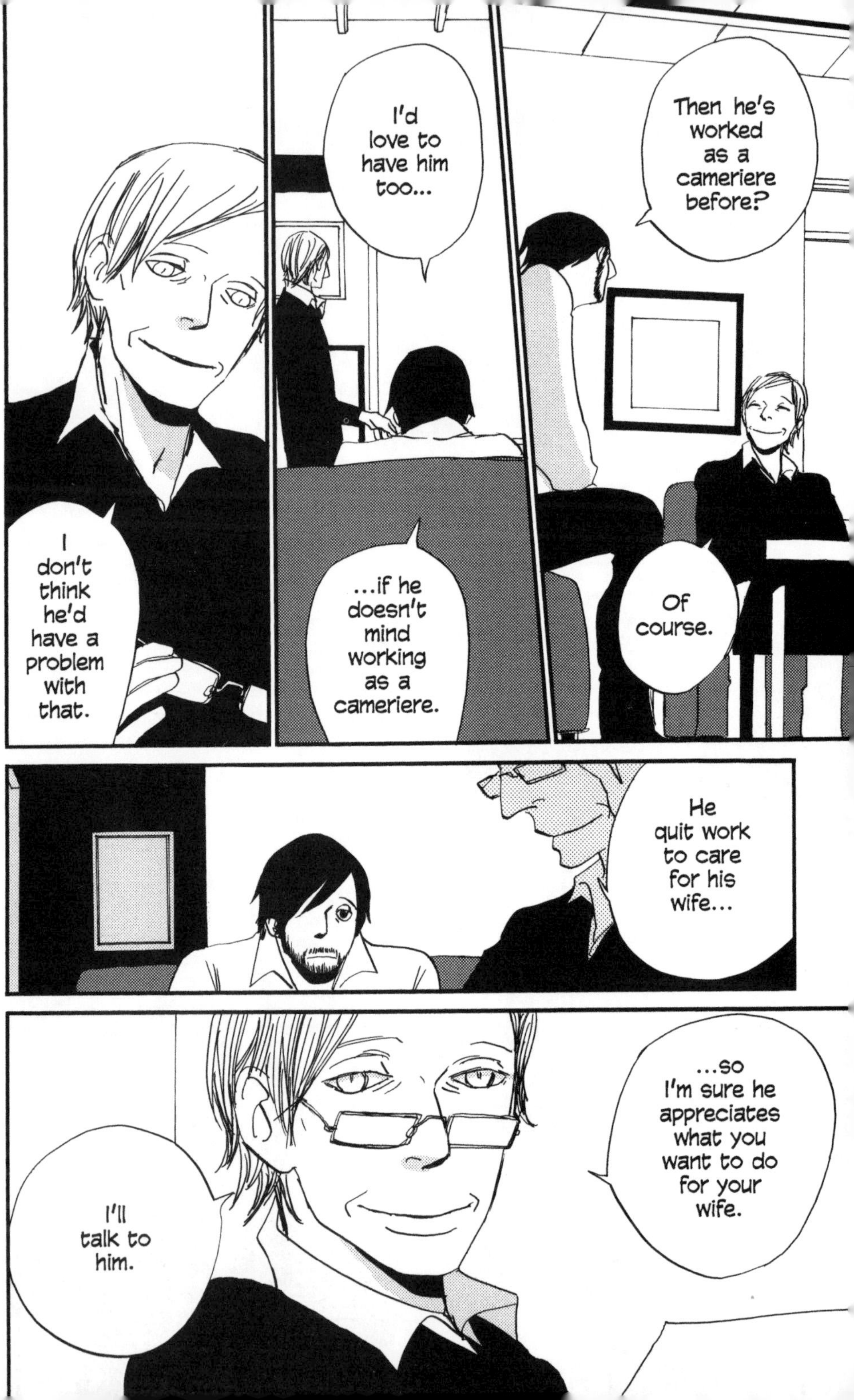
Then he's worked as a cameriere before?
Of course.
I'd love to have him too...
...if he doesn't mind working as a cameriere.
I don't think he'd have a problem with that.
He quit work to care for his wife...
...so I'm sure he appreciates what you want to do for your wife.
I'll talk to him.

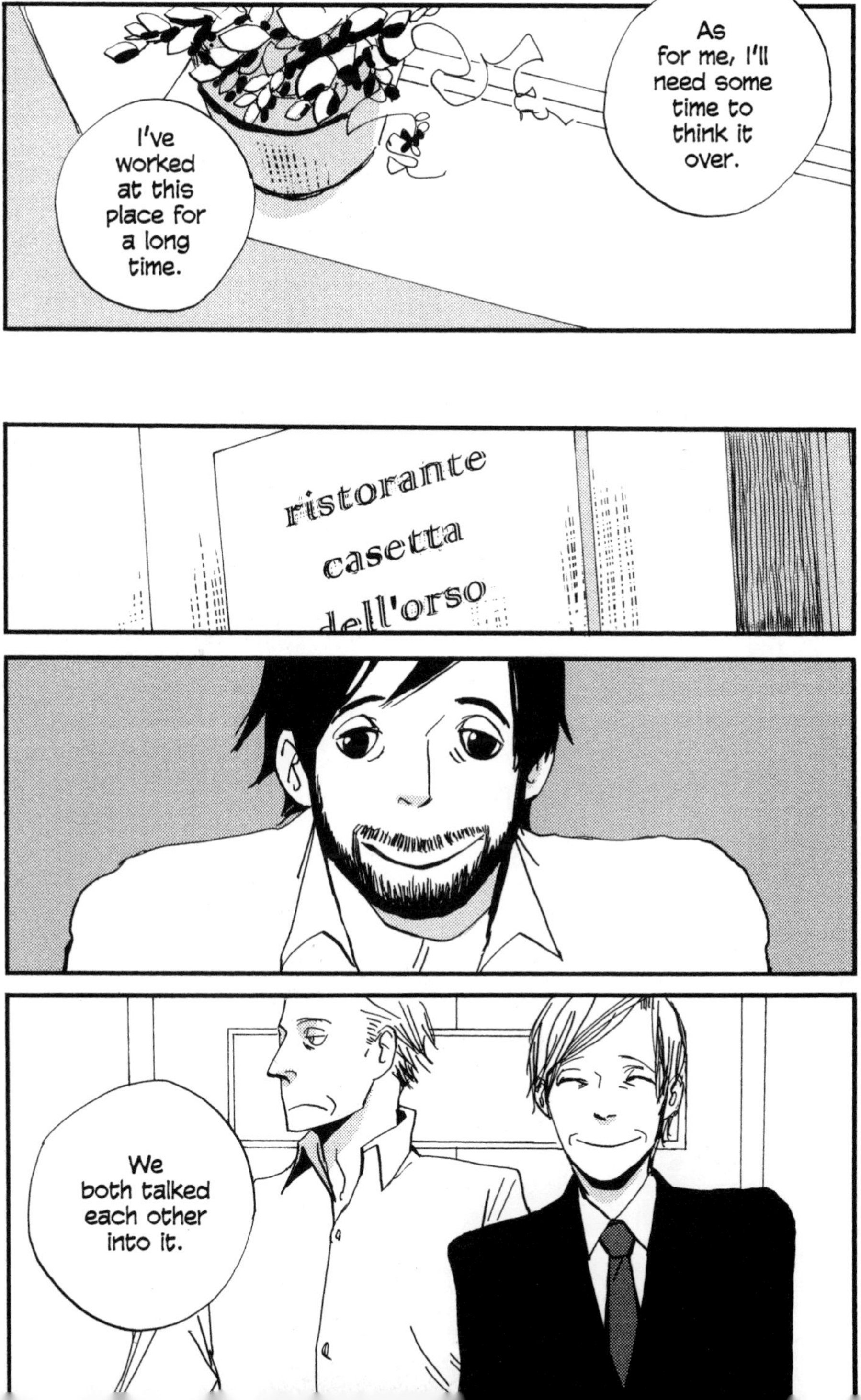
As for me, I'll need some time to think it over.
I've worked at this place for a long time.
ristorante casetta dell'orso
We both talked each other into it.

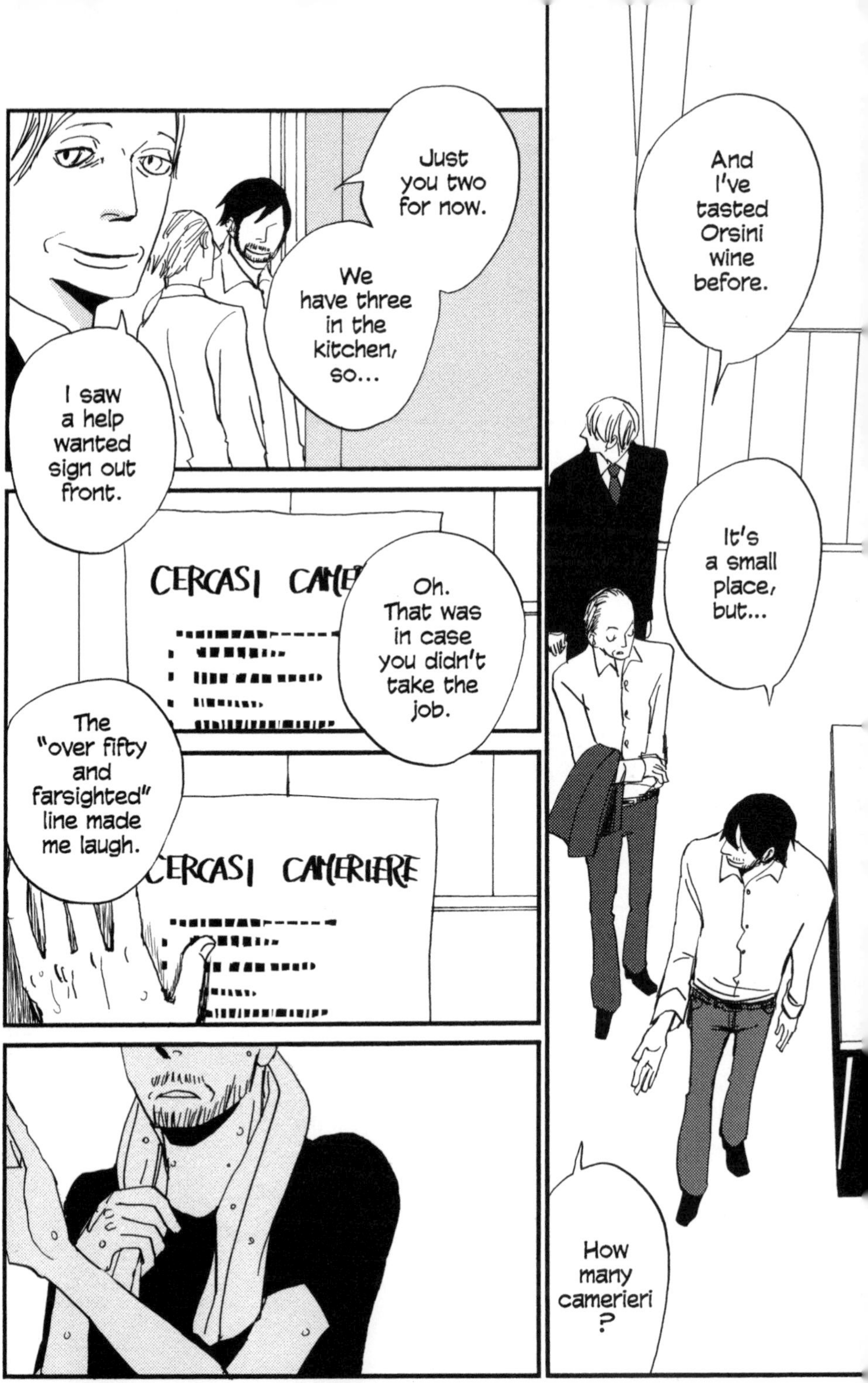
And I've tasted Orsini wine before.
It's a small place, but...
How many camerieri?
Just you two for now.
We have three in the kitchen, so...
I saw a help wanted sign out front.
CERCASI CAME
Oh. That was in case you didn't take the job.
The "over fifty and farsighted" line made me laugh.
CERCASI CAMERIERE

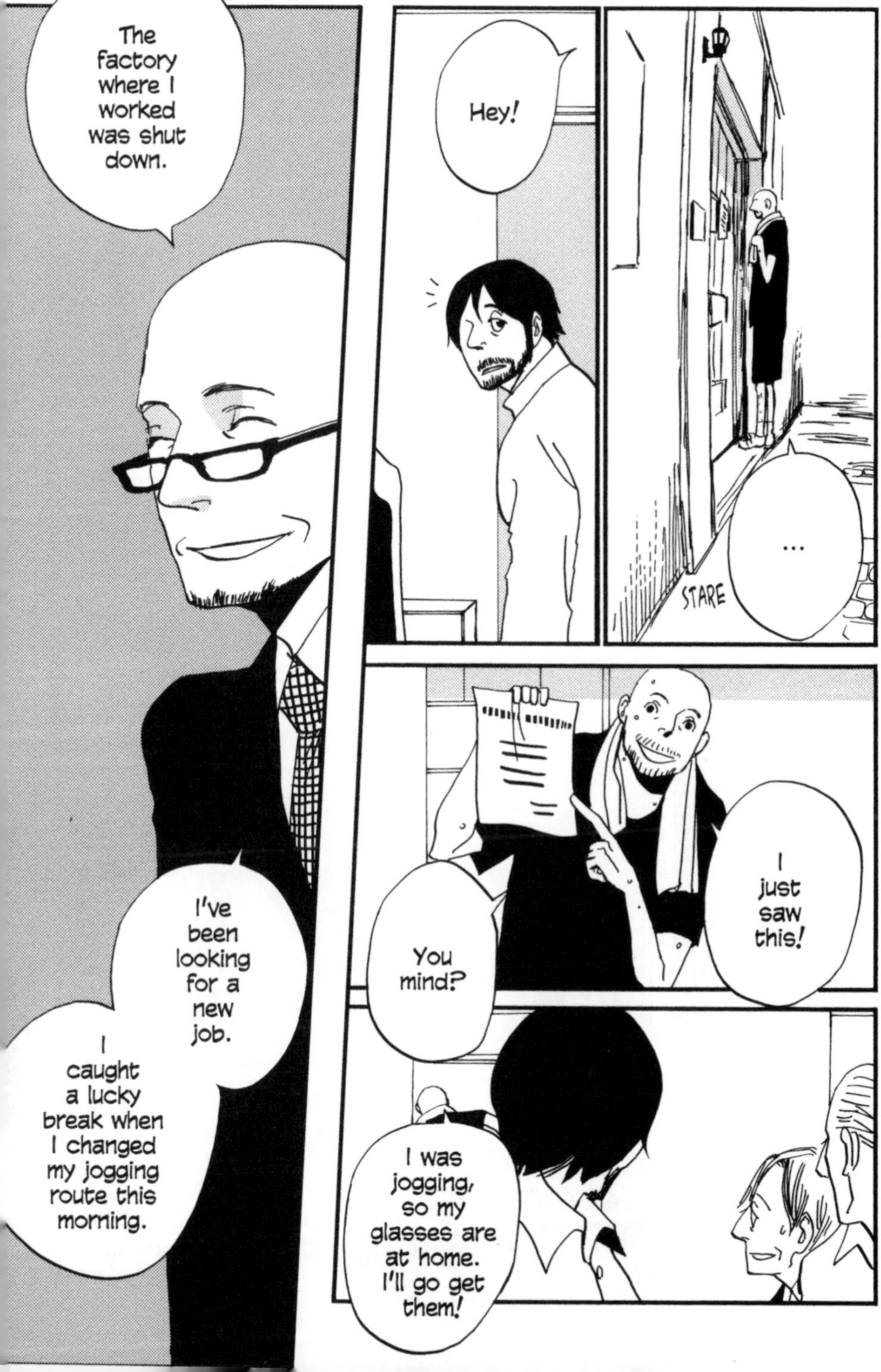
STARE
...
Hey!
I just saw this!
You mind?
I was jogging, so my glasses are at home. I'll go get them!
The factory where I worked was shut down.
I've been looking for a new job.
I caught a lucky break when I changed my jogging route this morning.

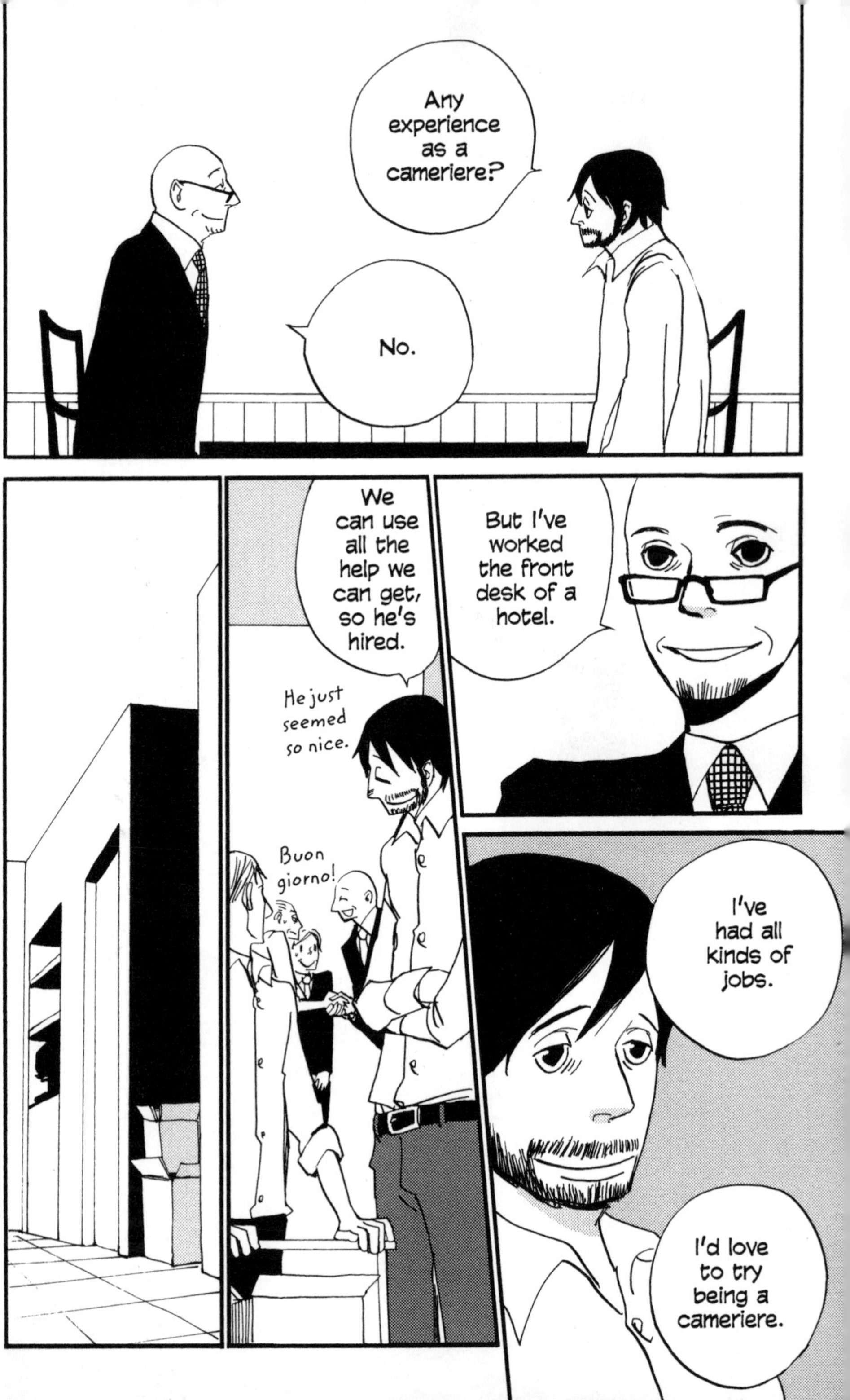
Any experience as a cameriere?
No.
But I've worked the front desk of a hotel.
I've had all kinds of jobs.
I'd love to try being a cameriere.
We can use all the help we can get, so he's hired.
He just seemed so nice.
Buon giorno!

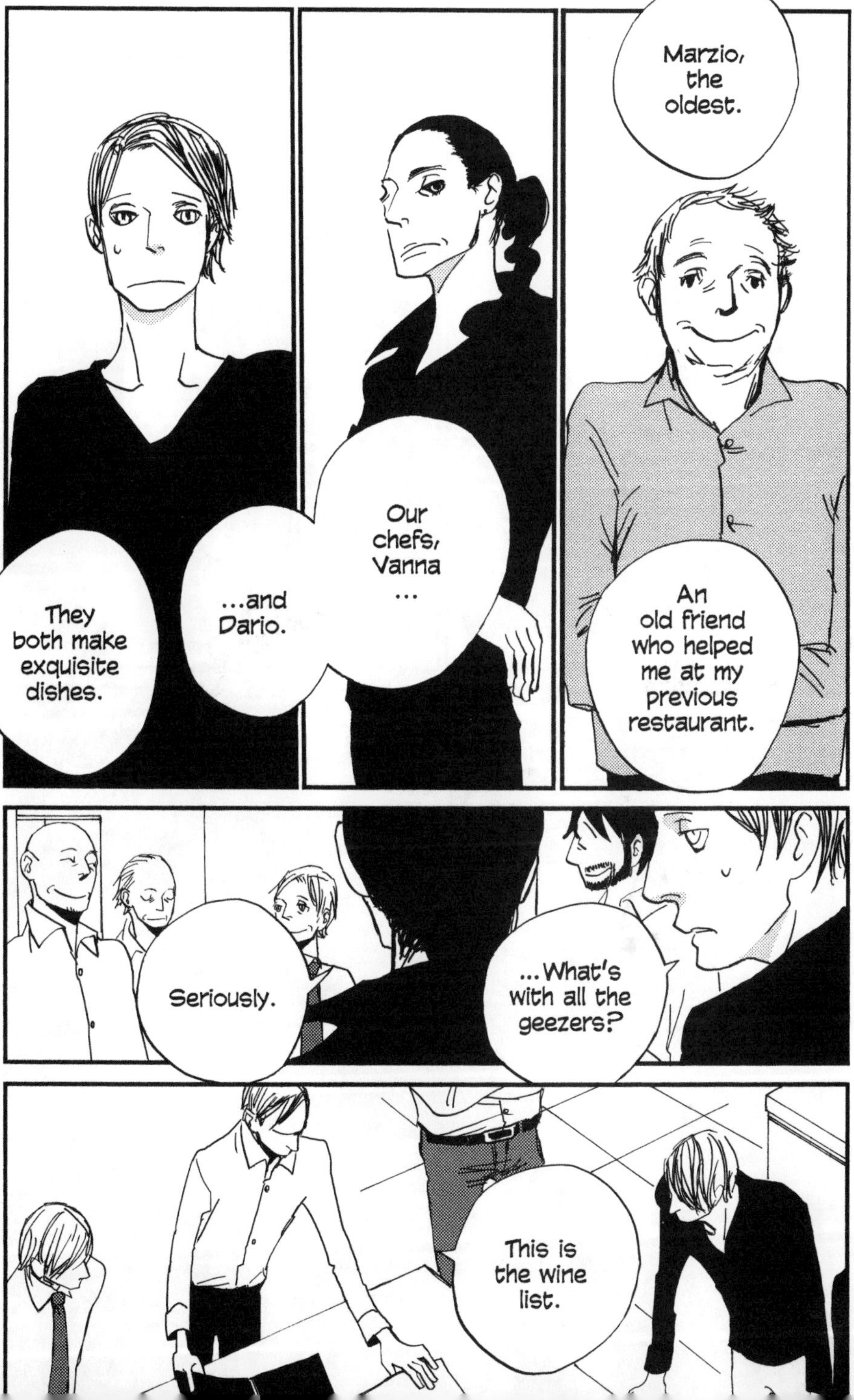
Marzio, the oldest.
An old friend who helped me at my previous restaurant.
Our chefs, Vanna ...
...and Dario.
They both make exquisite dishes.
...What's with all the geezers?
Seriously.
This is the wine list.

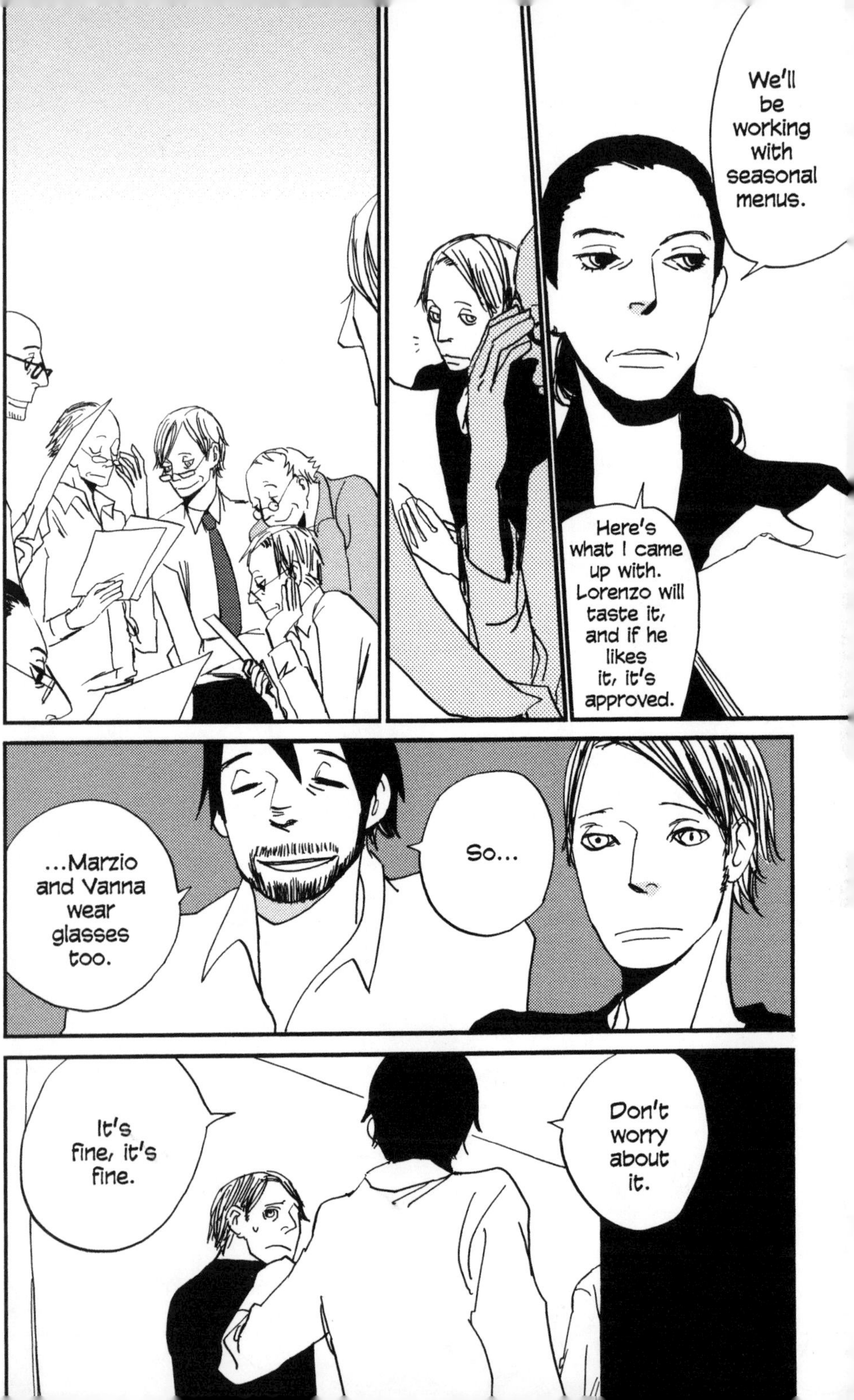
We'll be working with seasonal menus.
Here's what I came up with. Lorenzo will taste it, and if he likes it, it's approved.
So...
...Marzio and Vanna wear glasses too.
Don't worry about it.
It's fine, it's fine.

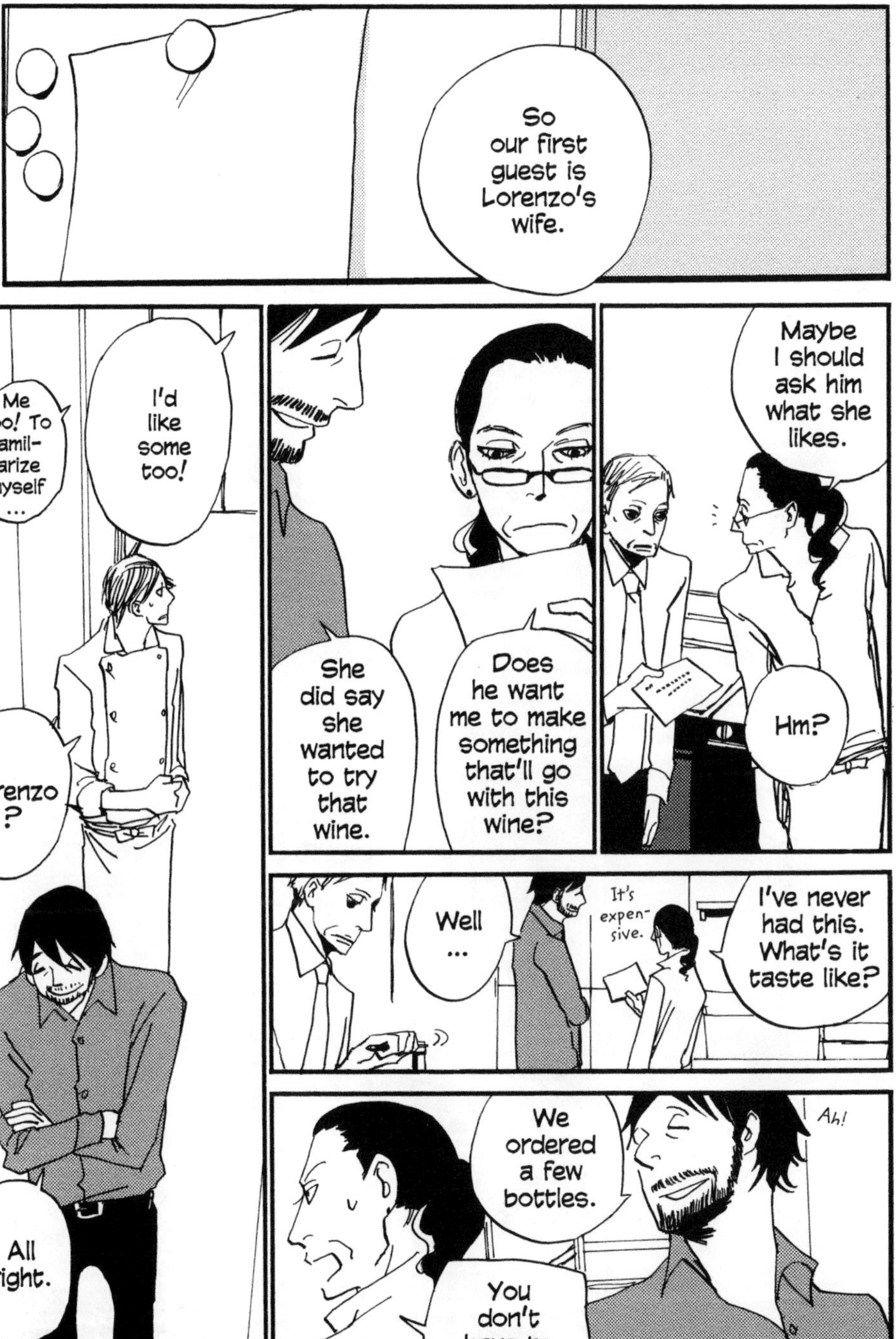
So our first guest is Lorenzo's wife.
Maybe I should ask him what she likes.
Hm?
Does he want me to make something that'll go with this wine?
She did say she wanted to try that wine.
I've never had this. What's it taste like?
It's expen-sive.
Well ...
Ah!
We ordered a few bottles.
You don't have to open one!
I'd like some too!
Me too! To famil-iarize myself ...
Lorenzo?
All right.

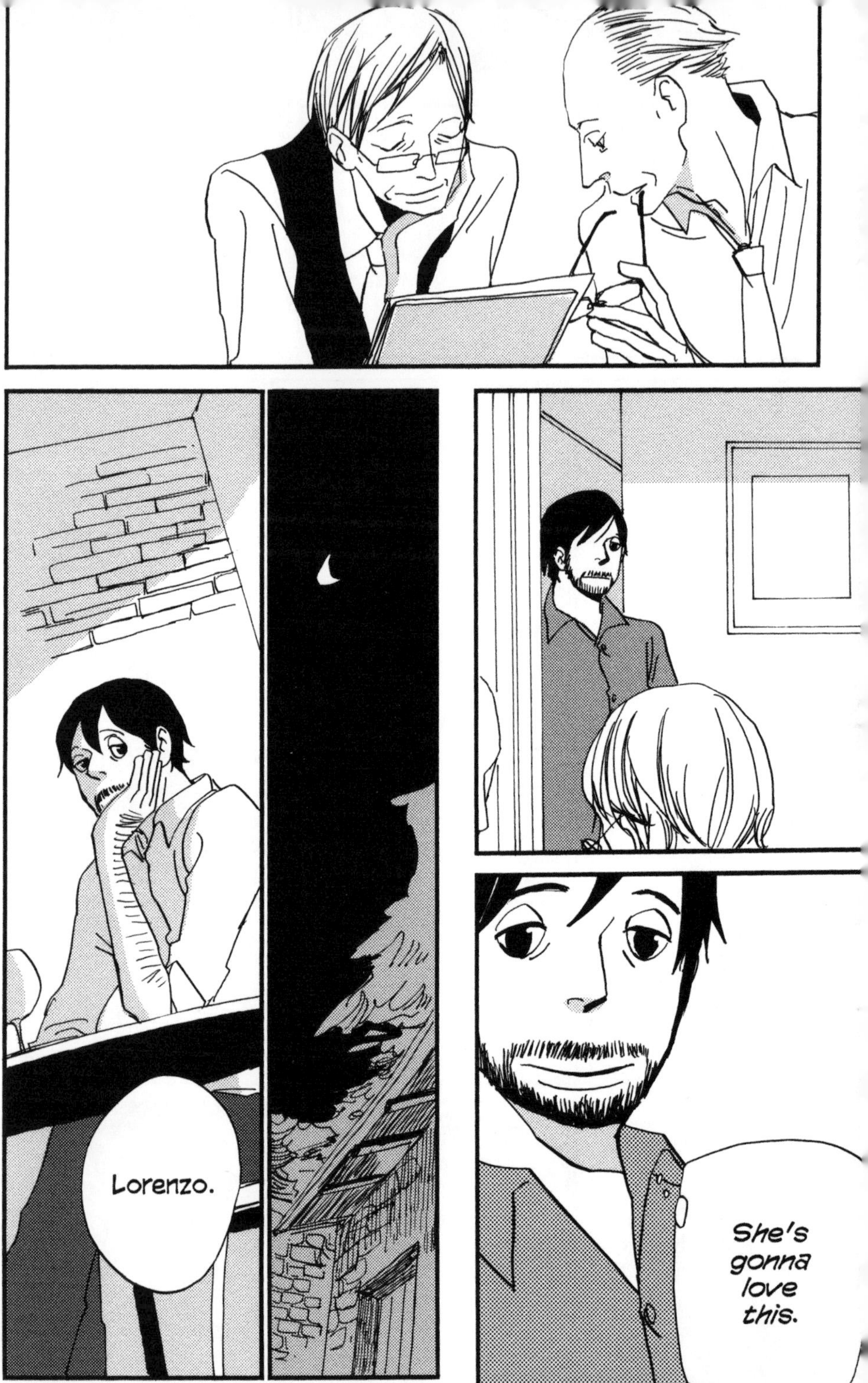
She's gonna love this.
Lorenzo.

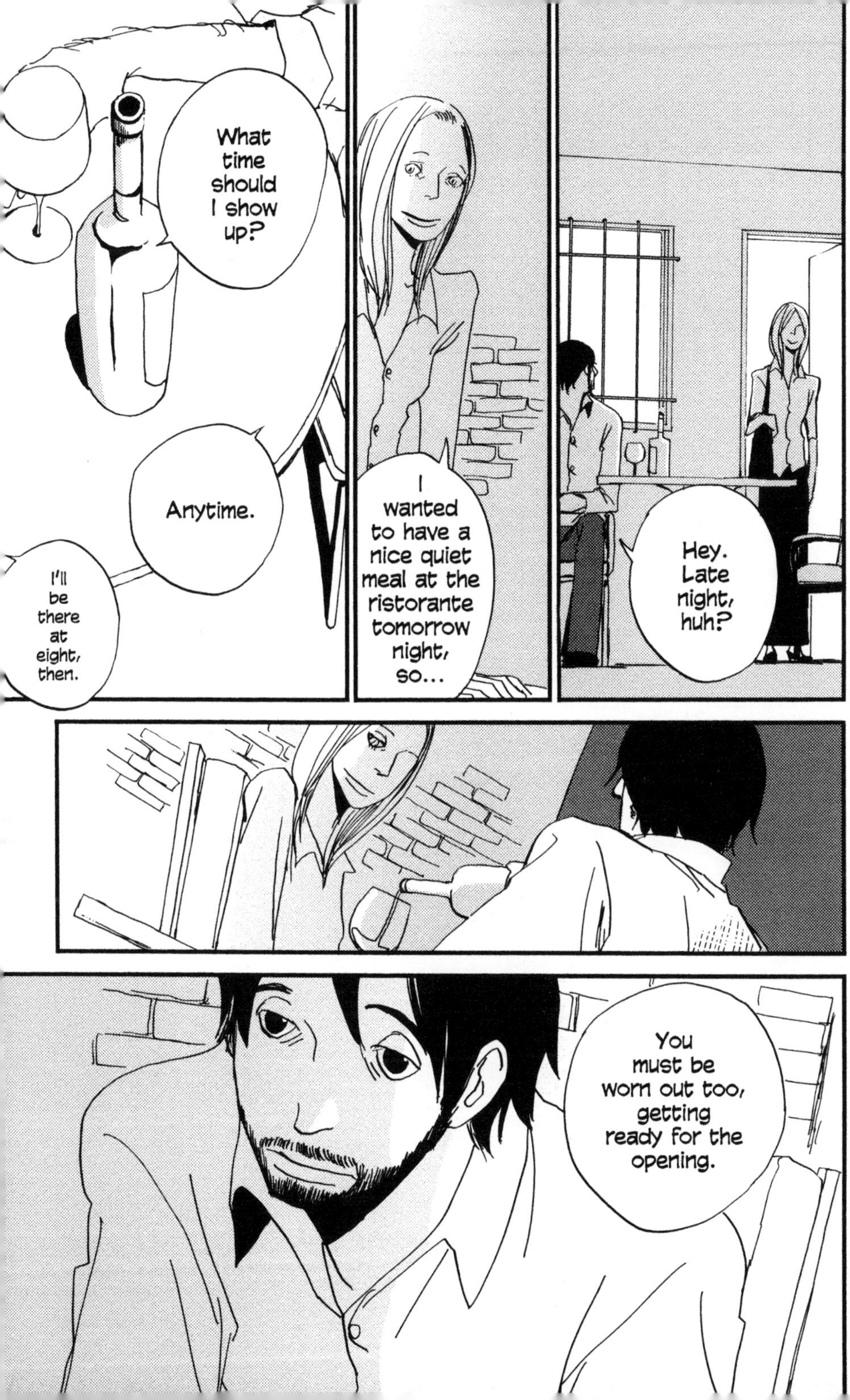
Hey. Late night, huh?
I wanted to have a nice quiet meal at the ristorante tomorrow night, so...
What time should I show up?
Anytime.
I'll be there at eight, then.
You must be worn out too, getting ready for the opening.

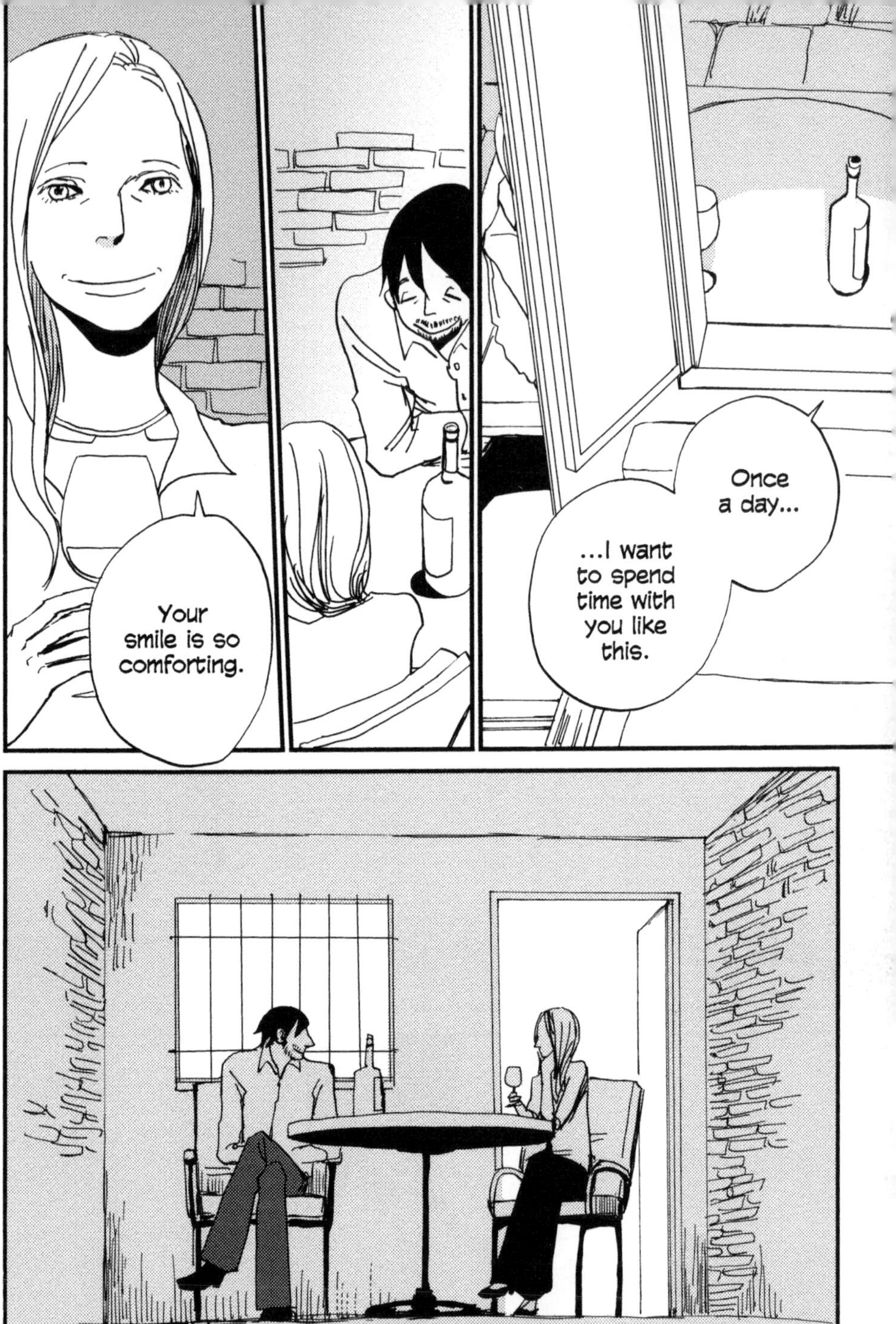
Once a day...
...I want to spend time with you like this.
Your smile is so comforting.

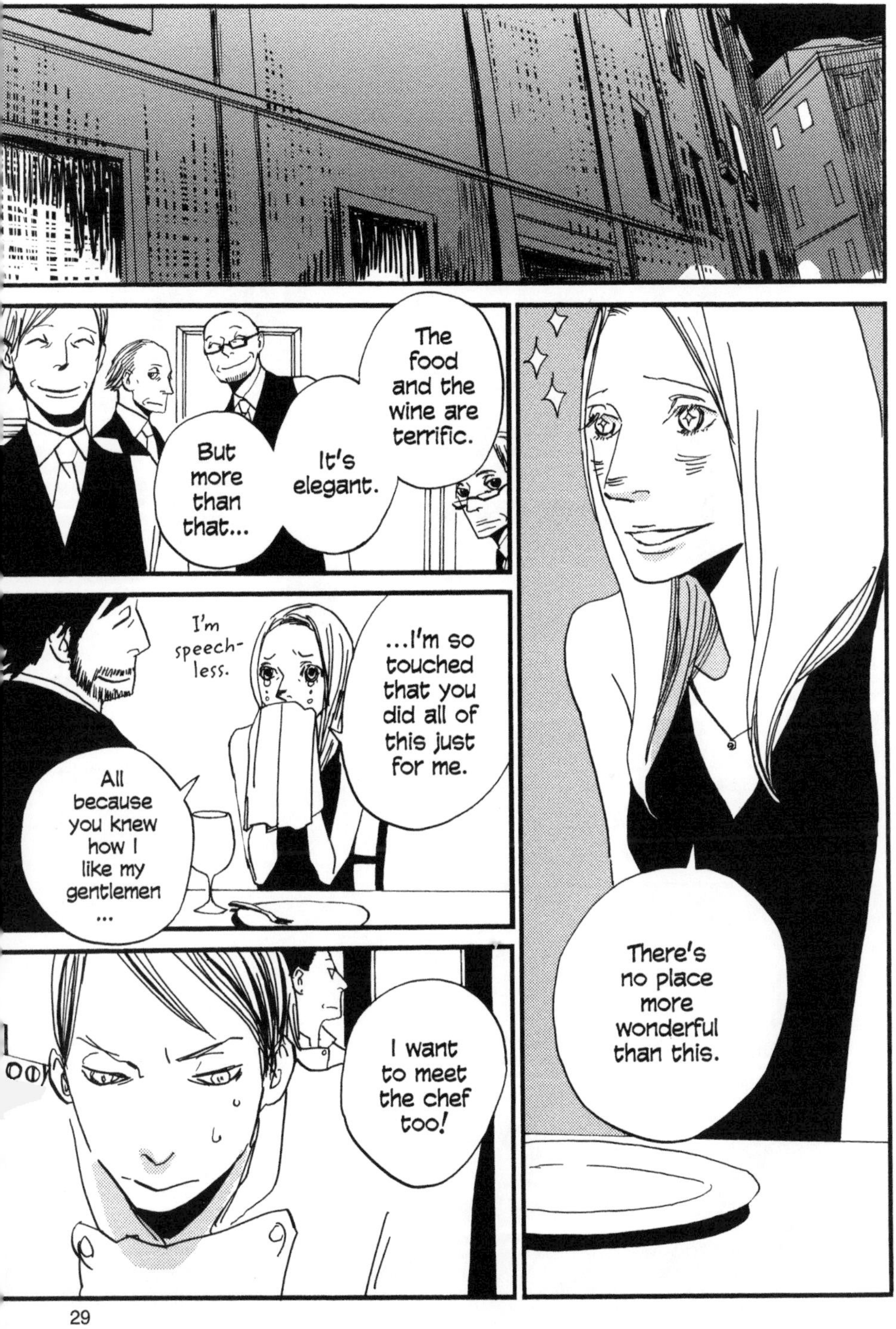
There's no place more wonderful than this.
The food and the wine are terrific.
It's elegant.
But more than that...
...I'm so touched that you did all of this just for me.
I'm speechless.
All because you knew how I like my gentlemen...
I want to meet the chef too!

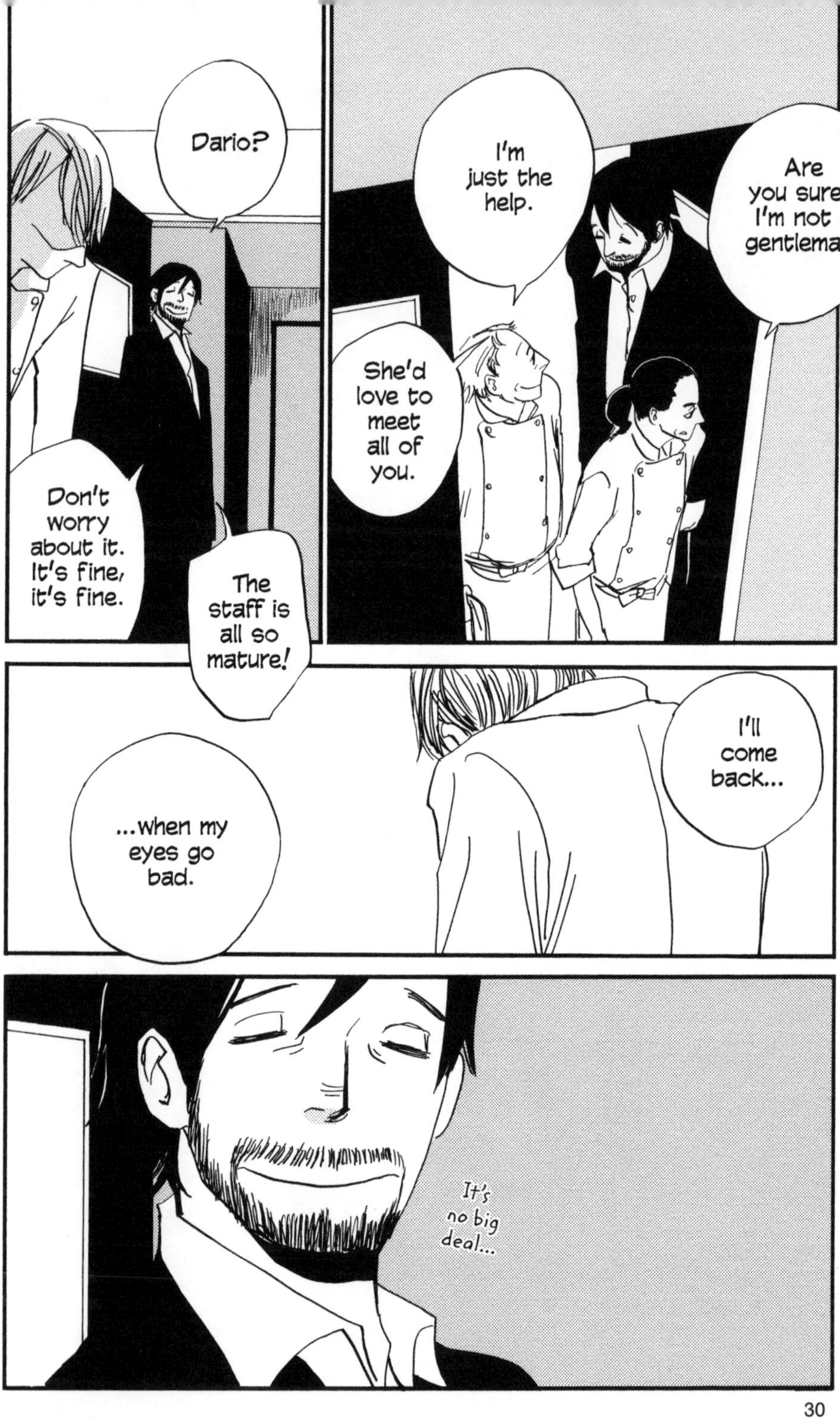
Are you sure? I'm not a gentleman.
I'm just the help.
She'd love to meet all of you.
Dario?
Don't worry about it. It's fine, it's fine.
The staff is all so mature!
I'll come back...
...when my eyes go bad.
It's no big deal...

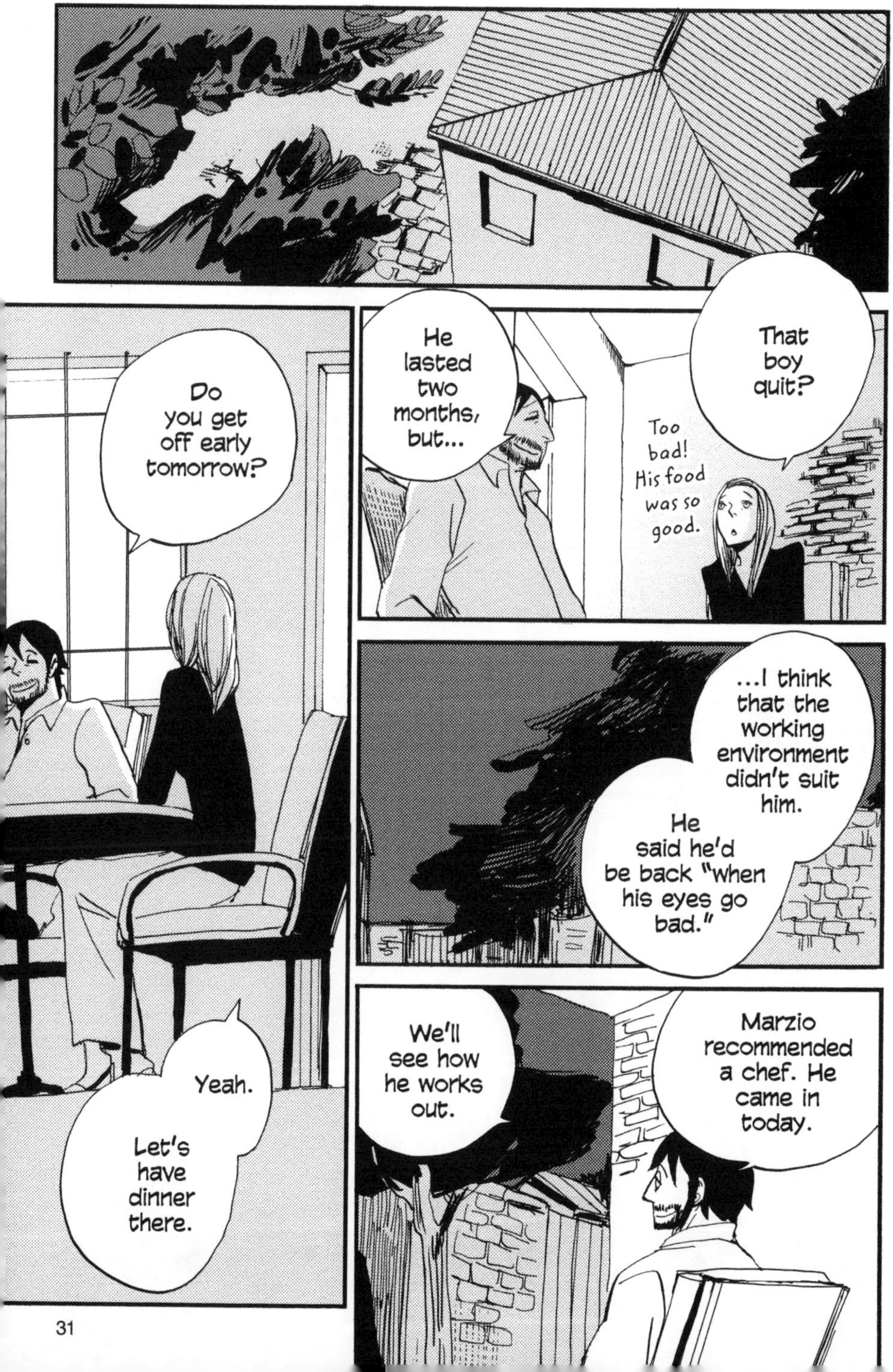
That boy quit?
Too bad! His food was so good.
He lasted two months, but...
...I think that the working environment didn't suit him.
He said he'd be back "when his eyes go bad."
Marzio recommended a chef. He came in today.
We'll see how he works out.
Do you get off early tomorrow?
Yeah.
Let's have dinner there.

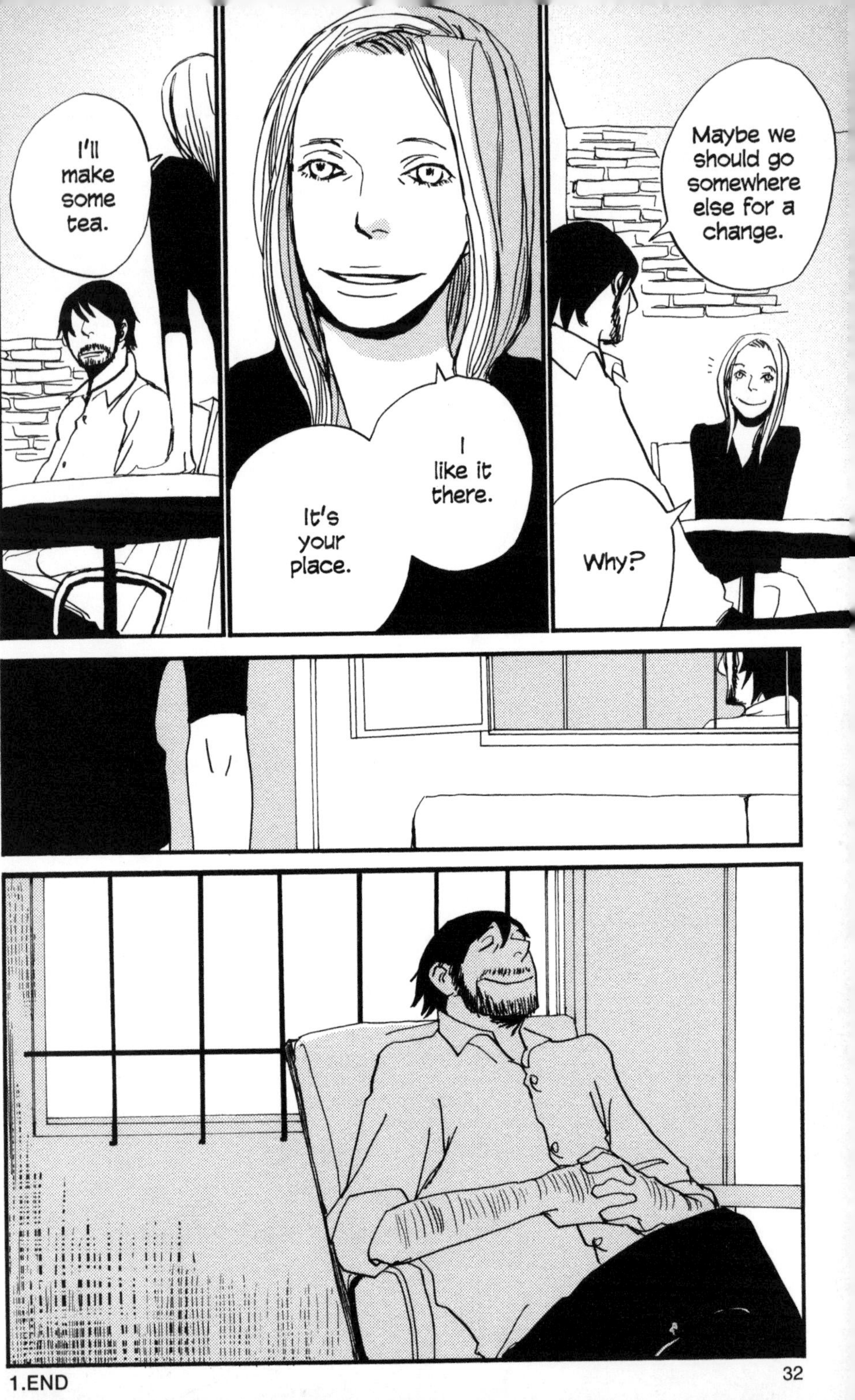
Maybe we should go somewhere else for a change.
Why?
I like it there.
It's your place.
I'll make some tea.

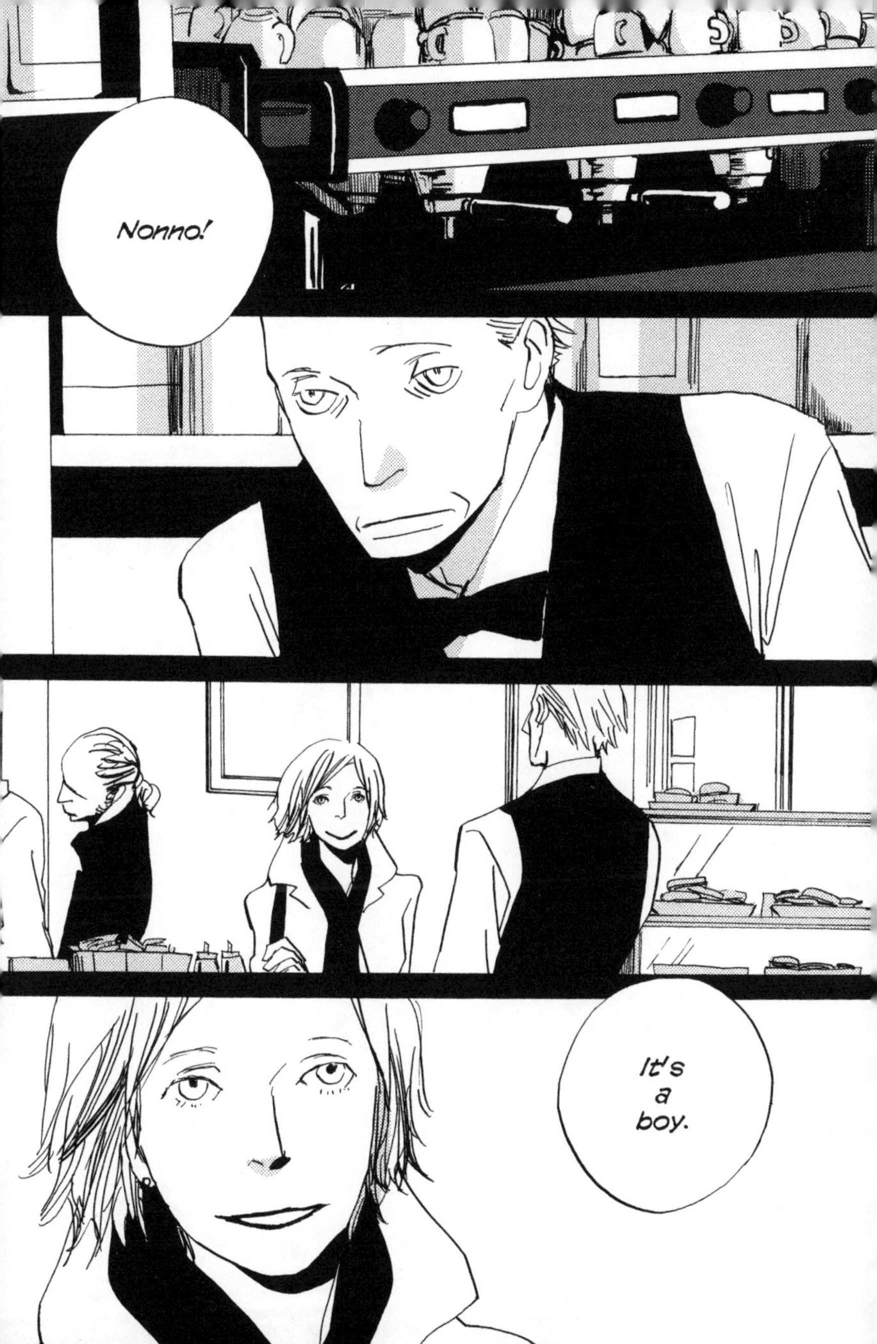
Nonno!
It's a boy.

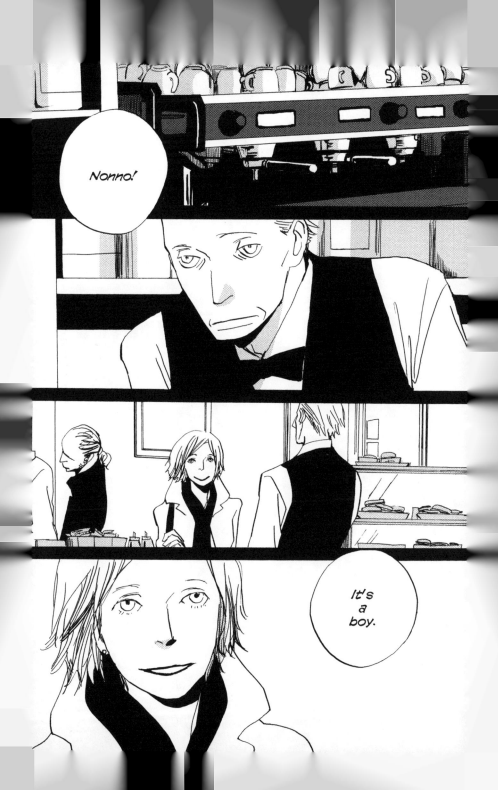

2. Luciano

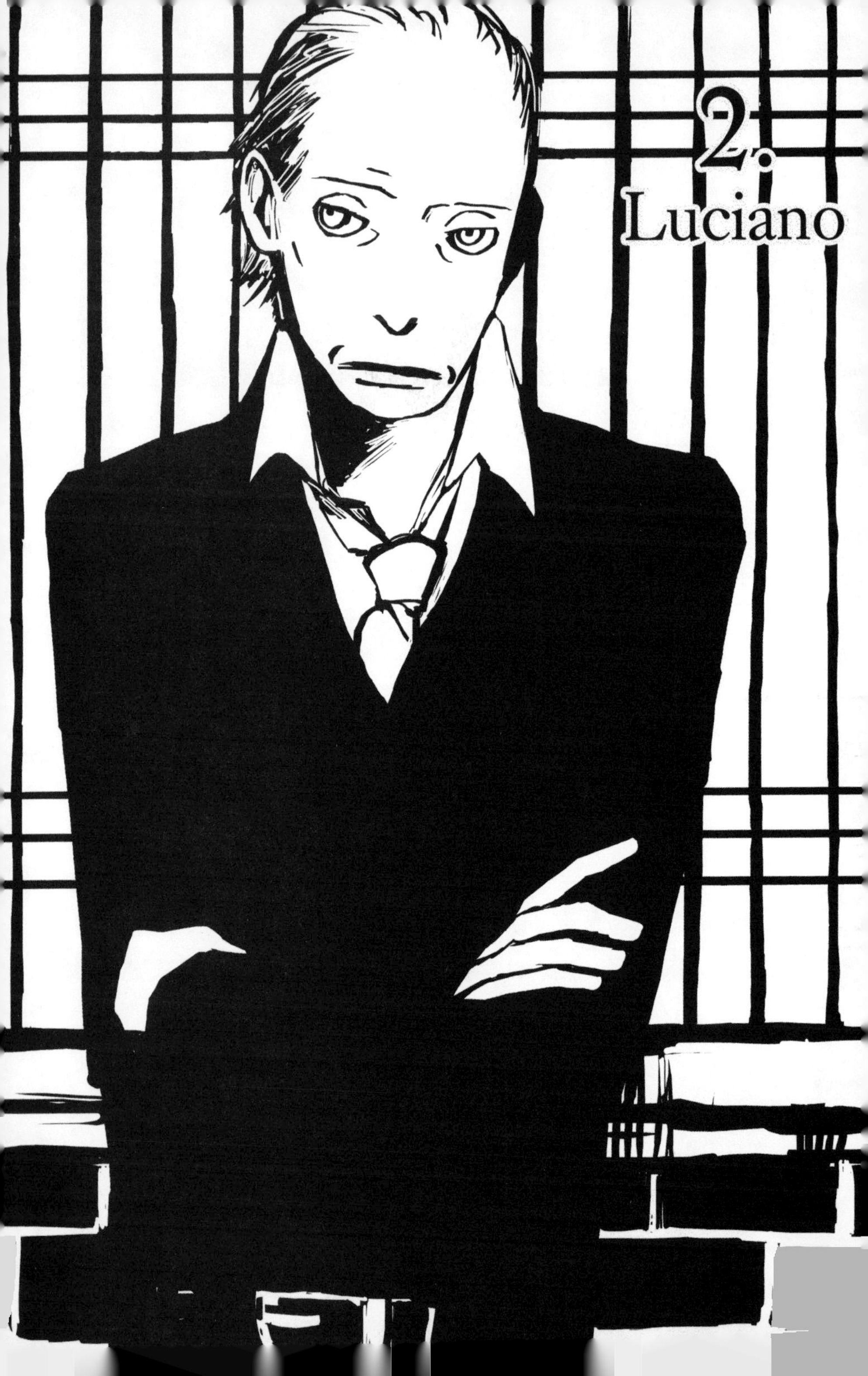

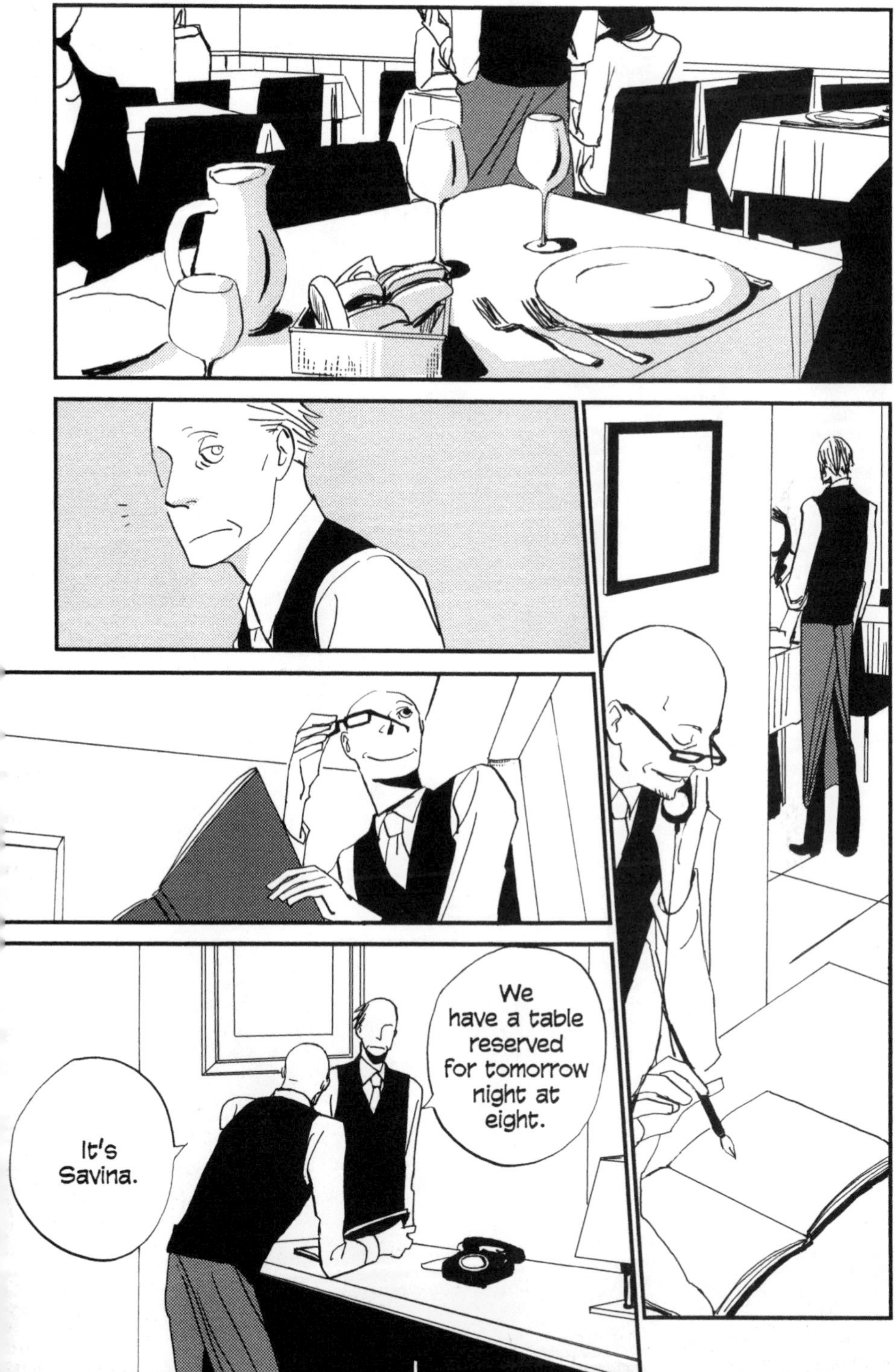
We have a table reserved for tomorrow night at eight.
It's Savina.

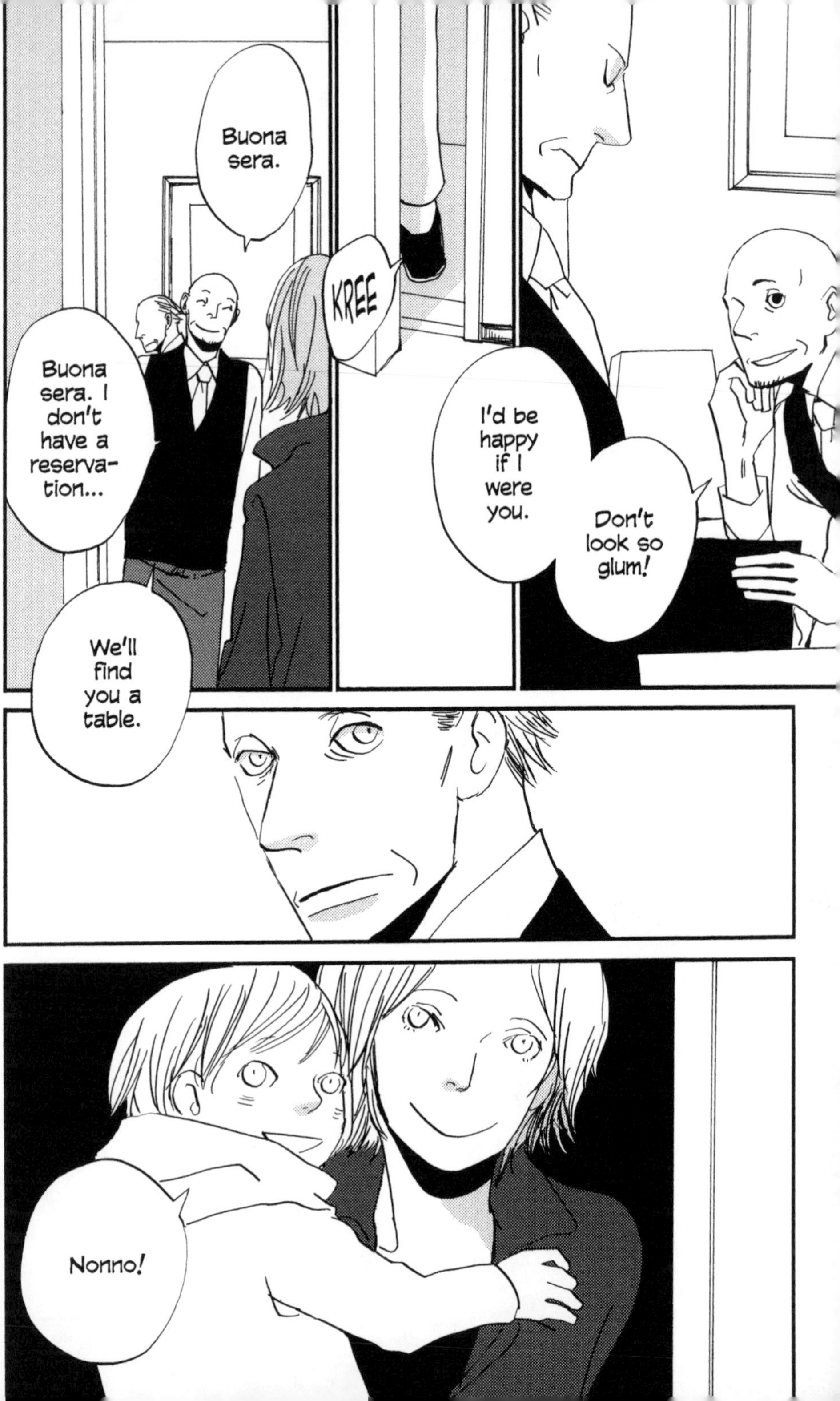
Don't look so glum!
I'd be happy if I were you.
KREE
Buona sera.
Buona sera. I don't have a reservation...
We'll find you a table.
Nonno!

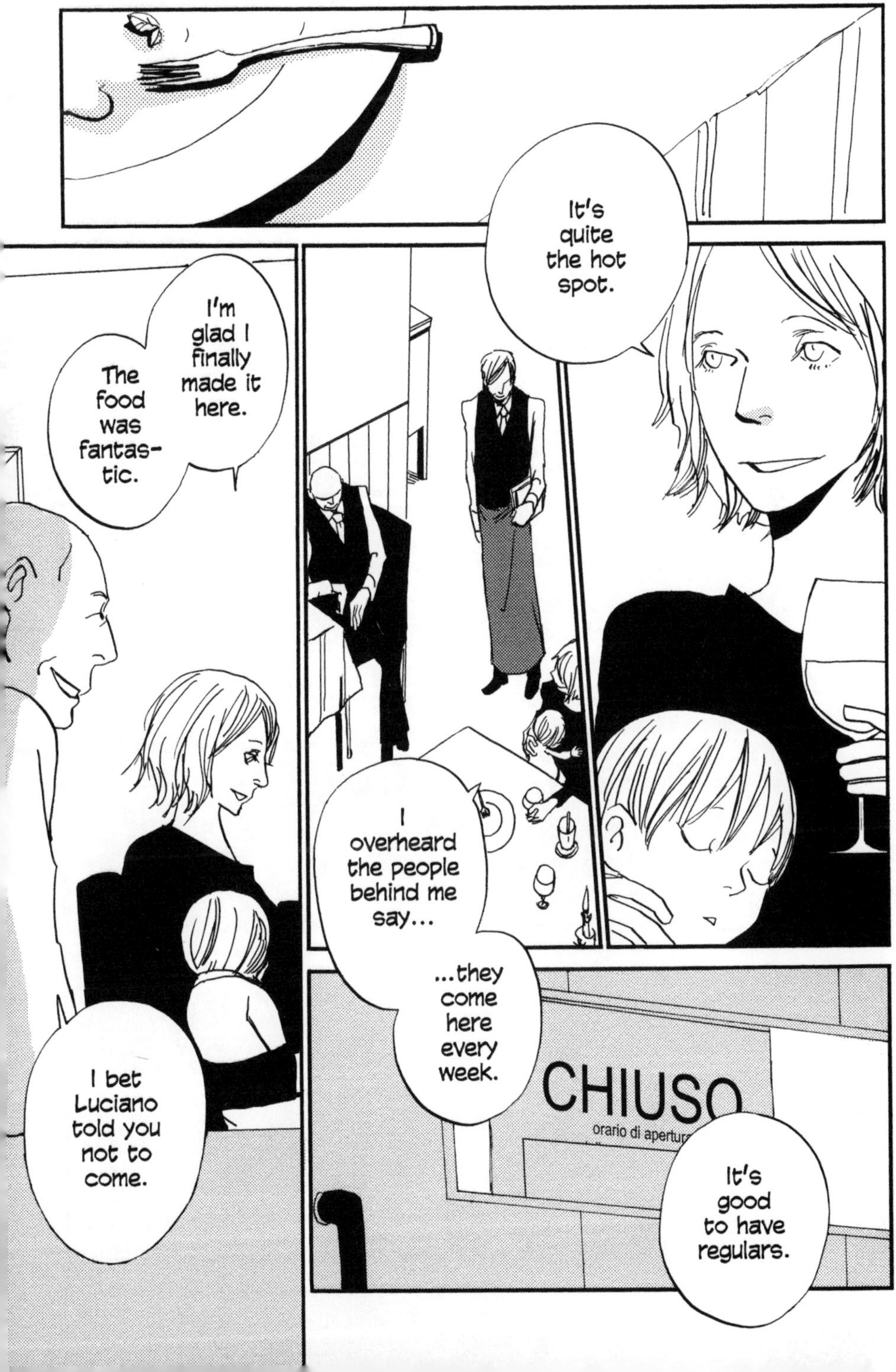
It's quite the hot spot.
I overheard the people behind me say...
...they come here every week.
CHIUSO
orario di apertura
It's good to have regulars.
I'm glad I finally made it here.
The food was fantastic.
I bet Luciano told you not to come.

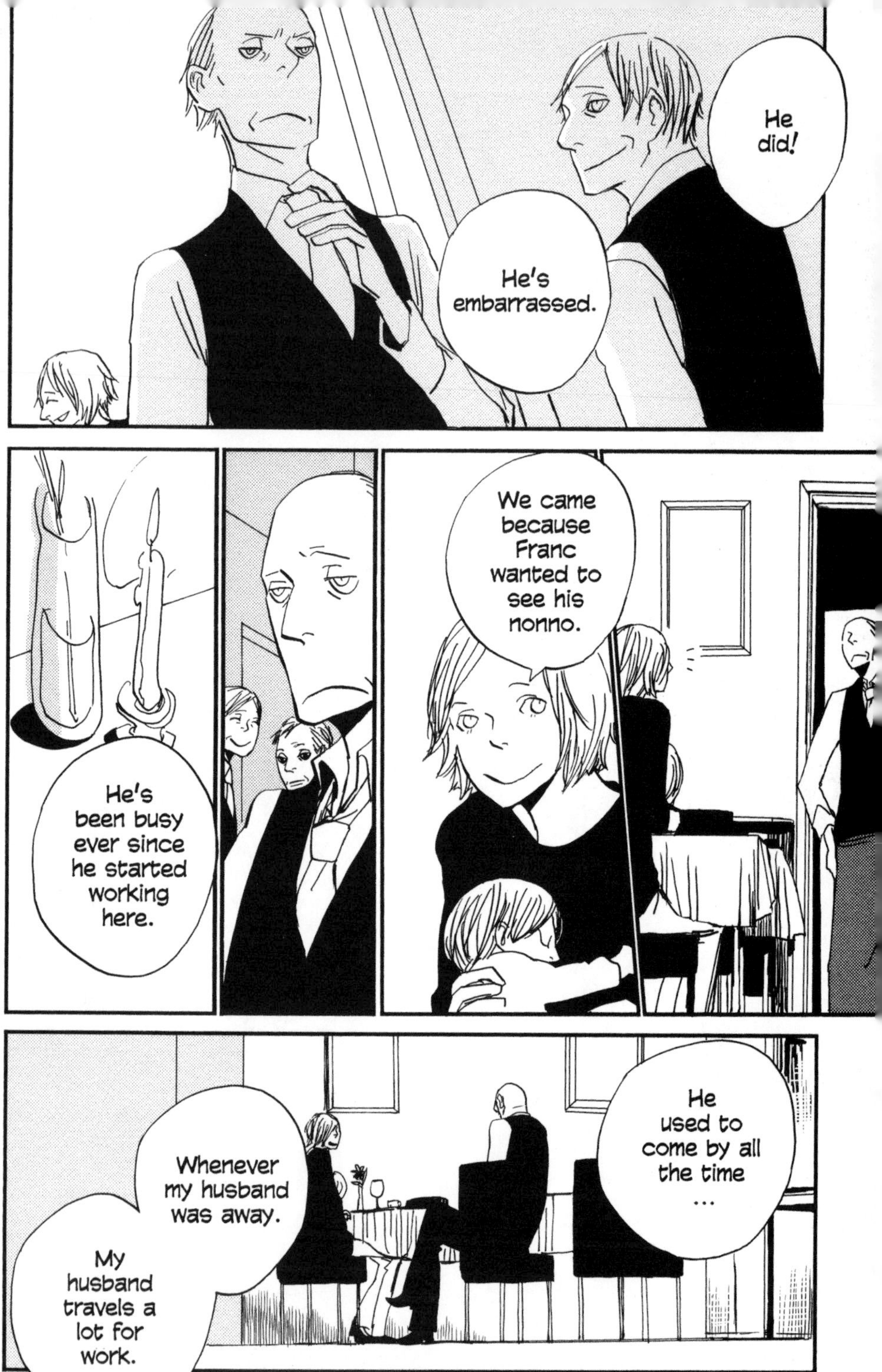
He did!
He's embarrassed.
We came because Franc wanted to see his nonno.
He's been busy ever since he started working here.
He used to come by all the time ...
Whenever my husband was away.
My husband travels a lot for work.

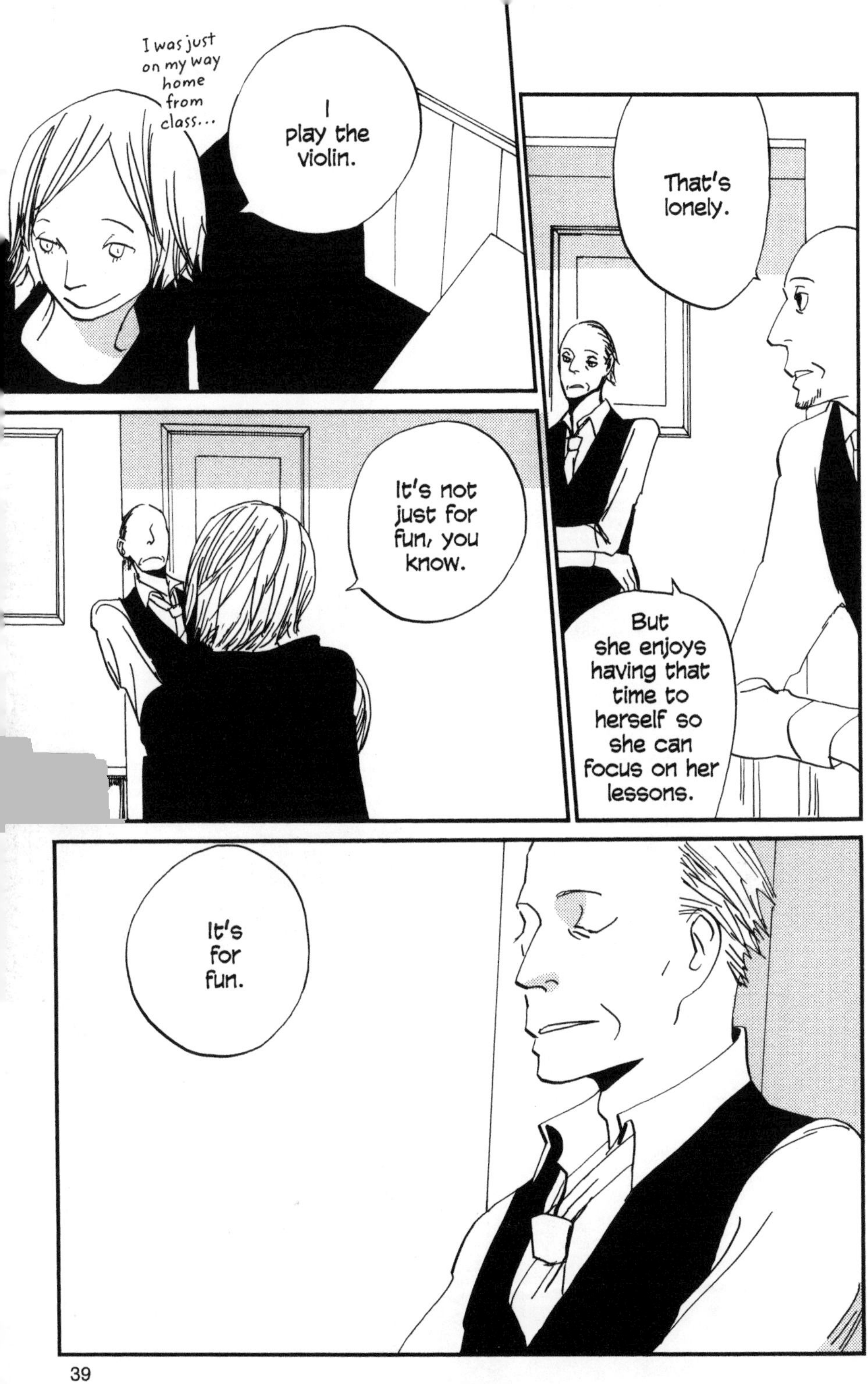
That's lonely.
But she enjoys having that time to herself so she can focus on her lessons.
I was just on my way home from class...
I play the violin.
It's not just for fun, you know.
It's for fun.

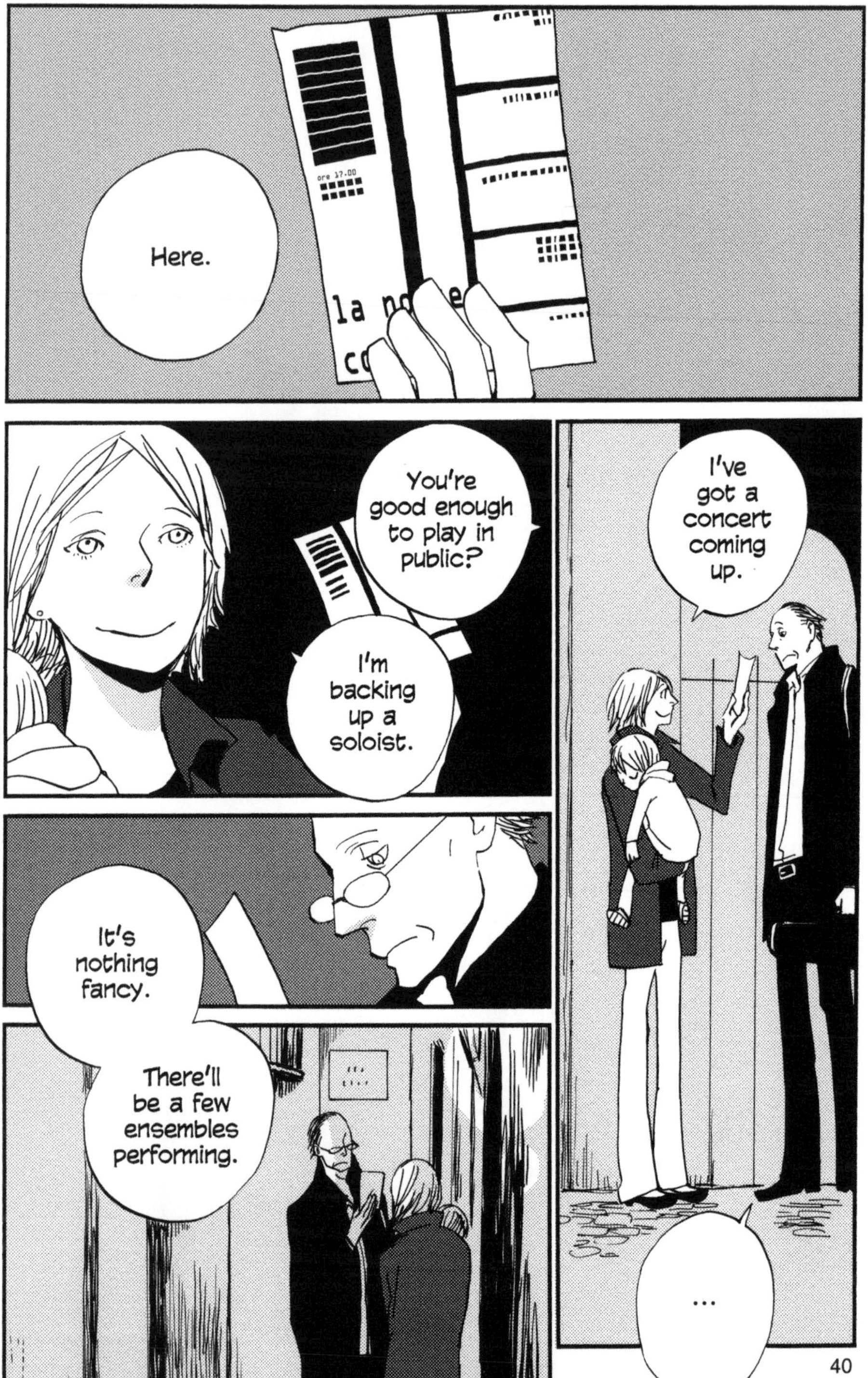
Here.
I've got a concert coming up.
...
You're good enough to play in public?
I'm backing up a soloist.
It's nothing fancy.
There'll be a few ensembles performing.

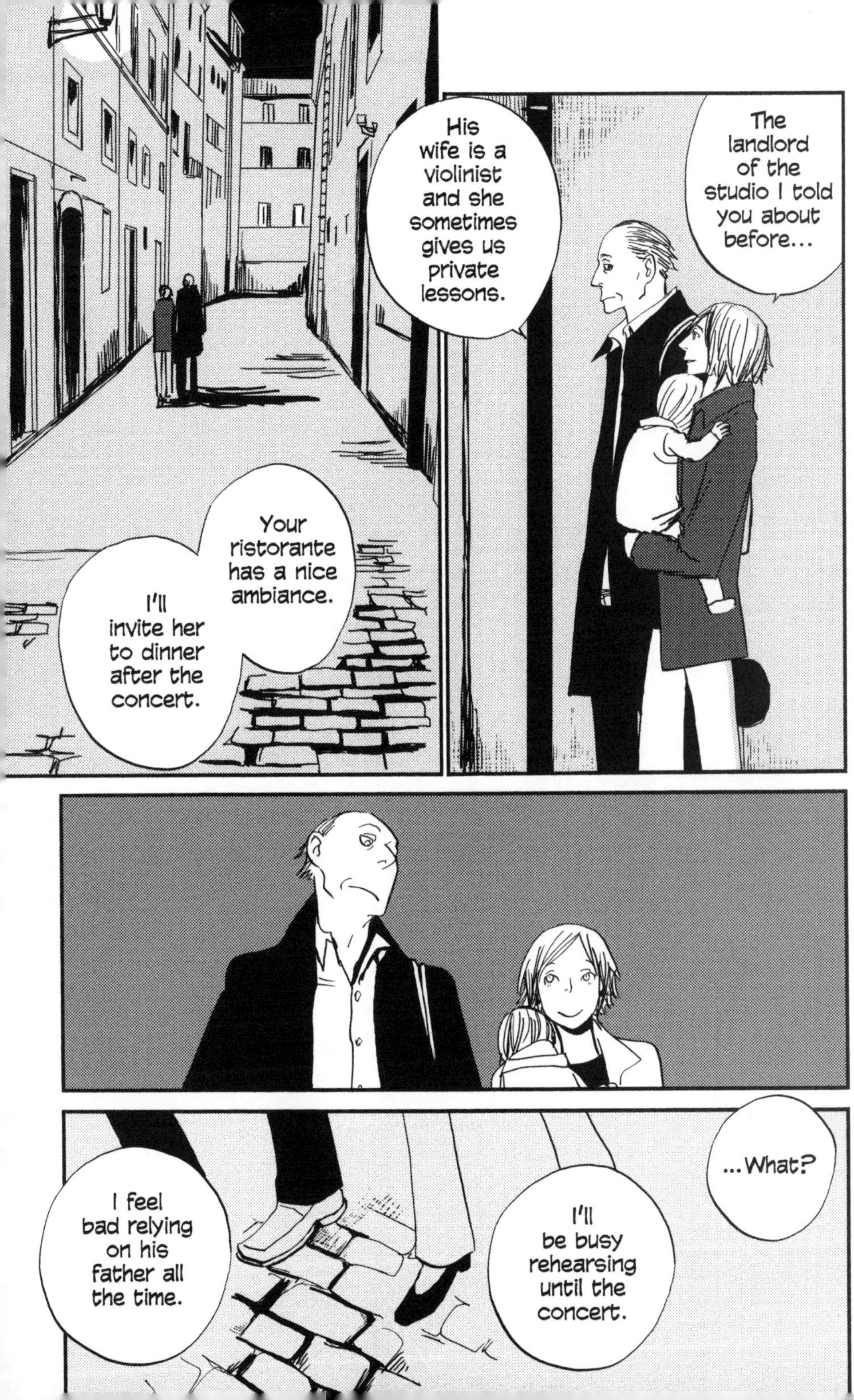
The landlord of the studio I told you about before...
His wife is a violinist and she sometimes gives us private lessons.
Your ristorante has a nice ambiance.
I'll invite her to dinner after the concert.
...What?
I'll be busy rehearsing until the concert.
I feel bad relying on his father all the time.

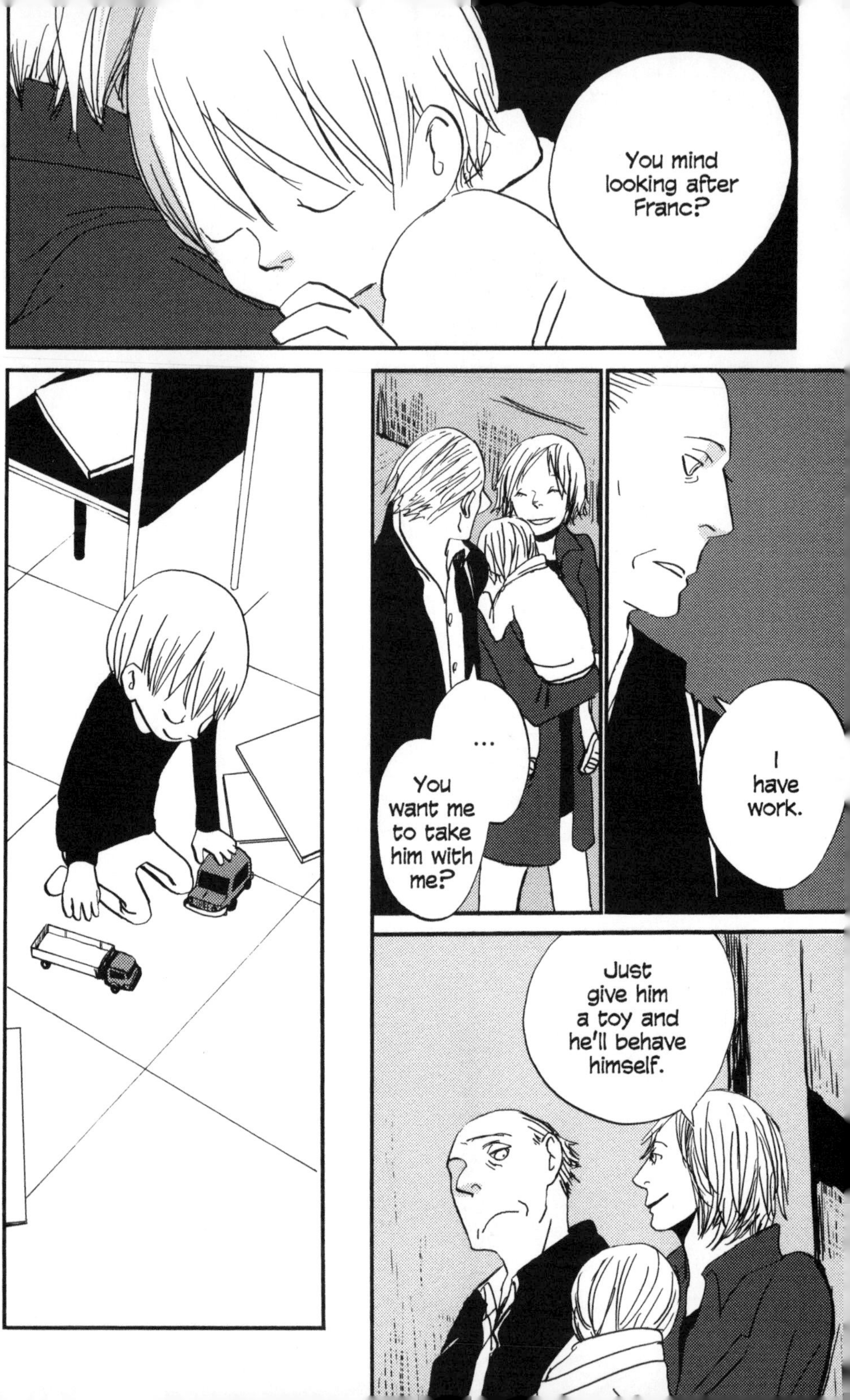
You mind looking after Franc?
I have work.
...
You want me to take him with me?
Just give him a toy and he'll behave himself.

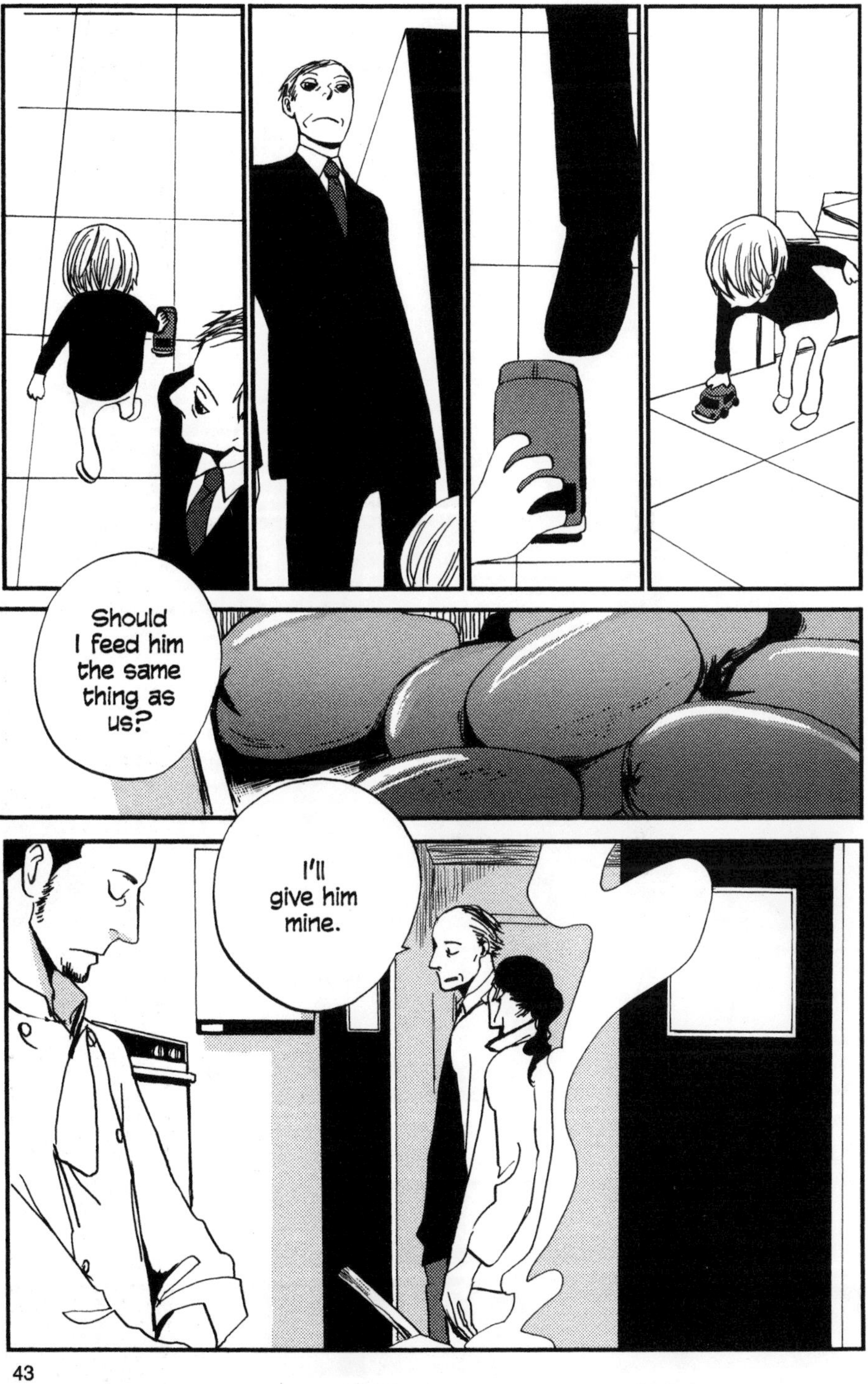
Should I feed him the same thing as us?
I'll give him mine.

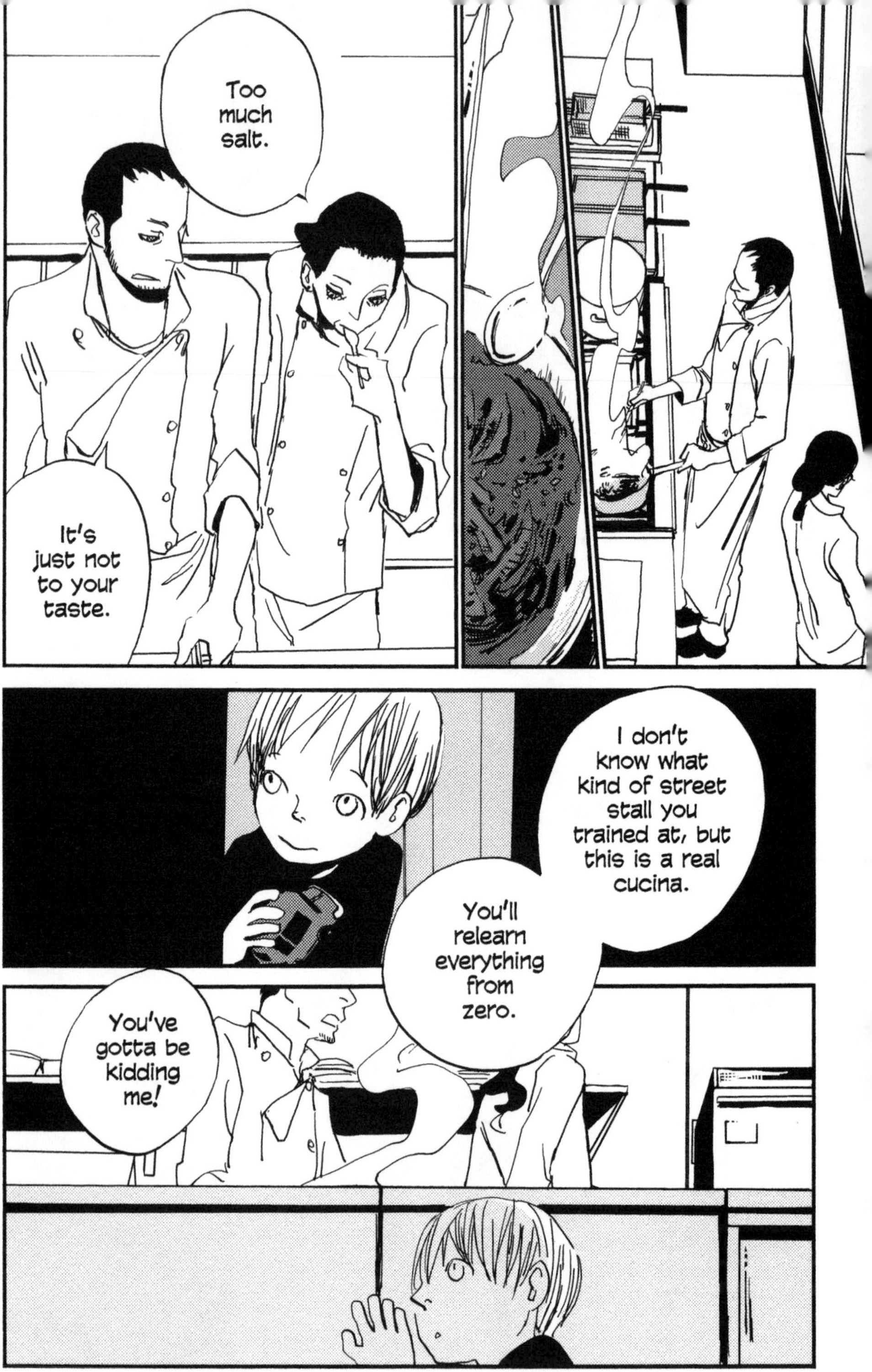
Too much salt.
It's just not to your taste.
I don't know what kind of street stall you trained at, but this is a real cucina.
You'll relearn everything from zero.
You've gotta be kidding me!

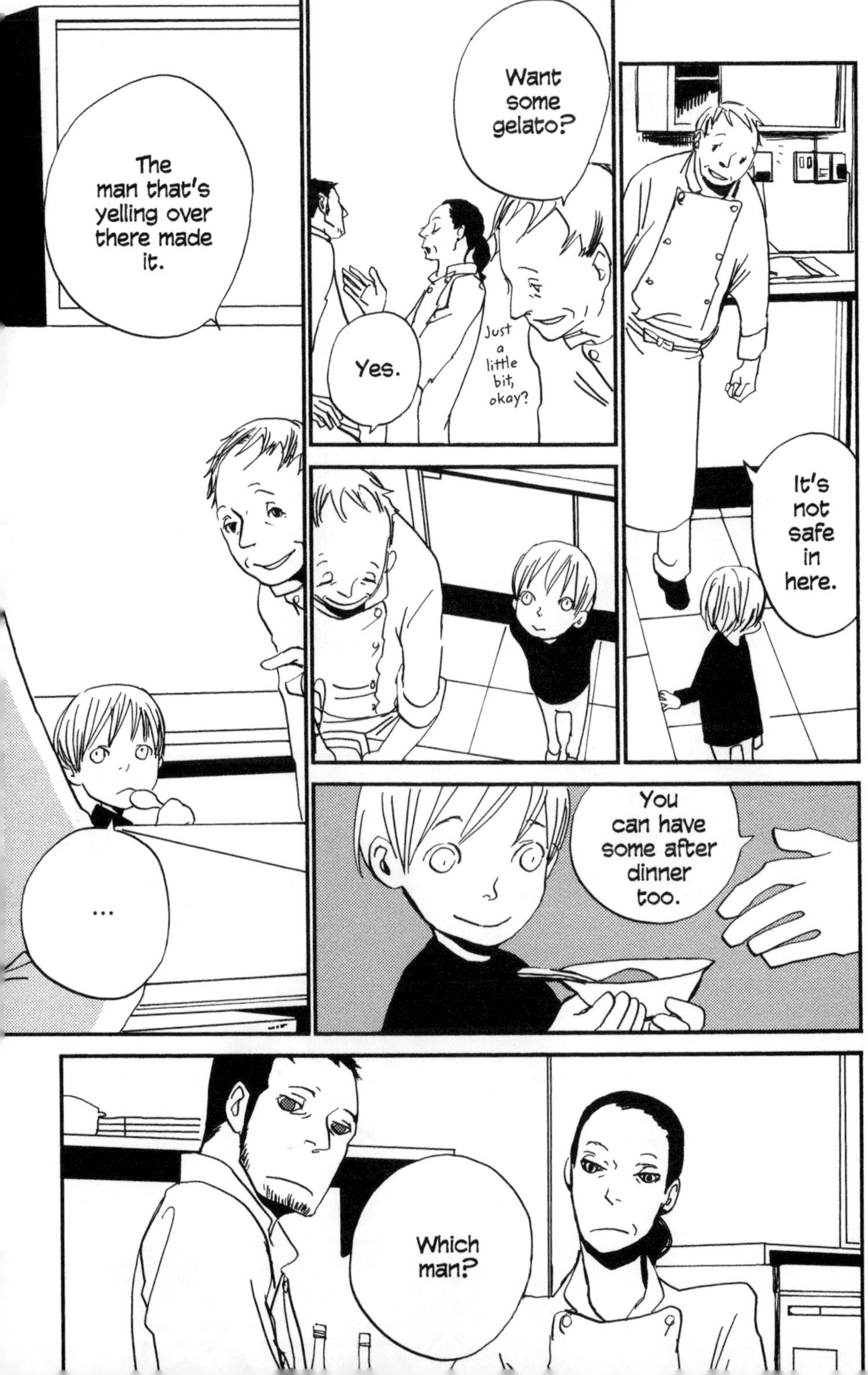
Want some gelato?
Just a little bit, okay?
Yes.
It's not safe in here.
You can have some after dinner too.
The man that's yelling over there made it.
...
Which man?

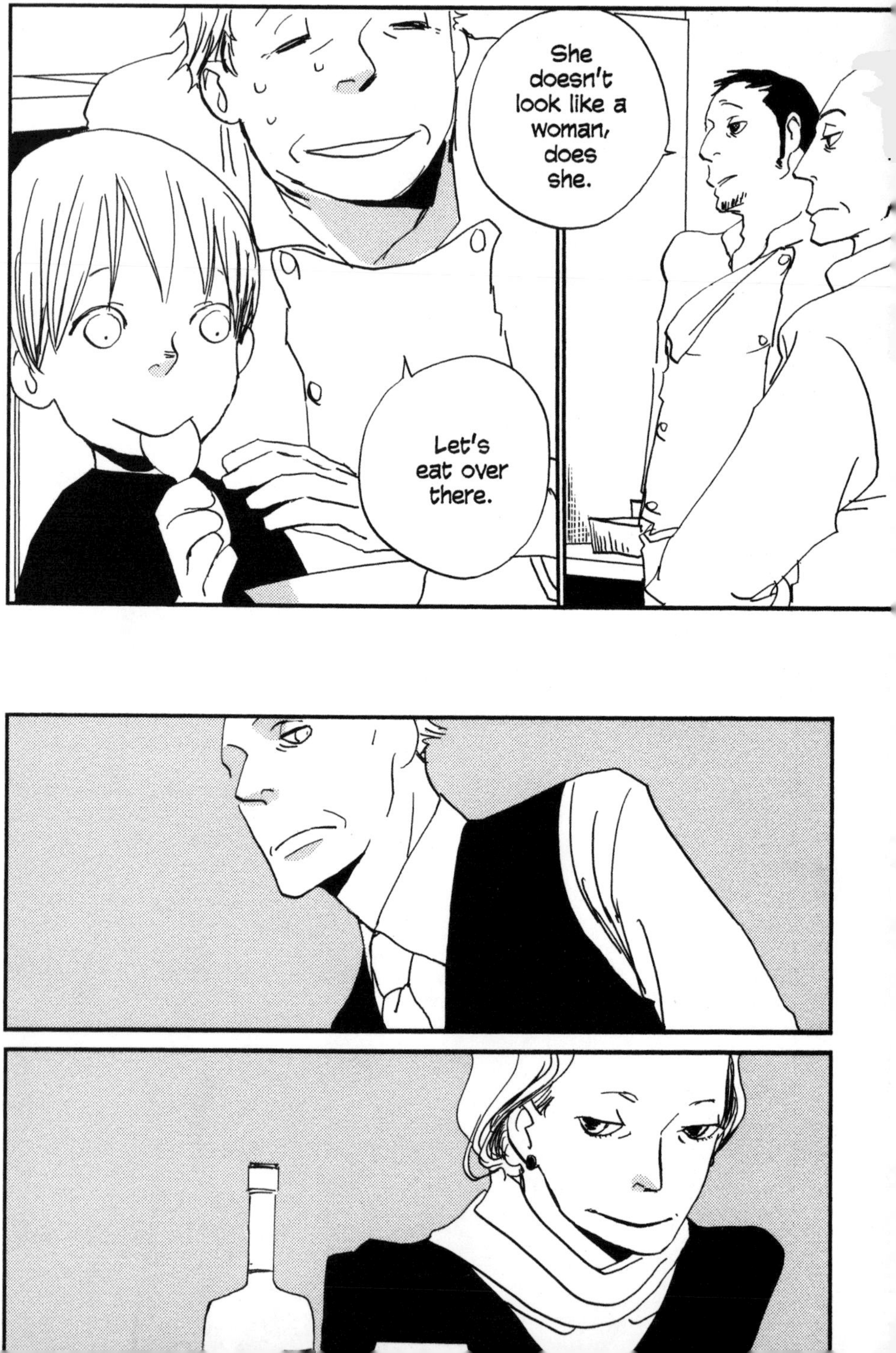
She doesn't look like a woman, does she.
Let's eat over there.

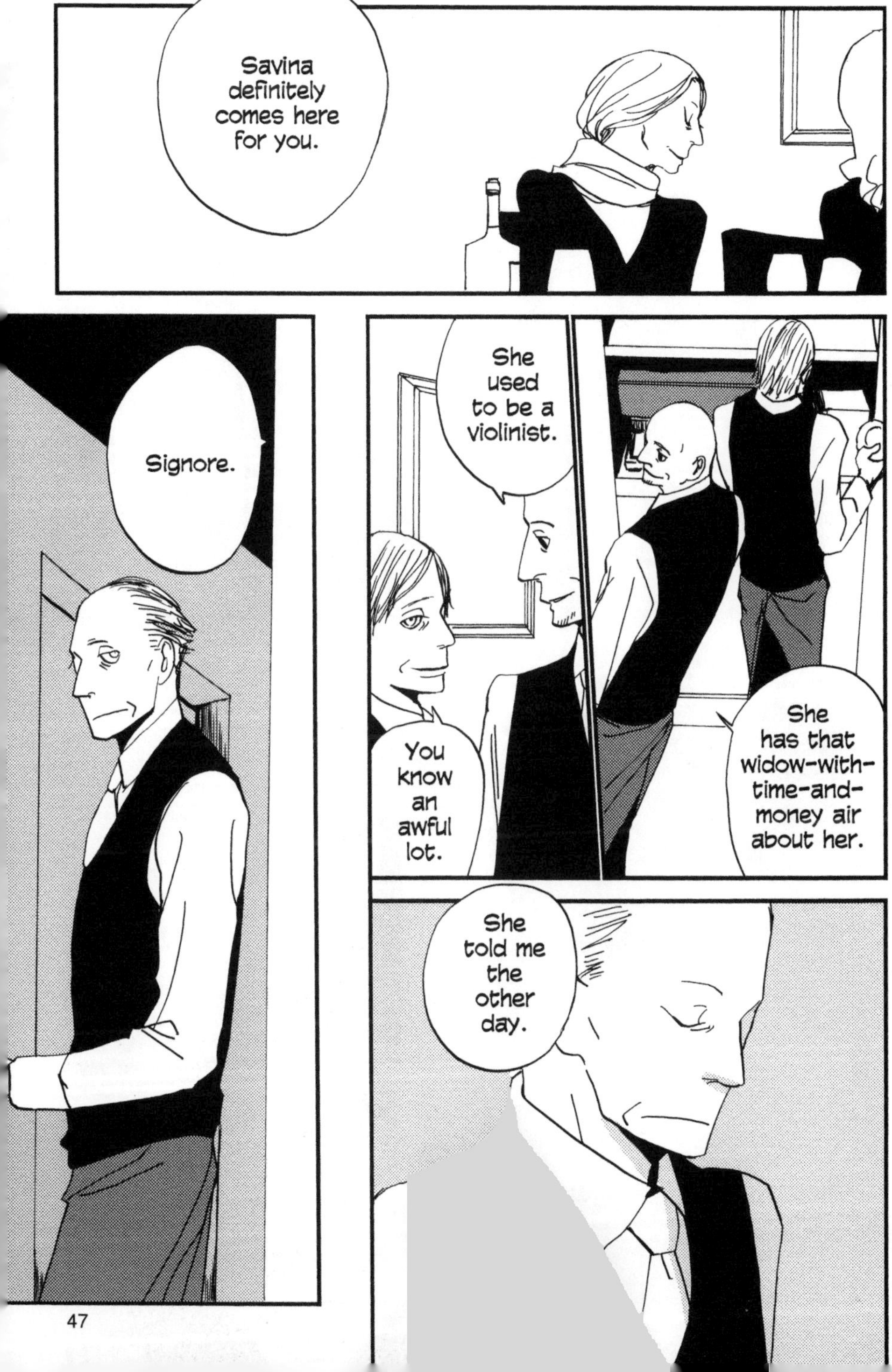
Savina definitely comes here for you.
She has that widow-with-time-and-money air about her.
She used to be a violinist.
You know an awful lot.
She told me the other day.
Signore.

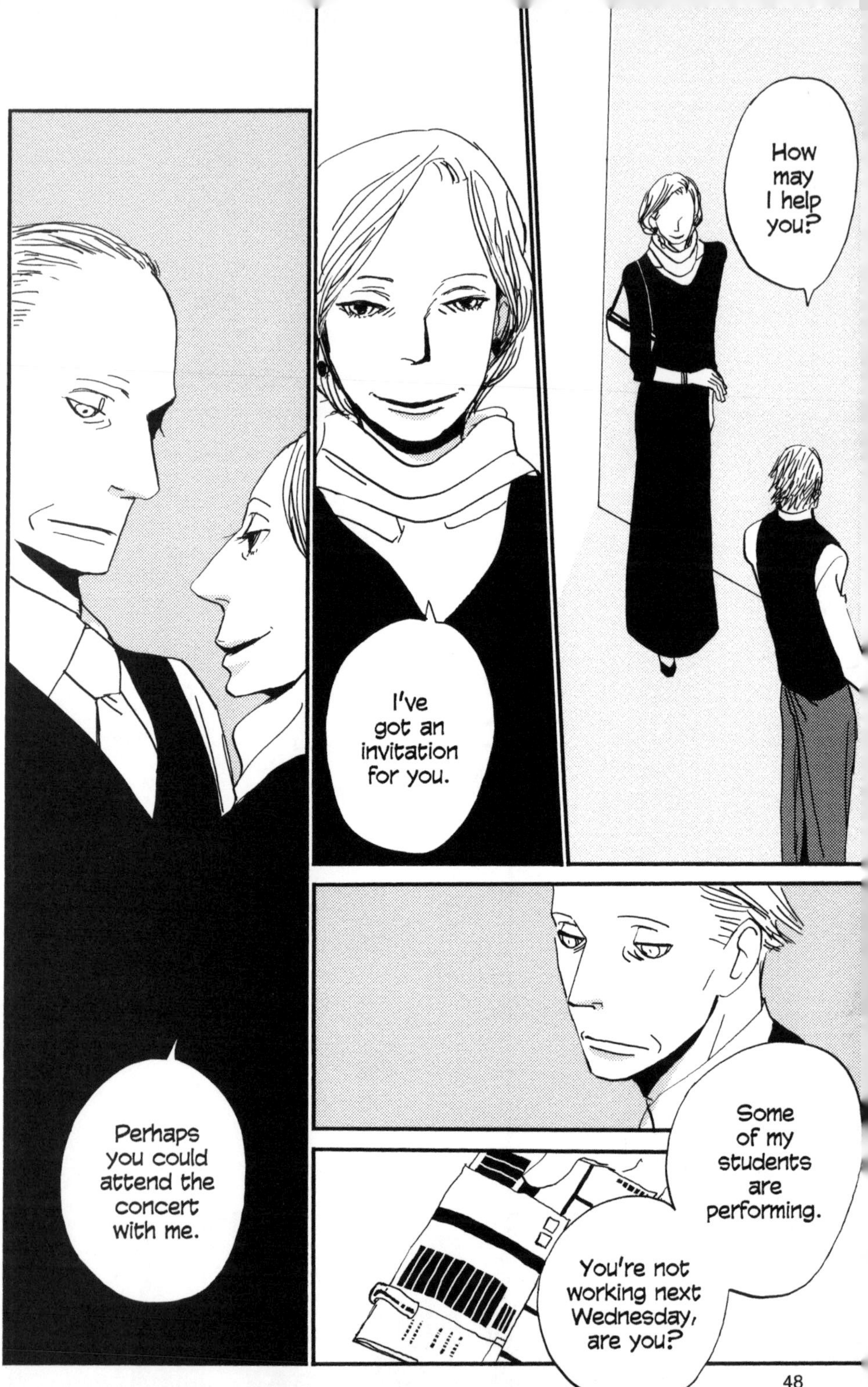
How may I help you?
I've got an invitation for you.
Some of my students are performing.
You're not working next Wednesday, are you?
Perhaps you could attend the concert with me.

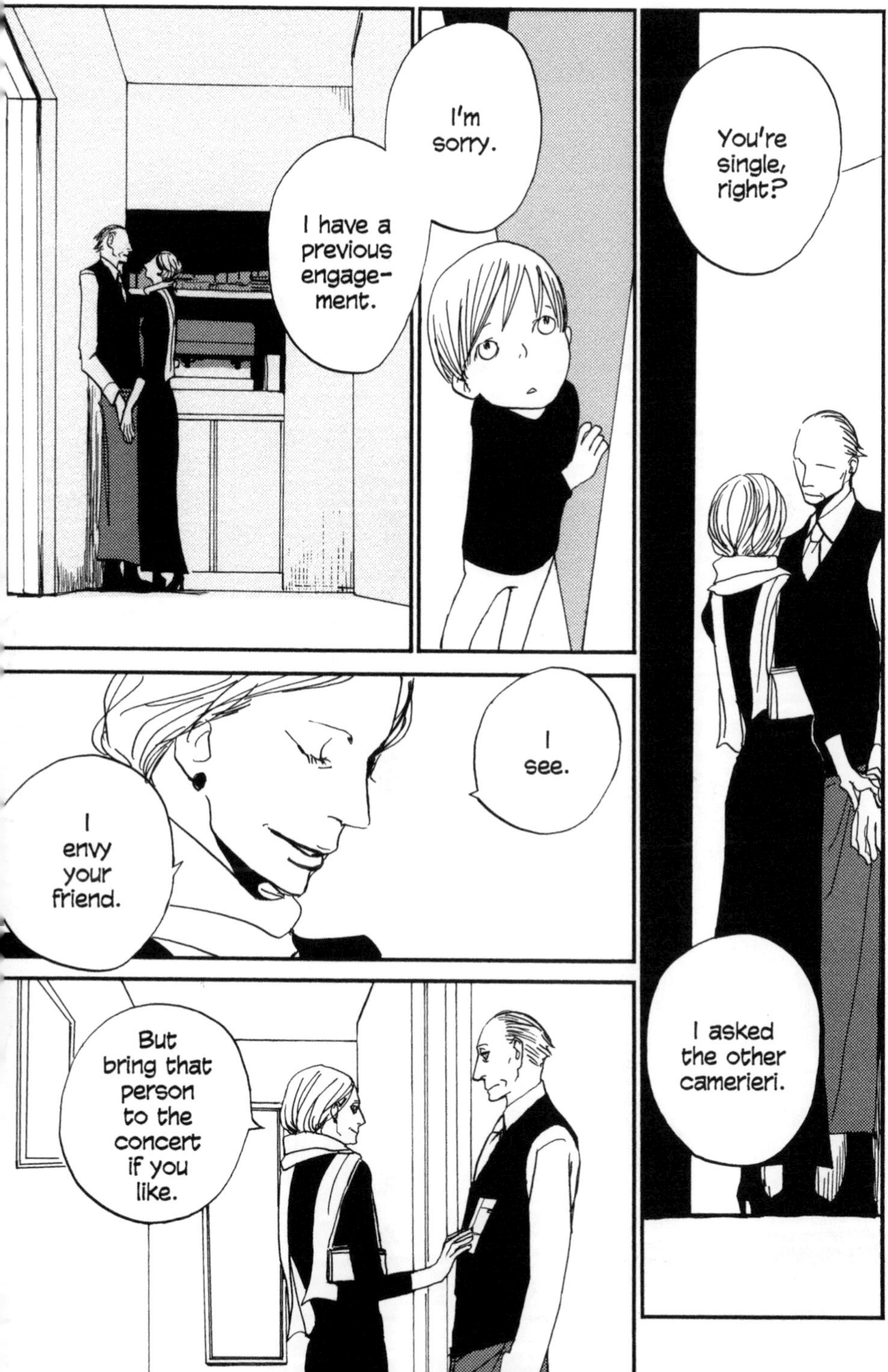
You're single, right?
I asked the other camerieri.
I'm sorry.
I have a previous engagement.
I see.
I envy your friend.
But bring that person to the concert if you like.

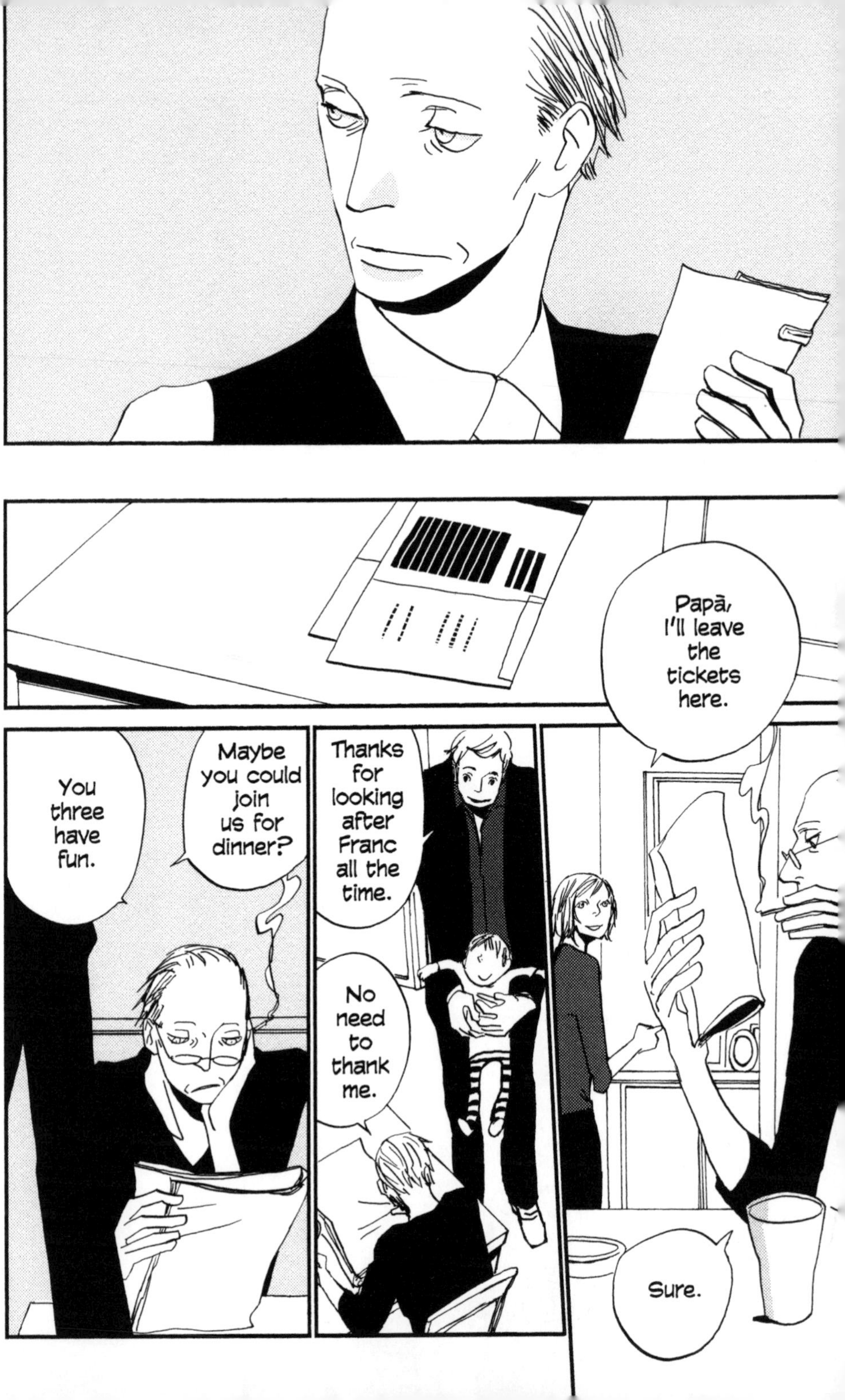
Papā, I'll leave the tickets here.
Sure.
Thanks for looking after Franc all the time.
No need to thank me.
Maybe you could join us for dinner?
You three have fun.

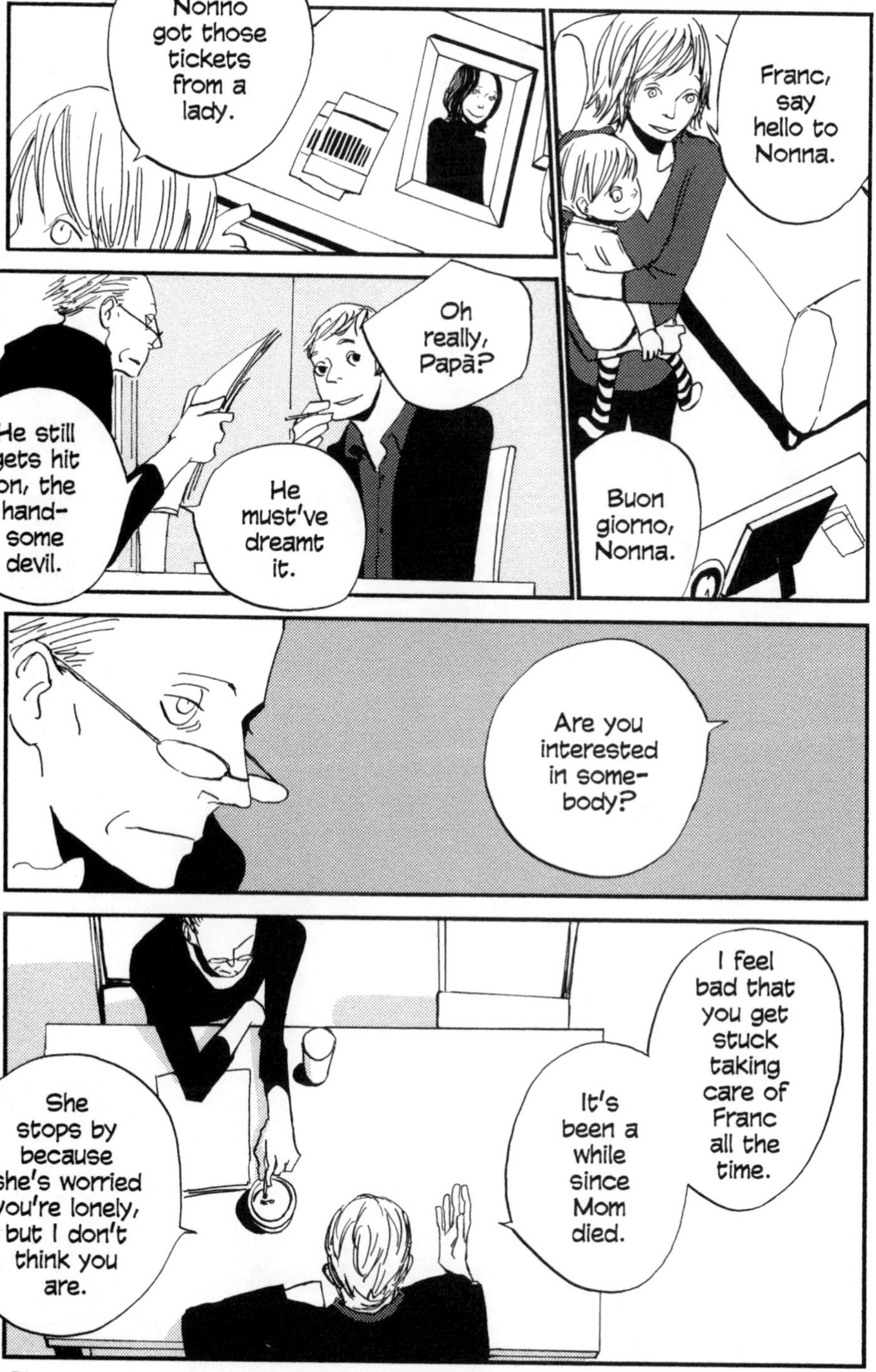
Franc, say hello to Nonna.
Buon giorno, Nonna.
Nonno got those tickets from a lady.
Oh really, Papà?
He must've dreamt it.
He still gets hit on, the hand-some devil.
Are you interested in some-body?
I feel bad that you get stuck taking care of Franc all the time.
It's been a while since Mom died.
She stops by because she's worried you're lonely, but I don't think you are.

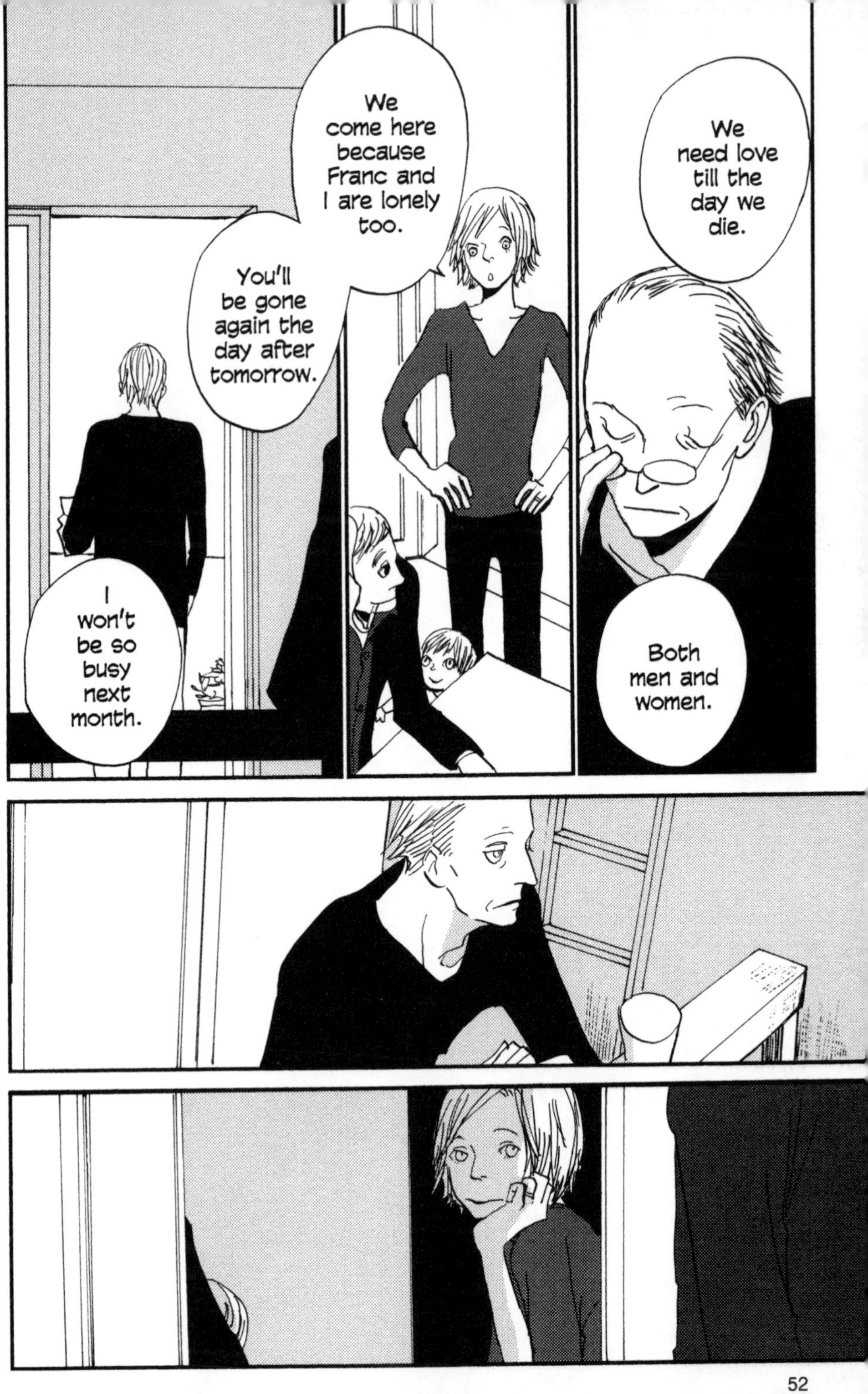
We need love till the day we die.
Both men and women.
We come here because Franc and I are lonely too.
You'll be gone again the day after tomorrow.
I won't be so busy next month.

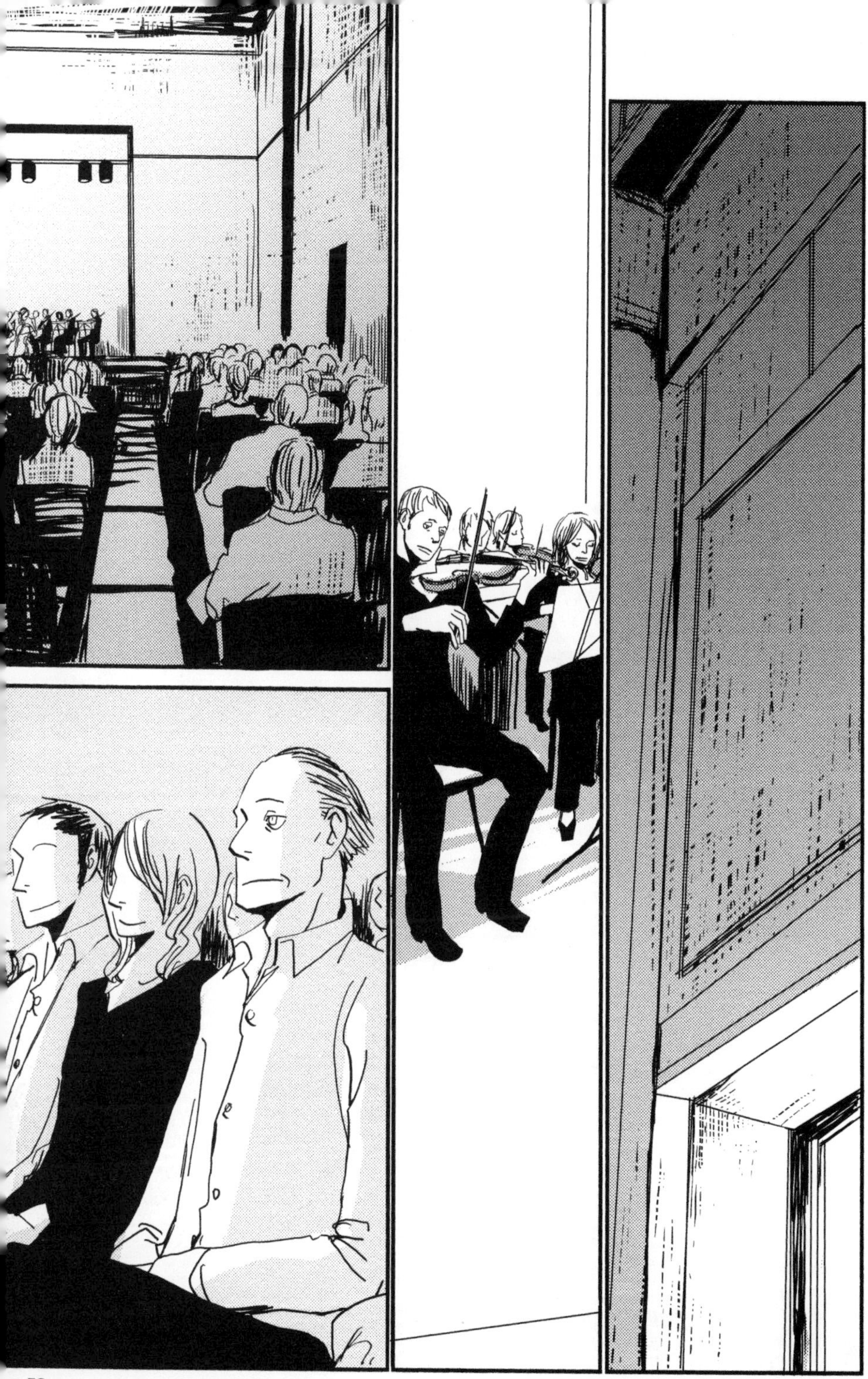

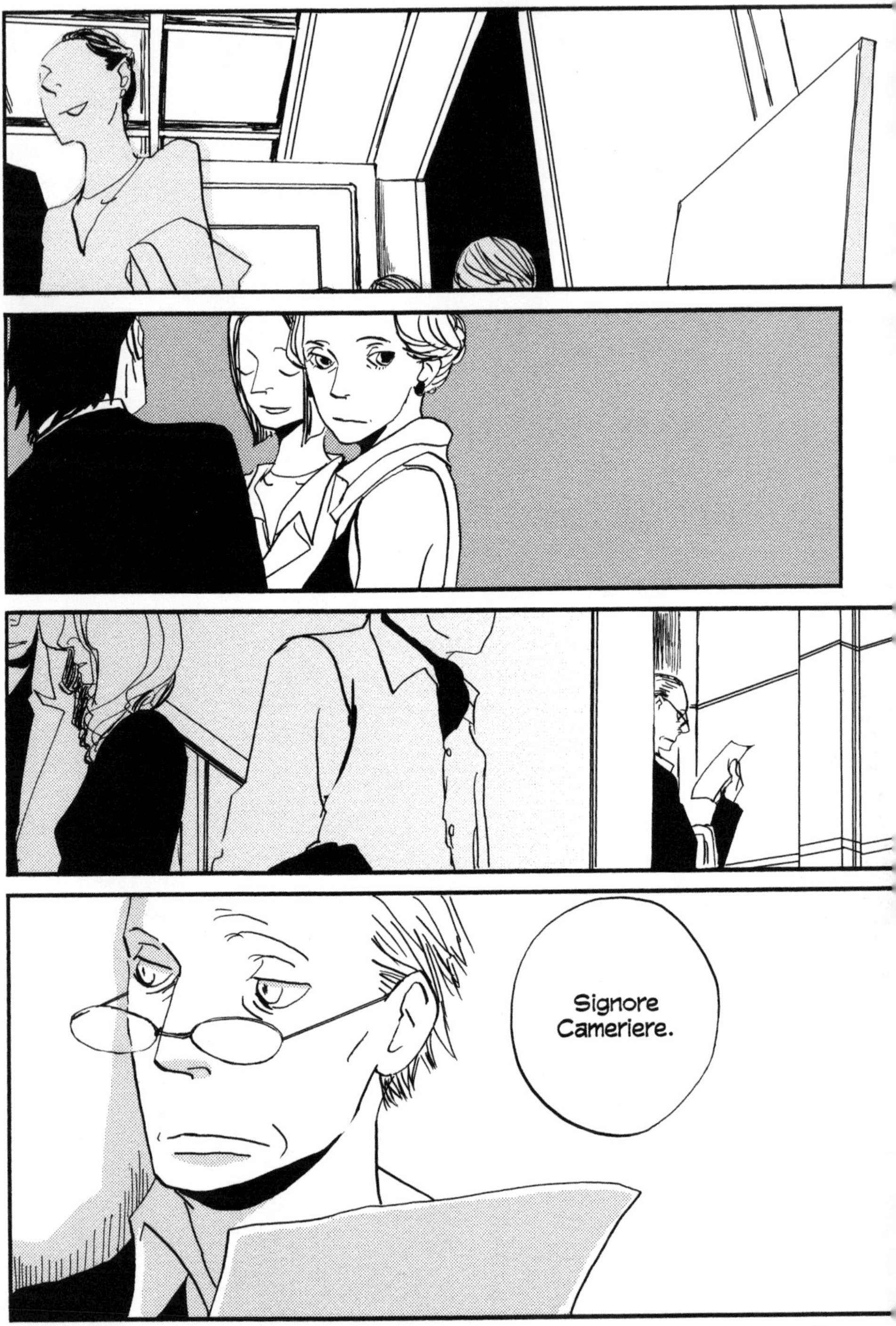
Signore
Cameriere.

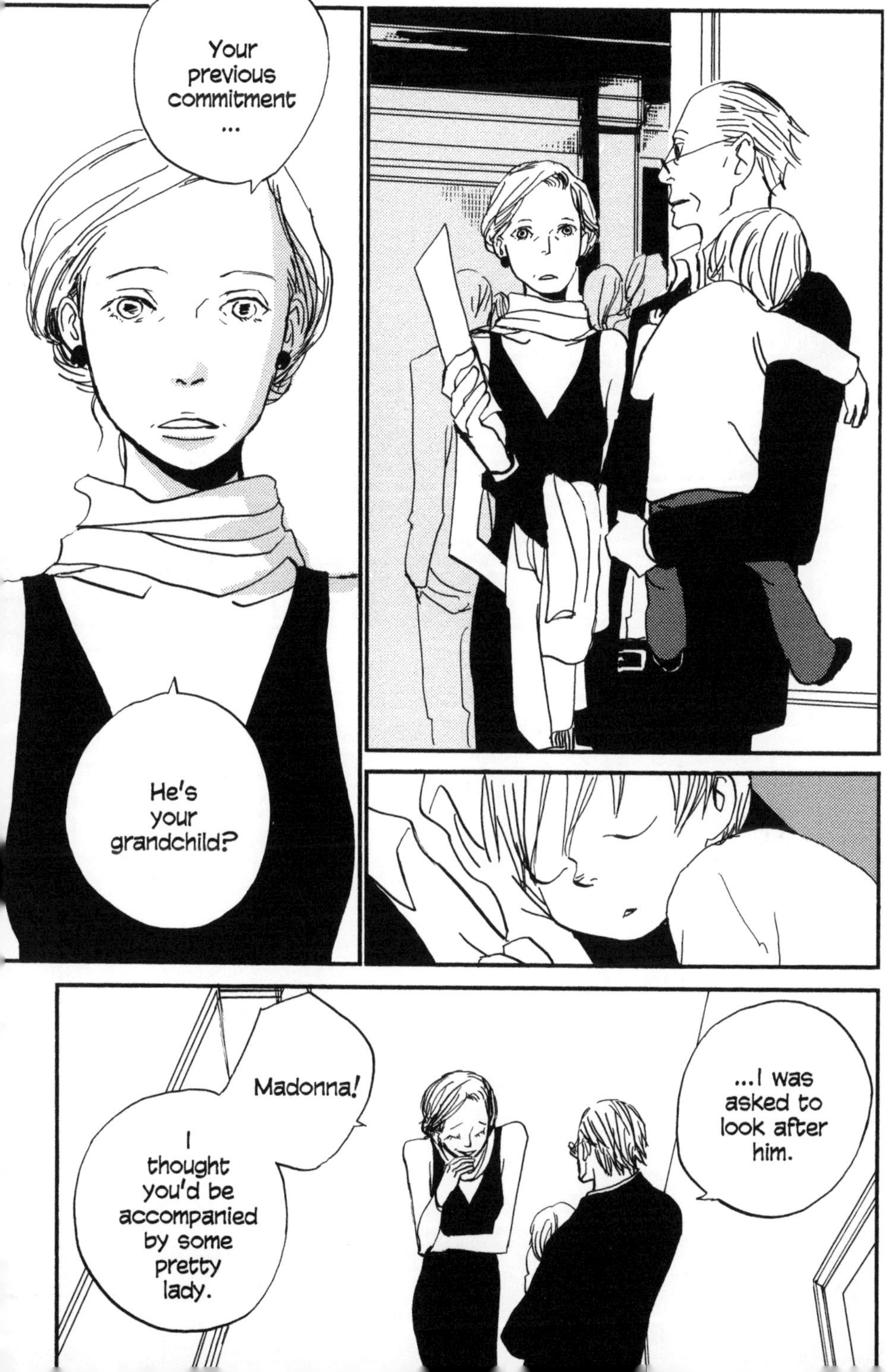
Your previous commitment ...
He's your grandchild?
...I was asked to look after him.
Madonna!
I thought you'd be accompanied by some pretty lady.

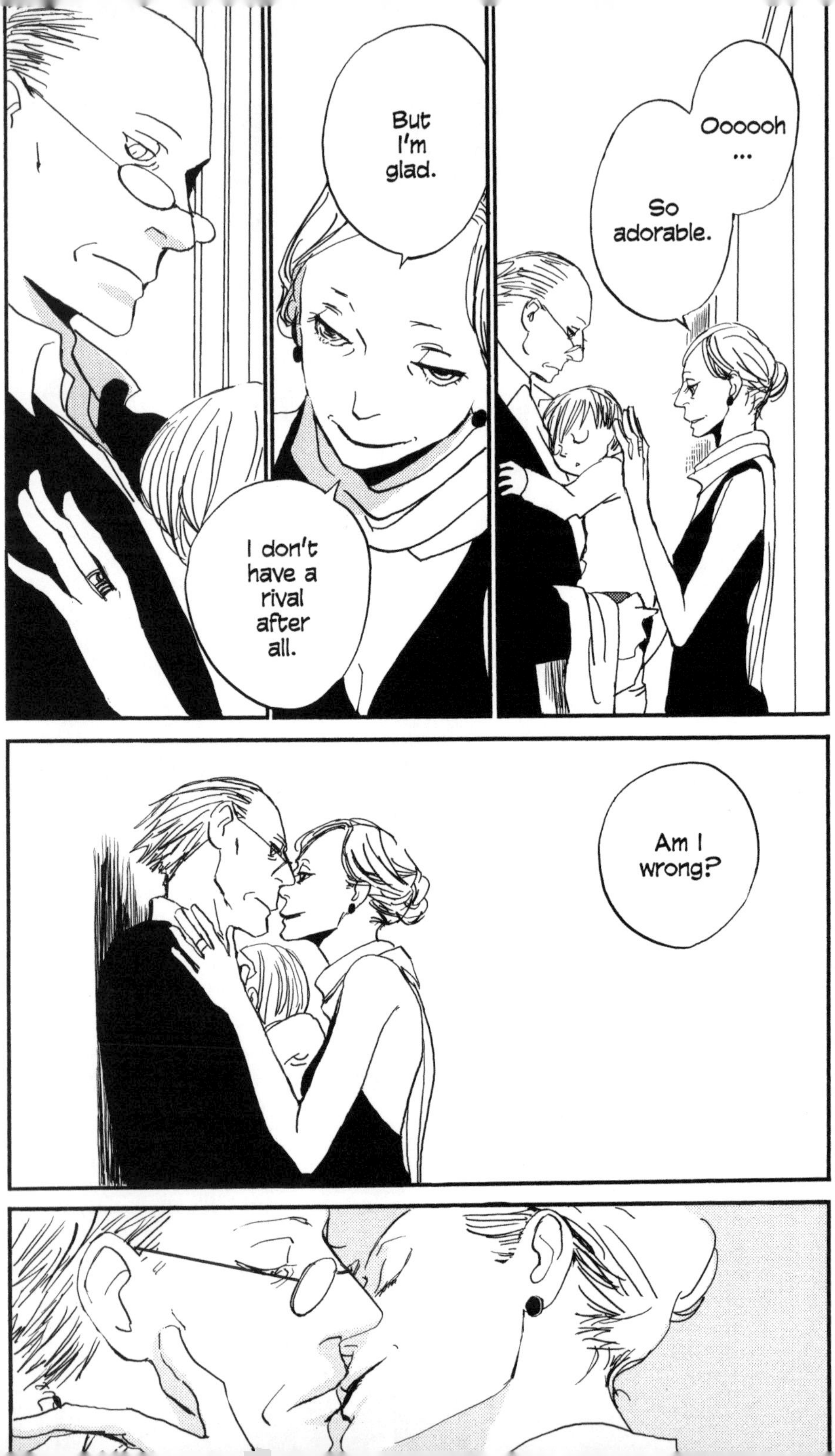
Oooooh ...
So adorable.
But I'm glad.
I don't have a rival after all.
Am I wrong?

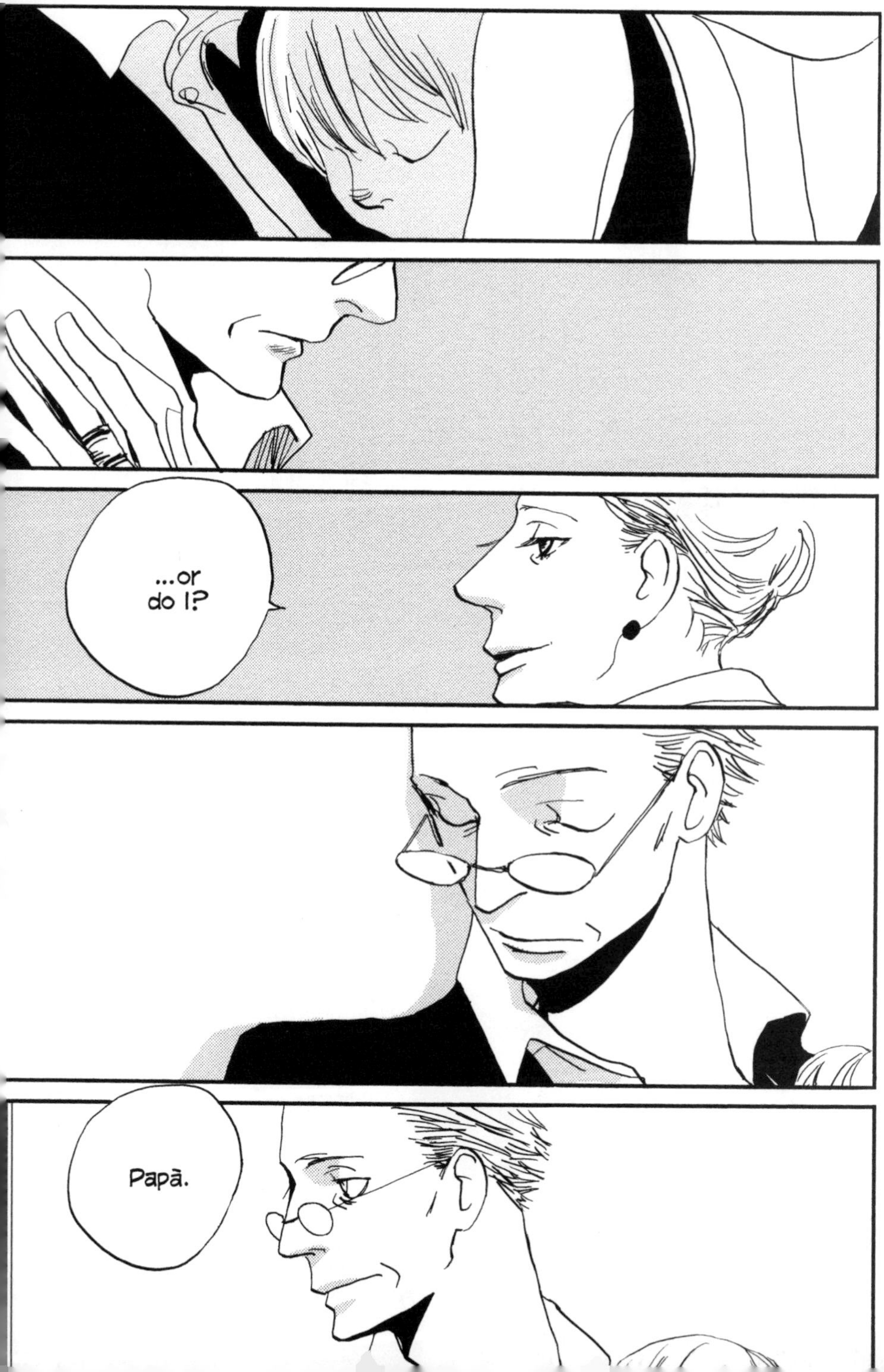
...or do I?
Papà.

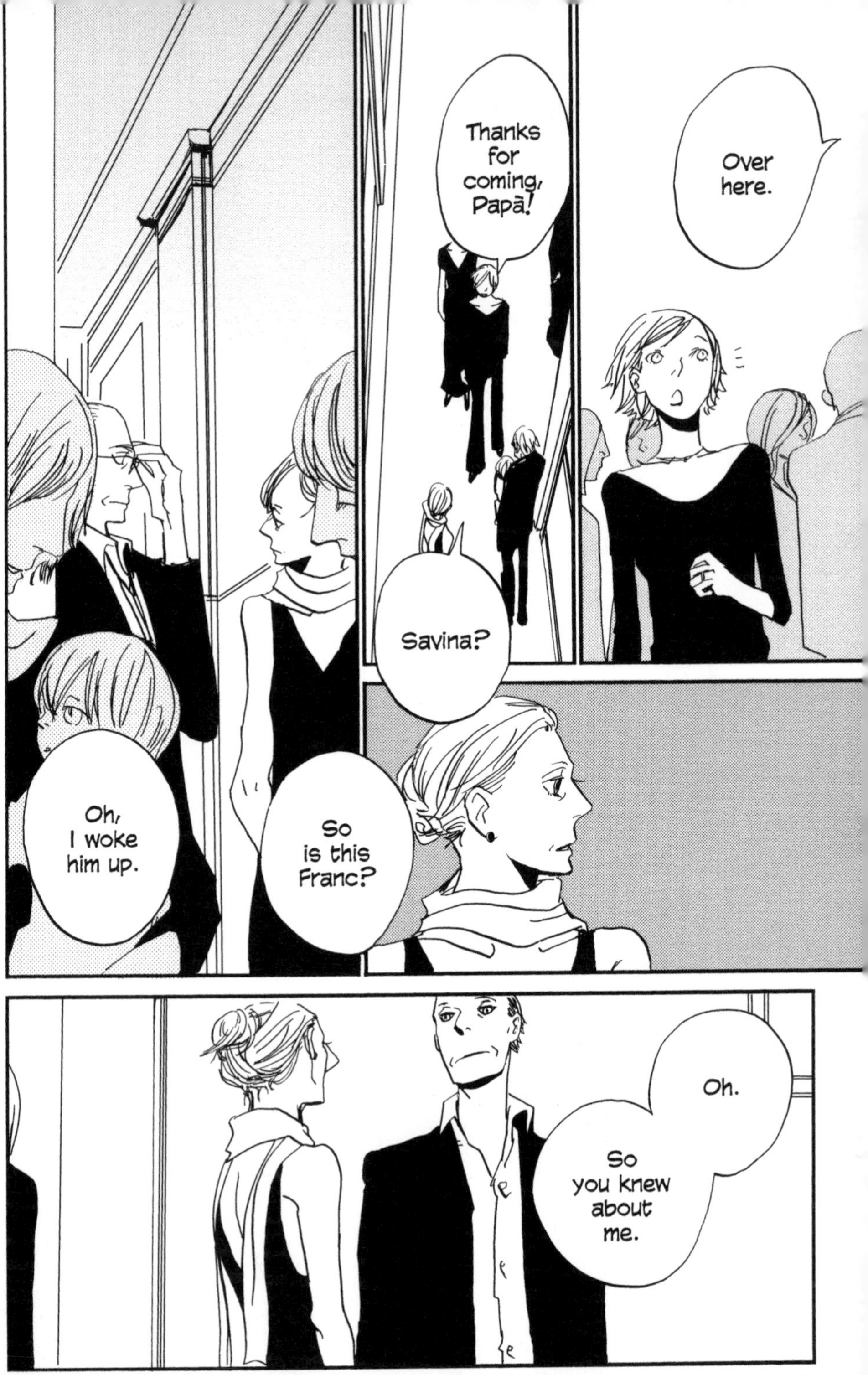
Over here.
Thanks for coming, Papà!
Savina?
So is this Franc?
Oh, I woke him up.
Oh.
So you knew about me.

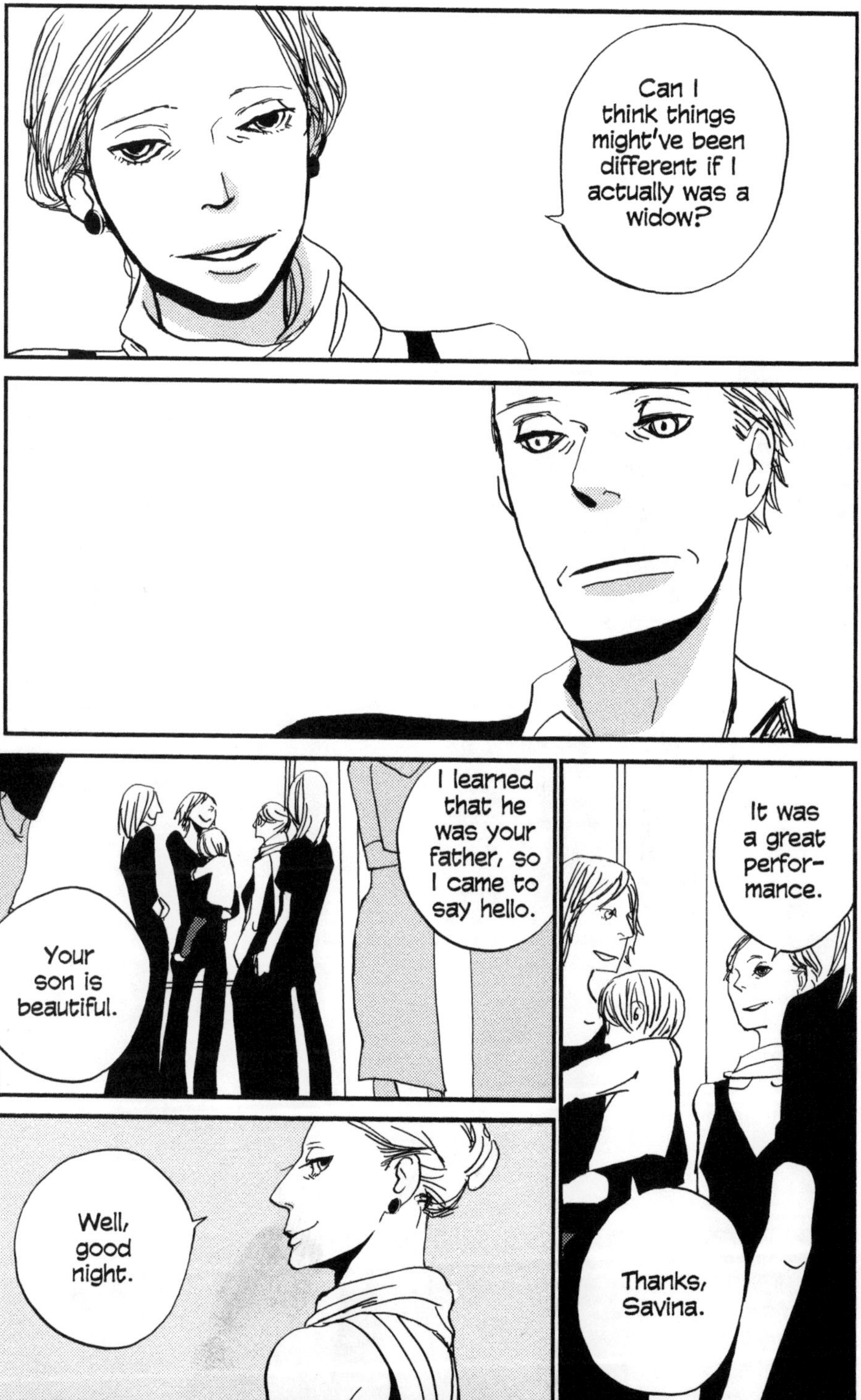
Can I think things might've been different if I actually was a widow?
It was a great performance.
Thanks, Savina.
I learned that he was your father, so I came to say hello.
Your son is beautiful.
Well, good night.

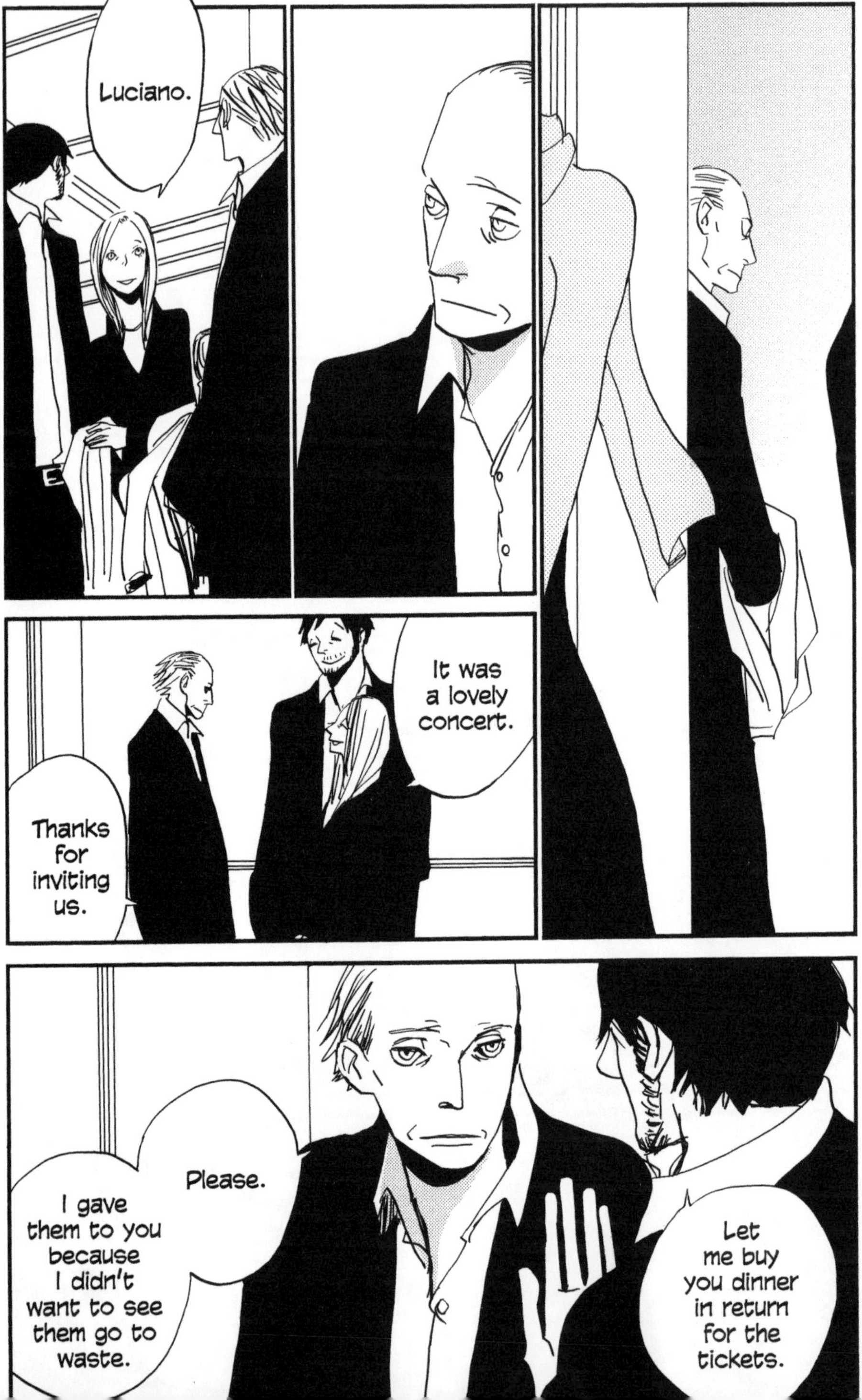
Luciano.
It was a lovely concert.
Thanks for inviting us.
Let me buy you dinner in return for the tickets.
Please.
I gave them to you because I didn't want to see them go to waste.

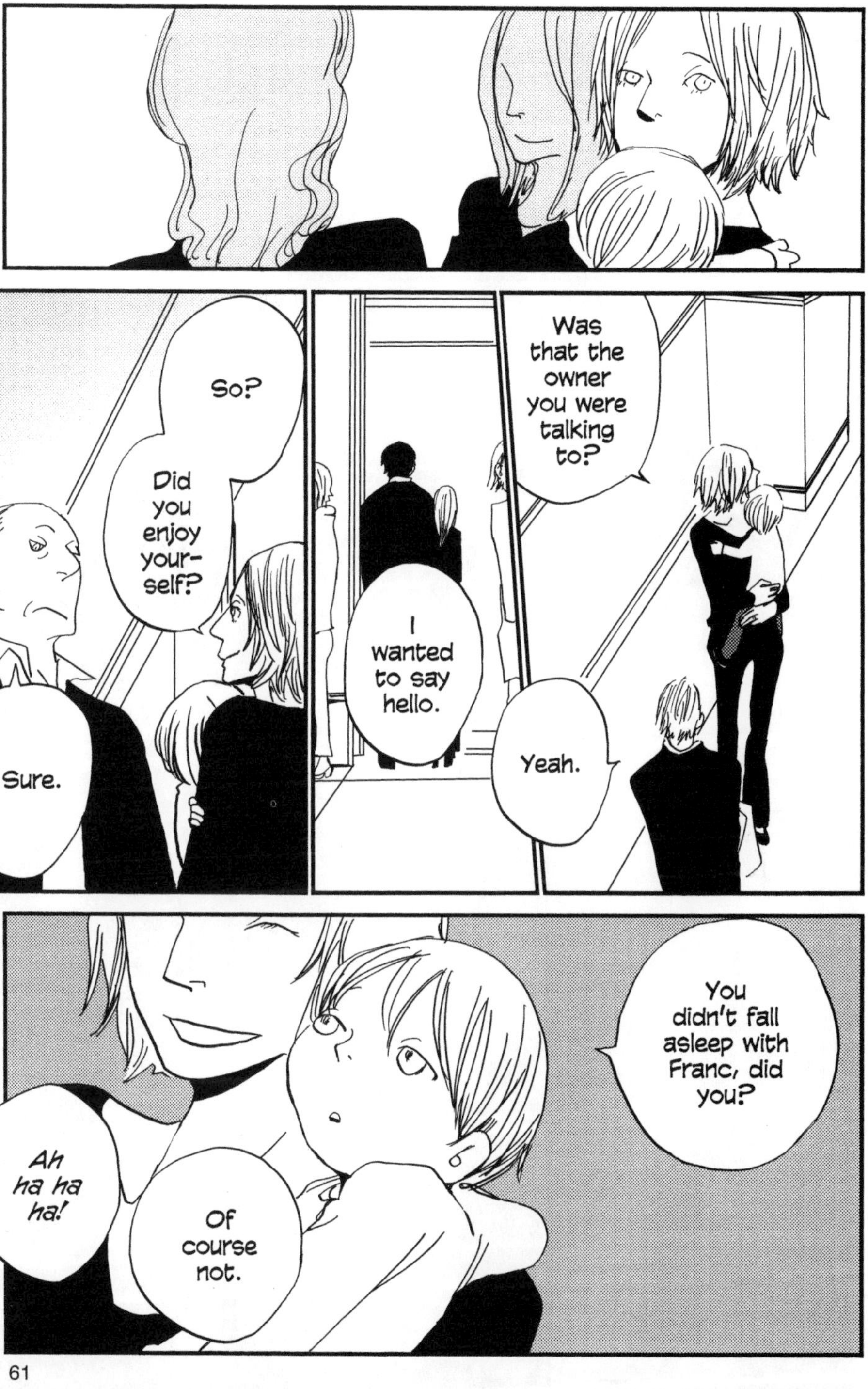
Was that the owner you were talking to?
Yeah.
I wanted to say hello.
So?
Did you enjoy your-self?
...Sure.
You didn't fall asleep with Franc, did you?
Of course not.
Ah ha ha ha!

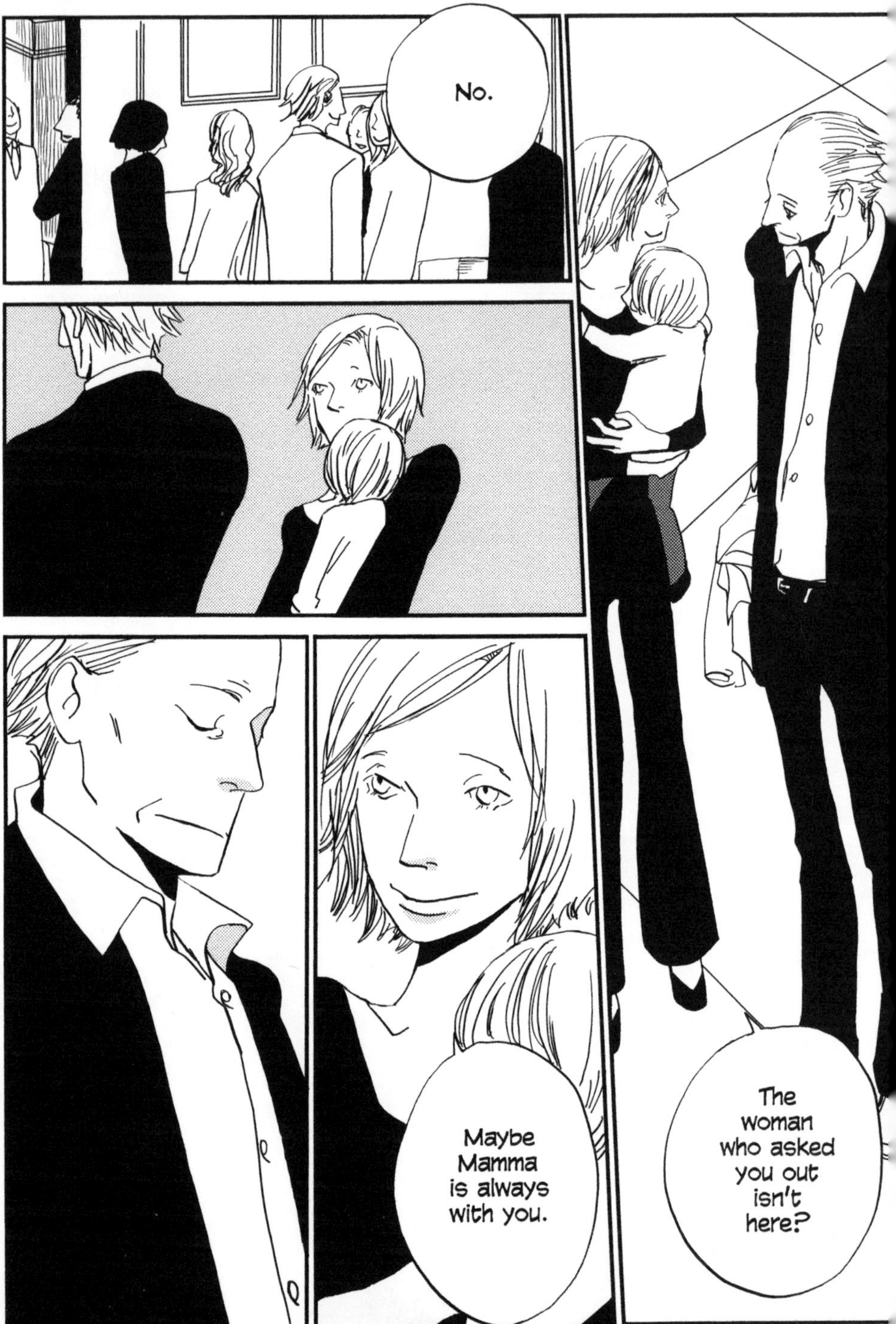
The woman who asked you out isn't here?
No.
Maybe Mamma is always with you.

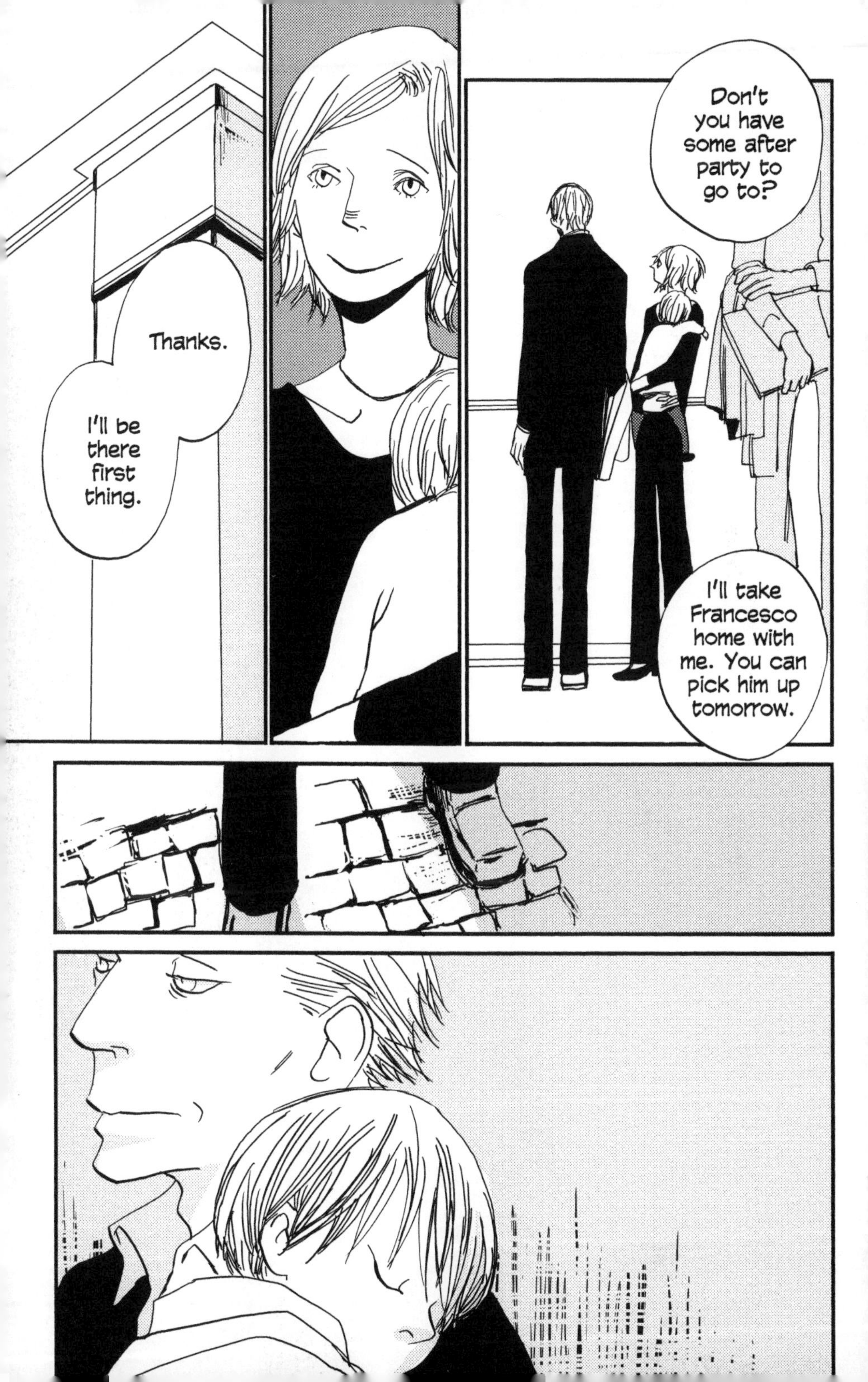

Don't you have some after party to go to?
I'll take Francesco home with me. You can pick him up tomorrow.
Thanks.
I'll be there first thing.

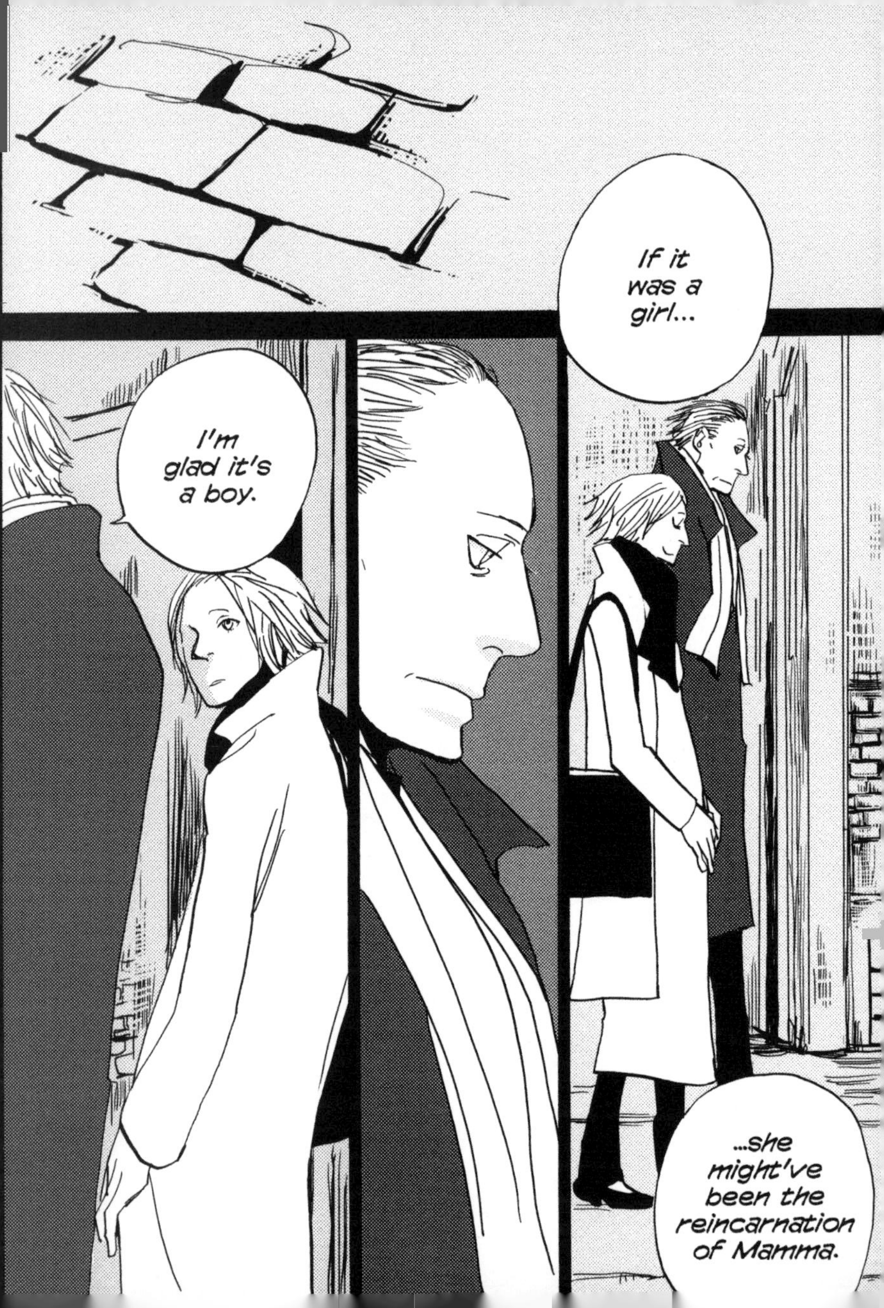
If it was a girl...
...she might've been the reincarnation of Mamma.
I'm glad it's a boy.

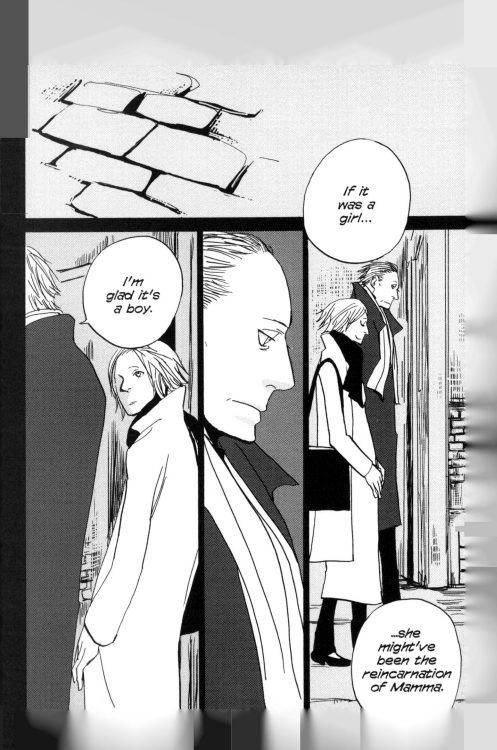

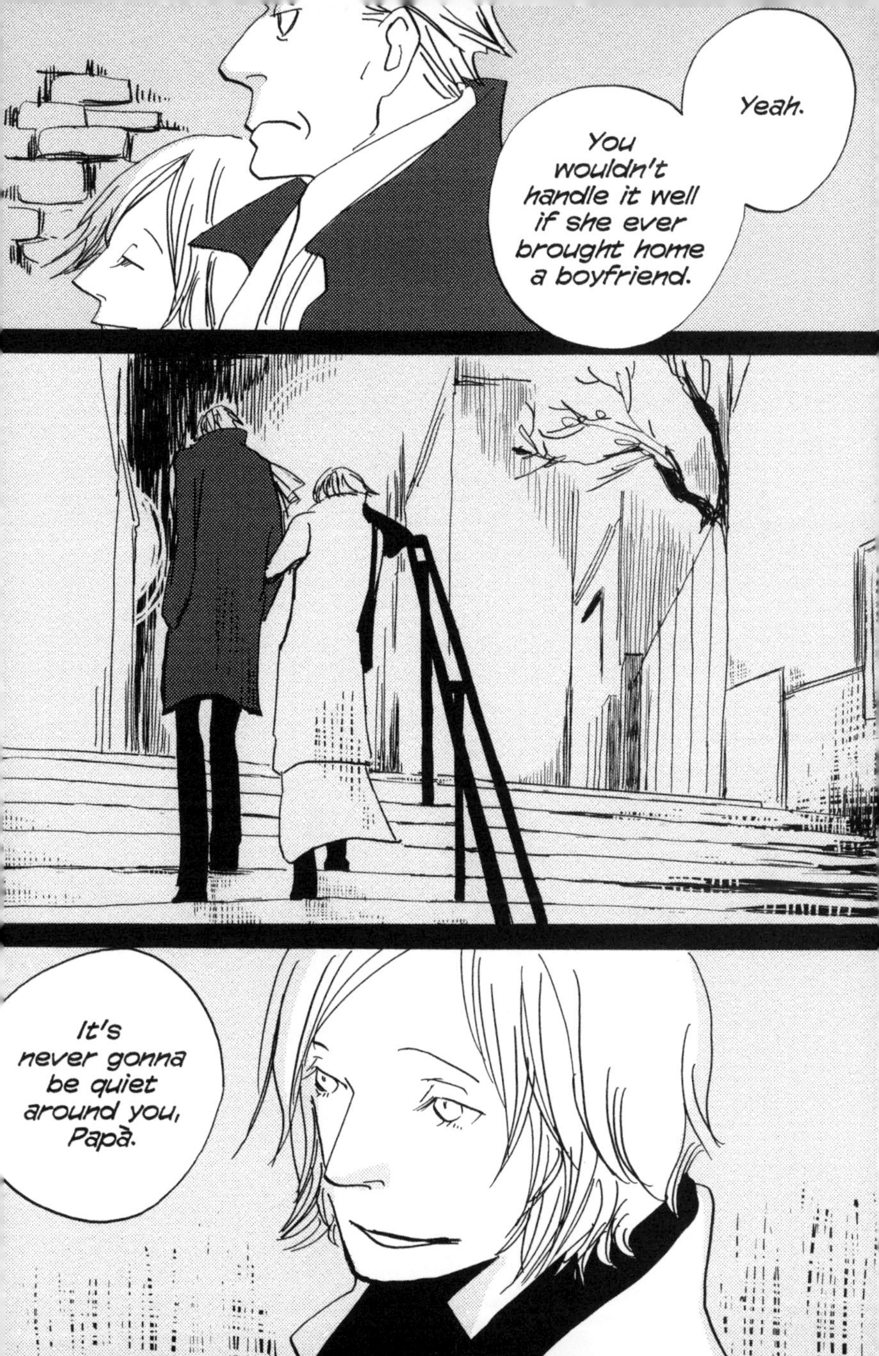
Yeah.
You wouldn't handle it well if she ever brought home a boyfriend.
It's never gonna be quiet around you, Papà.

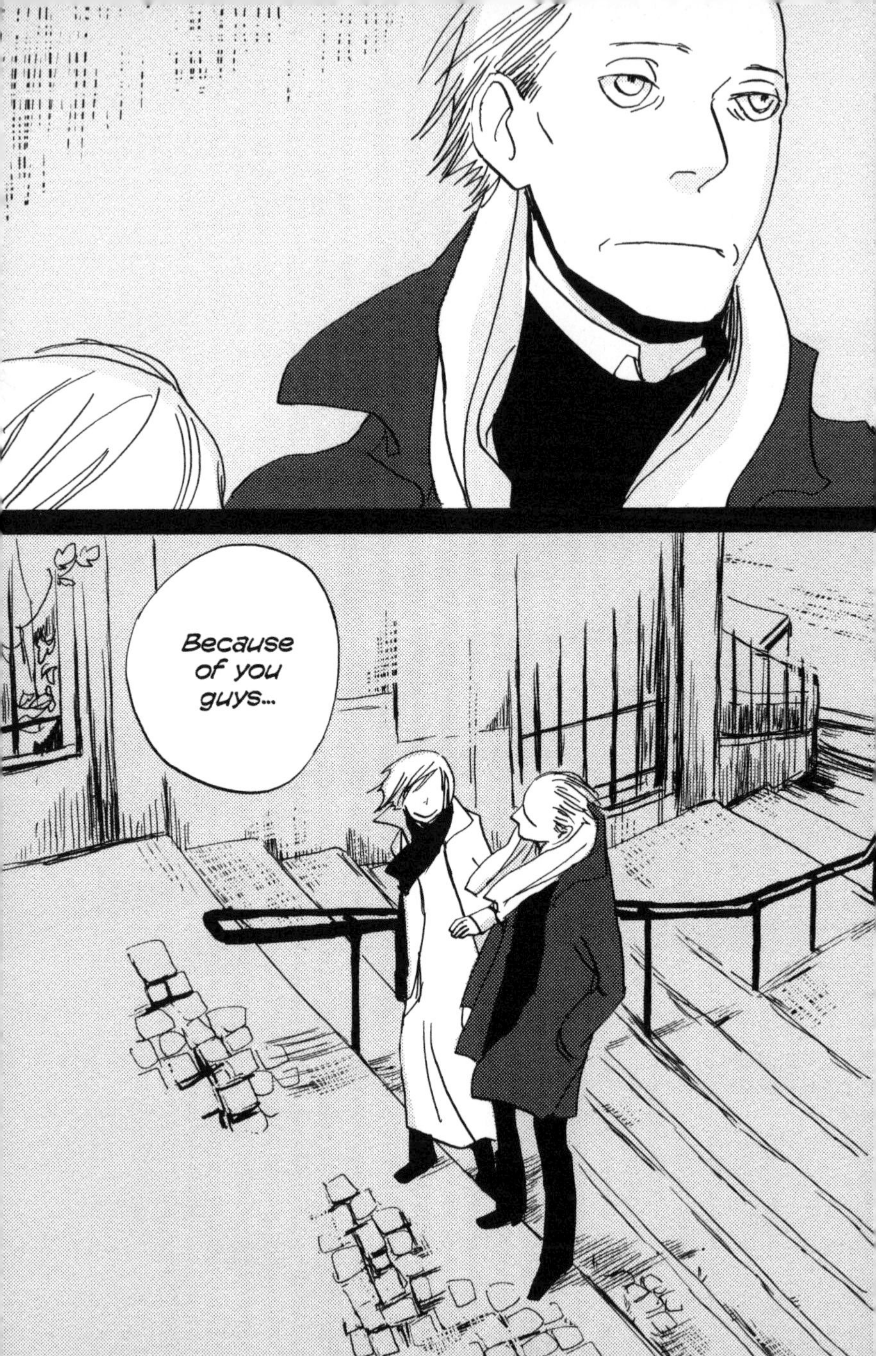
Because of you guys...

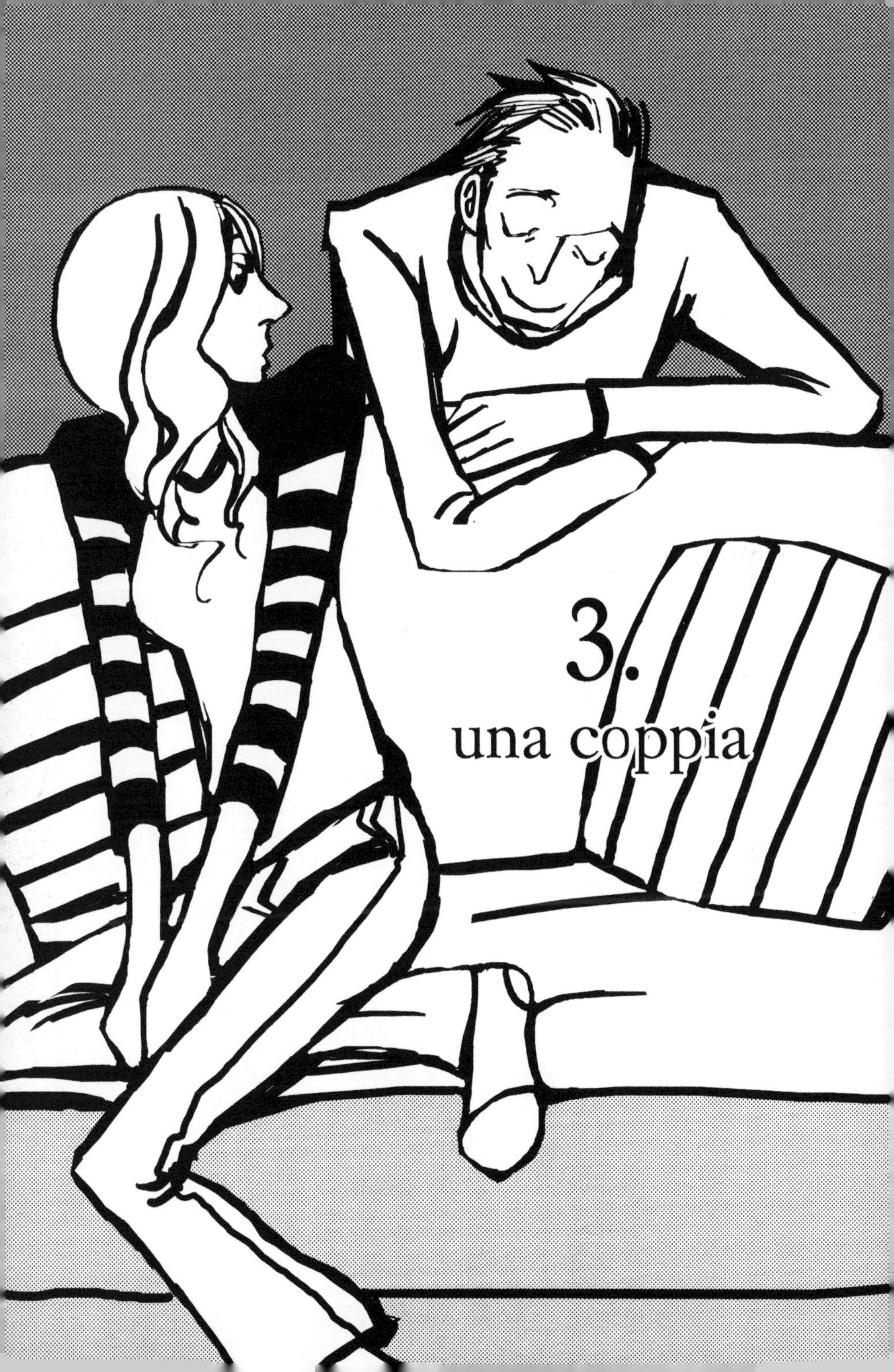
3.
una coppia

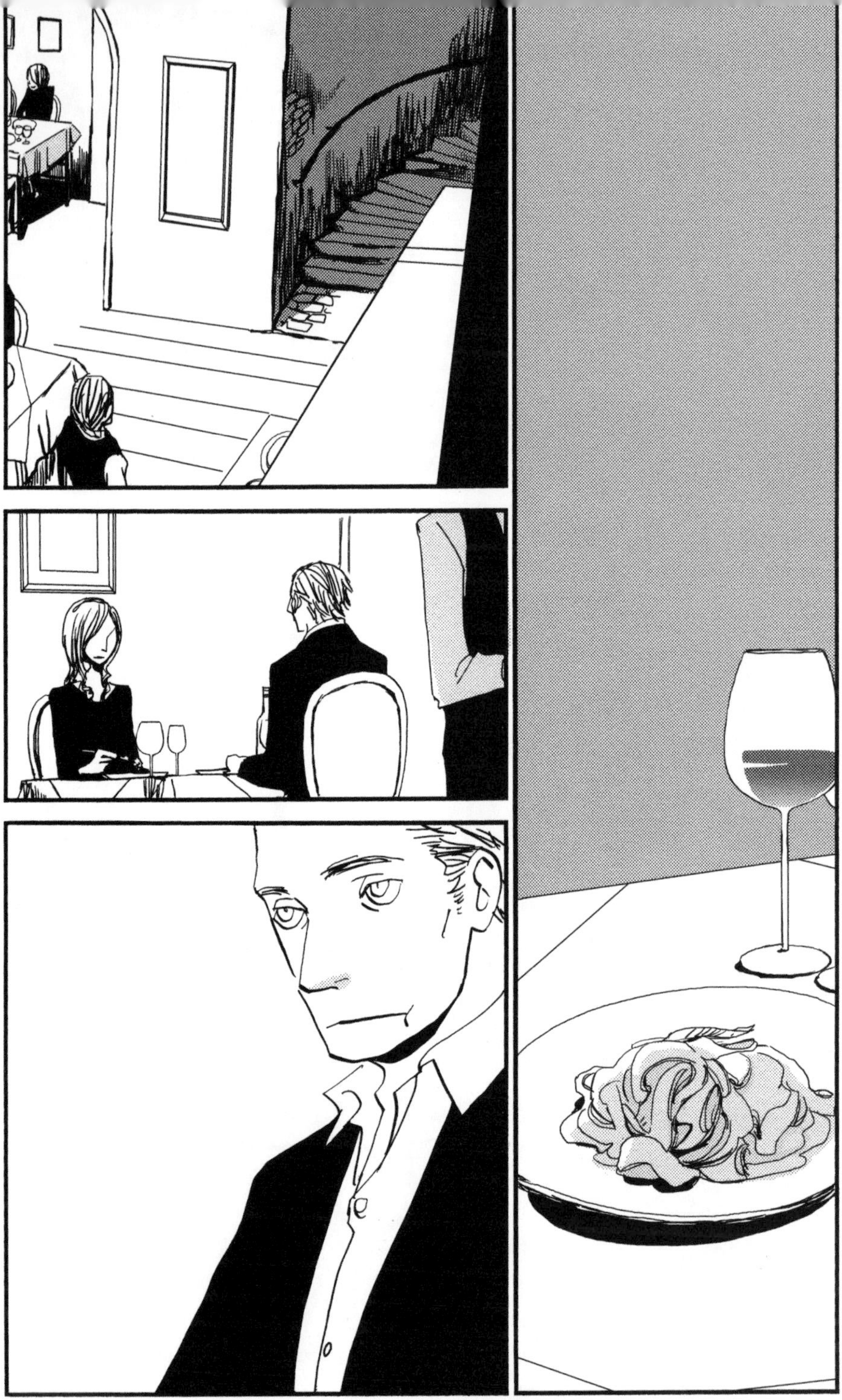

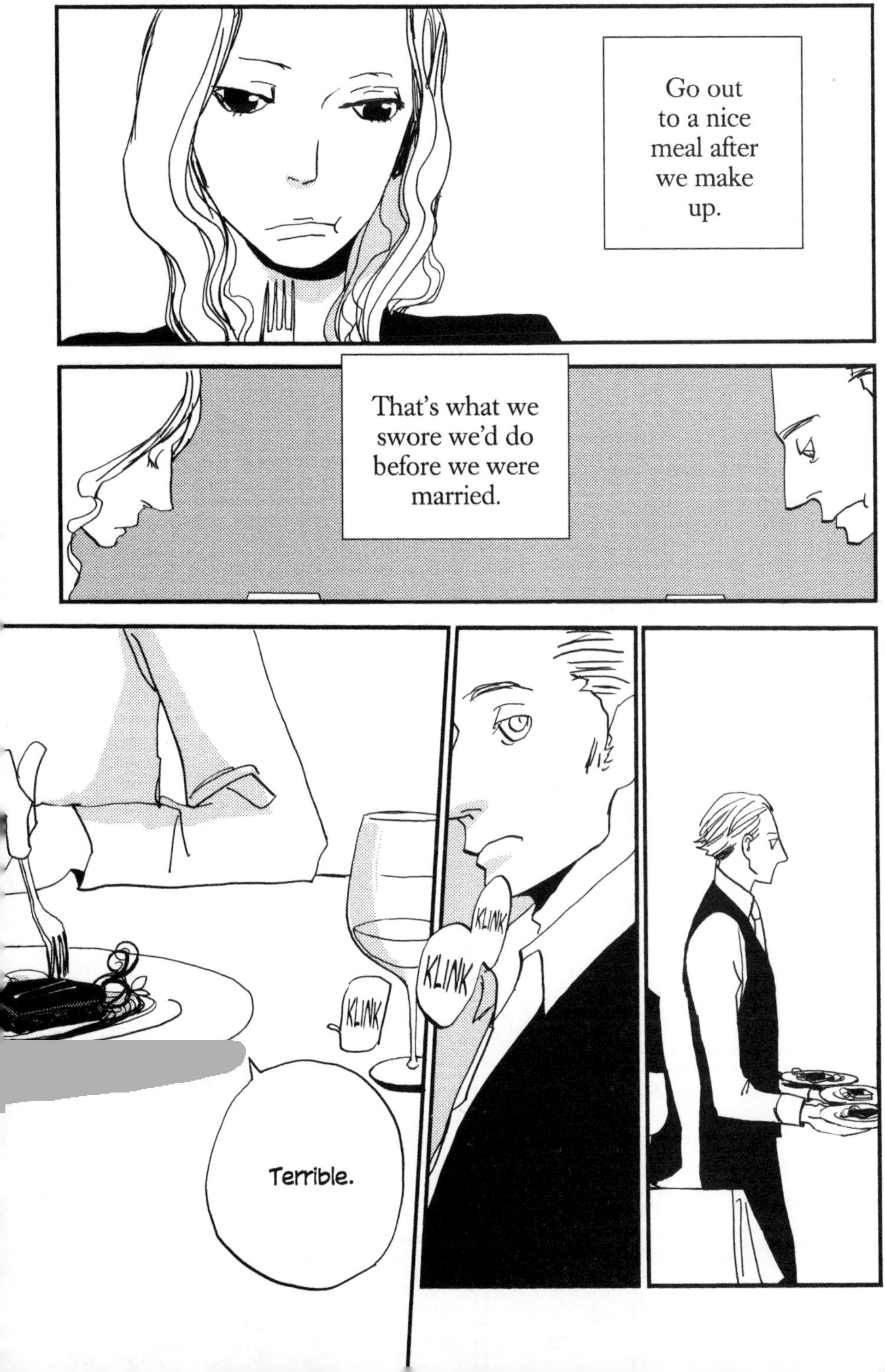
Go out to a nice meal after we make up.
That's what we swore we'd do before we were married.
KLINK
KLINK
KLINK
Terrible.

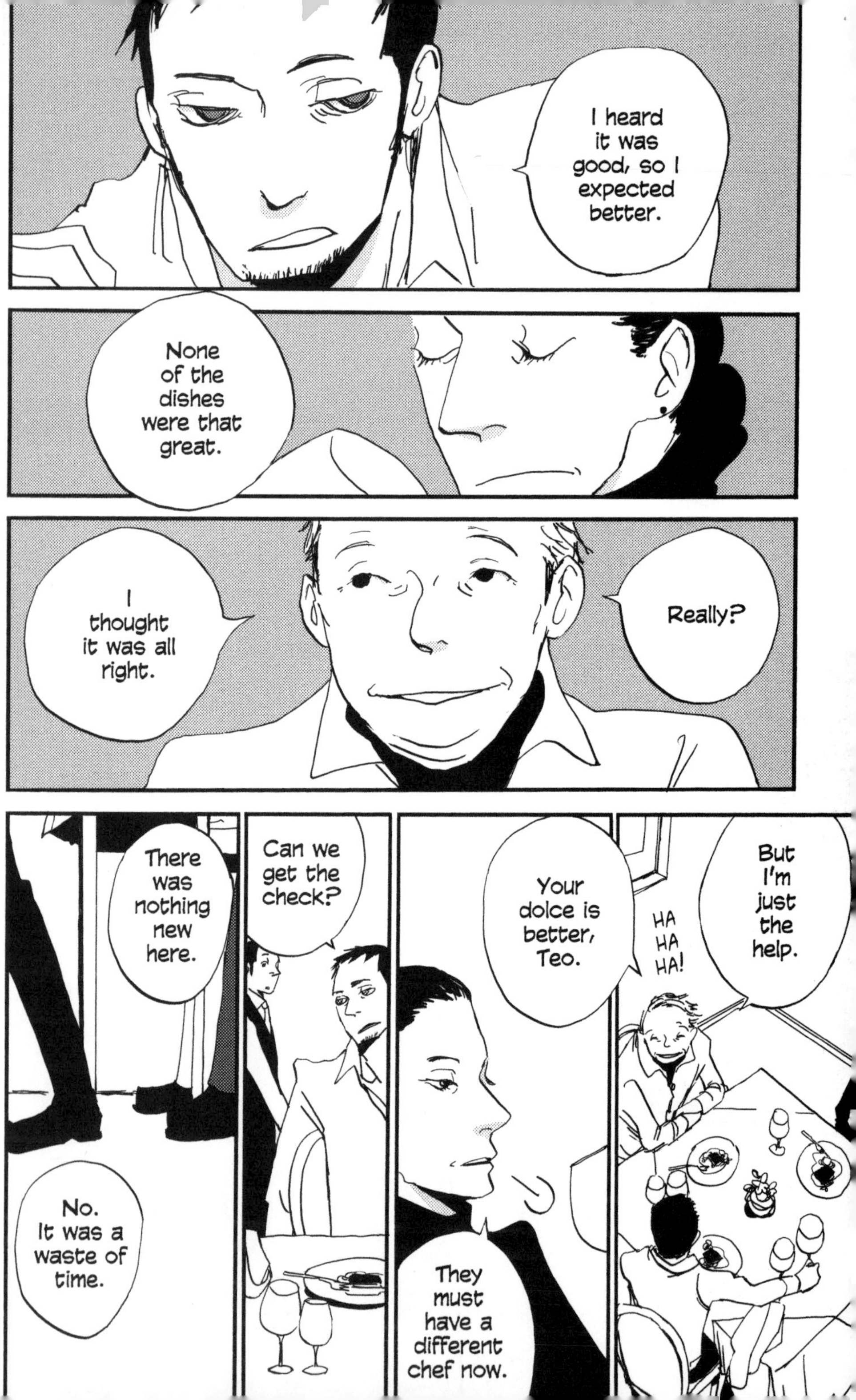
I heard it was good, so I expected better.
None of the dishes were that great.
Really?
I thought it was all right.
Your dolce is better, Teo.
But I'm just the help.
HA HA HA!
They must have a different chef now.
Can we get the check?
There was nothing new here.
No. It was a waste of time.

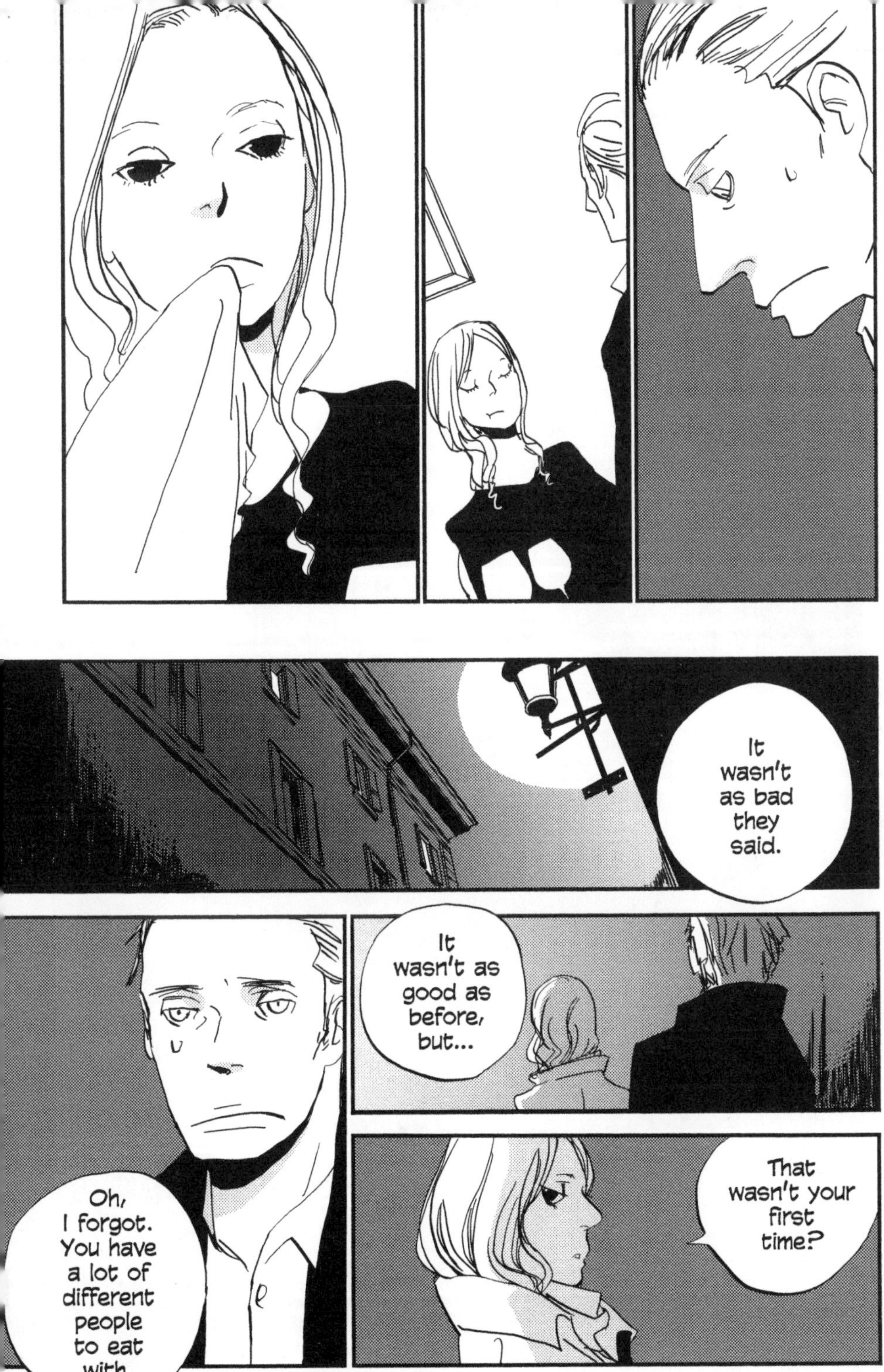
It wasn't as bad they said.
It wasn't as good as before, but...
That wasn't your first time?
Oh, I forgot. You have a lot of different people to eat with.

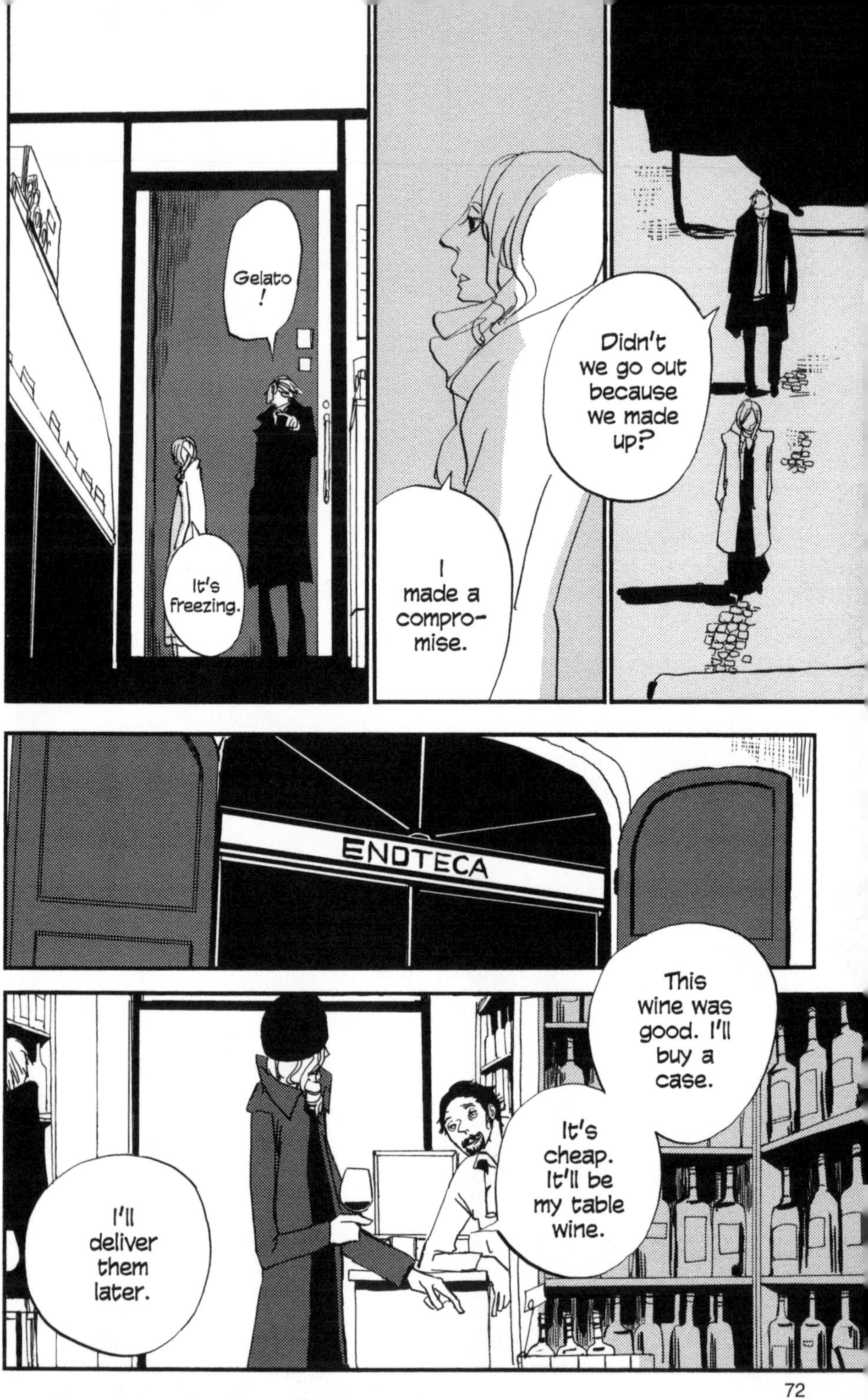
Didn't we go out because we made up?
I made a compromise.
Gelato!
It's freezing.
ENDTECA
This wine was good. I'll buy a case.
It's cheap. It'll be my table wine.
I'll deliver them later.

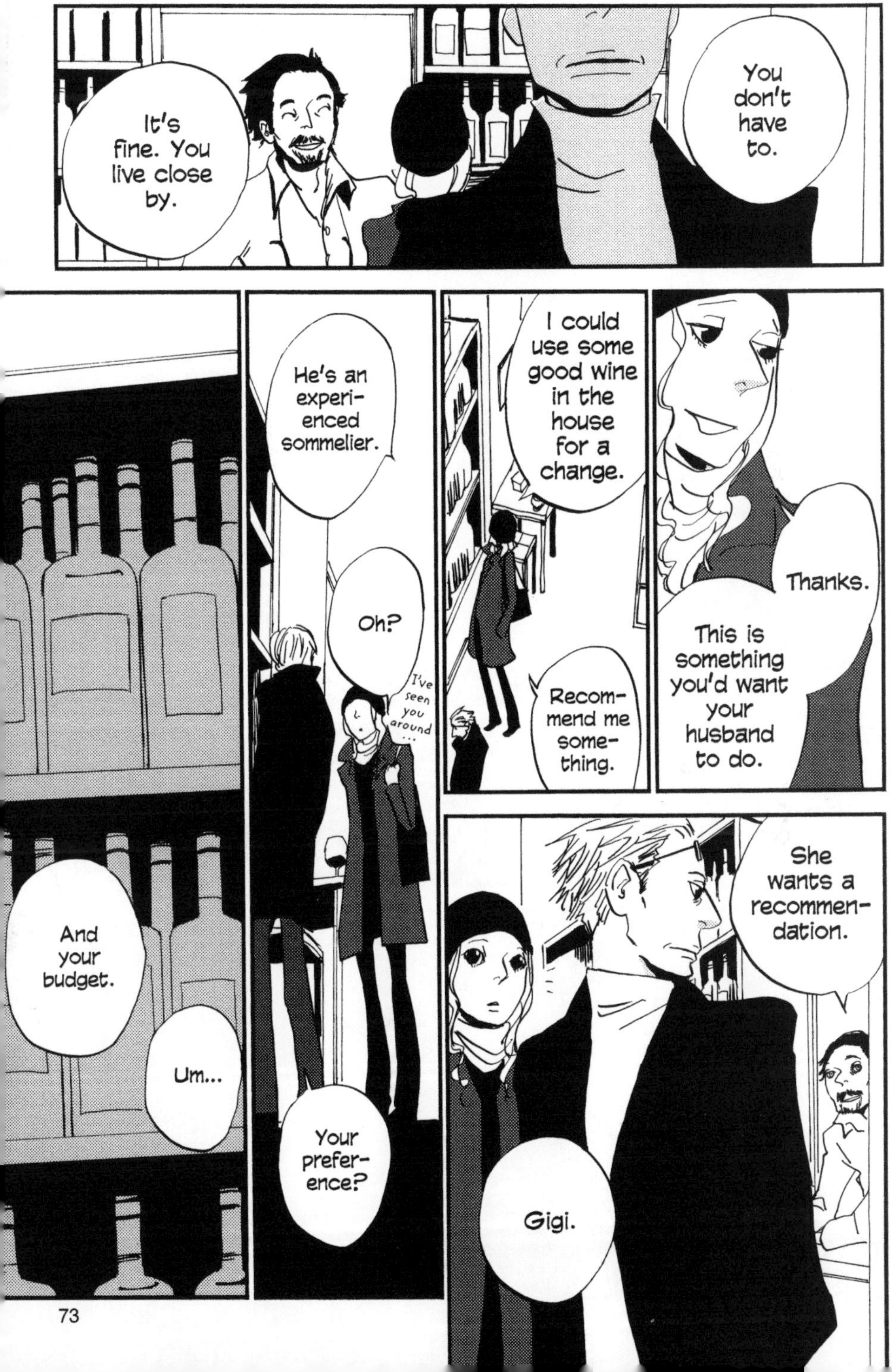
You don't have to.
It's fine. You live close by.
Thanks.
This is something you'd want your husband to do.
I could use some good wine in the house for a change.
Recommend me something.
She wants a recommendation.
Gigi.
He's an experienced sommelier.
Oh?
I've seen you around...
Your preference?
And your budget.
Um...

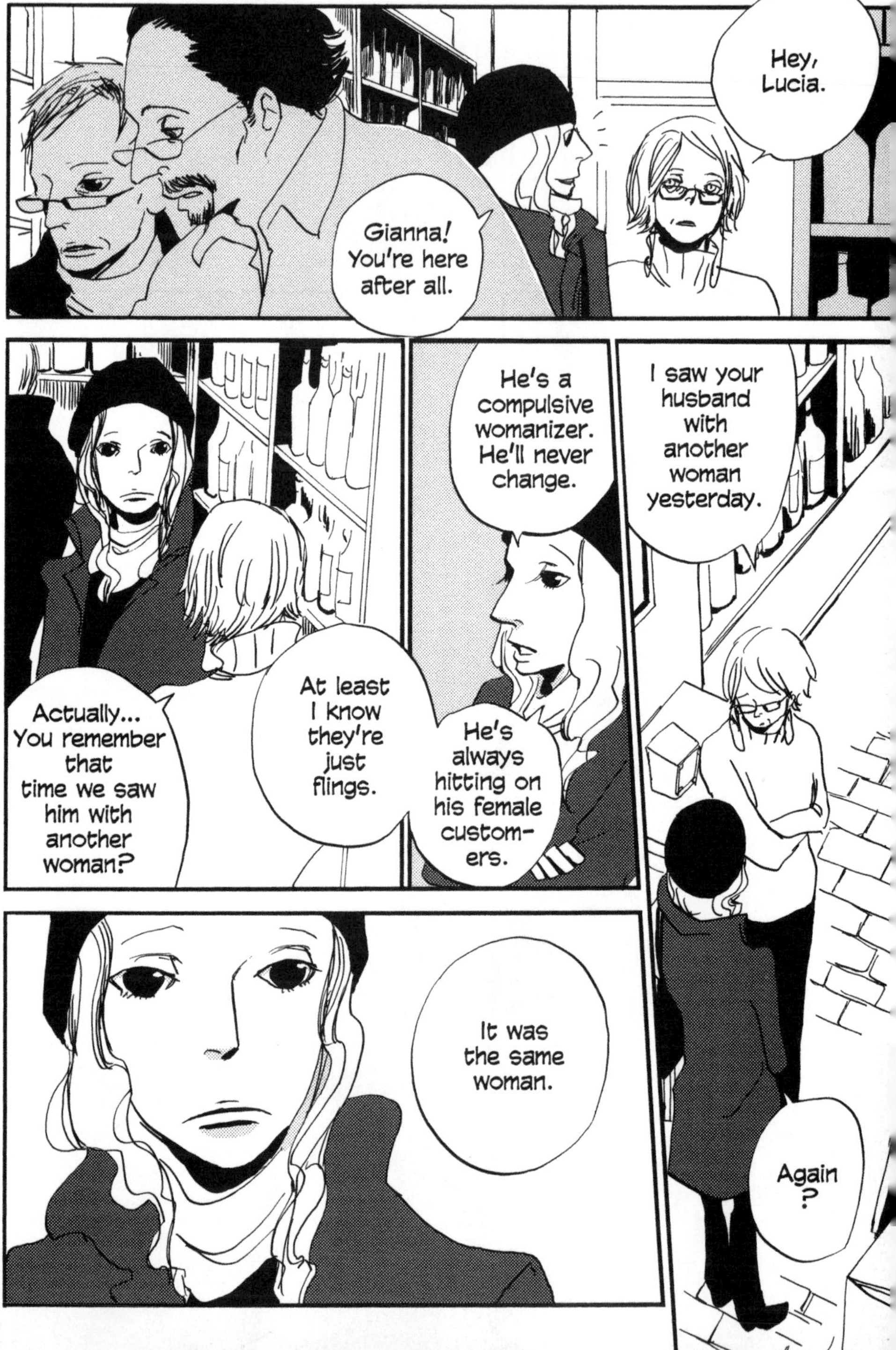
Hey, Lucia.
Gianna! You're here after all.
I saw your husband with another woman yesterday.
Again?
He's a compulsive womanizer. He'll never change.
He's always hitting on his female custom-ers.
At least I know they're just flings.
Actually... You remember that time we saw him with another woman?
It was the same woman.

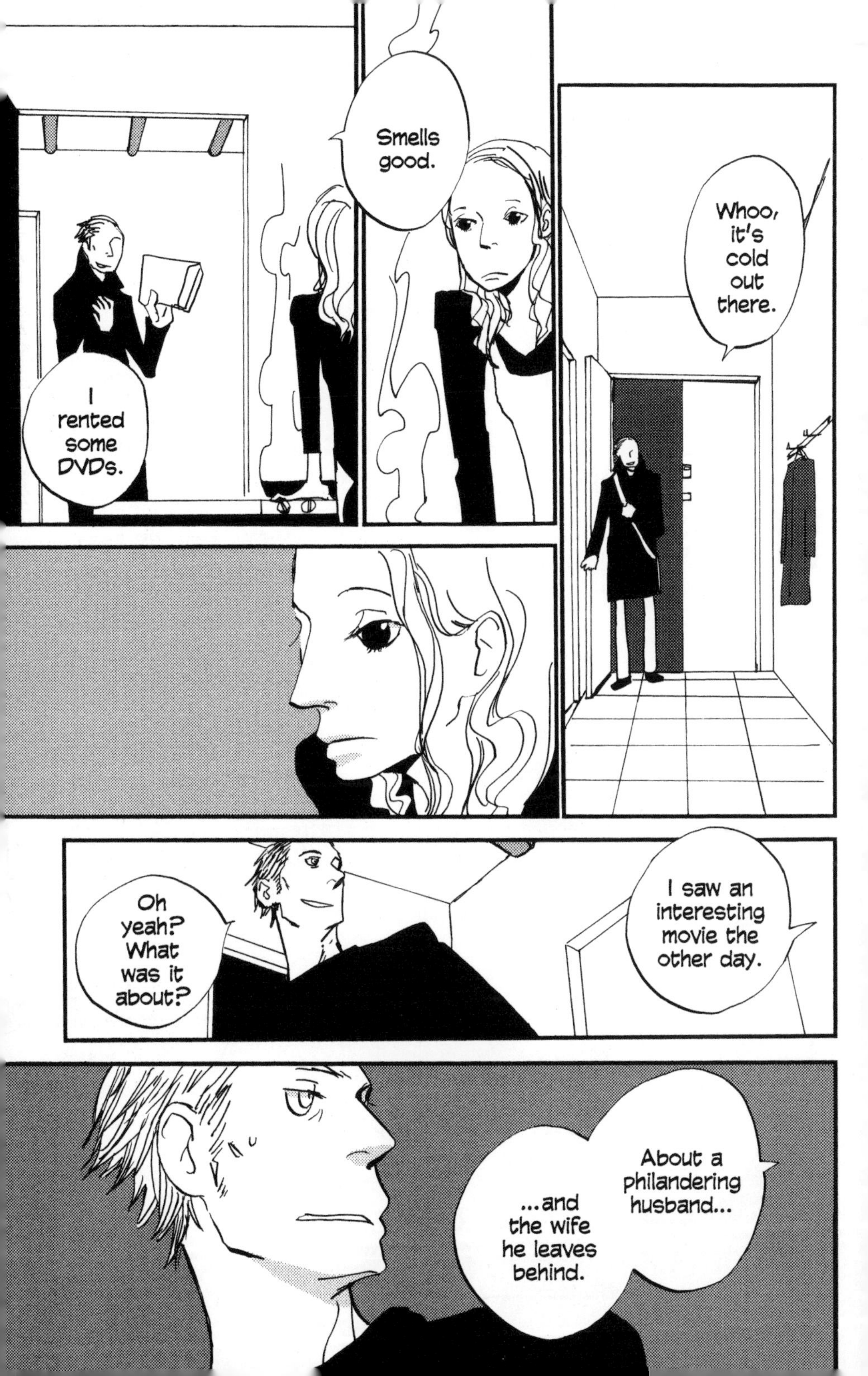
Whoo, it's cold out there.
Smells good.
I rented some DVDs.
I saw an interesting movie the other day.
Oh yeah? What was it about?
About a philandering husband...
...and the wife he leaves behind.

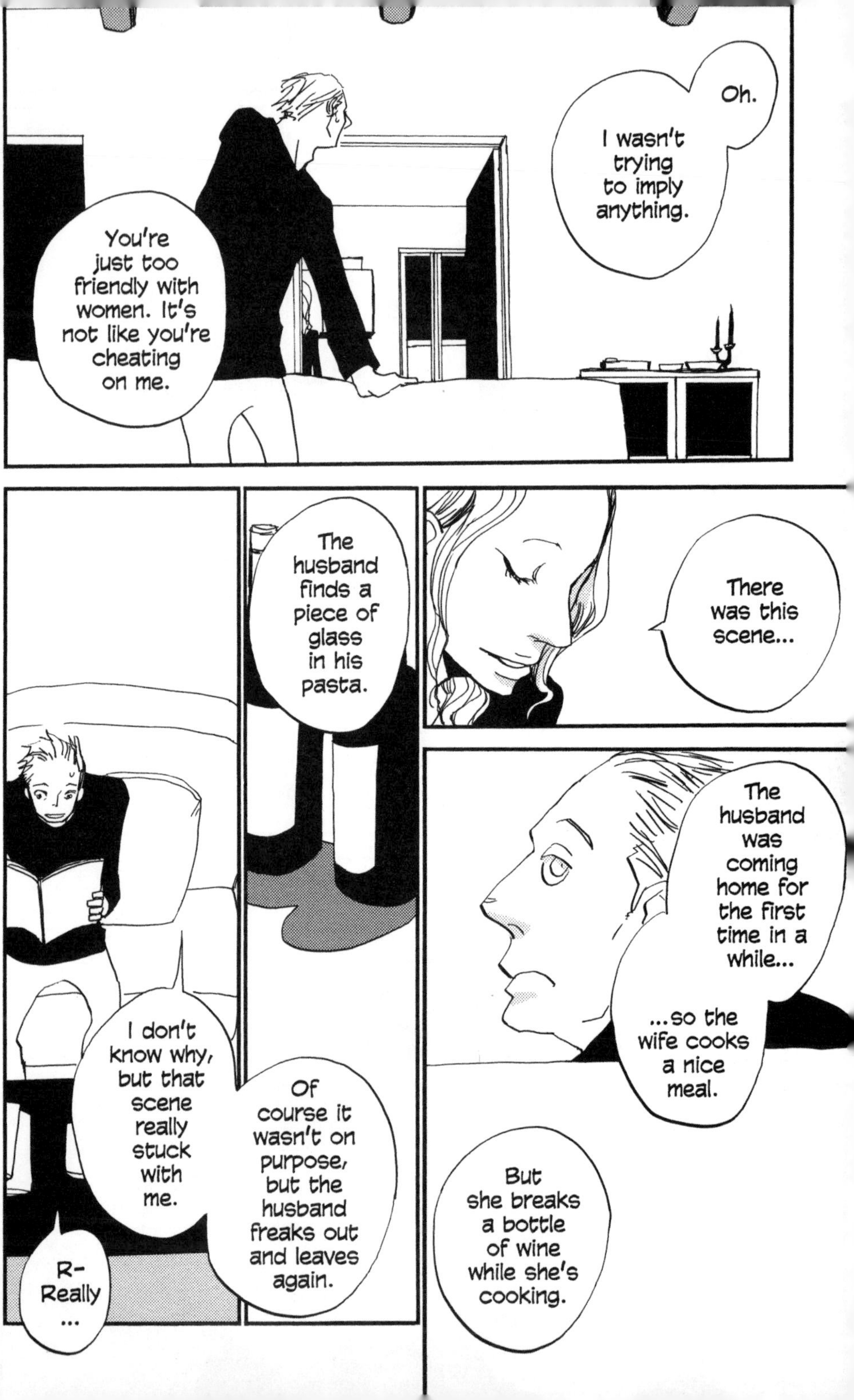
Oh.
I wasn't trying to imply anything.
You're just too friendly with women. It's not like you're cheating on me.
There was this scene...
The husband was coming home for the first time in a while...
...so the wife cooks a nice meal.
But she breaks a bottle of wine while she's cooking.
The husband finds a piece of glass in his pasta.
Of course it wasn't on purpose, but the husband freaks out and leaves again.
I don't know why, but that scene really stuck with me.
R-Really...

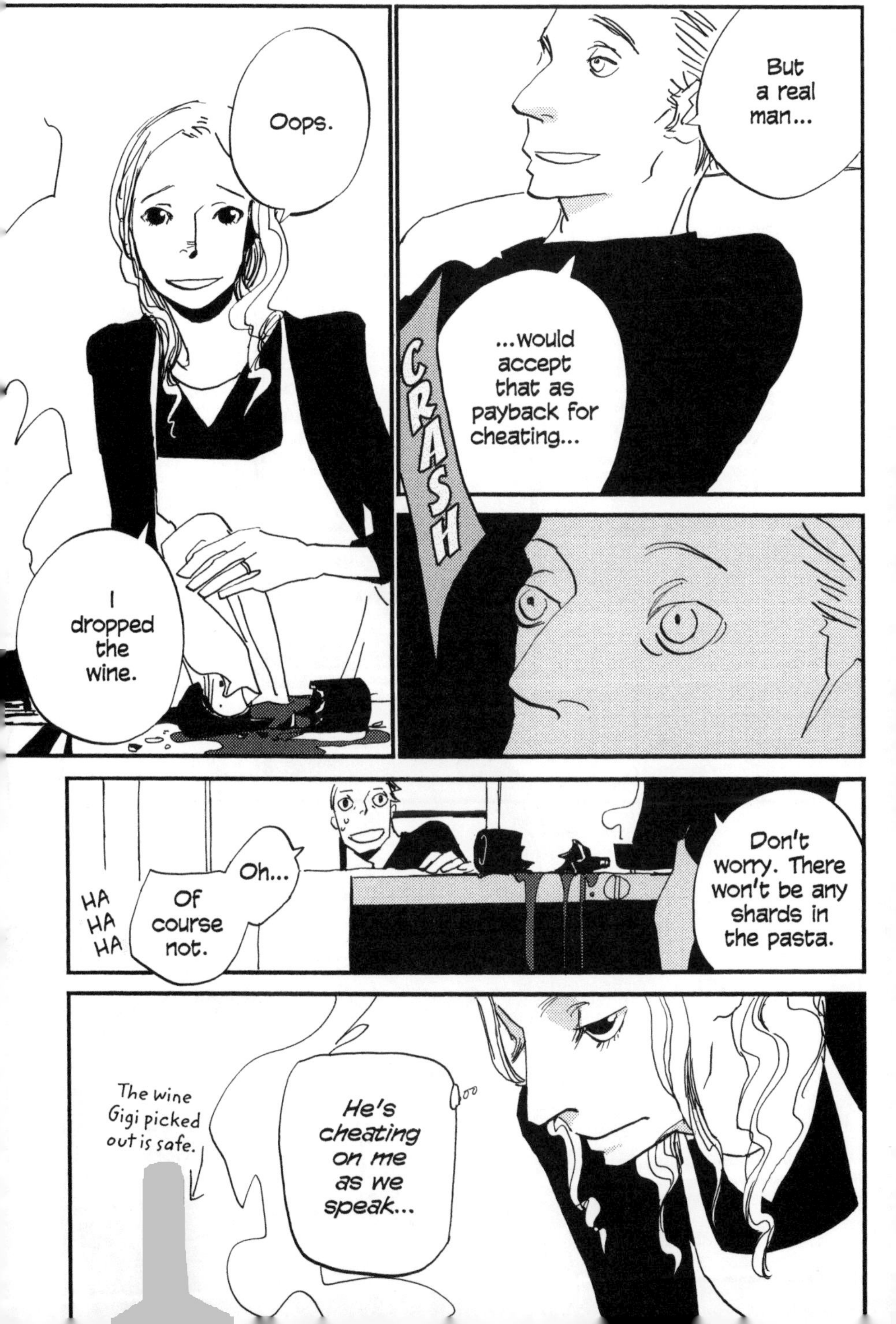
But a real man...
...would accept that as payback for cheating...
CRASH
Oops.
I dropped the wine.
Don't worry. There won't be any shards in the pasta.
Oh...
Of course not.
HA HA HA
He's cheating on me as we speak...
The wine Gigi picked out is safe.

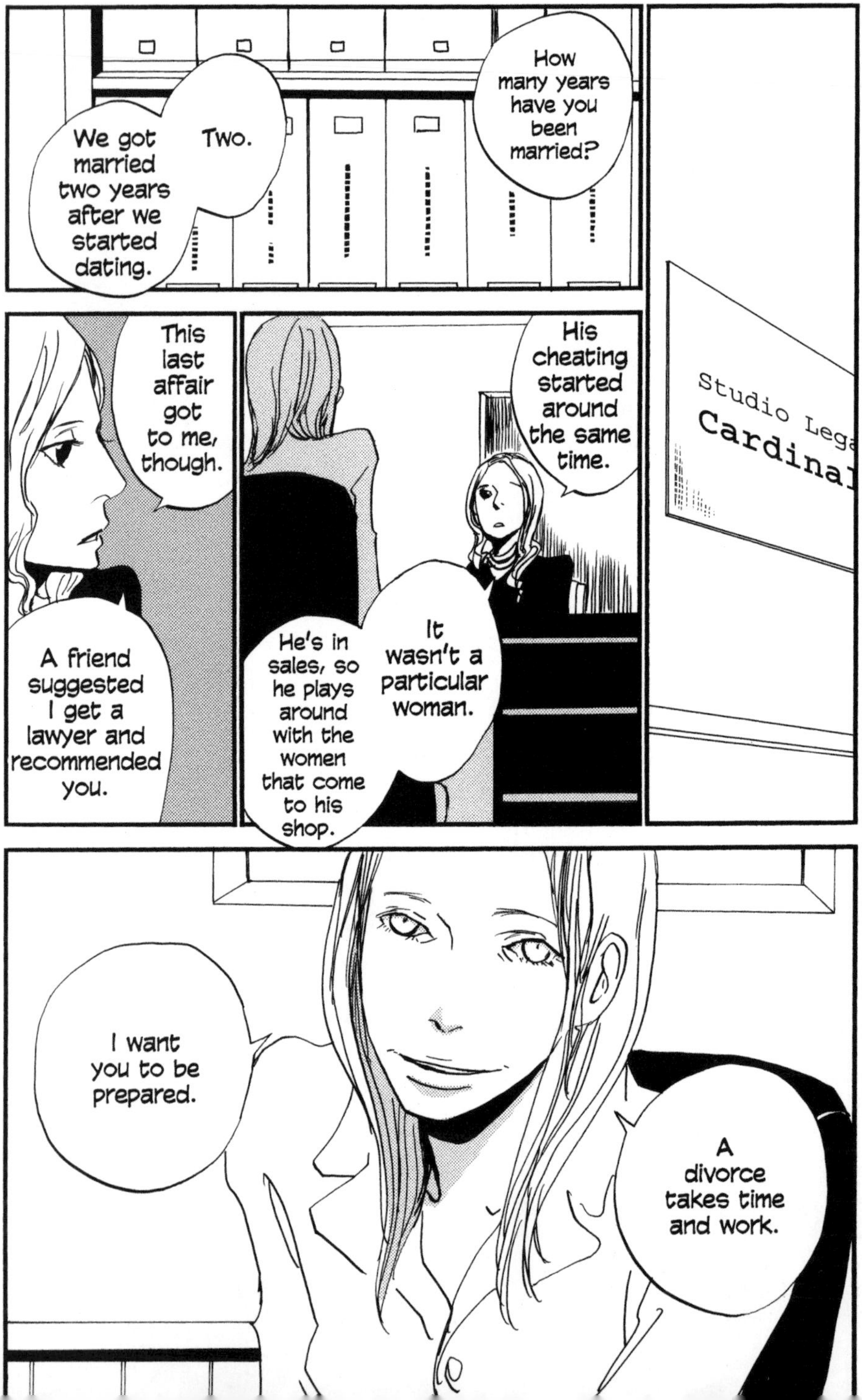
Studio Lega
Cardina
How many years have you been married?
Two.
We got married two years after we started dating.
His cheating started around the same time.
It wasn't a particular woman.
He's in sales, so he plays around with the women that come to his shop.
This last affair got to me, though.
A friend suggested I get a lawyer and recommended you.
A divorce takes time and work.
I want you to be prepared.

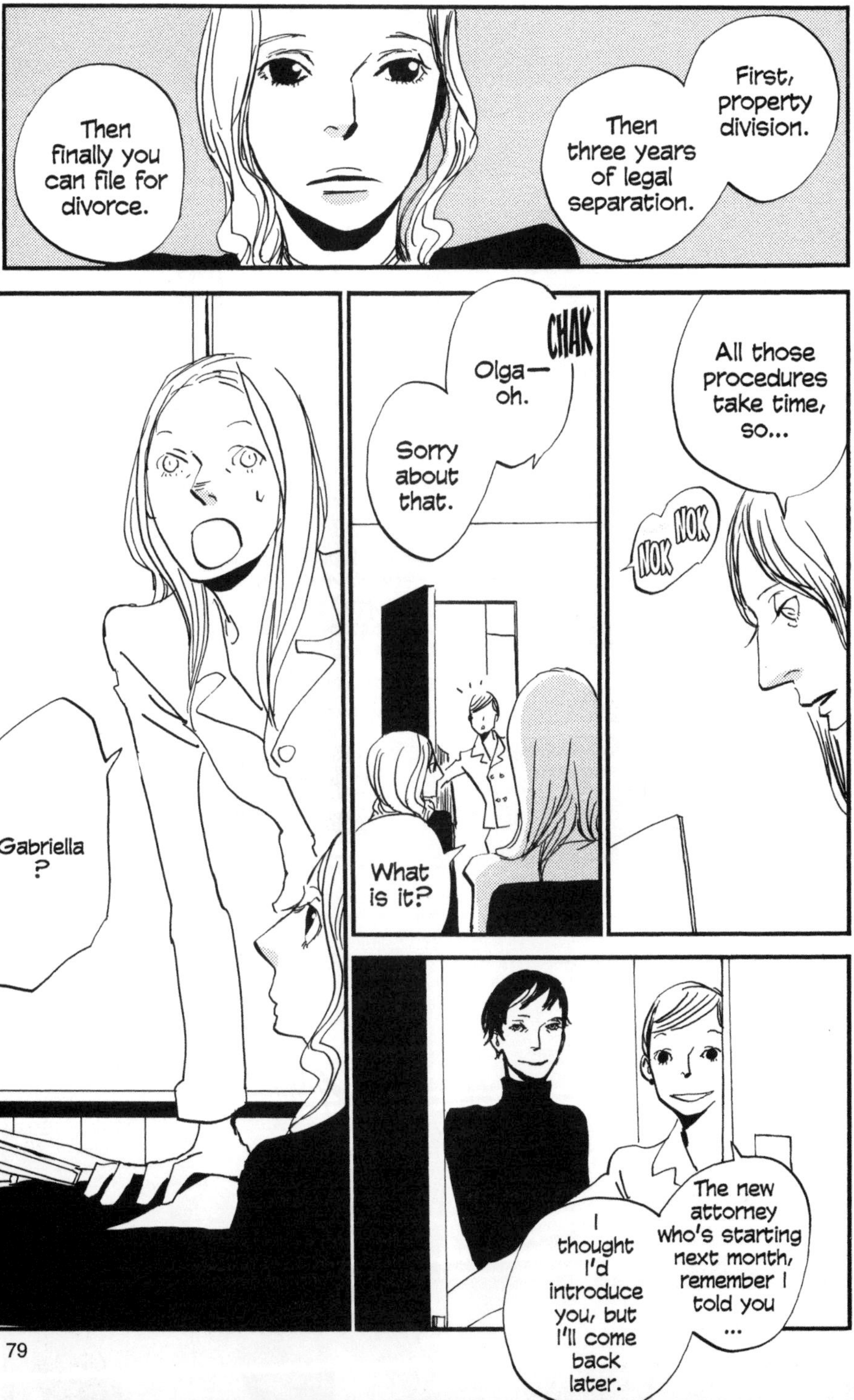
First, property division.
Then three years of legal separation.
Then finally you can file for divorce.
All those procedures take time, so...
NOK NOK
CHAK
Olga— oh.
Sorry about that.
What is it?
The new attorney who's starting next month, remember I told you ...
I thought I'd introduce you, but I'll come back later.
Gabriella ?

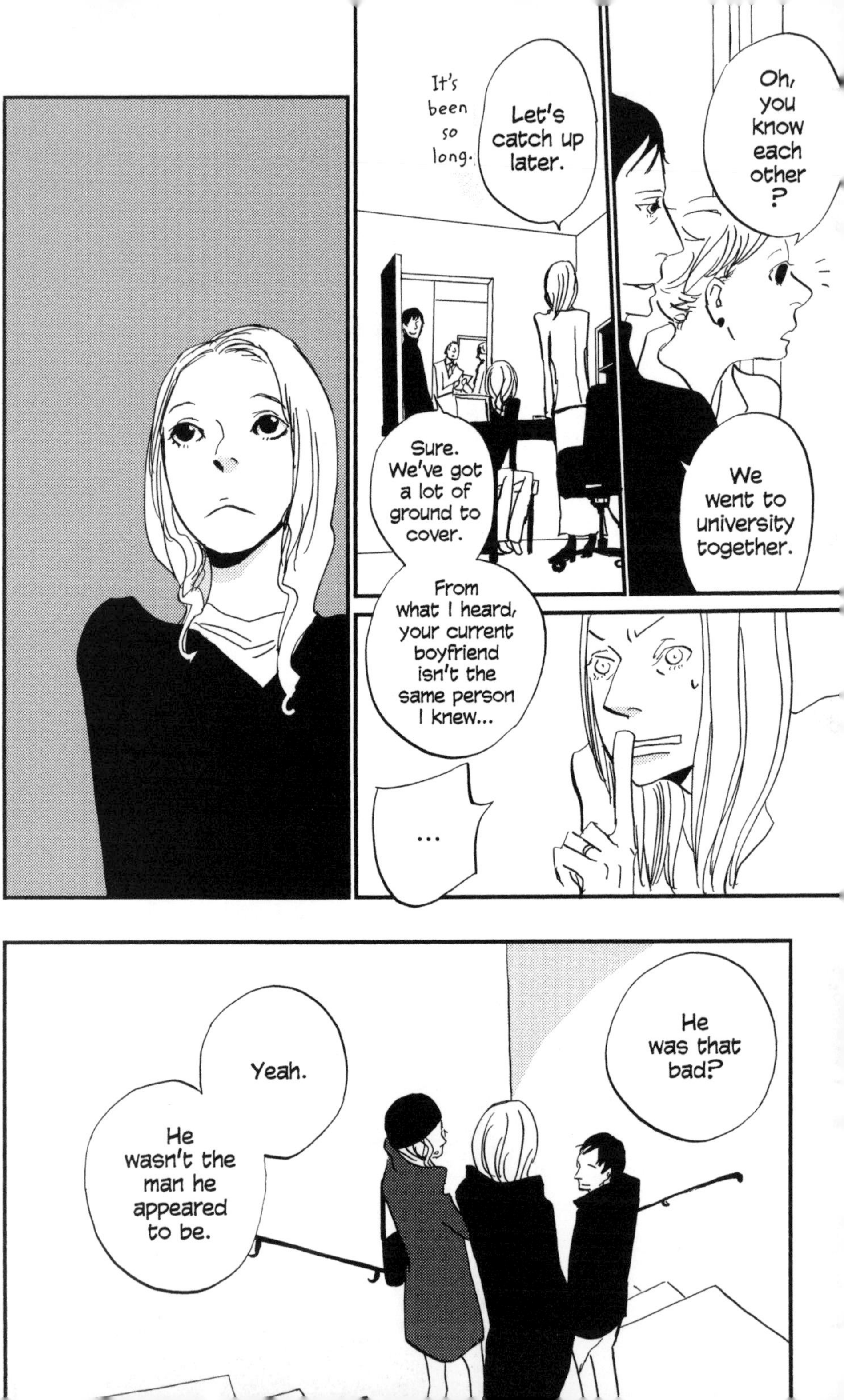
Oh, you know each other?
We went to university together.
Let's catch up later.
It's been so long.
Sure. We've got a lot of ground to cover.
From what I heard, your current boyfriend isn't the same person I knew...
...
He was that bad?
Yeah.
He wasn't the man he appeared to be.

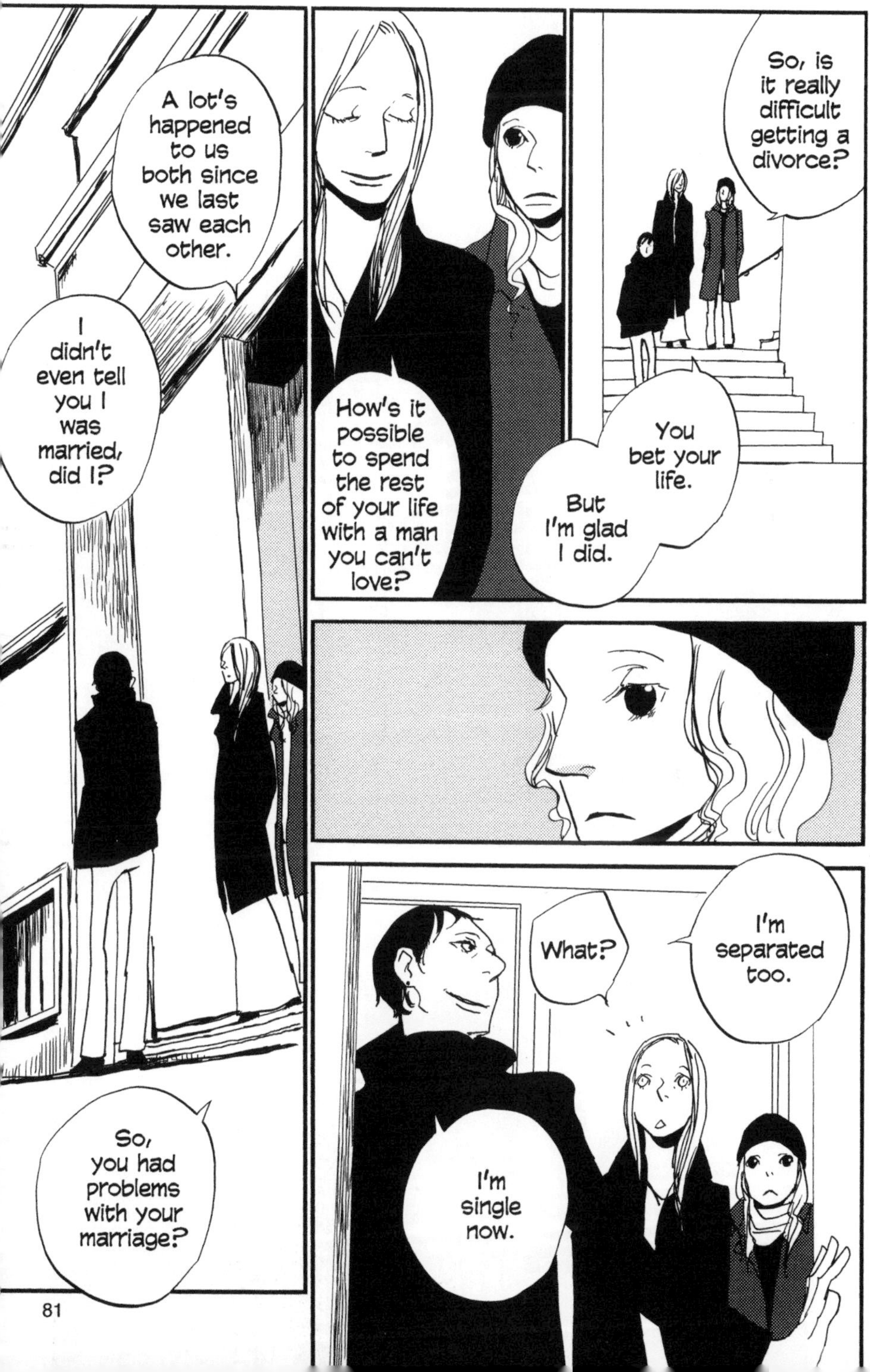
So, is it really difficult getting a divorce?
You bet your life.
But I'm glad I did.
How's it possible to spend the rest of your life with a man you can't love?
I'm separated too.
What?
I'm single now.
A lot's happened to us both since we last saw each other.
I didn't even tell you I was married, did I?
So, you had problems with your marriage?

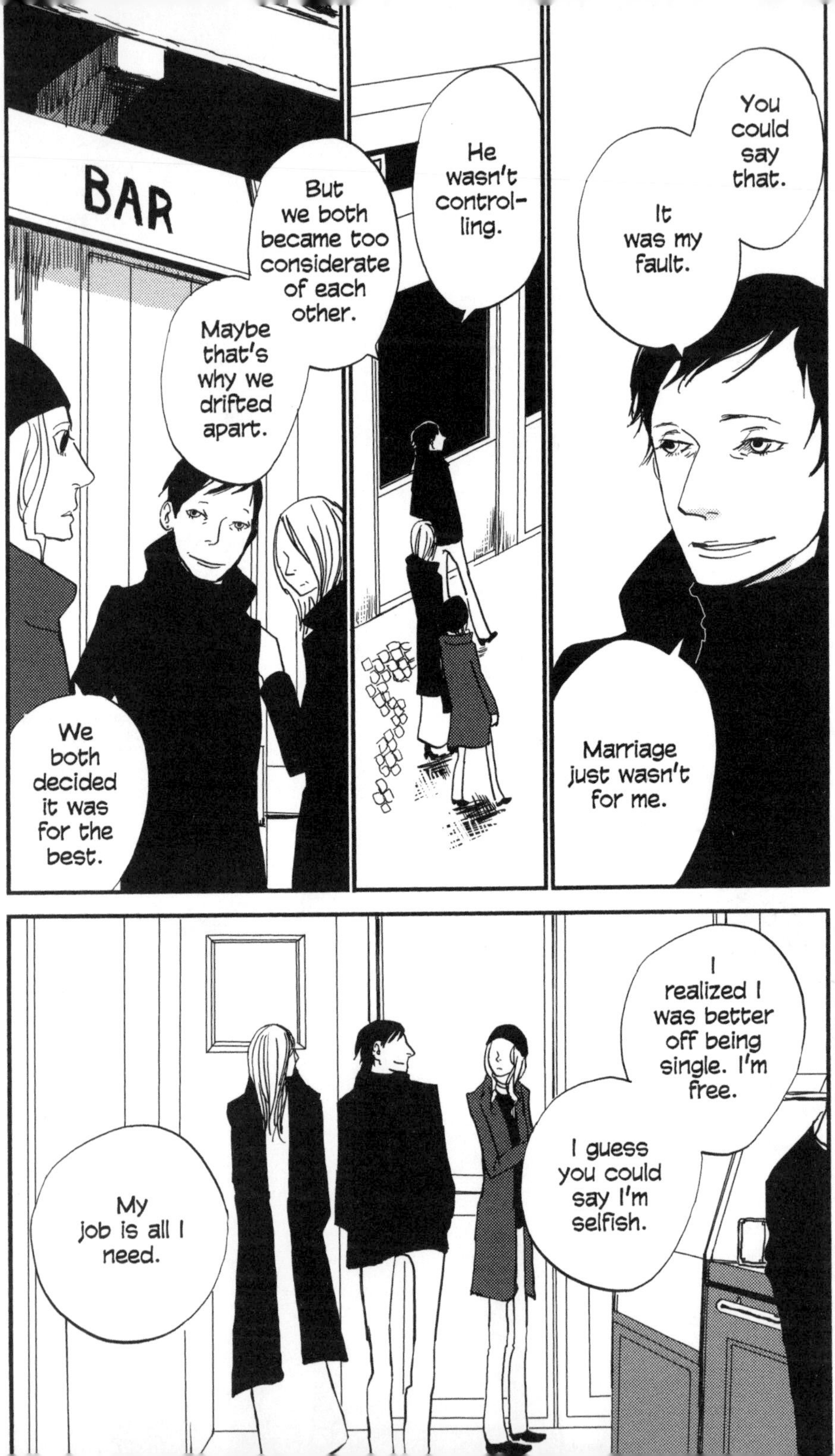
You could say that.
It was my fault.
Marriage just wasn't for me.
He wasn't controlling.
BAR
But we both became too considerate of each other.
Maybe that's why we drifted apart.
We both decided it was for the best.
I realized I was better off being single. I'm free.
I guess you could say I'm selfish.
My job is all I need.

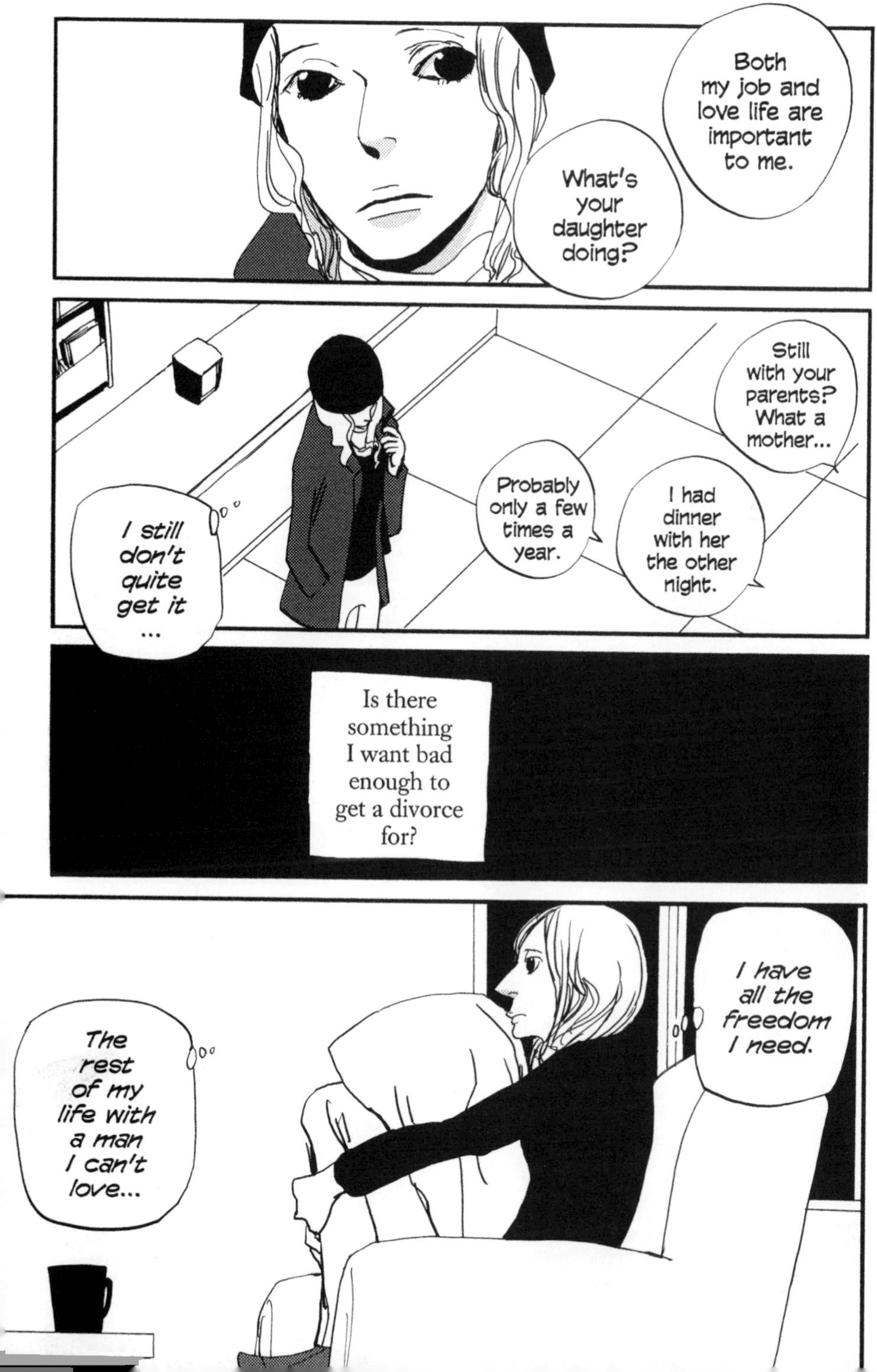

Both my job and love life are important to me.
What's your daughter doing?
Still with your parents? What a mother...
I had dinner with her the other night.
Probably only a few times a year.
I still don't quite get it...
Is there something I want bad enough to get a divorce for?
I have all the freedom I need.
The rest of my life with a man I can't love...

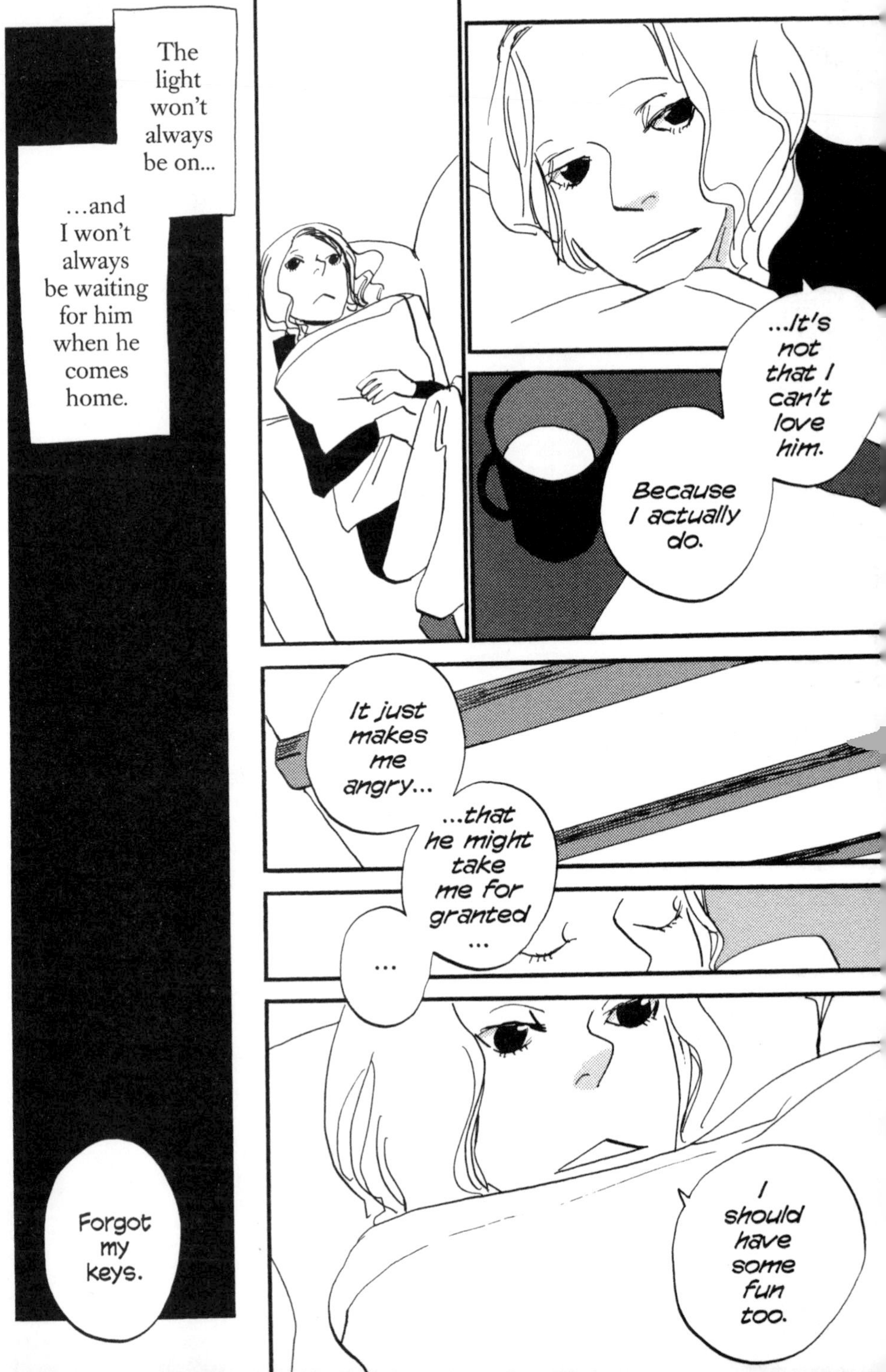
...It's not that I can't love him.
Because I actually do.
It just makes me angry...
...that he might take me for granted...
...
I should have some fun too.
The light won't always be on...
...and I won't always be waiting for him when he comes home.
Forgot my keys.

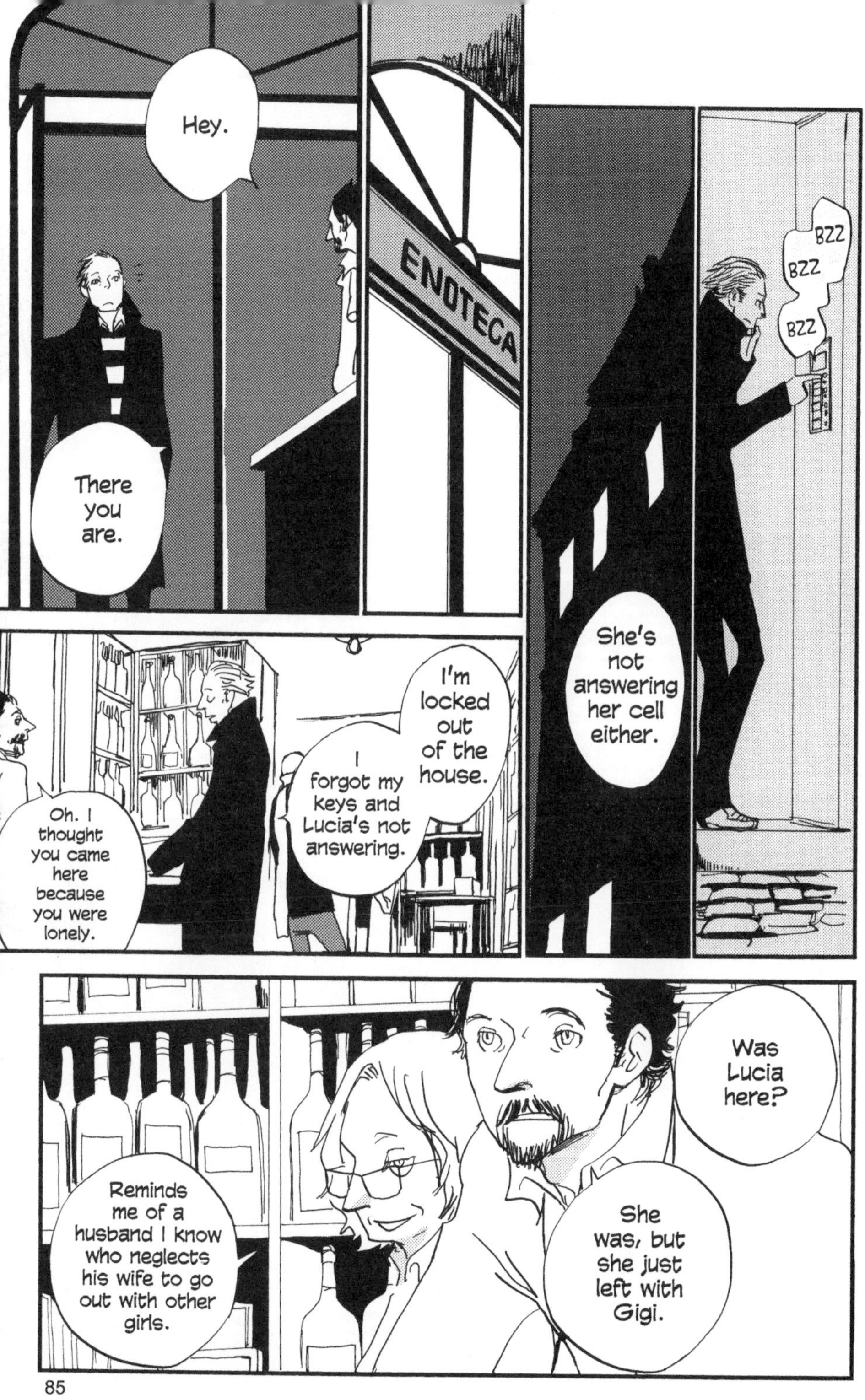
BZZ
BZZ
BZZ
She's not answering her cell either.
ENOTECA
Hey.
There you are.
I'm locked out of the house.
I forgot my keys and Lucia's not answering.
Oh. I thought you came here because you were lonely.
Was Lucia here?
She was, but she just left with Gigi.
Reminds me of a husband I know who neglects his wife to go out with other girls.

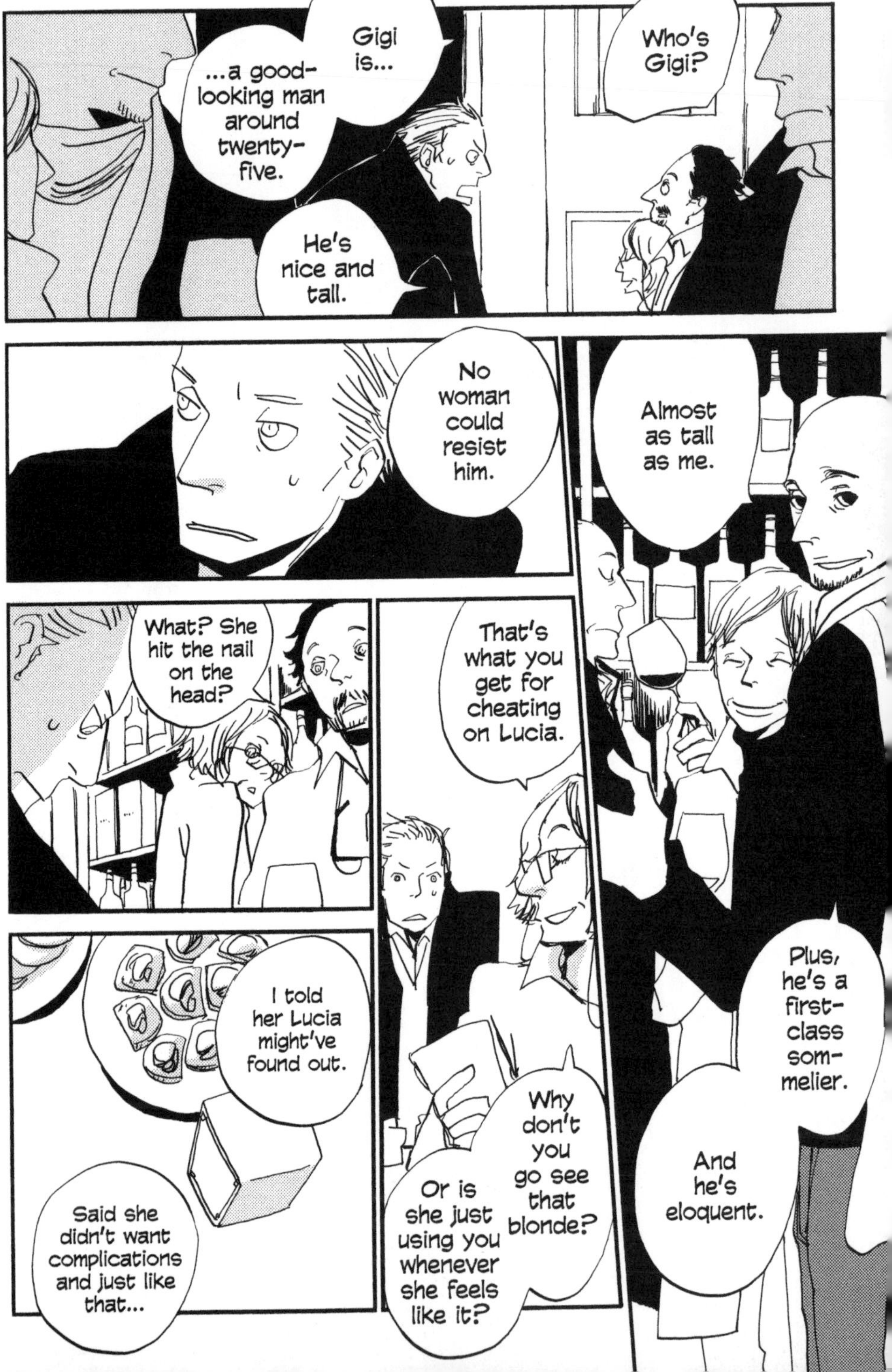
Who's Gigi?
Gigi is...
...a good-looking man around twenty-five.
He's nice and tall.
Almost as tall as me.
Plus, he's a first-class sommelier.
And he's eloquent.
No woman could resist him.
That's what you get for cheating on Lucia.
Why don't you go see that blonde?
Or is she just using you whenever she feels like it?
What? She hit the nail on the head?
I told her Lucia might've found out.
Said she didn't want complications and just like that...

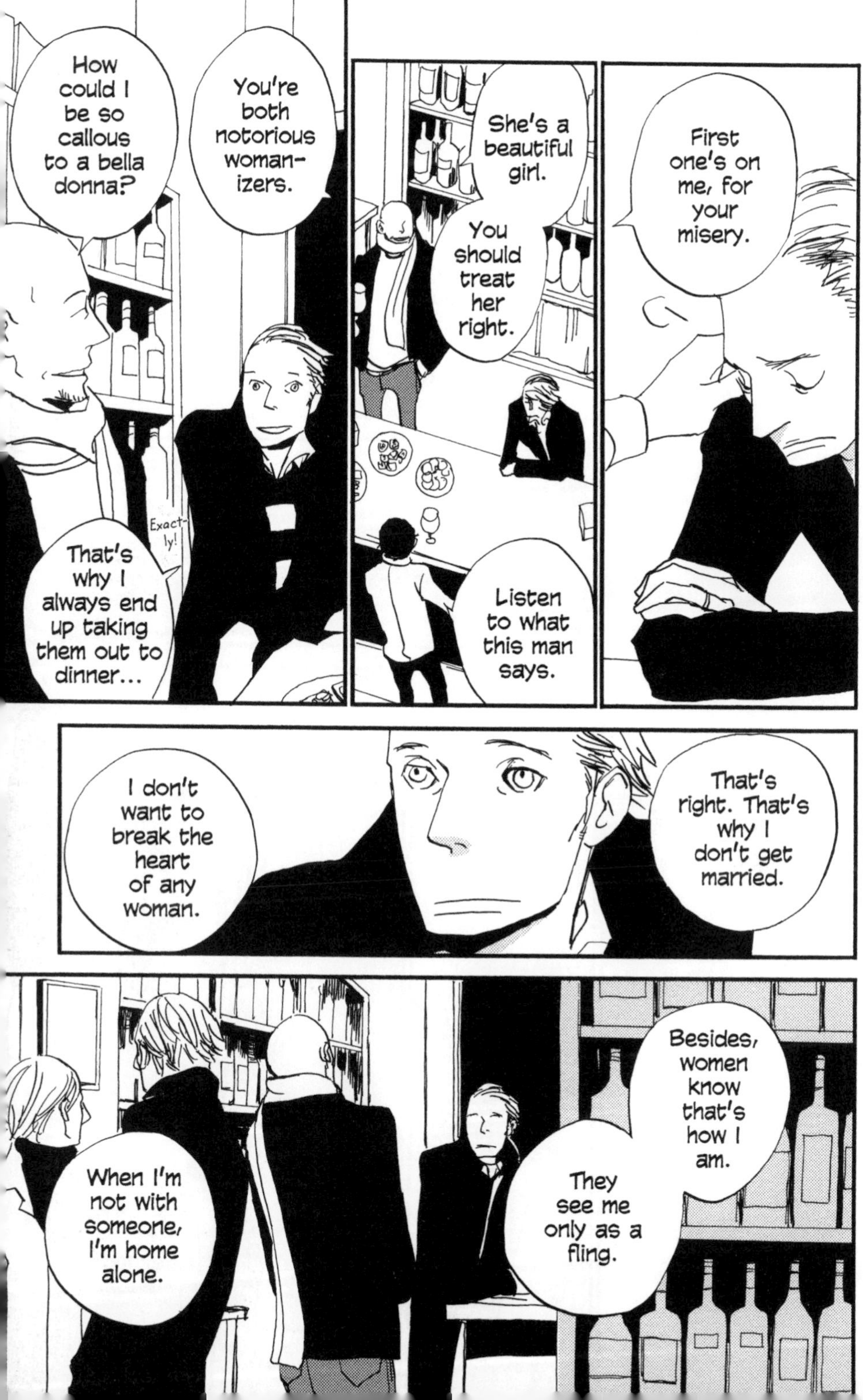
First one's on me, for your misery.
She's a beautiful girl.
You should treat her right.
Listen to what this man says.
You're both notorious woman-izers.
How could I be so callous to a bella donna?
Exact-ly!
That's why I always end up taking them out to dinner...
That's right. That's why I don't get married.
I don't want to break the heart of any woman.
Besides, women know that's how I am.
They see me only as a fling.
When I'm not with someone, I'm home alone.

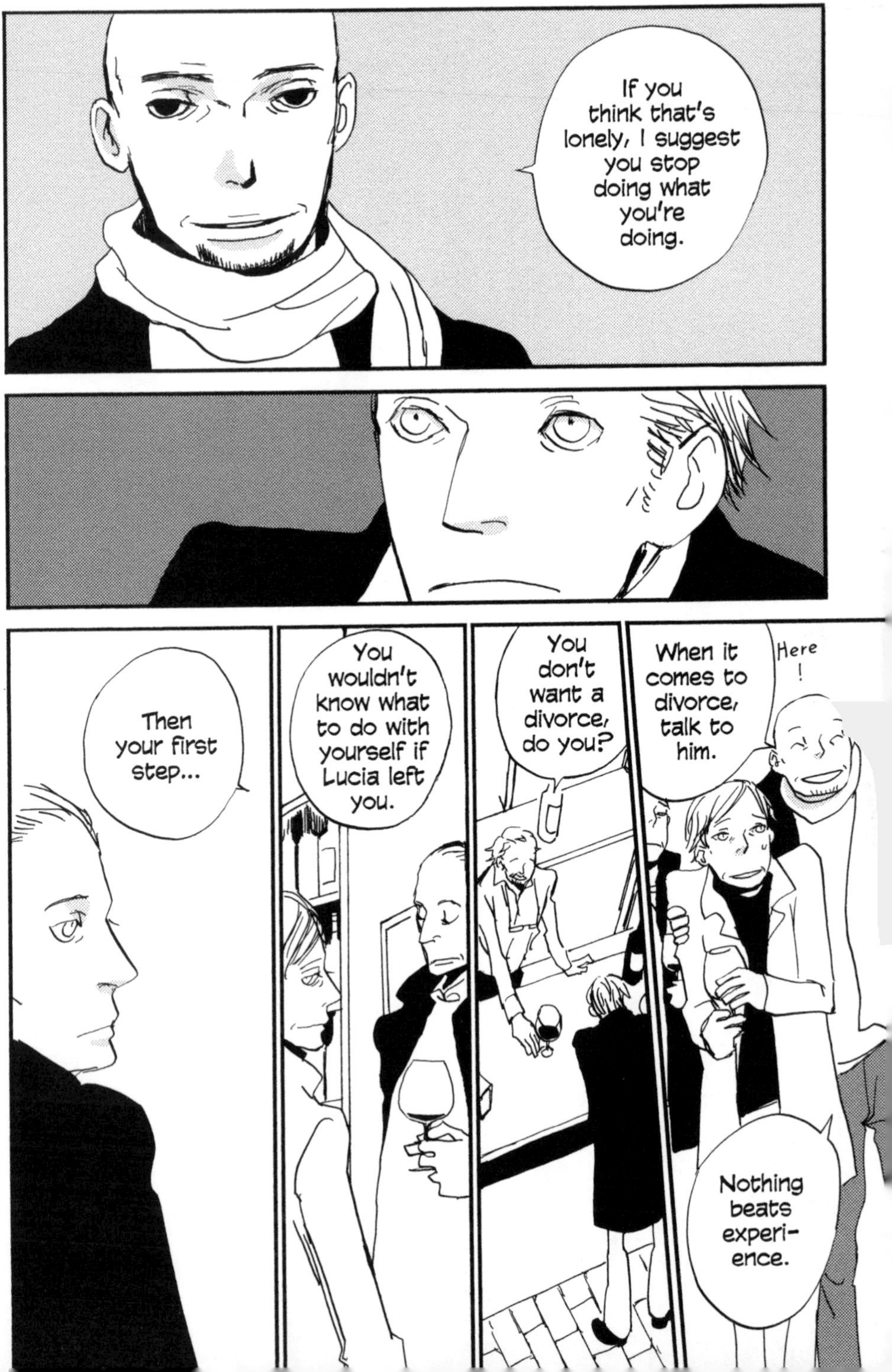
If you think that's lonely, I suggest you stop doing what you're doing.
Here !
When it comes to divorce, talk to him.
Nothing beats experi-ence.
You don't want a divorce, do you?
You wouldn't know what to do with yourself if Lucia left you.
Then your first step...

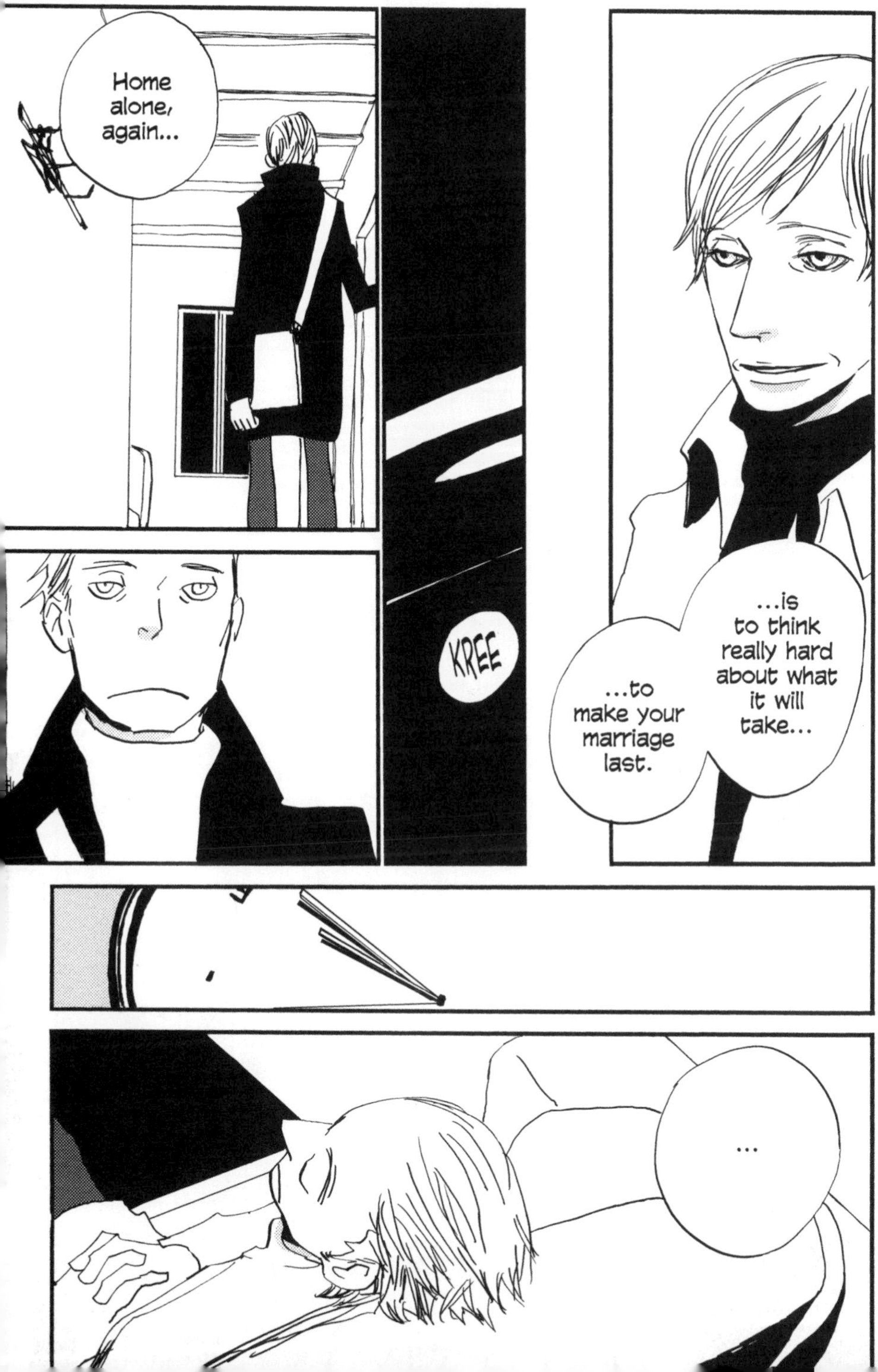
...is to think really hard about what it will take...
...to make your marriage last.
KREE
Home alone, again...
...

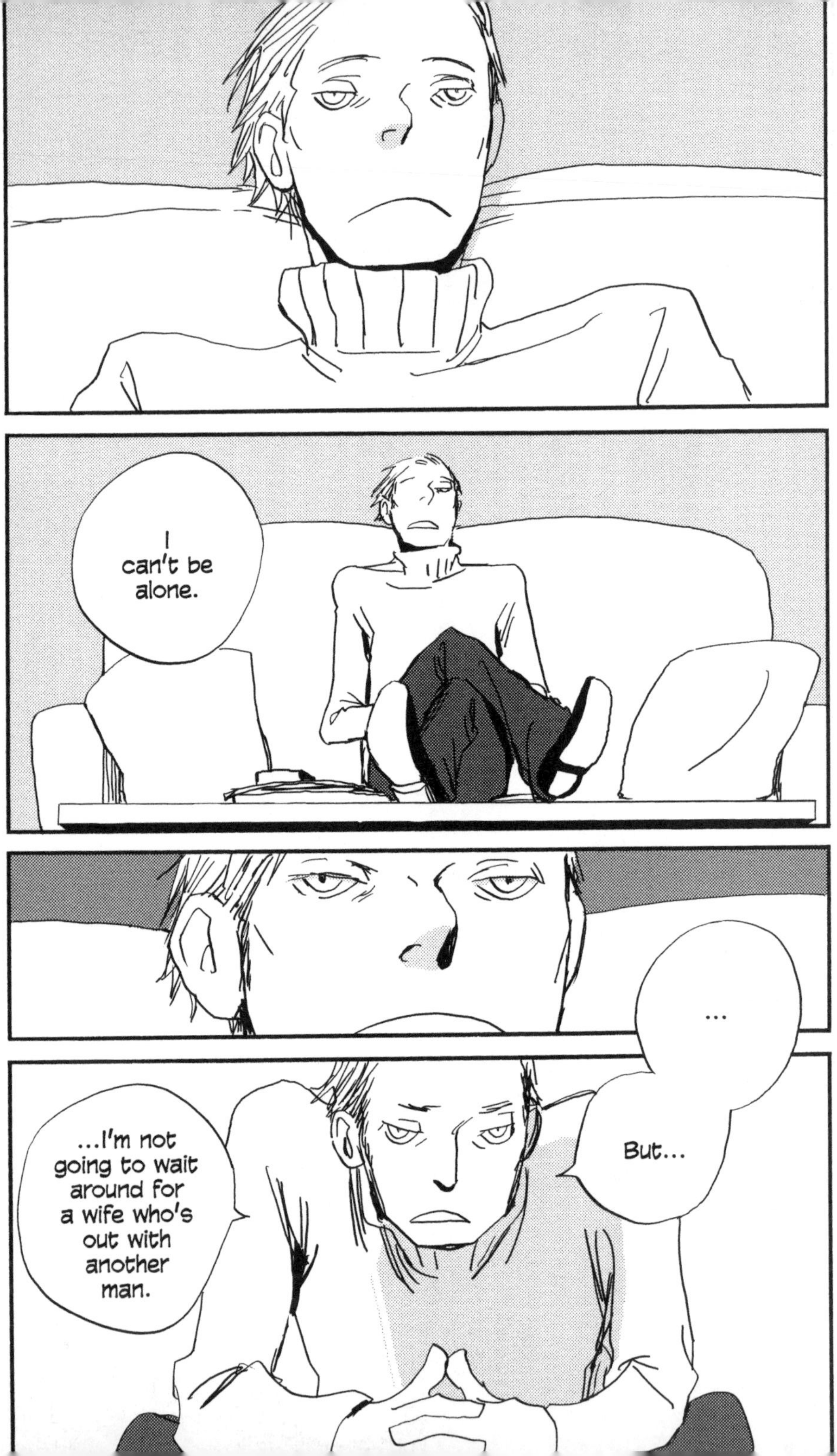
I can't be alone.
...
But...
...I'm not going to wait around for a wife who's out with another man.

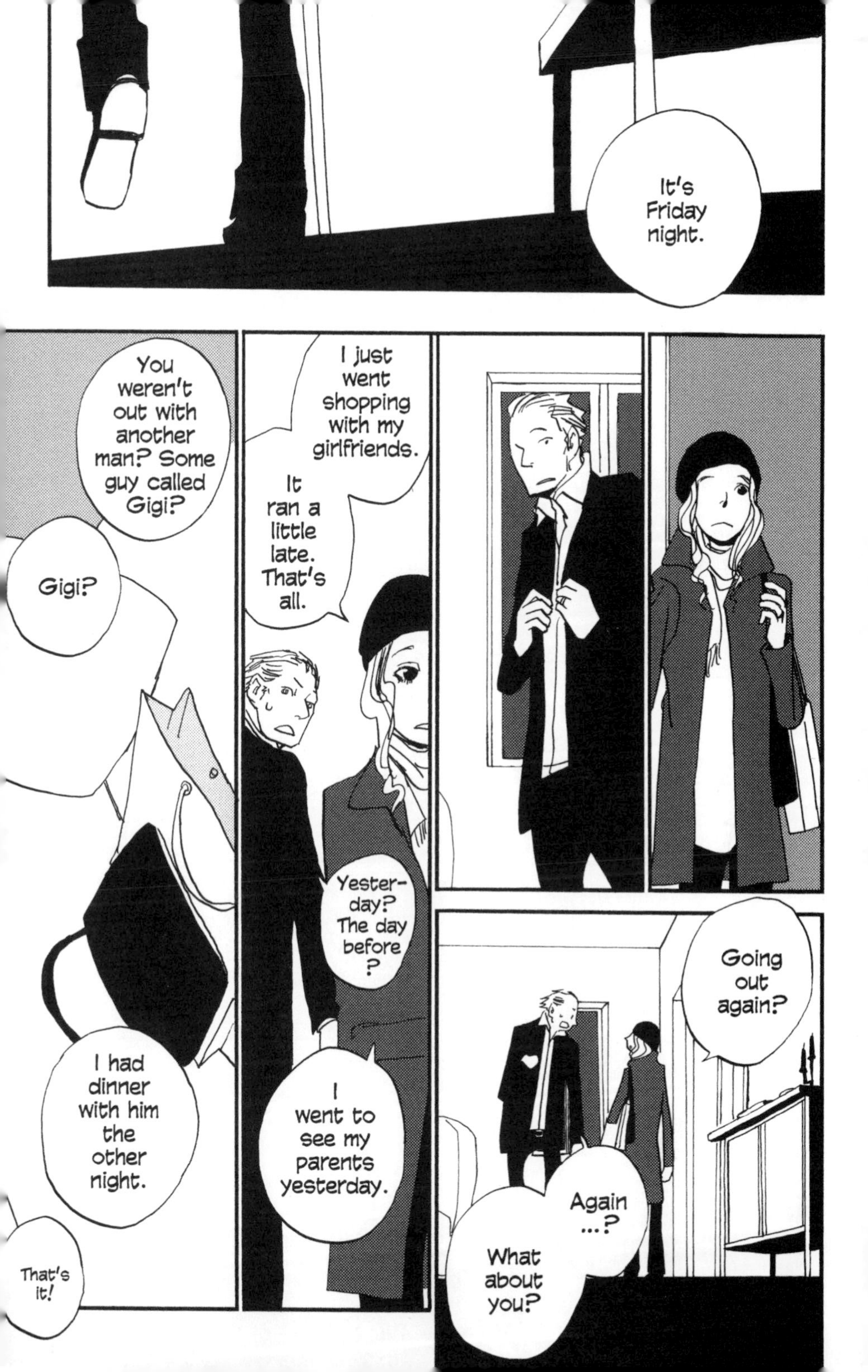

It's Friday night.
Going out again?
Again ...?
What about you?
I just went shopping with my girlfriends.
It ran a little late. That's all.
Yester-day? The day before?
I went to see my parents yesterday.
You weren't out with another man? Some guy called Gigi?
Gigi?
I had dinner with him the other night.
That's it!

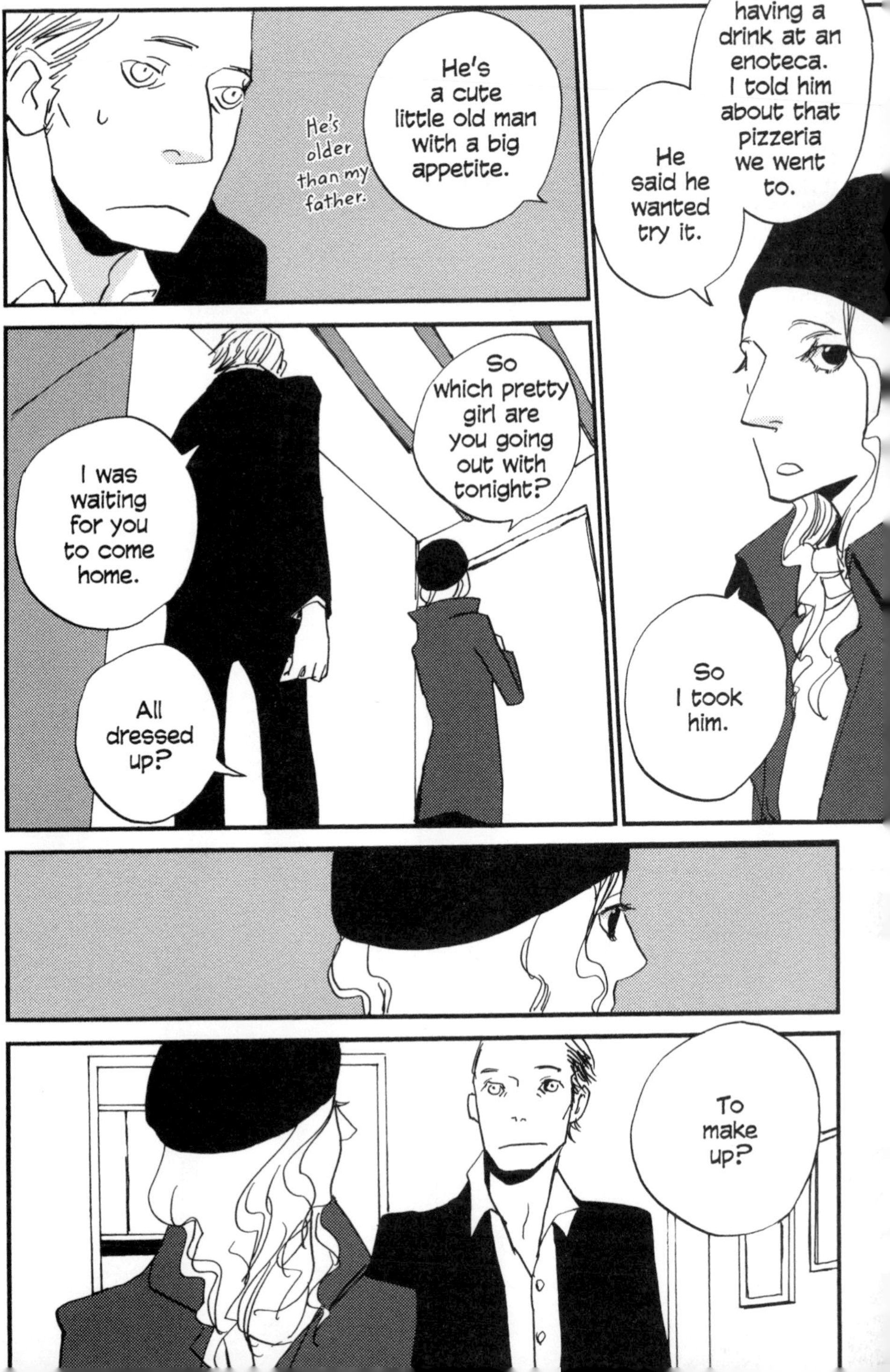
I was having a drink at an enoteca. I told him about that pizzeria we went to.
He said he wanted try it.
So I took him.
He's a cute little old man with a big appetite.
He's older than my father.
So which pretty girl are you going out with tonight?
I was waiting for you to come home.
All dressed up?
To make up?

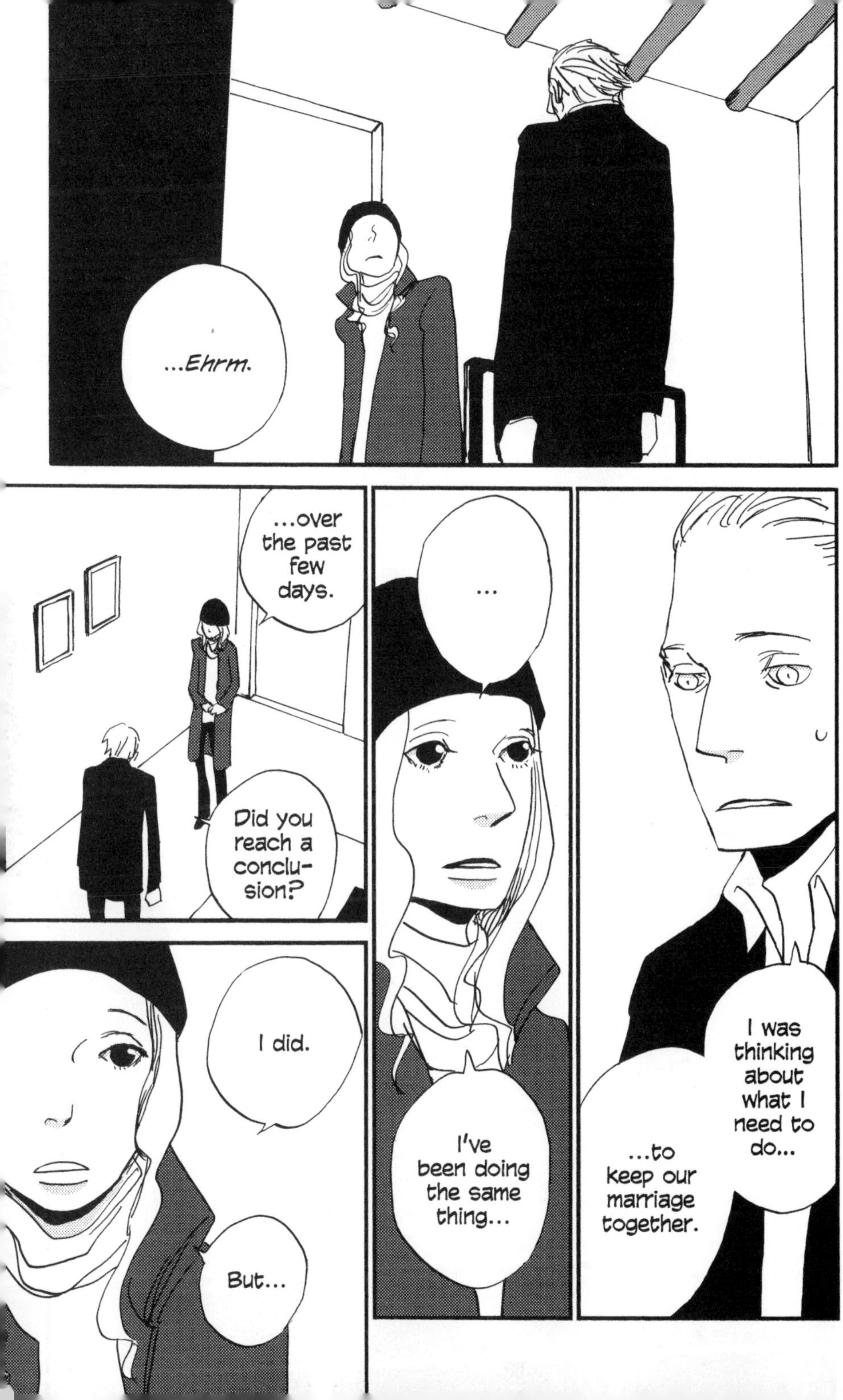
...Ehrm.
I was thinking about what I need to do...
...to keep our marriage together.
...
I've been doing the same thing...
...over the past few days.
Did you reach a conclusion?
I did.
But...

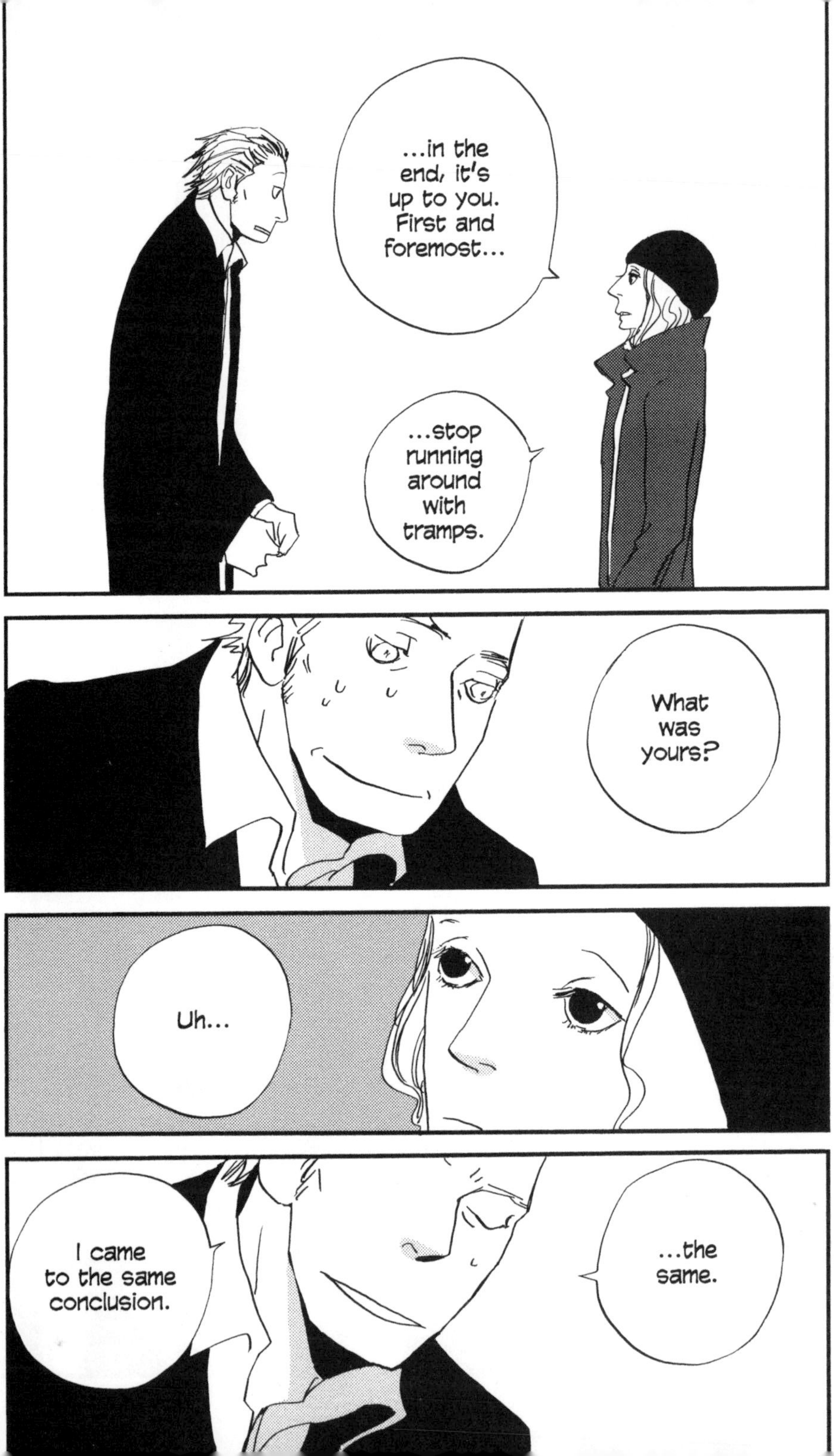
...in the end, it's up to you. First and foremost...
...stop running around with tramps.
What was yours?
Uh...
...the same.
I came to the same conclusion.

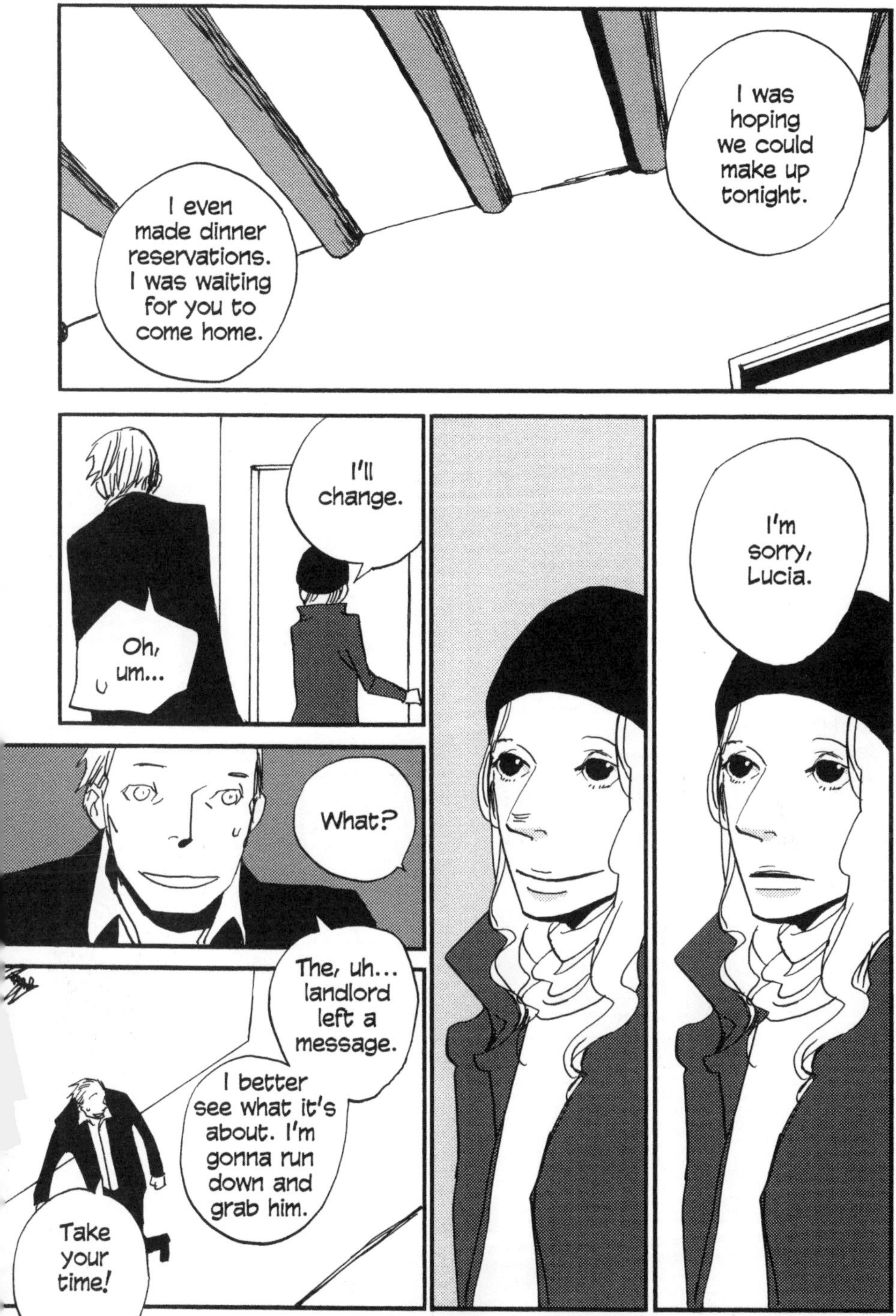
I was hoping we could make up tonight.
I even made dinner reservations. I was waiting for you to come home.
I'm sorry, Lucia.
I'll change.
Oh, um...
What?
The, uh... landlord left a message.
I better see what it's about. I'm gonna run down and grab him.
Take your time!

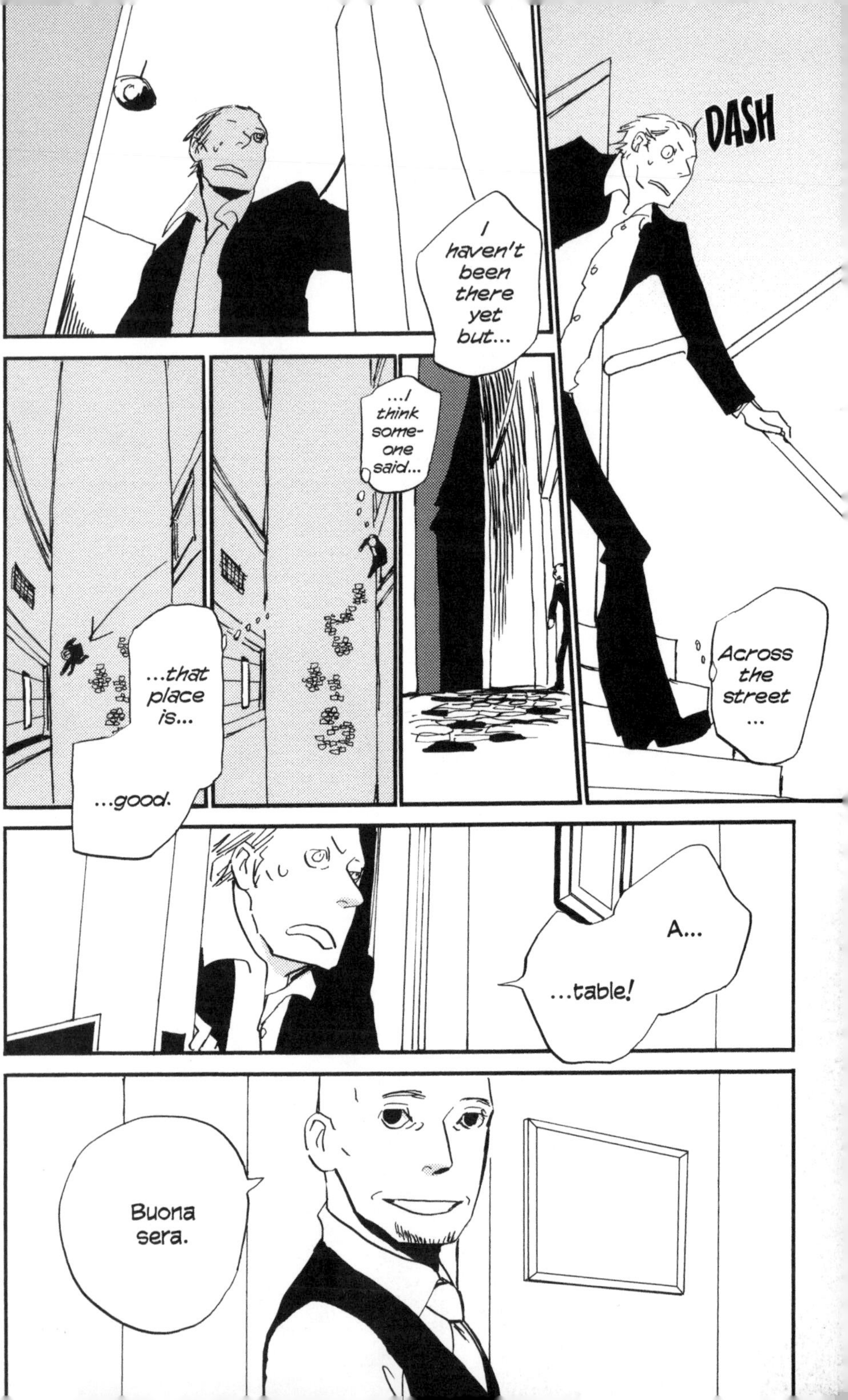
DASH
I haven't been there yet but...
Across the street ...
...I think some-one said...
...that place is...
...good.
A...
...table!
Buona sera.

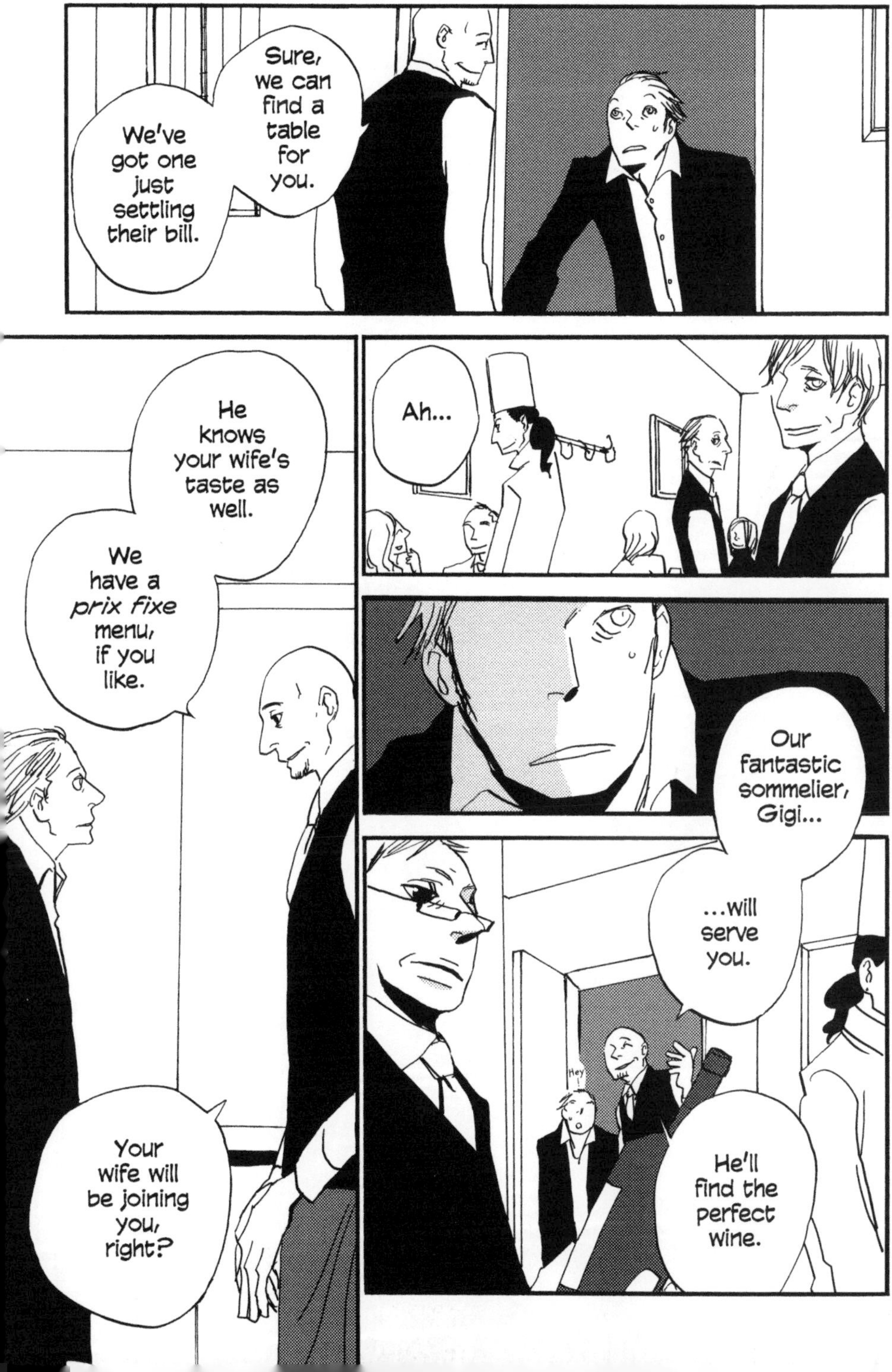
Sure, we can find a table for you.
We've got one just settling their bill.
Ah...
Our fantastic sommelier, Gigi...
...will serve you.
Hey
He'll find the perfect wine.
He knows your wife's taste as well.
We have a *prix fixe* menu, if you like.
Your wife will be joining you, right?

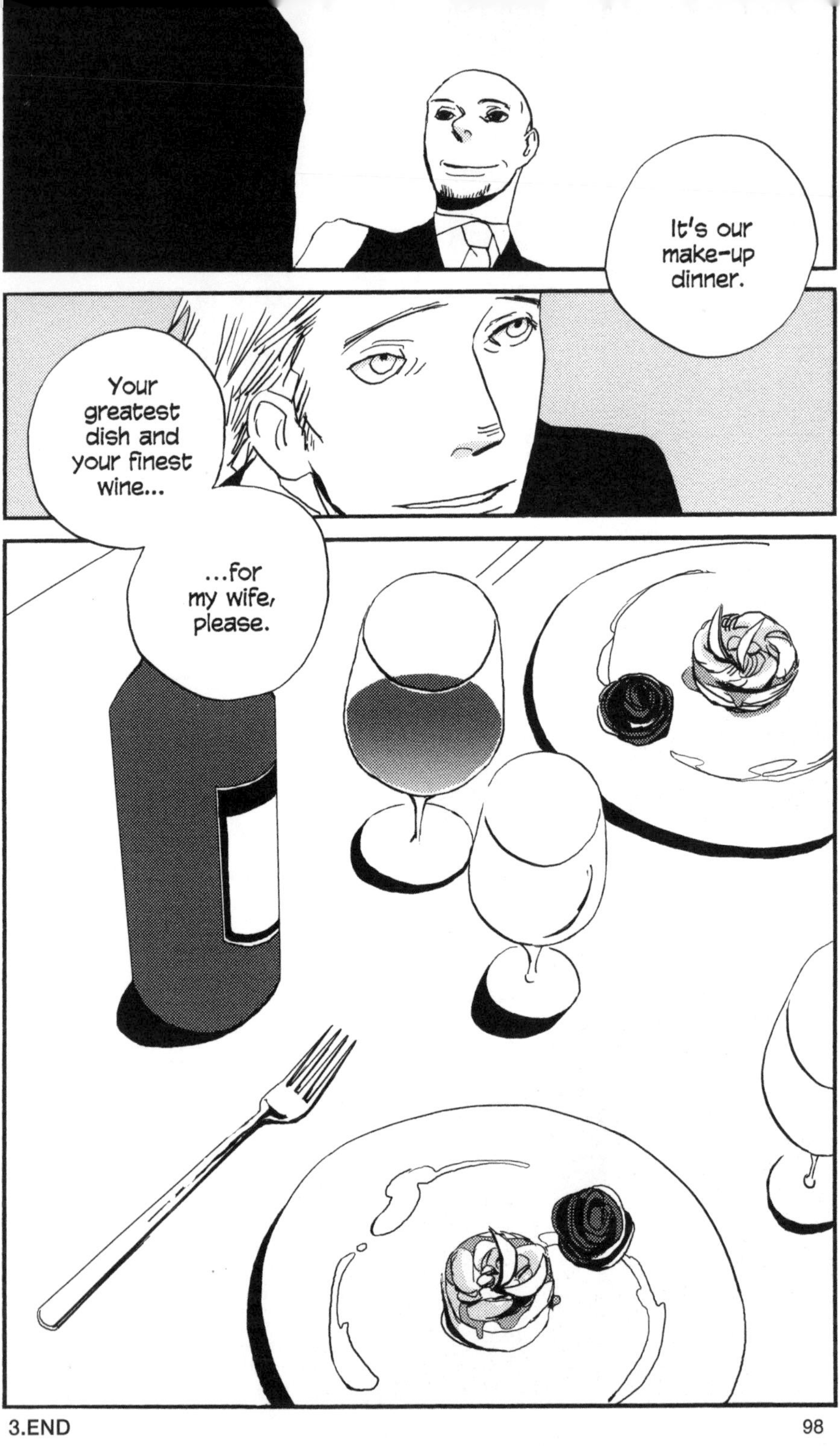
It's our make-up dinner.
Your greatest dish and your finest wine...
...for my wife, please.

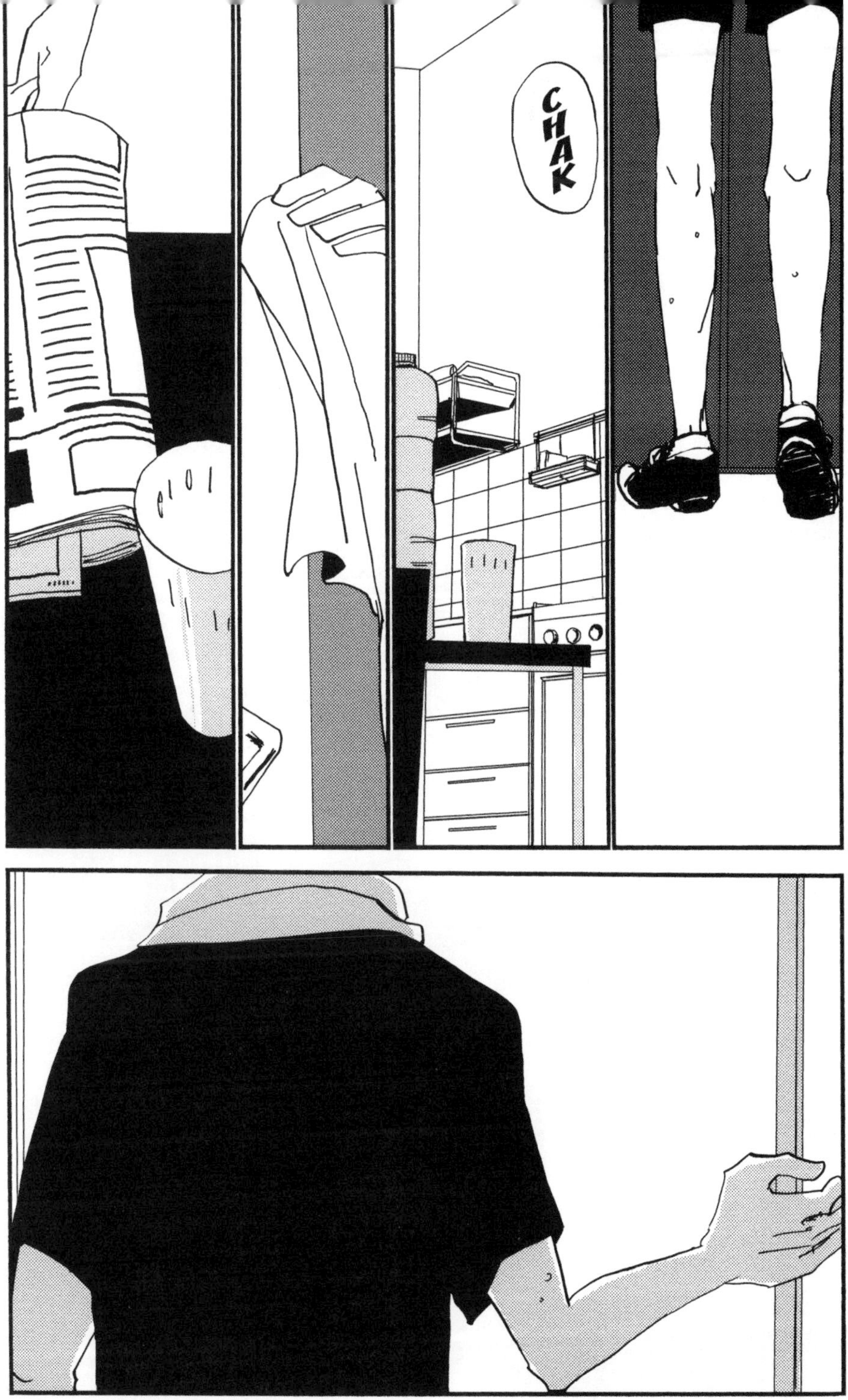
CHAK

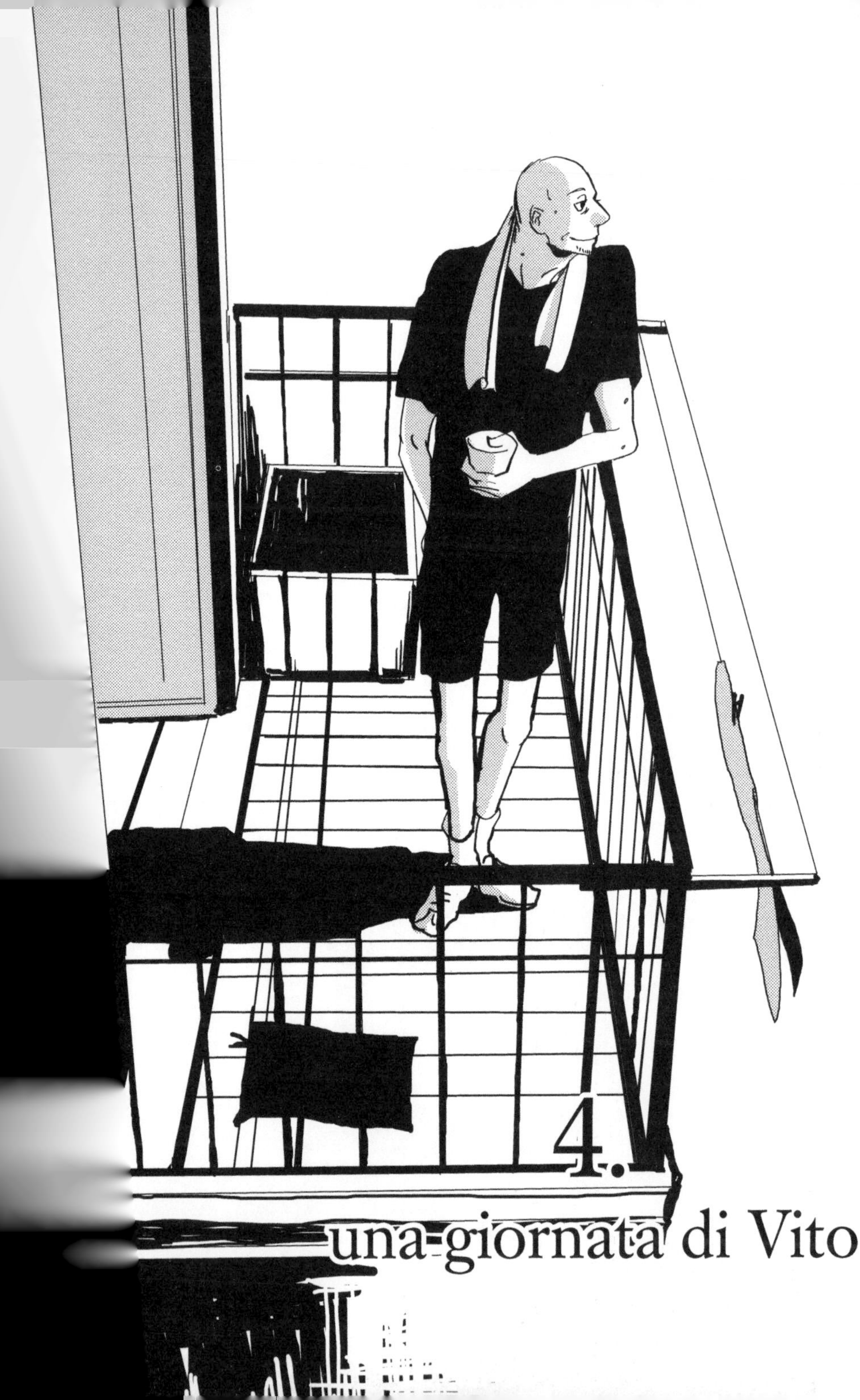

4. una giornata di Vito

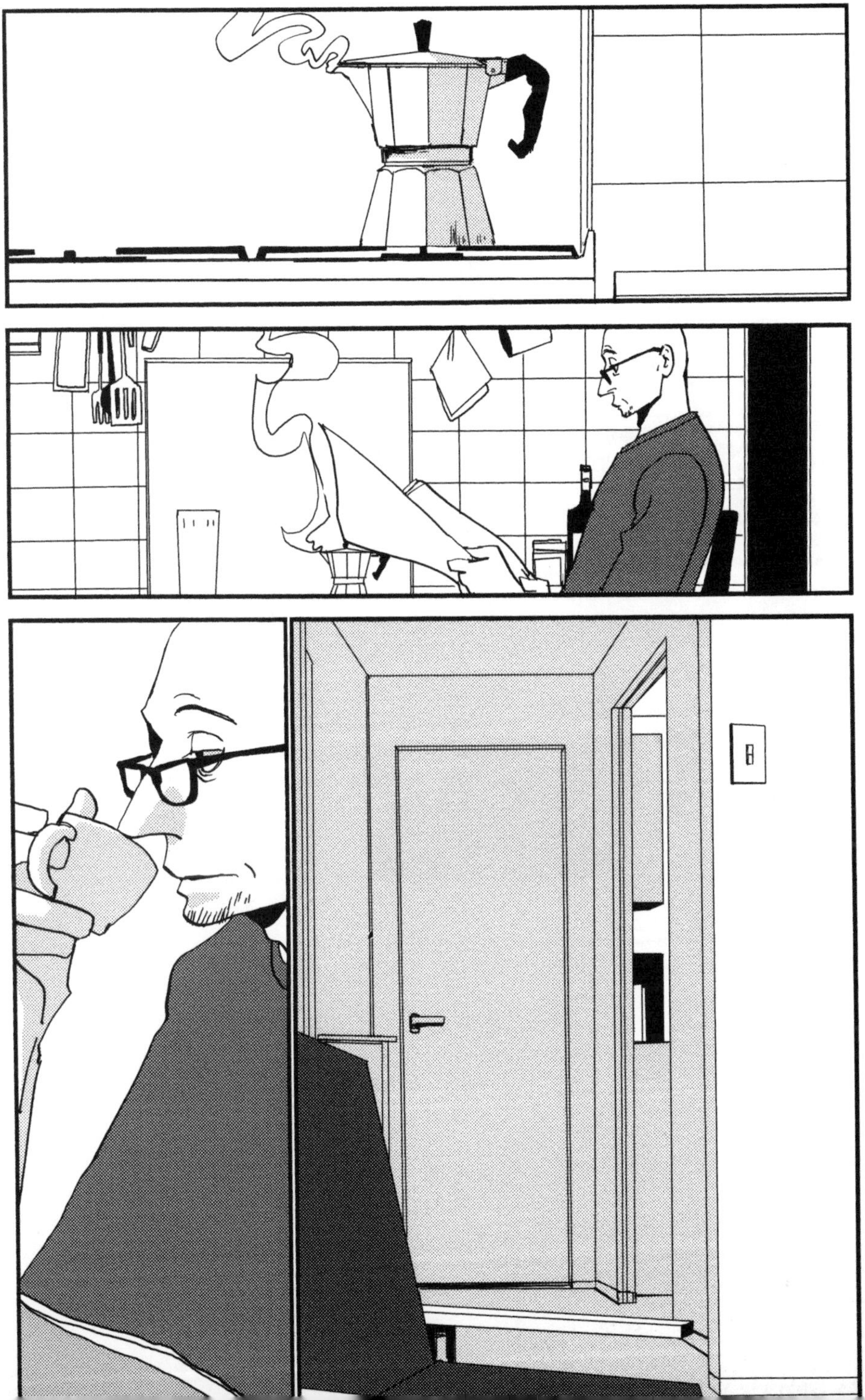

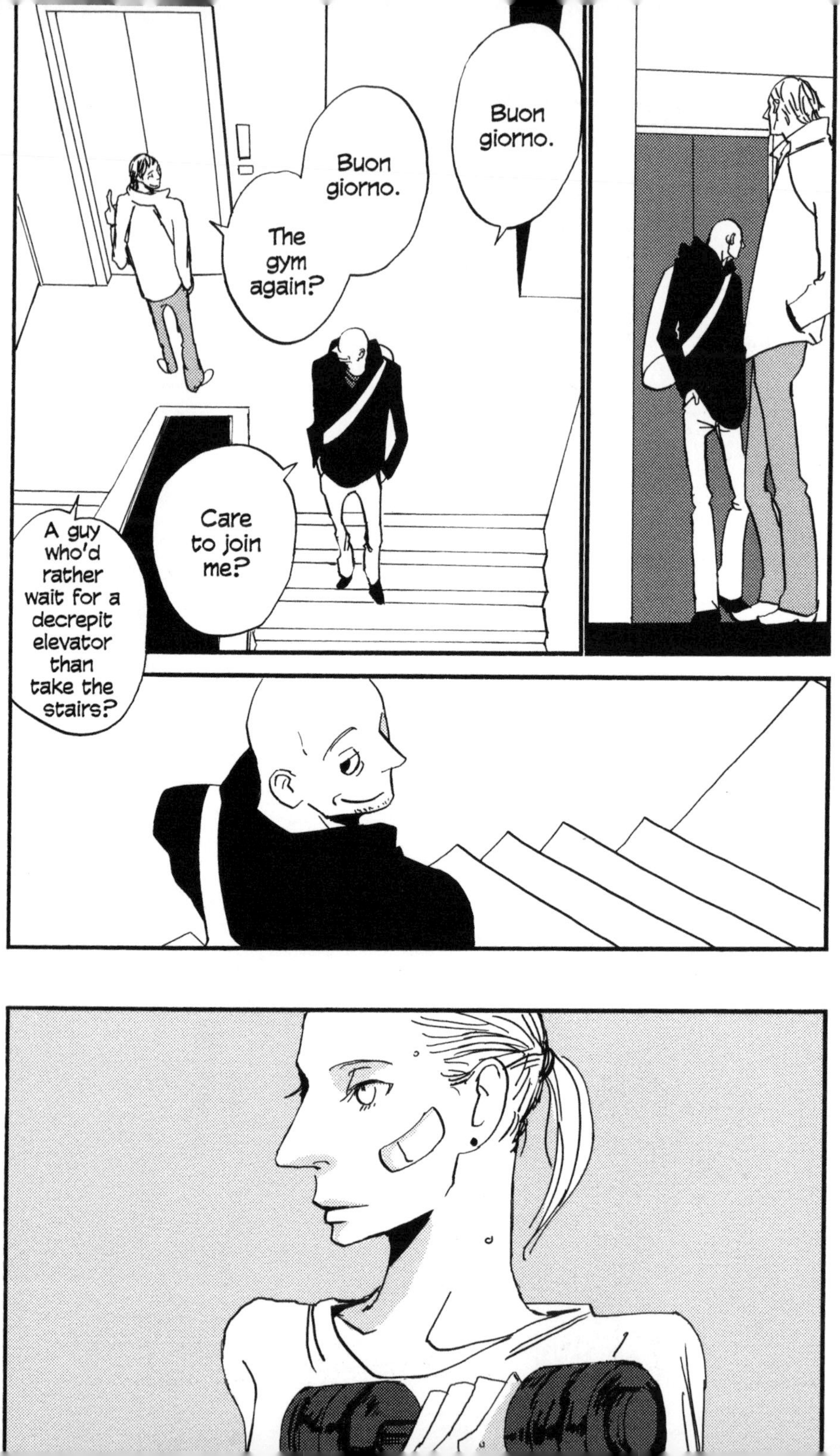
Buon giorno.
Buon giorno.
The gym again?
Care to join me?
A guy who'd rather wait for a decrepit elevator than take the stairs?

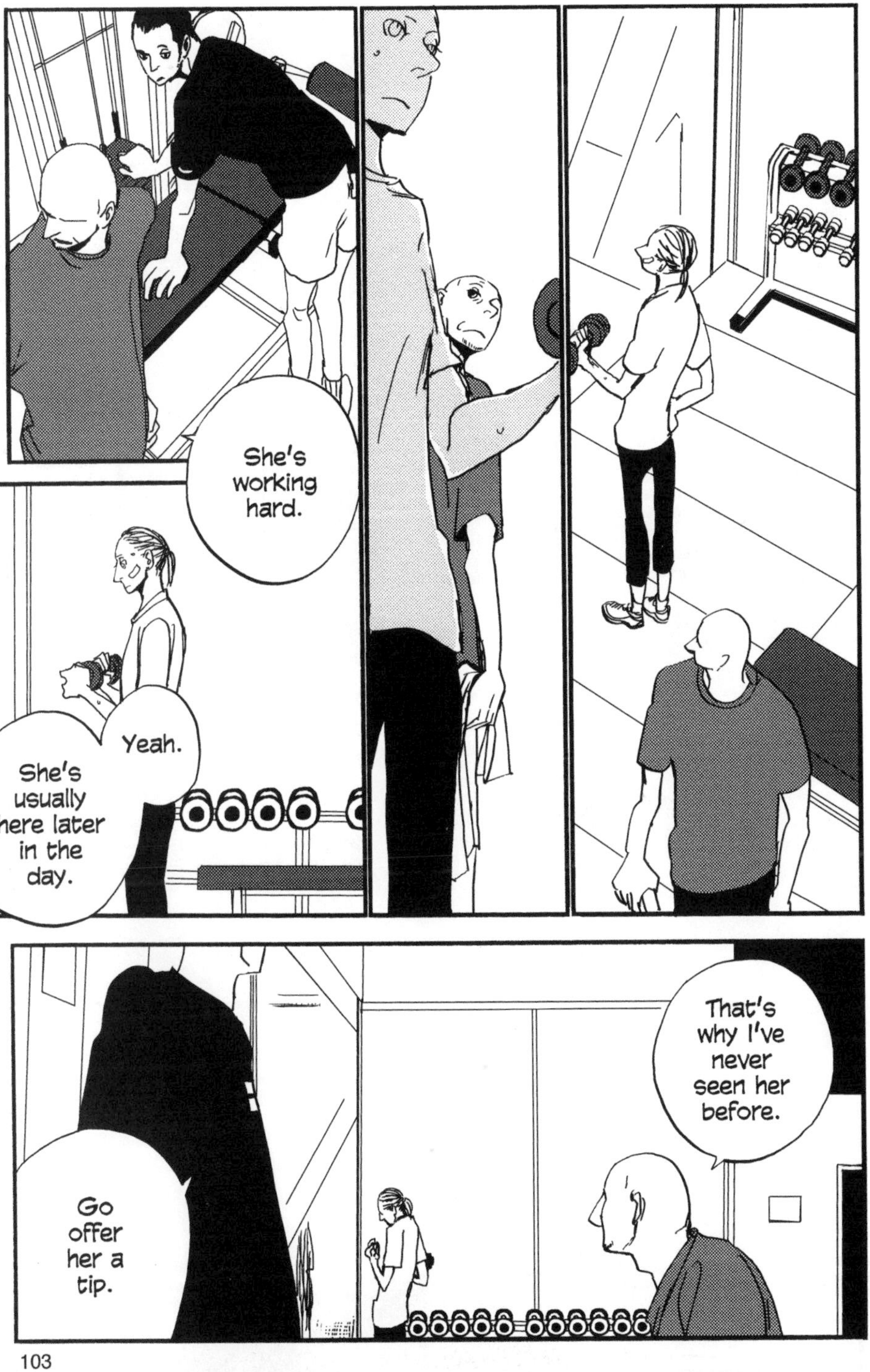
She's working hard.
Yeah.
She's usually here later in the day.
That's why I've never seen her before.
Go offer her a tip.

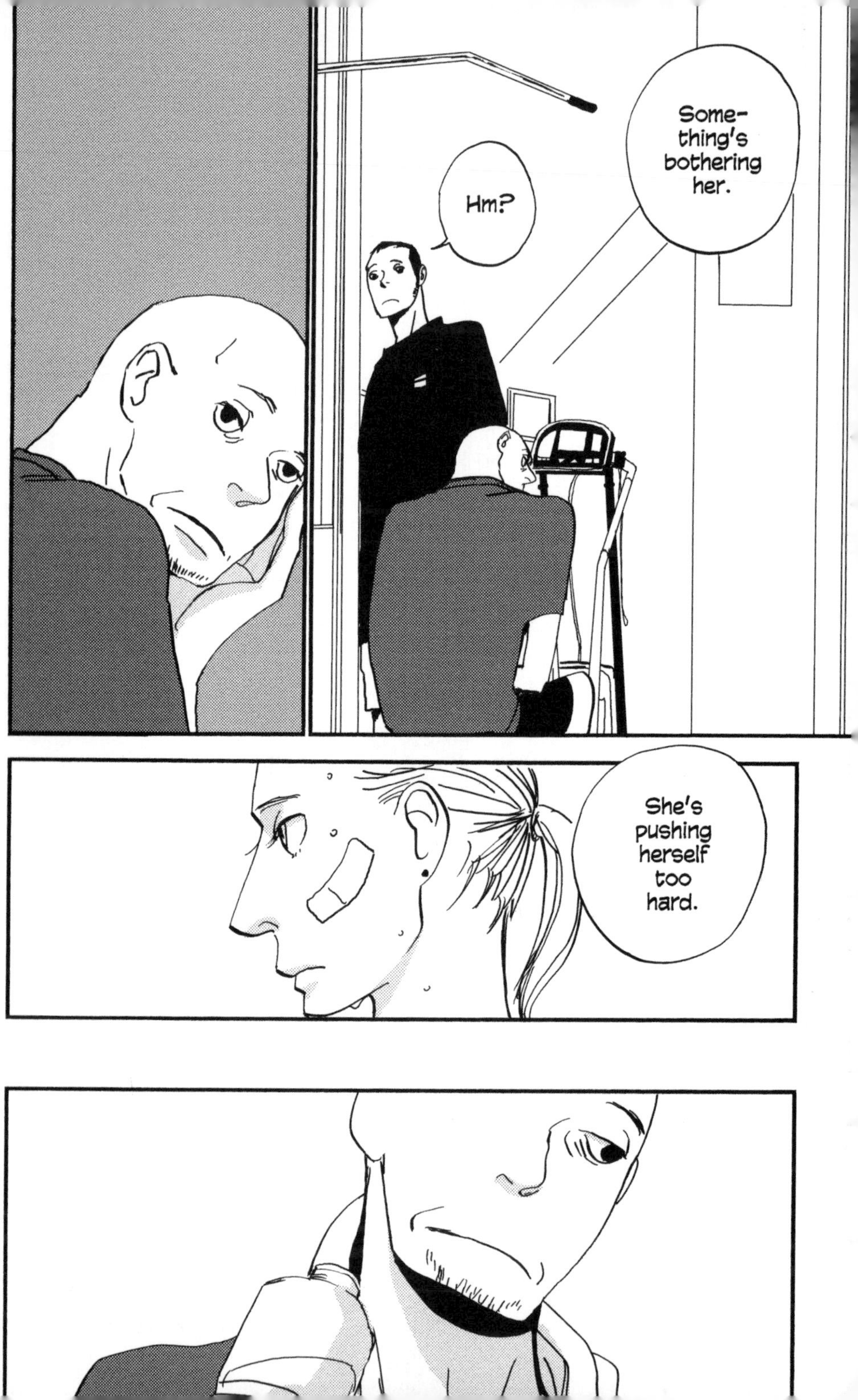
Some-thing's bothering her.
Hm?
She's pushing herself too hard.

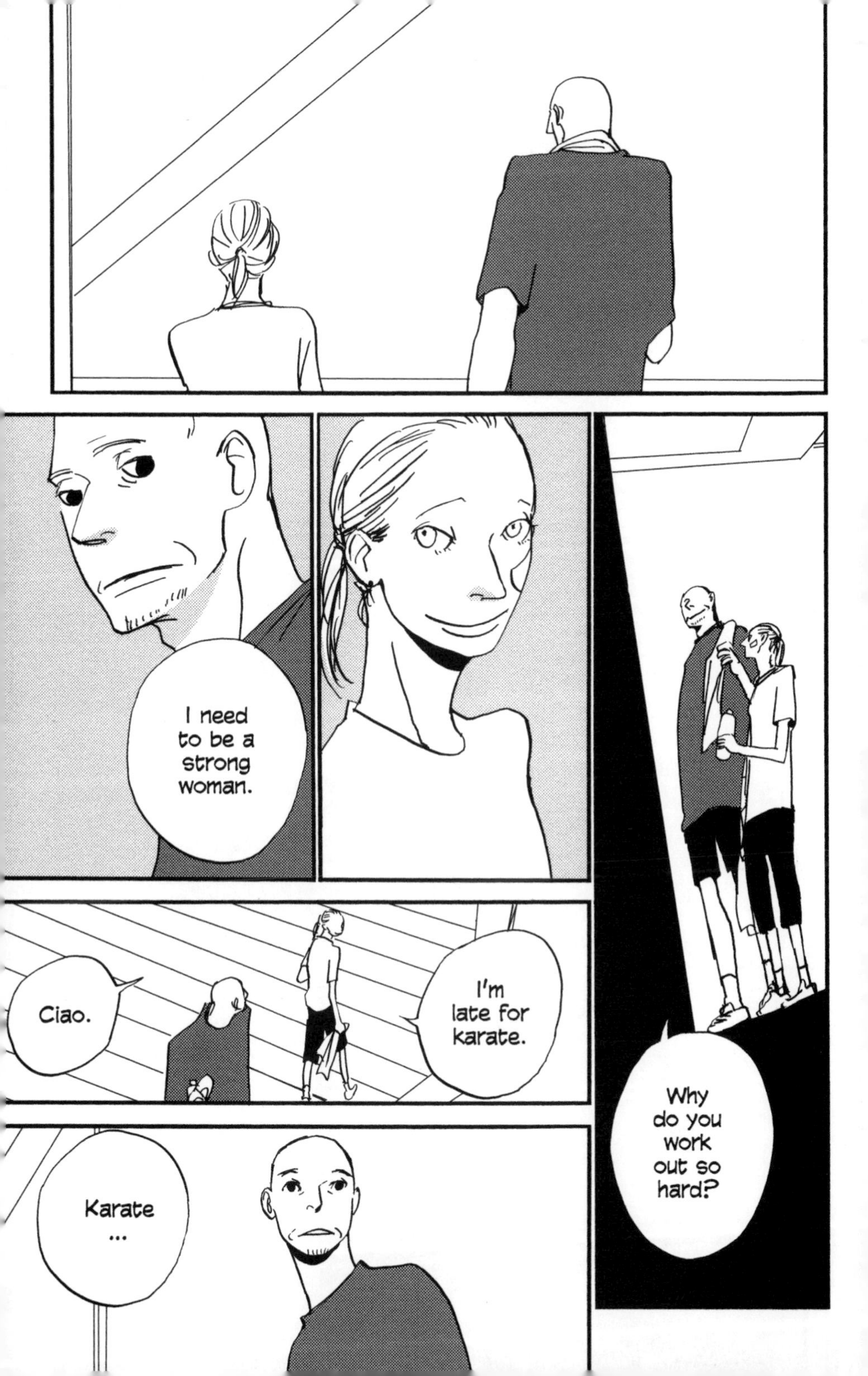
Why do you work out so hard?
I need to be a strong woman.
I'm late for karate.
Ciao.
Karate ...

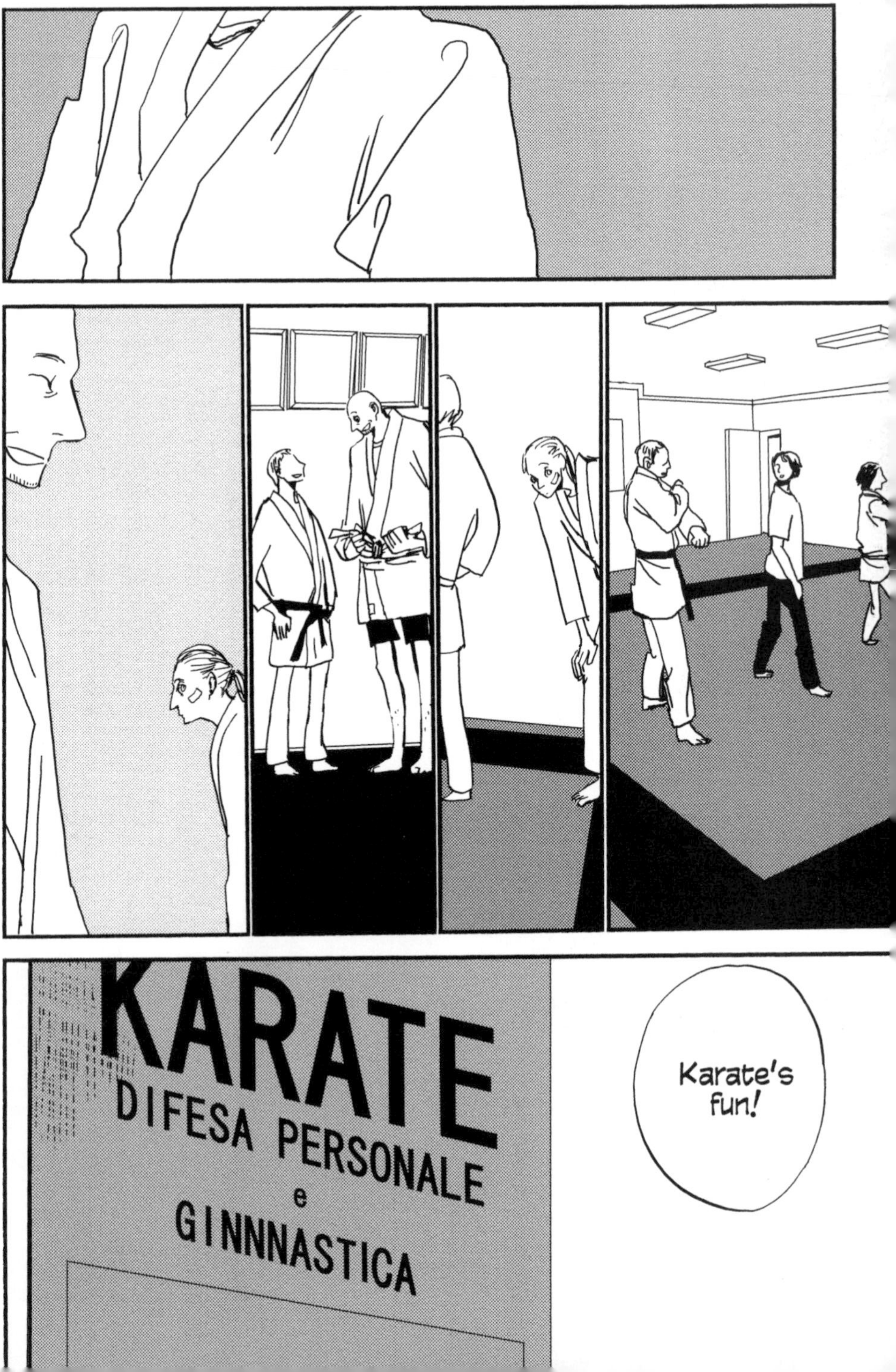
Karate's fun!
KARATE
DIFESA PERSONALE
e
GINNNASTICA

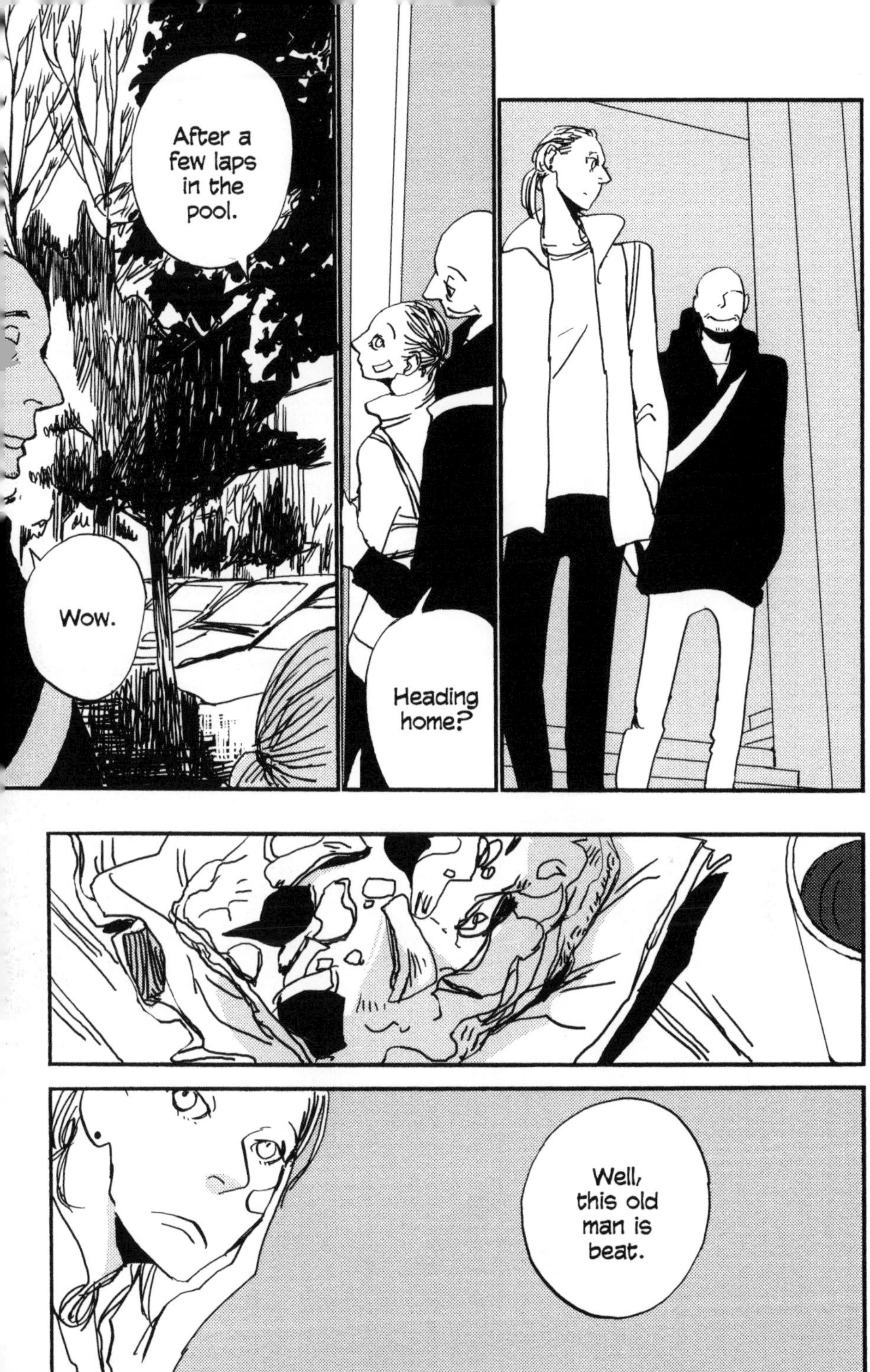
Heading home?
After a few laps in the pool.
Wow.
Well, this old man is beat.

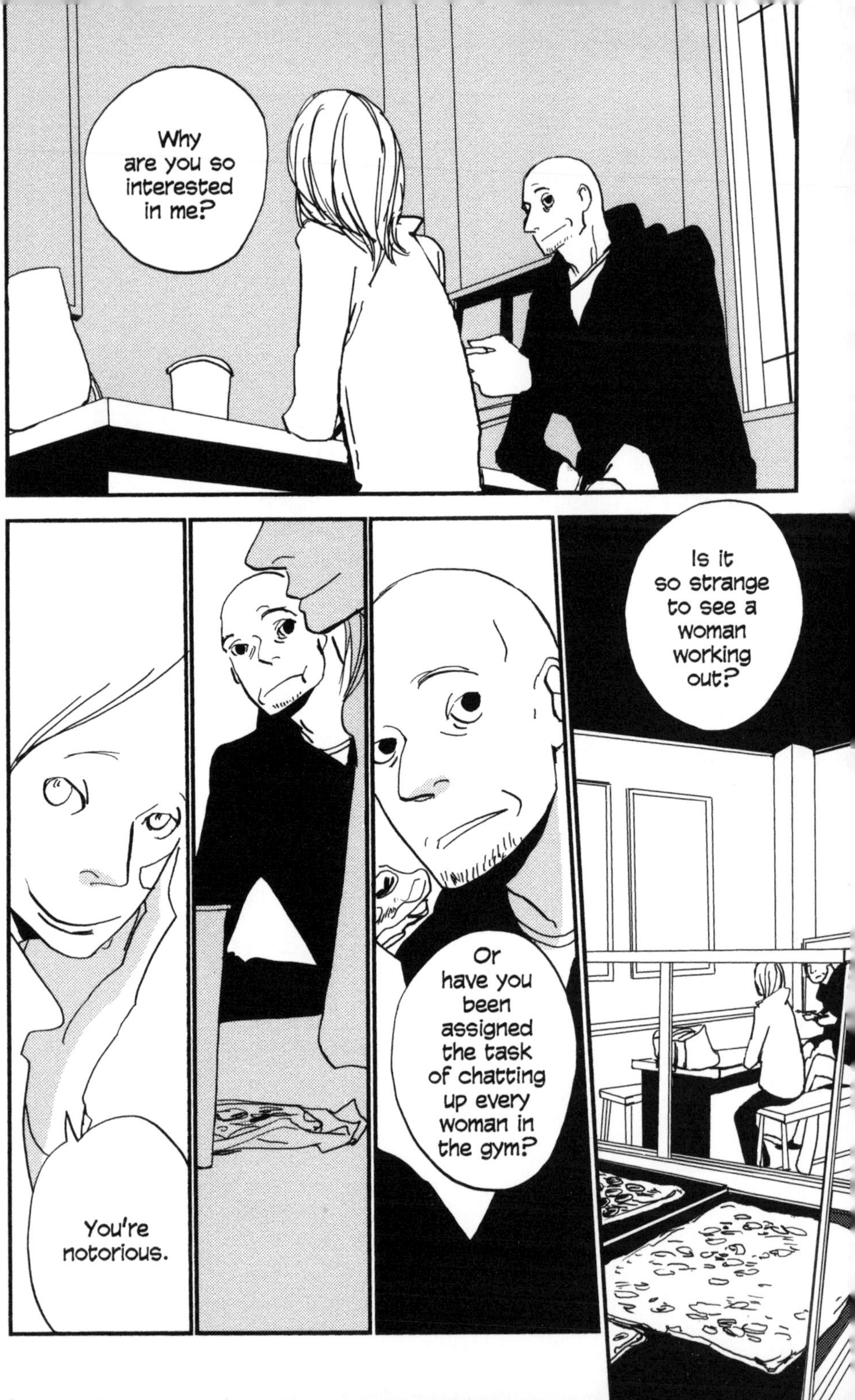
Why are you so interested in me?
Is it so strange to see a woman working out?
Or have you been assigned the task of chatting up every woman in the gym?
You're notorious.

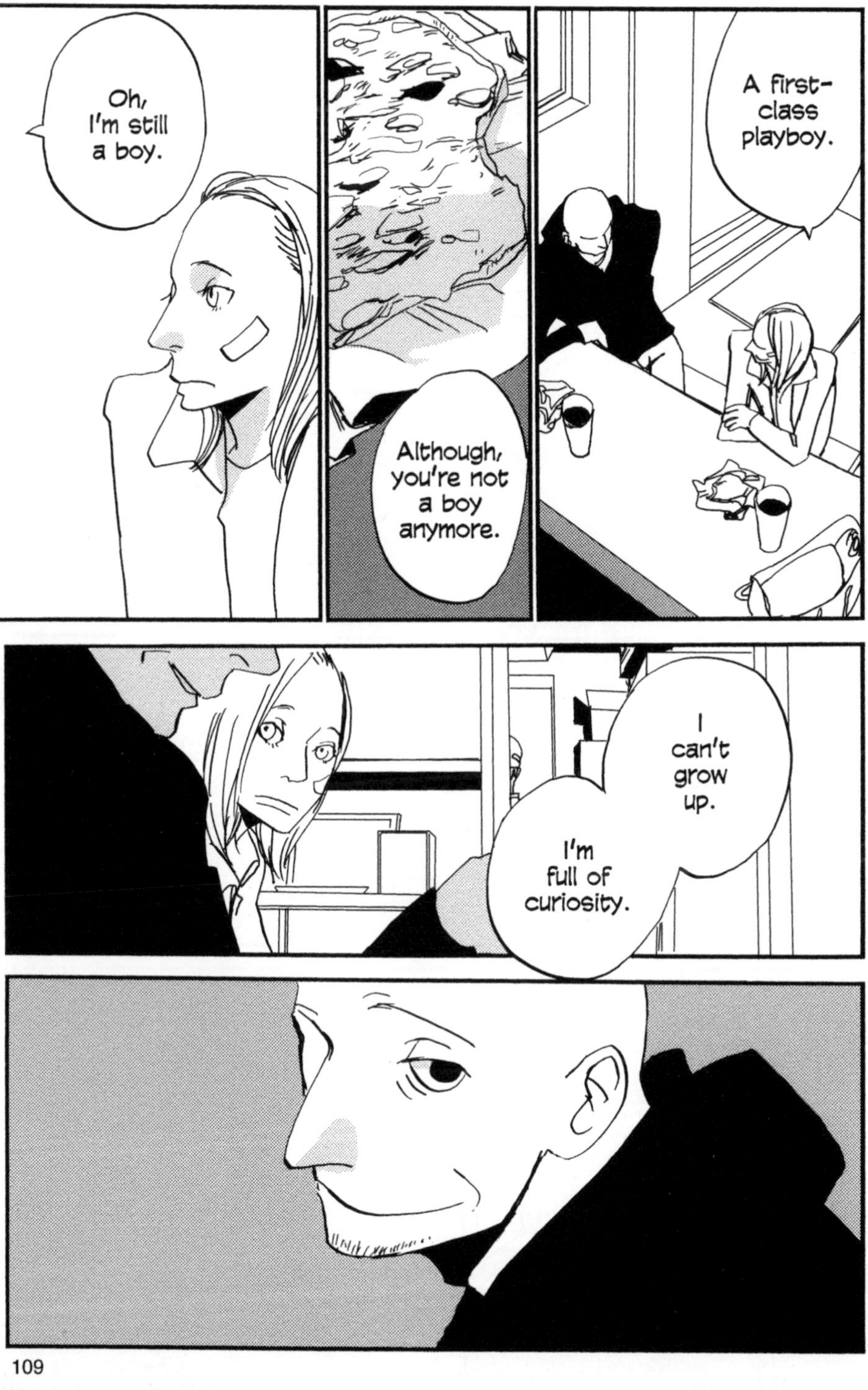
A first-class playboy.
Although, you're not a boy anymore.
Oh, I'm still a boy.
I can't grow up.
I'm full of curiosity.

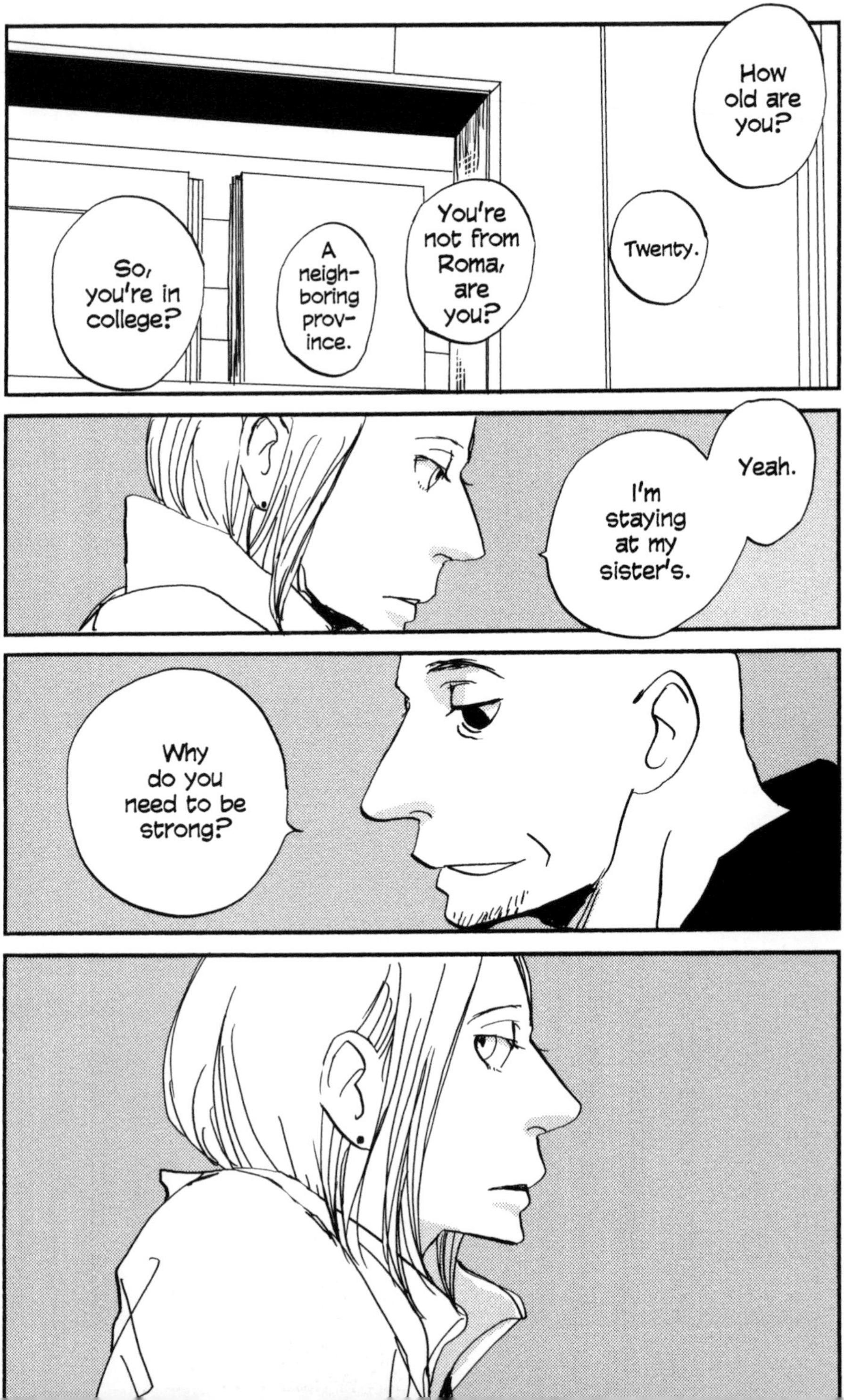
How old are you?
Twenty.
You're not from Roma, are you?
A neighboring province.
So, you're in college?
Yeah.
I'm staying at my sister's.
Why do you need to be strong?

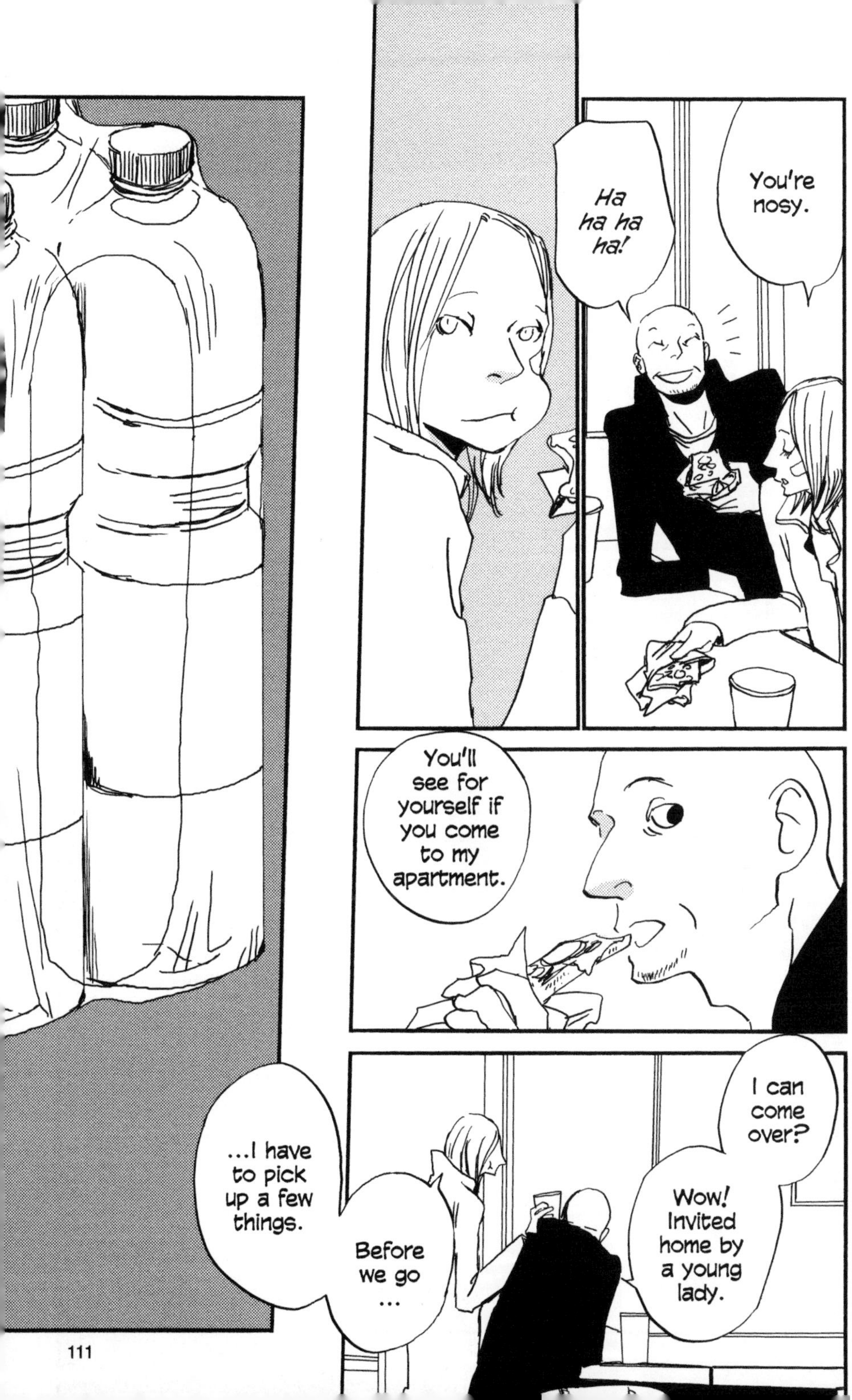
You're nosy.
Ha ha ha ha!
You'll see for yourself if you come to my apartment.
I can come over?
Wow! Invited home by a young lady.
Before we go ...
...I have to pick up a few things.

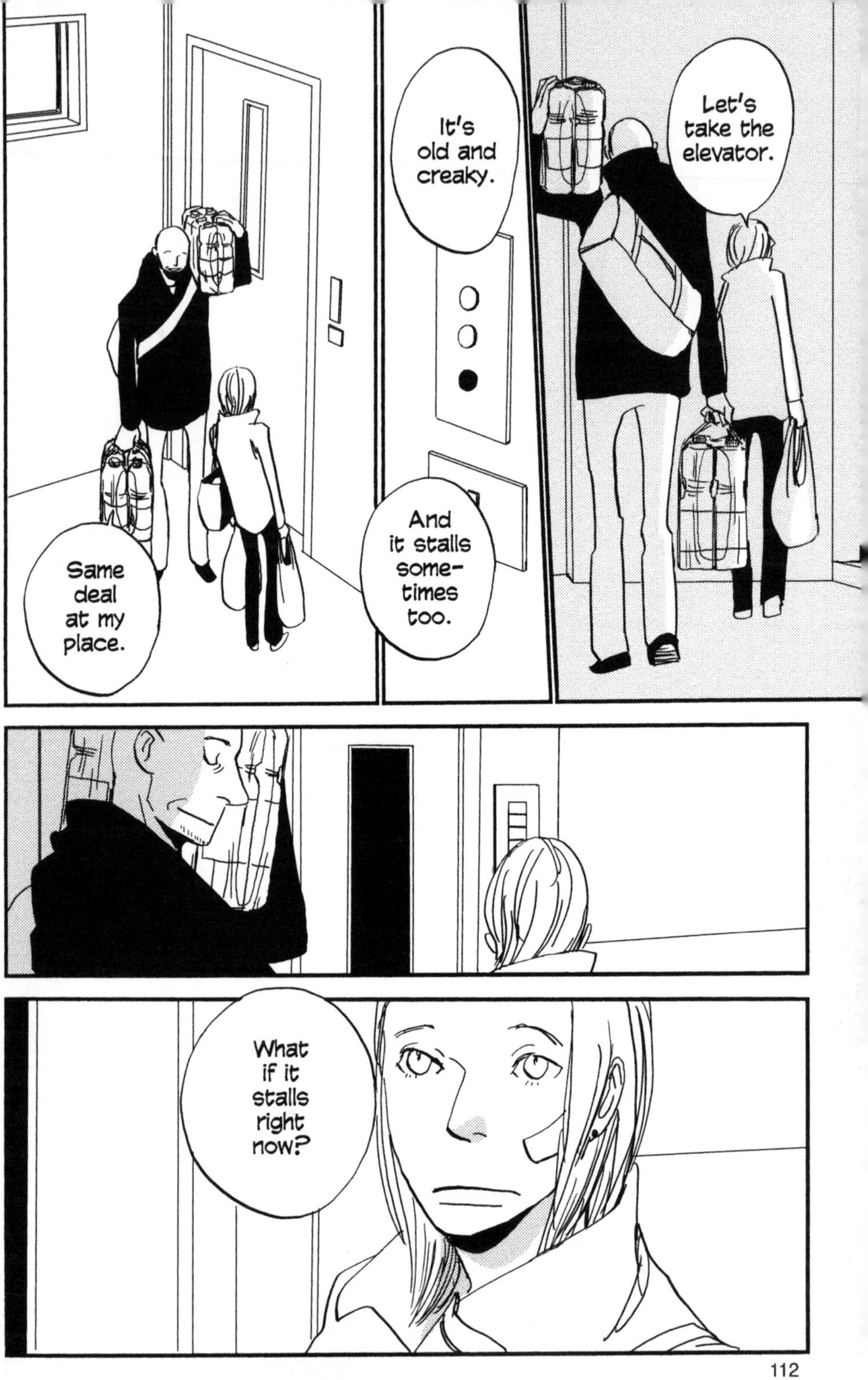
Let's take the elevator.
It's old and creaky.
And it stalls sometimes too.
Same deal at my place.
What if it stalls right now?

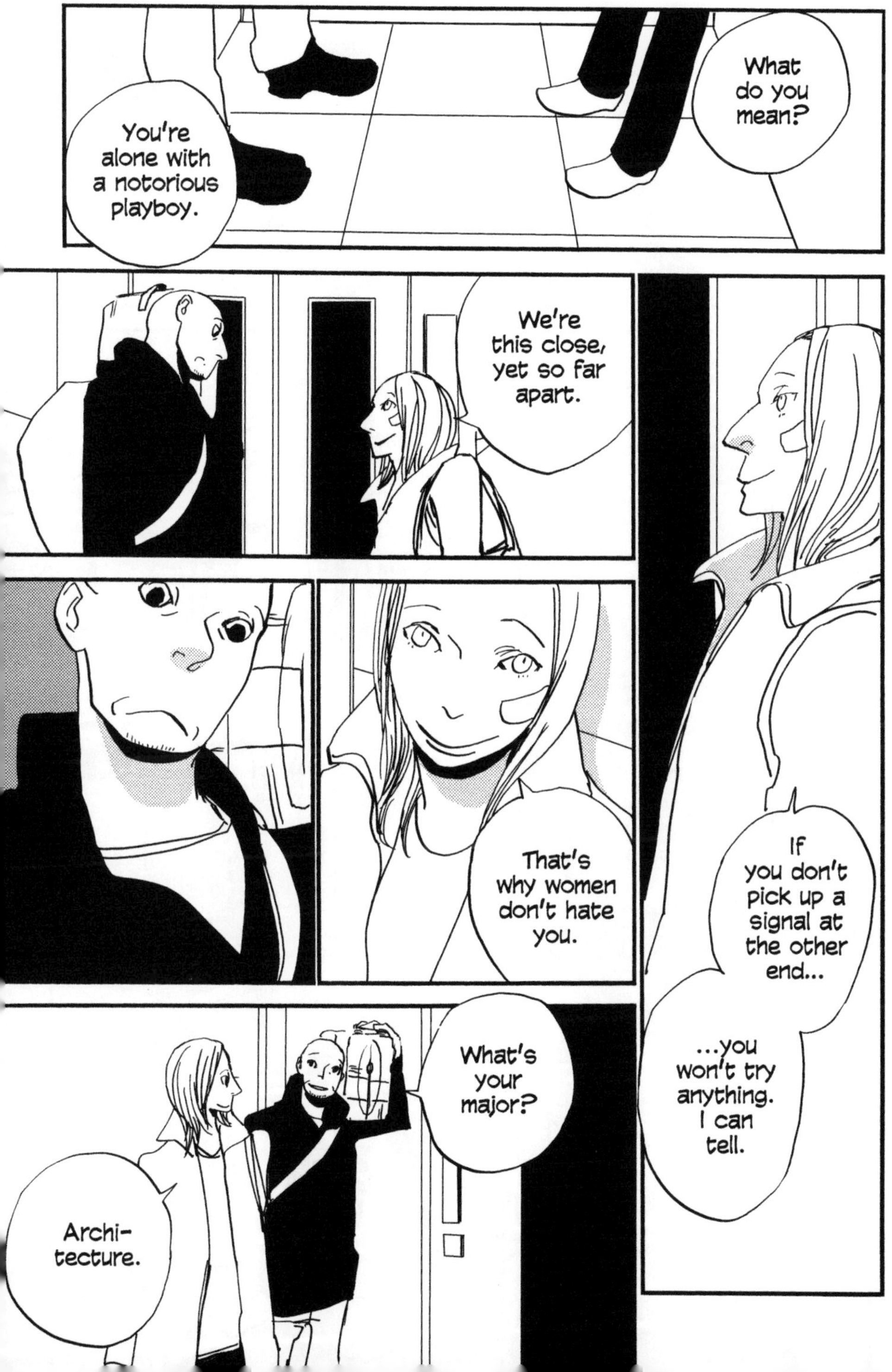
What do you mean?
You're alone with a notorious playboy.
If you don't pick up a signal at the other end...
...you won't try anything. I can tell.
We're this close, yet so far apart.
That's why women don't hate you.
What's your major?
Archi-tecture.

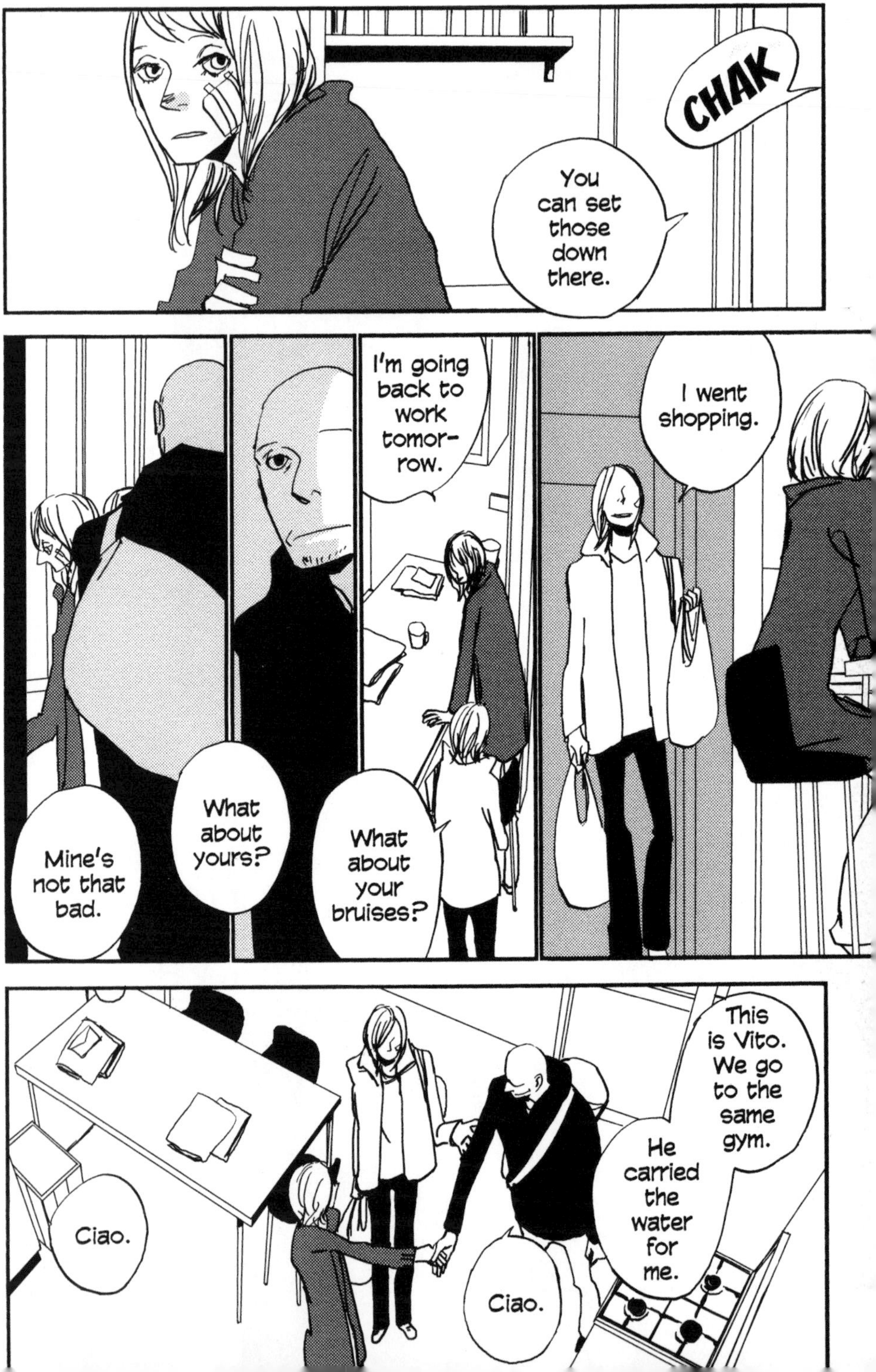
CHAK
You can set those down there.
I went shopping.
I'm going back to work tomorrow.
What about your bruises?
What about yours?
Mine's not that bad.
This is Vito. We go to the same gym.
He carried the water for me.
Ciao.
Ciao.

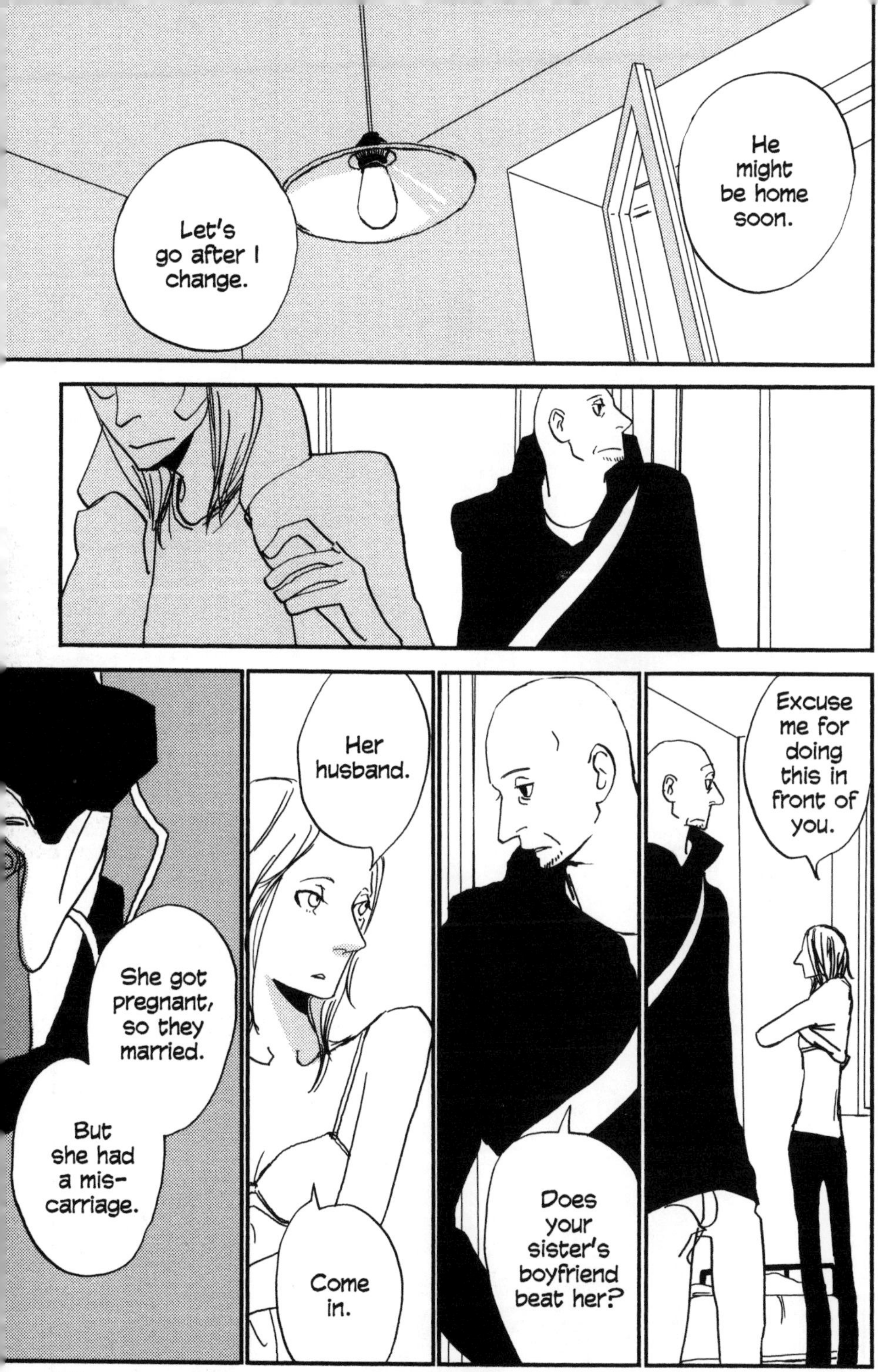
He might be home soon.
Let's go after I change.
Excuse me for doing this in front of you.
Does your sister's boyfriend beat her?
Her husband.
Come in.
She got pregnant, so they married.
But she had a mis-carriage.

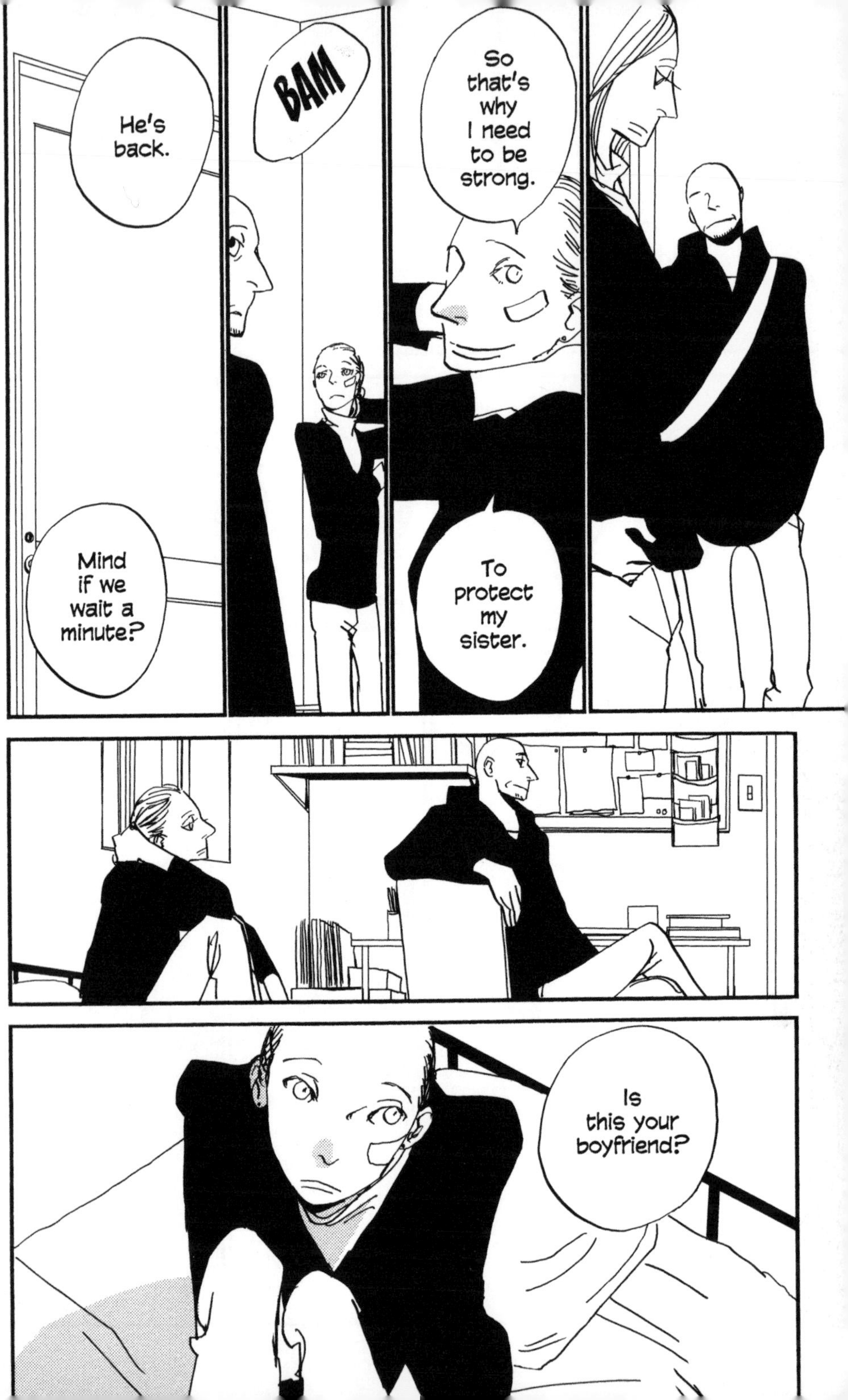
So that's why I need to be strong.
To protect my sister.
BAM
He's back.
Mind if we wait a minute?
Is this your boyfriend?

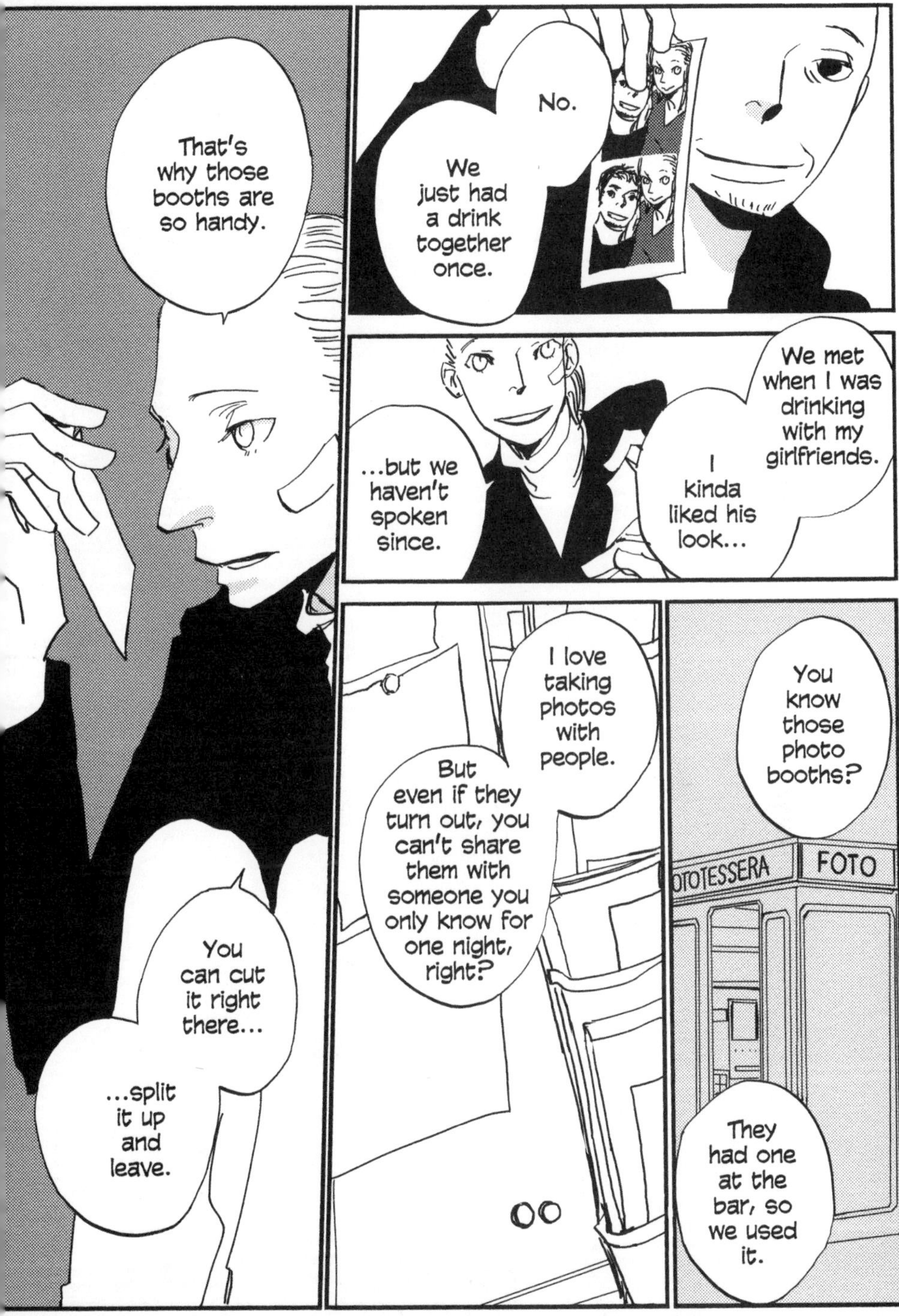
No.
We just had a drink together once.
We met when I was drinking with my girlfriends.
I kinda liked his look...
...but we haven't spoken since.
You know those photo booths?
OTOTESSERA
FOTO
They had one at the bar, so we used it.
I love taking photos with people.
But even if they turn out, you can't share them with someone you only know for one night, right?
That's why those booths are so handy.
You can cut it right there...
...split it up and leave.

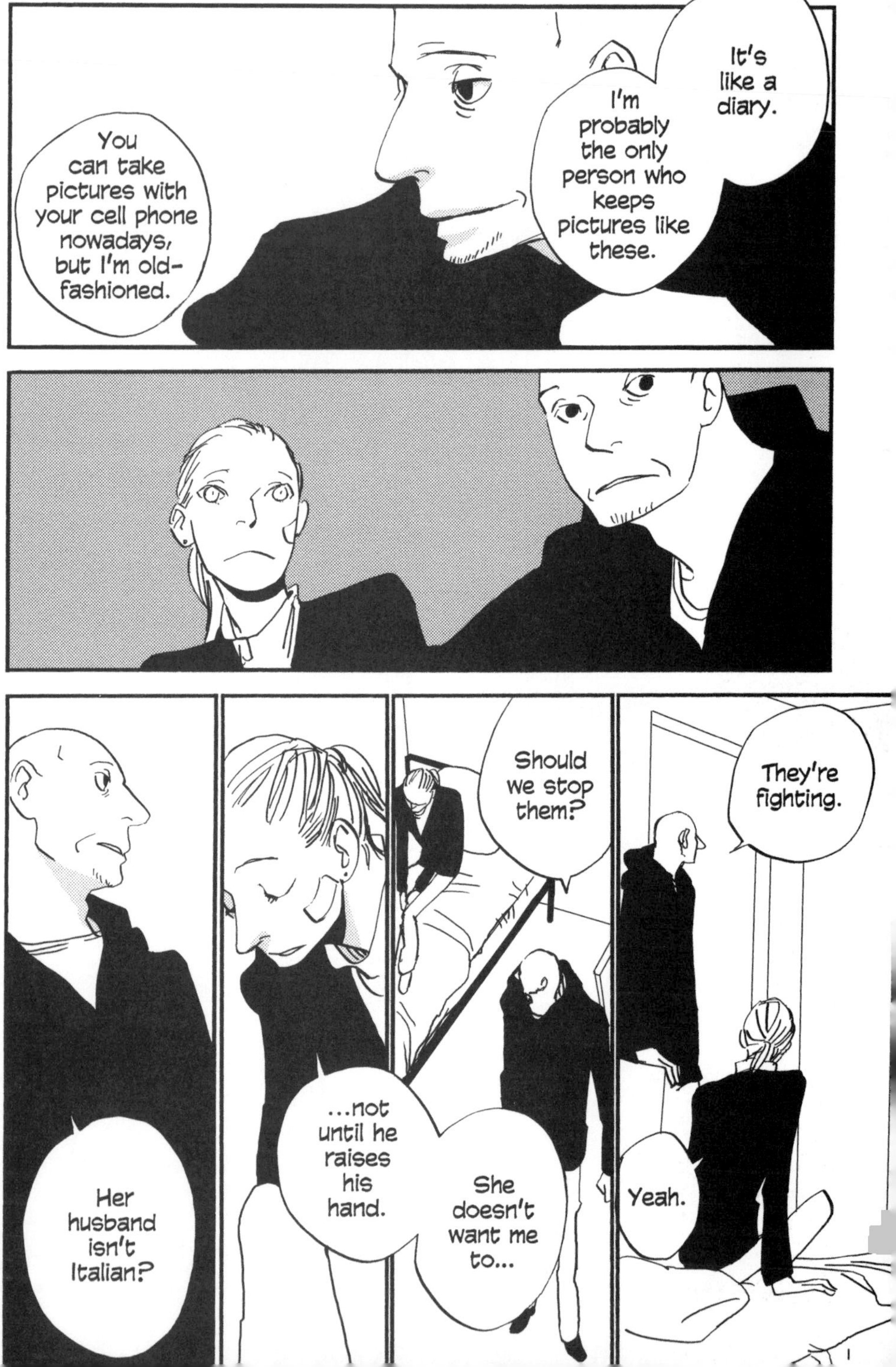
It's like a diary.
I'm probably the only person who keeps pictures like these.
You can take pictures with your cell phone nowadays, but I'm old-fashioned.
They're fighting.
Yeah.
Should we stop them?
She doesn't want me to...
...not until he raises his hand.
Her husband isn't Italian?

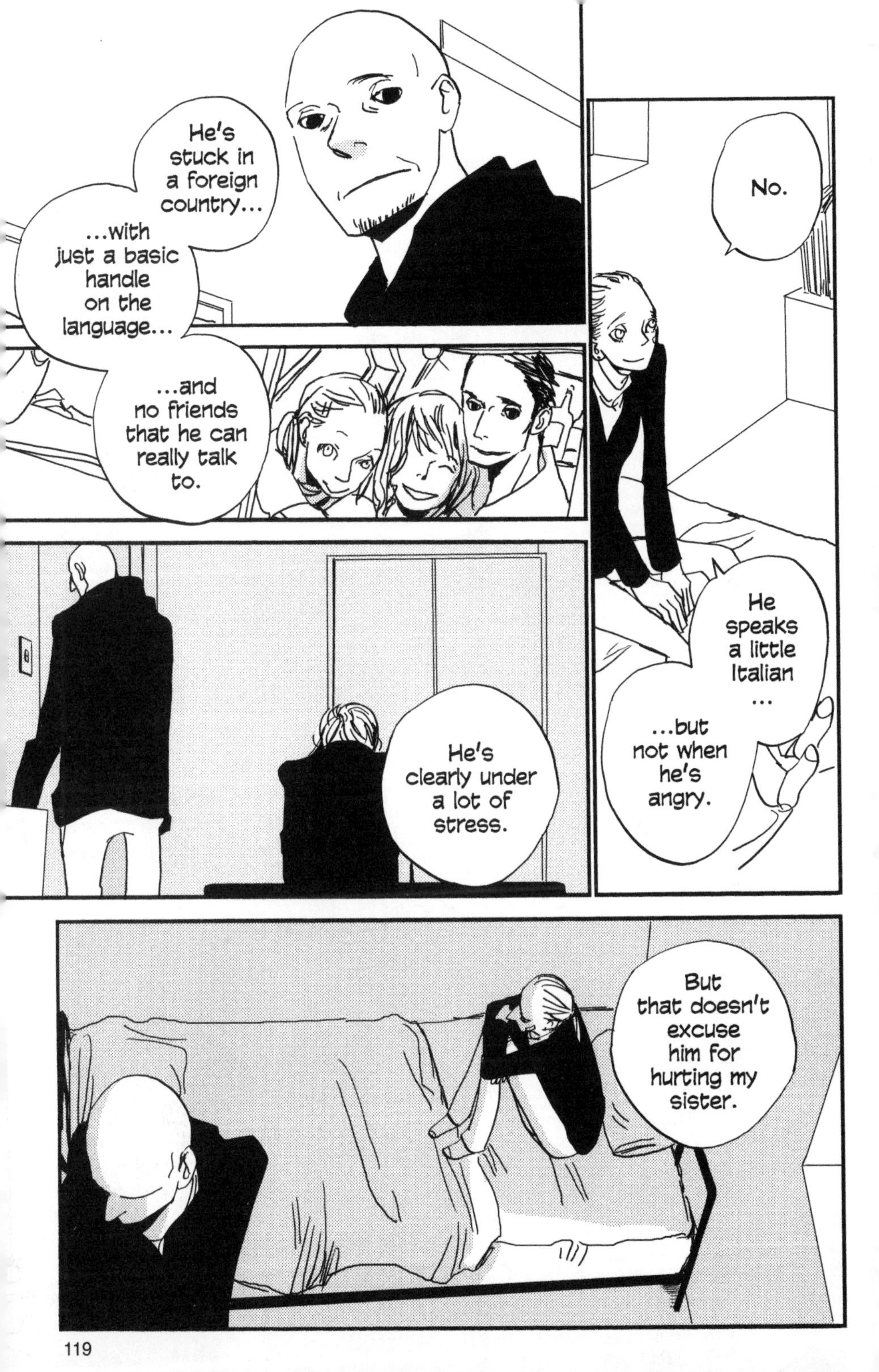
No.
He speaks a little Italian ...
...but not when he's angry.
He's stuck in a foreign country...
...with just a basic handle on the language...
...and no friends that he can really talk to.
He's clearly under a lot of stress.
But that doesn't excuse him for hurting my sister.

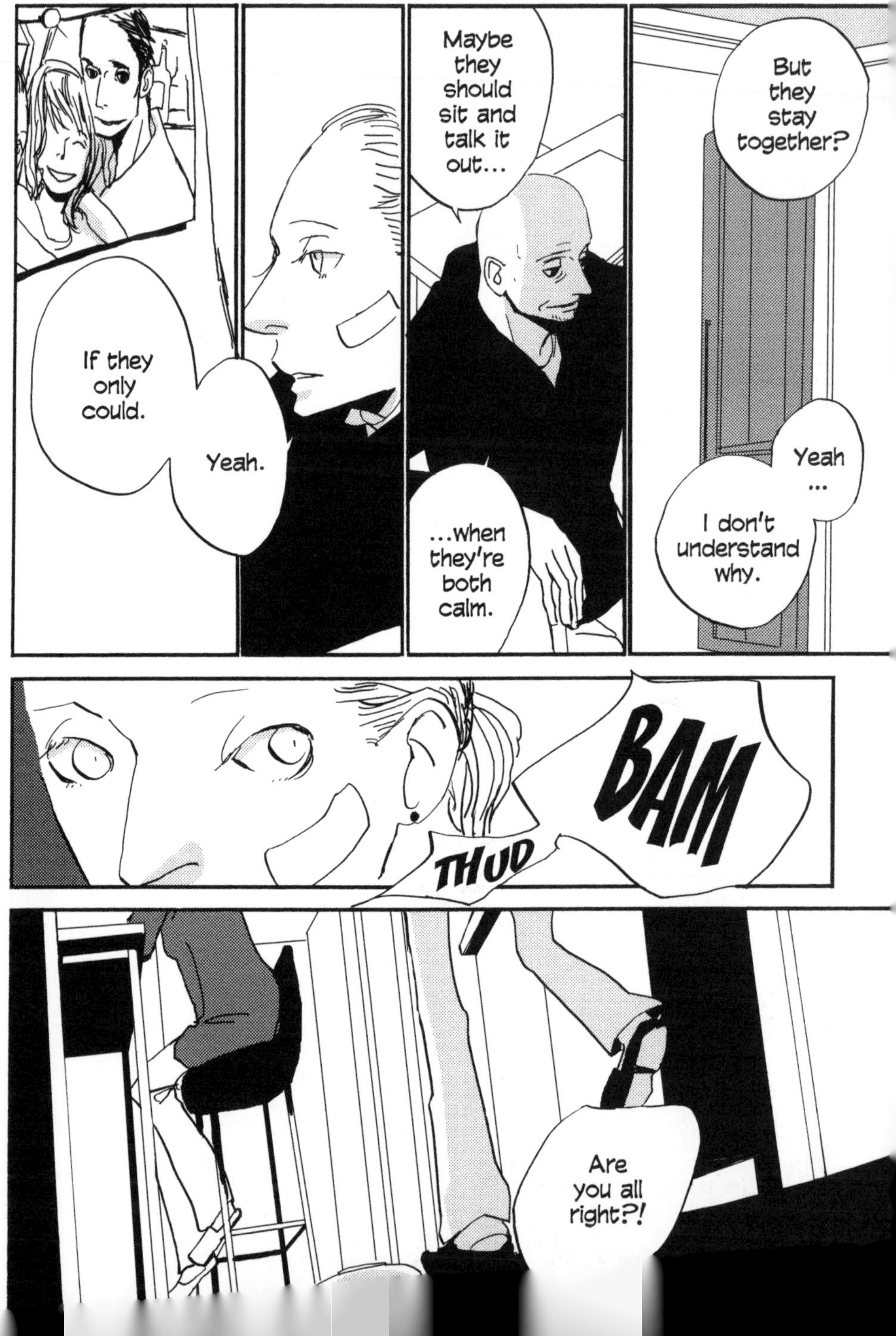
But they stay together?
Yeah ...
I don't understand why.
Maybe they should sit and talk it out...
...when they're both calm.
Yeah.
If they only could.
BAM
THUD
Are you all right?!

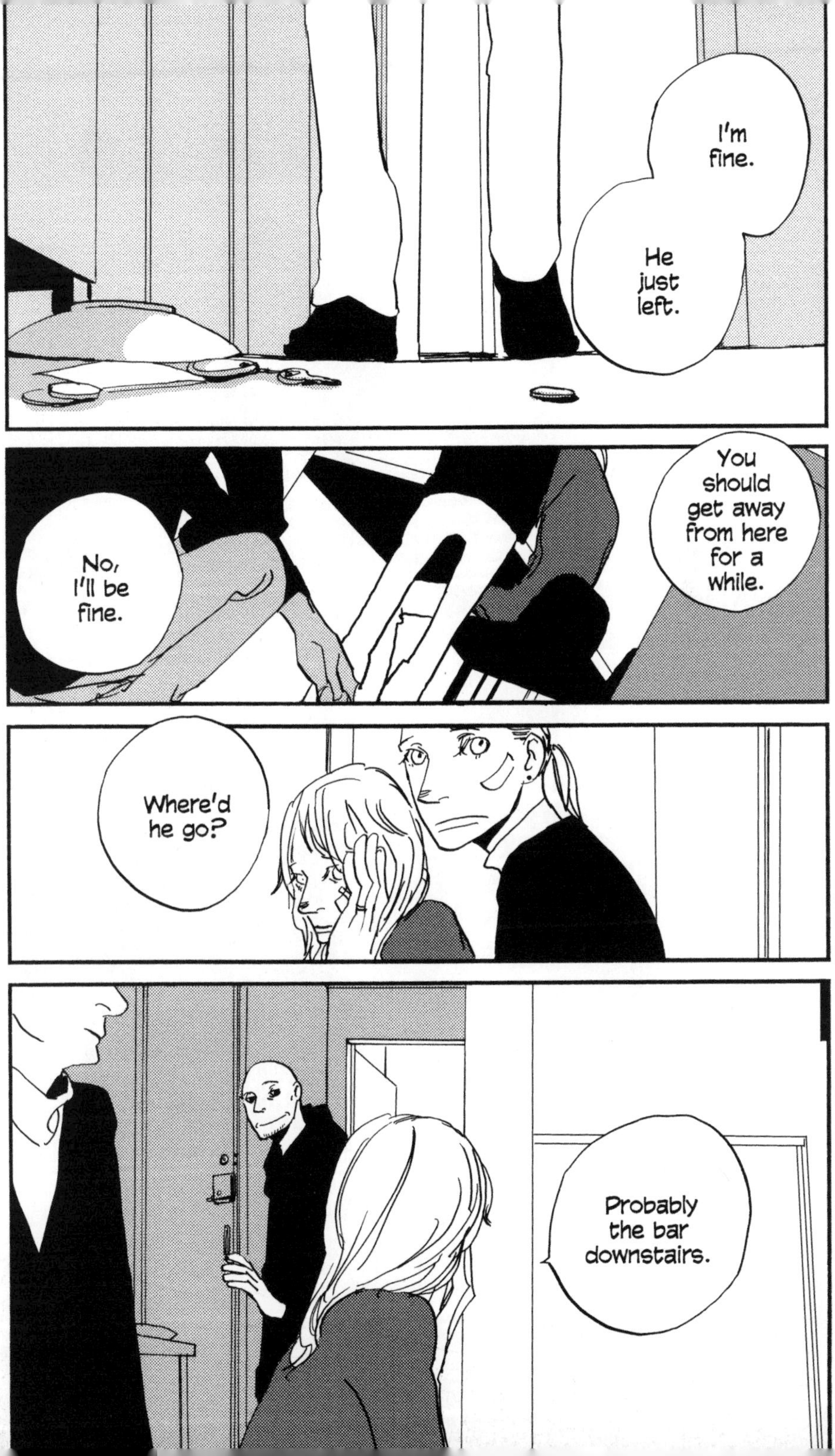
I'm fine.
He just left.
You should get away from here for a while.
No, I'll be fine.
Where'd he go?
Probably the bar downstairs.

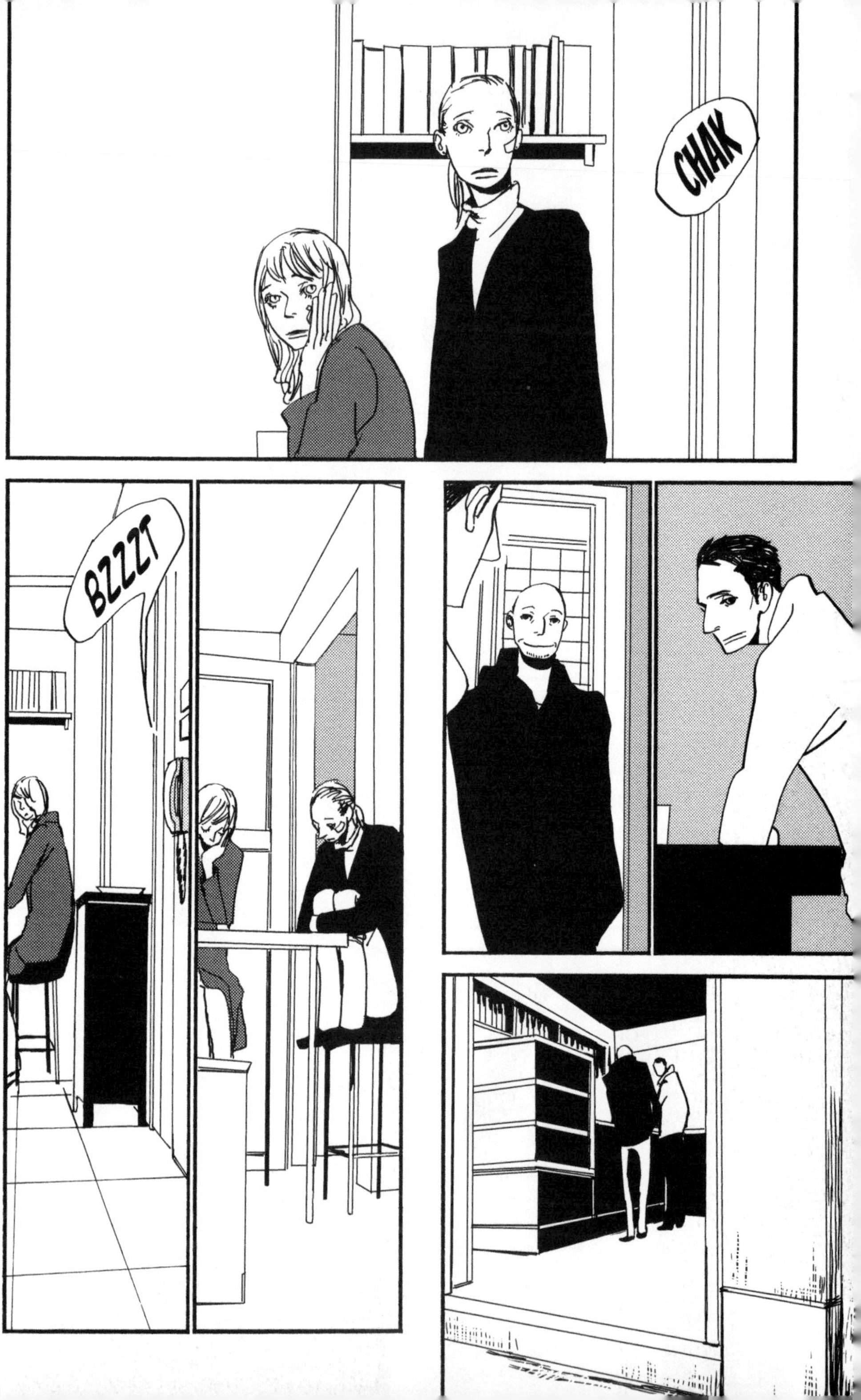
CHAK
BZZZT

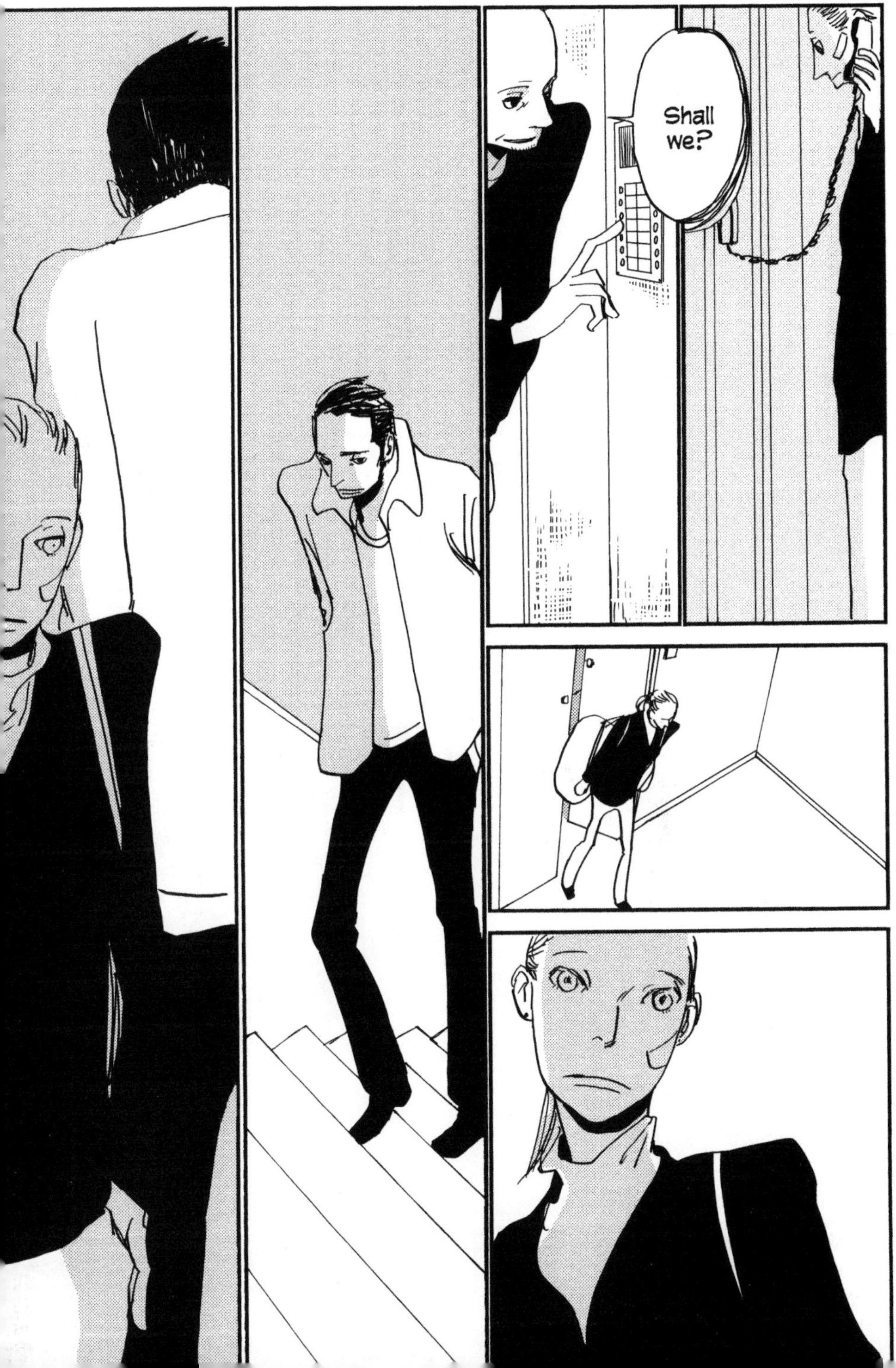
Shall we?

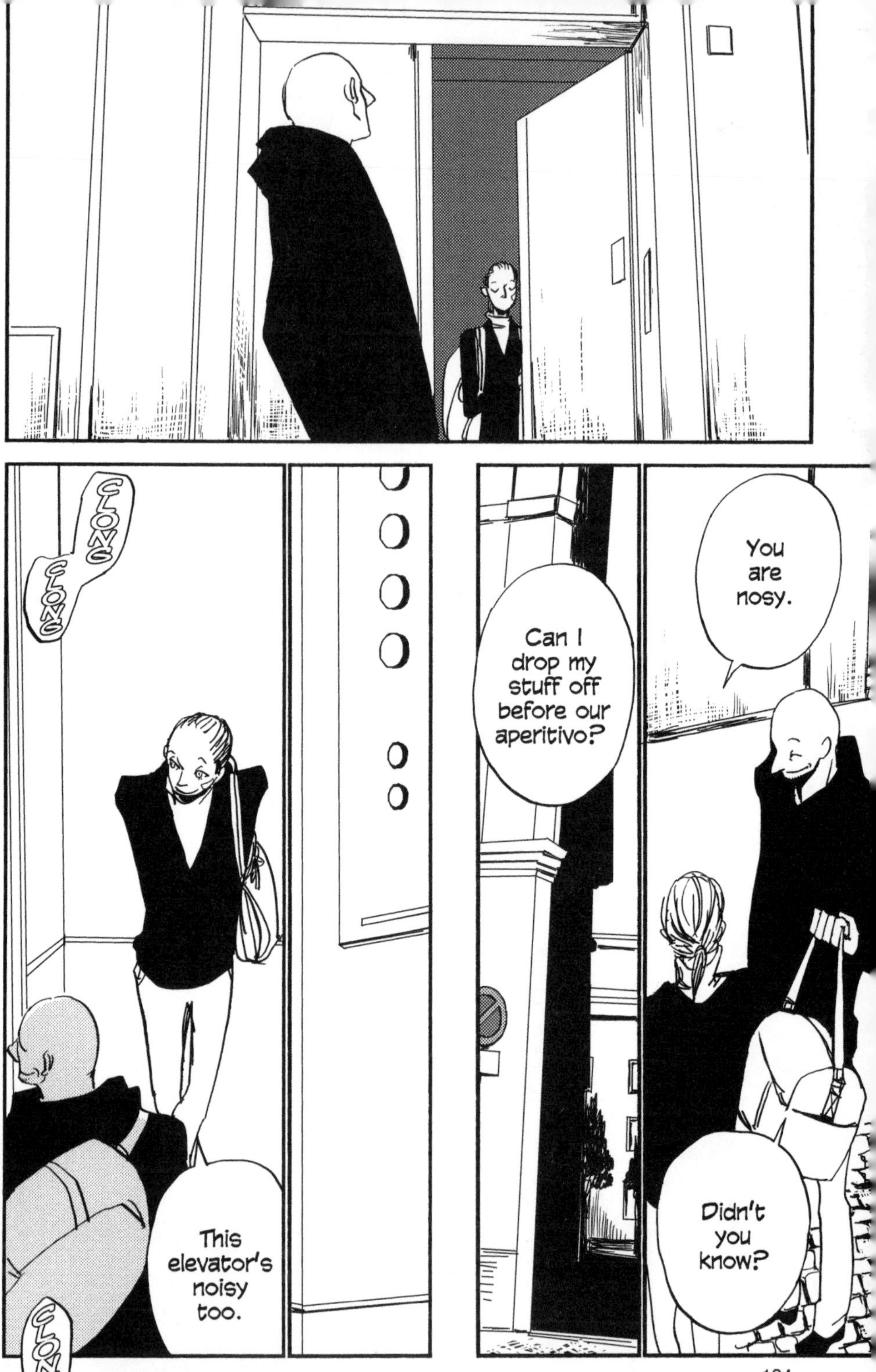
You are nosy.
Didn't you know?
Can I drop my stuff off before our aperitivo?
CLONG
CLONG
This elevator's noisy too.
CLONG

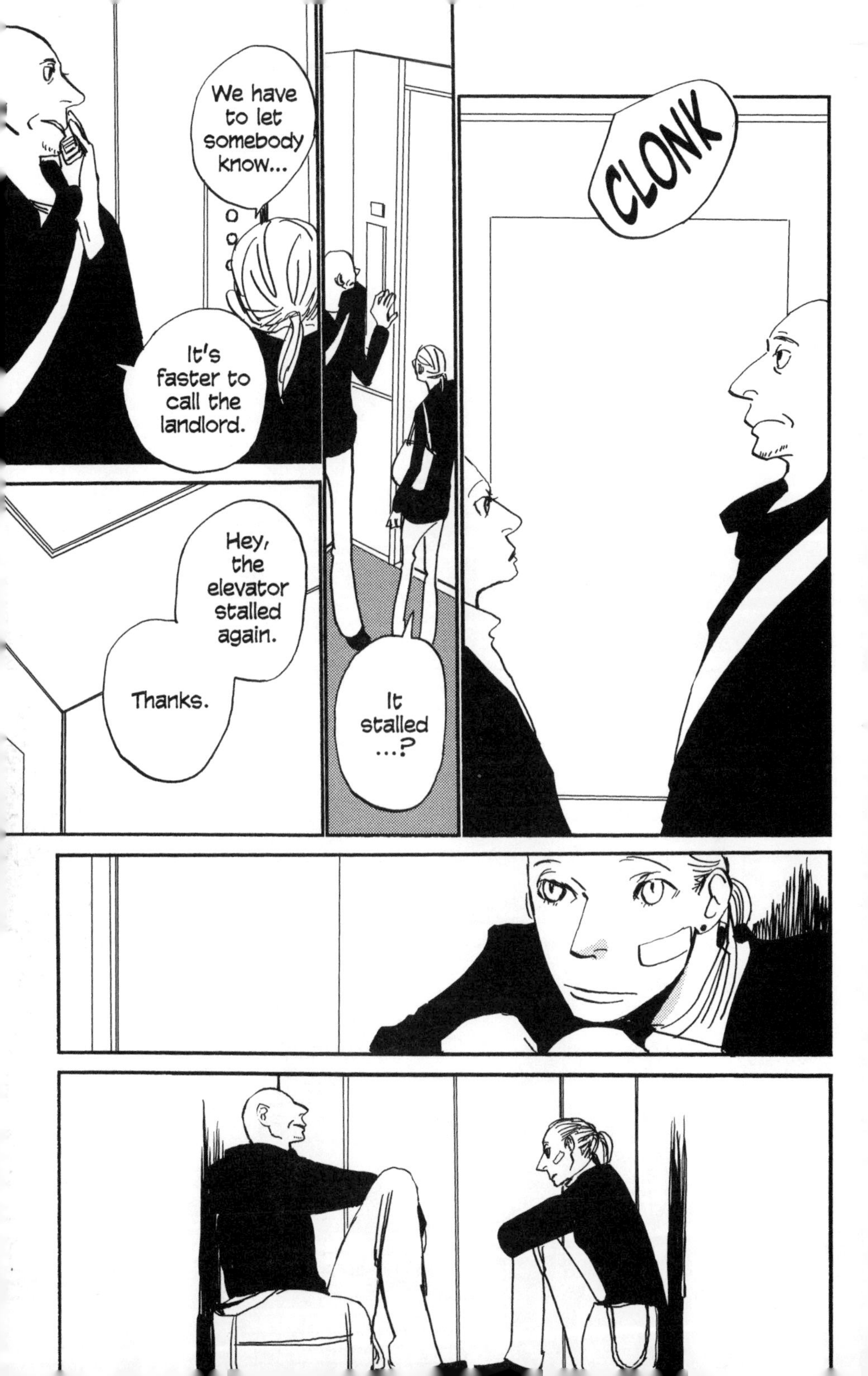
CLONK
It stalled ...?
We have to let somebody know...
It's faster to call the landlord.
Hey, the elevator stalled again.
Thanks.

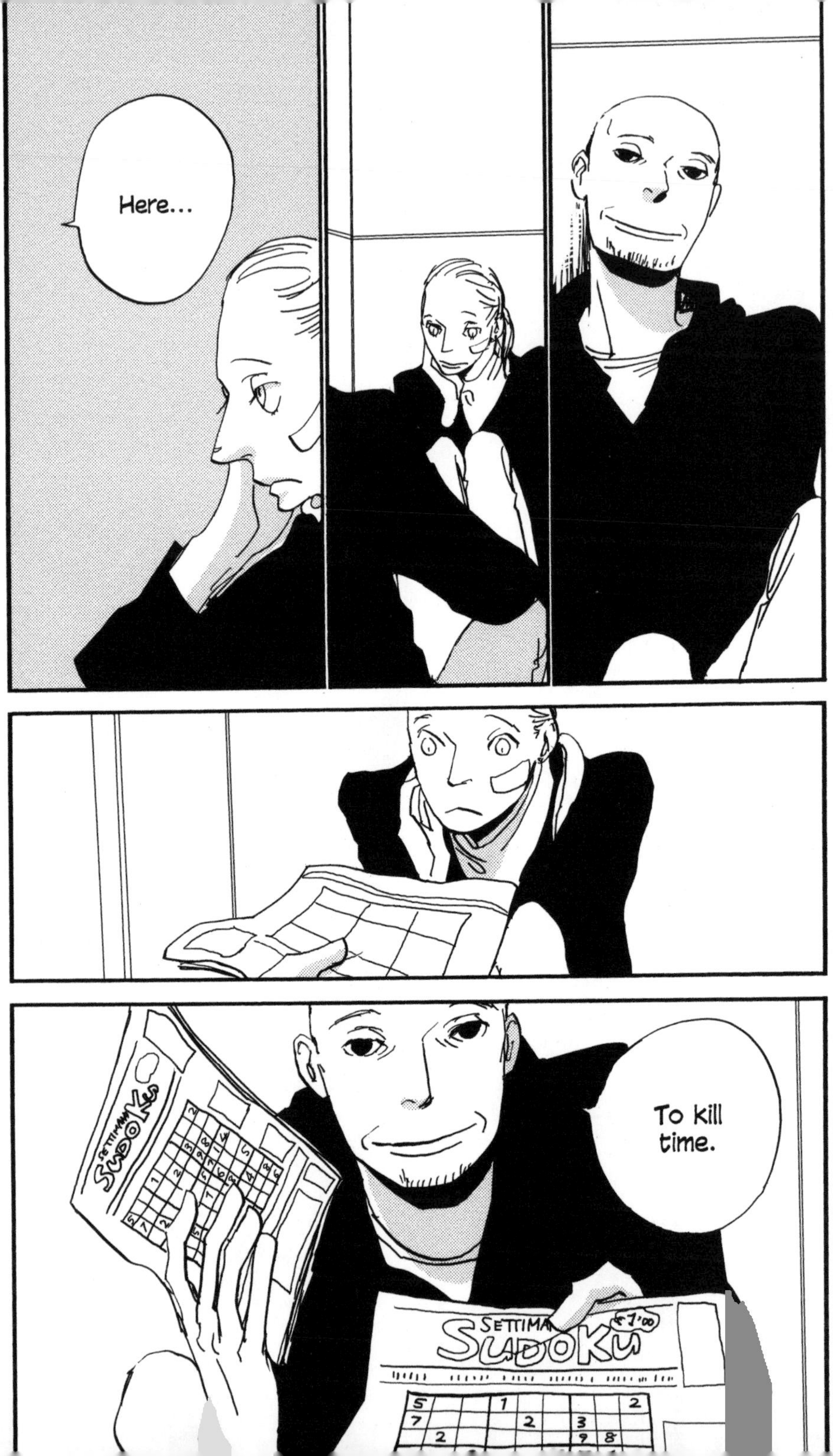
Here...
To kill time.
SUDOKU

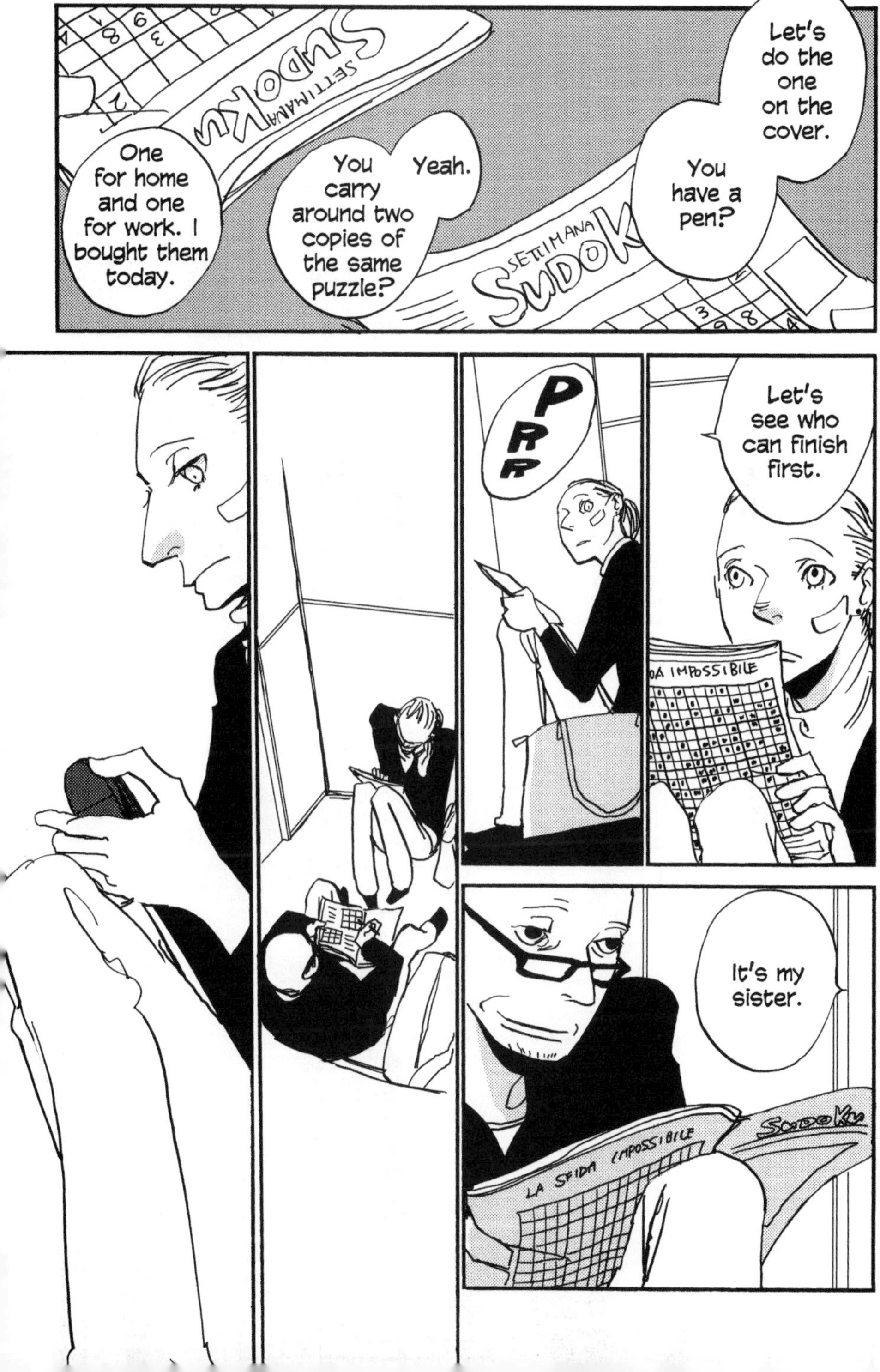
Let's do the one on the cover.
You have a pen?
SETTIMANA SUDOKU
Yeah.
You carry around two copies of the same puzzle?
One for home and one for work. I bought them today.
Let's see who can finish first.
PRR
It's my sister.
SUDOKU
LA SFIDA IMPOSSIBILE

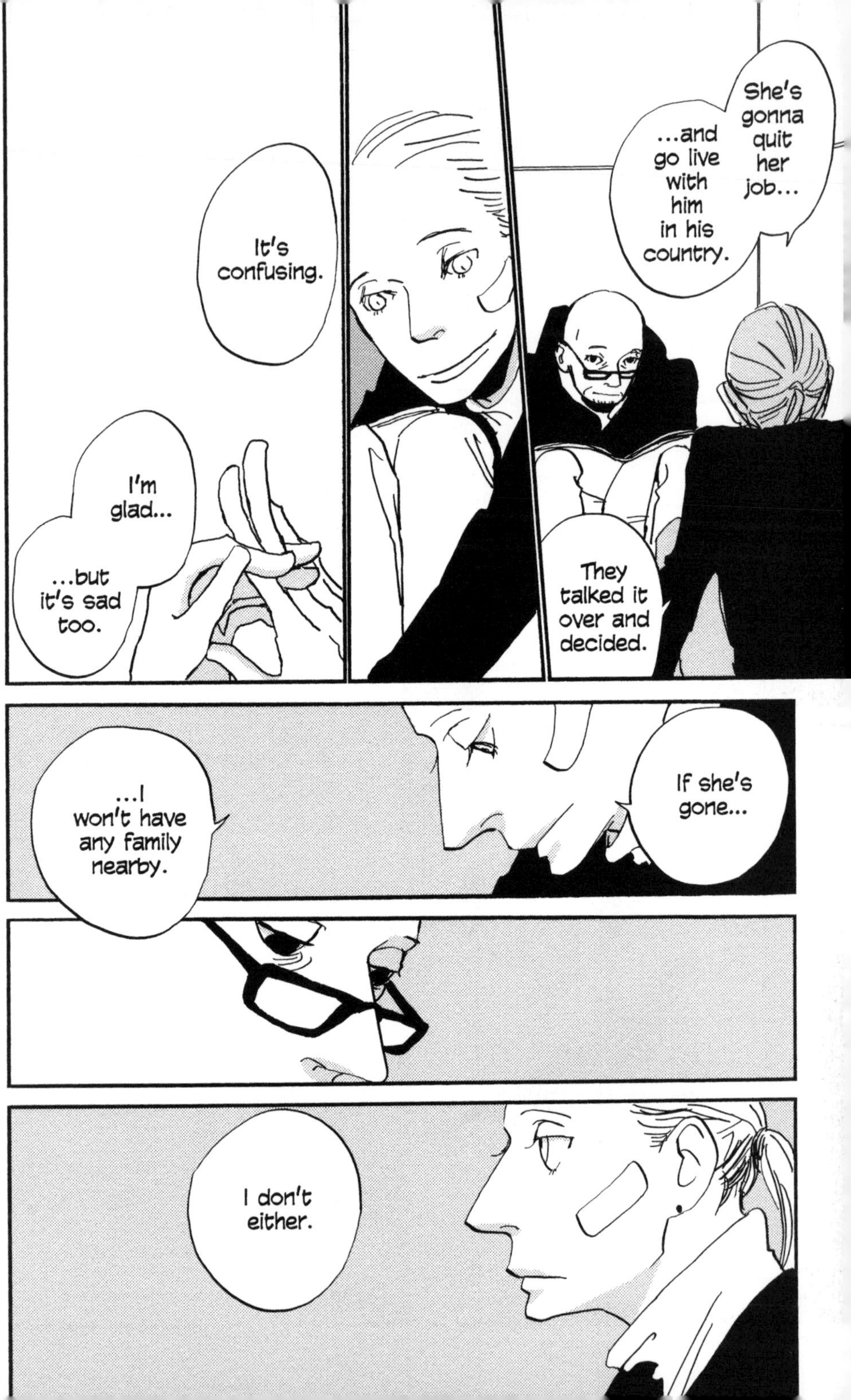
She's gonna quit her job...
...and go live with him in his country.
They talked it over and decided.
It's confusing.
I'm glad...
...but it's sad too.
If she's gone...
...I won't have any family nearby.
I don't either.

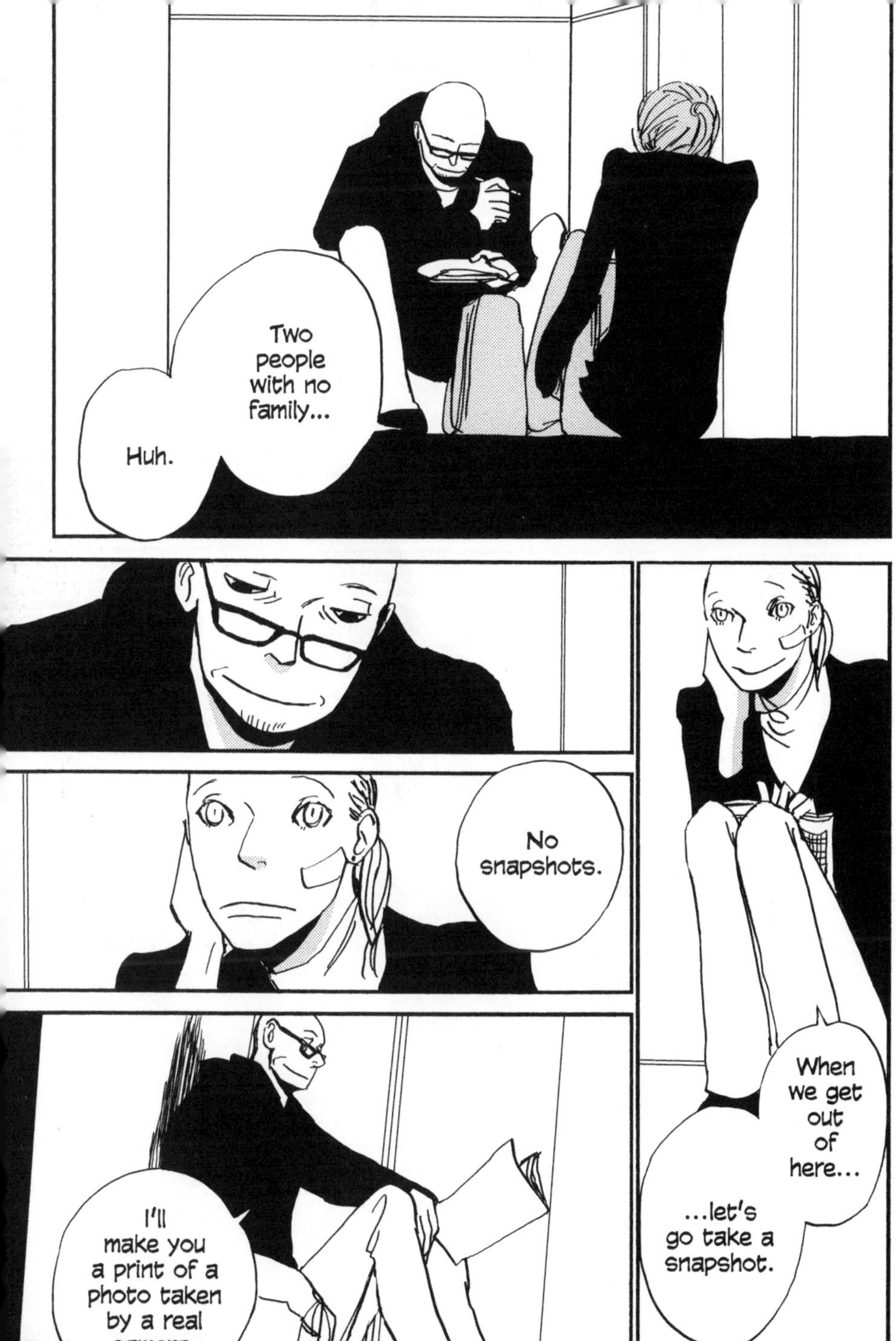
Two people with no family...
Huh.
When we get out of here...
...let's go take a snapshot.
No snapshots.
I'll make you a print of a photo taken by a real camera.

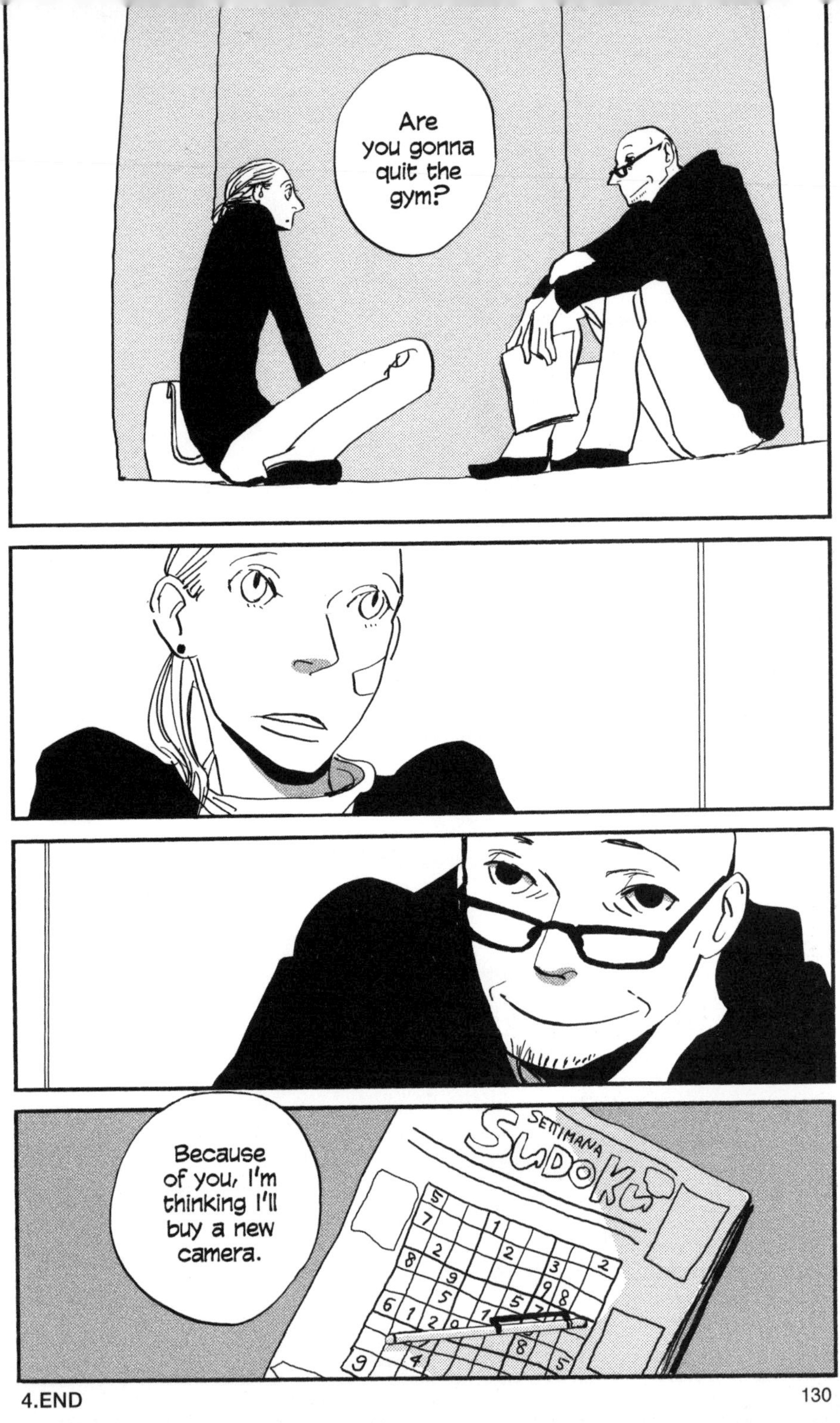
Are you gonna quit the gym?
Because of you, I'm thinking I'll buy a new camera.
SETTIMANA SUDOKU

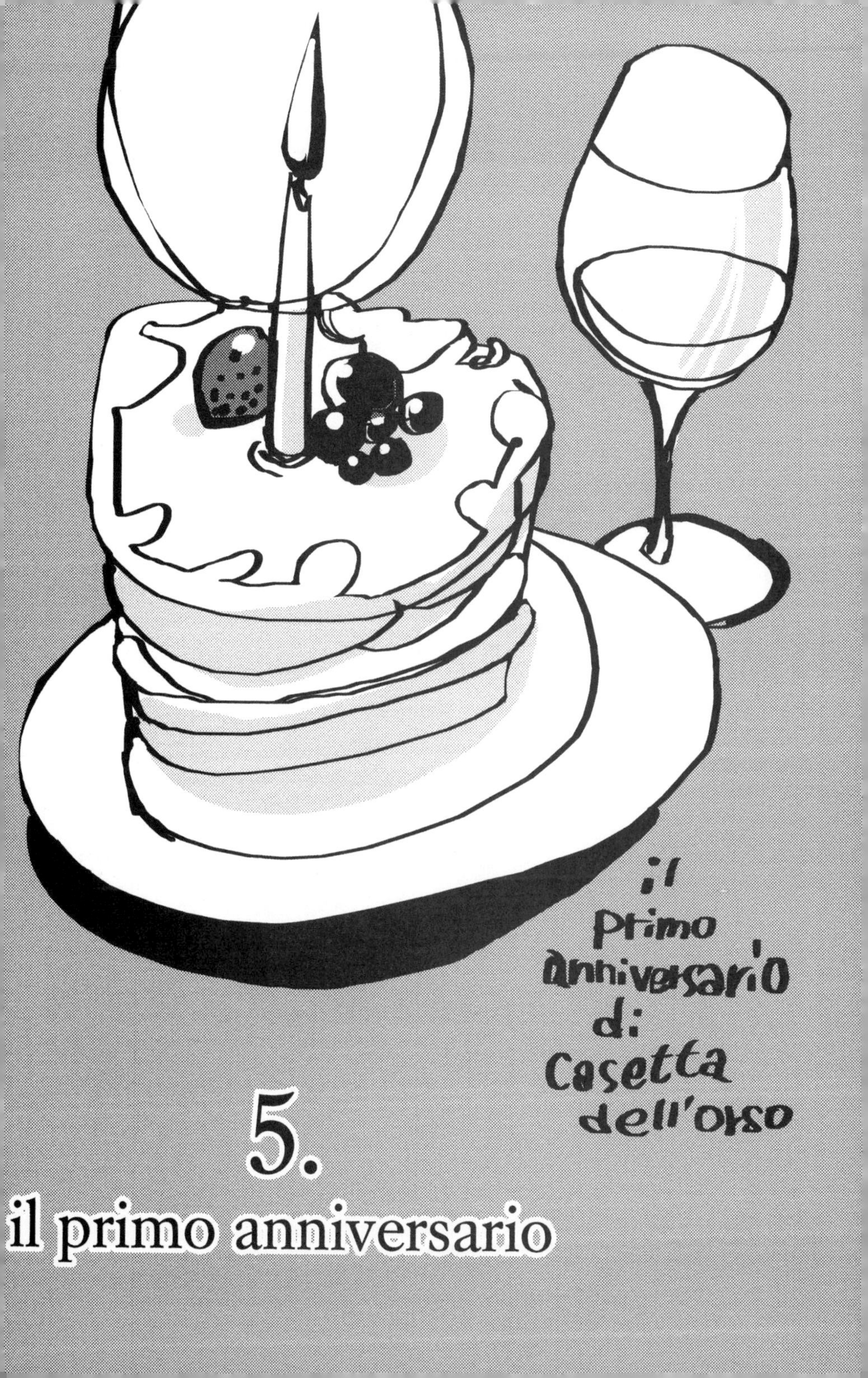
il primo anniversario di Casetta dell'orso

5.
il primo anniversario

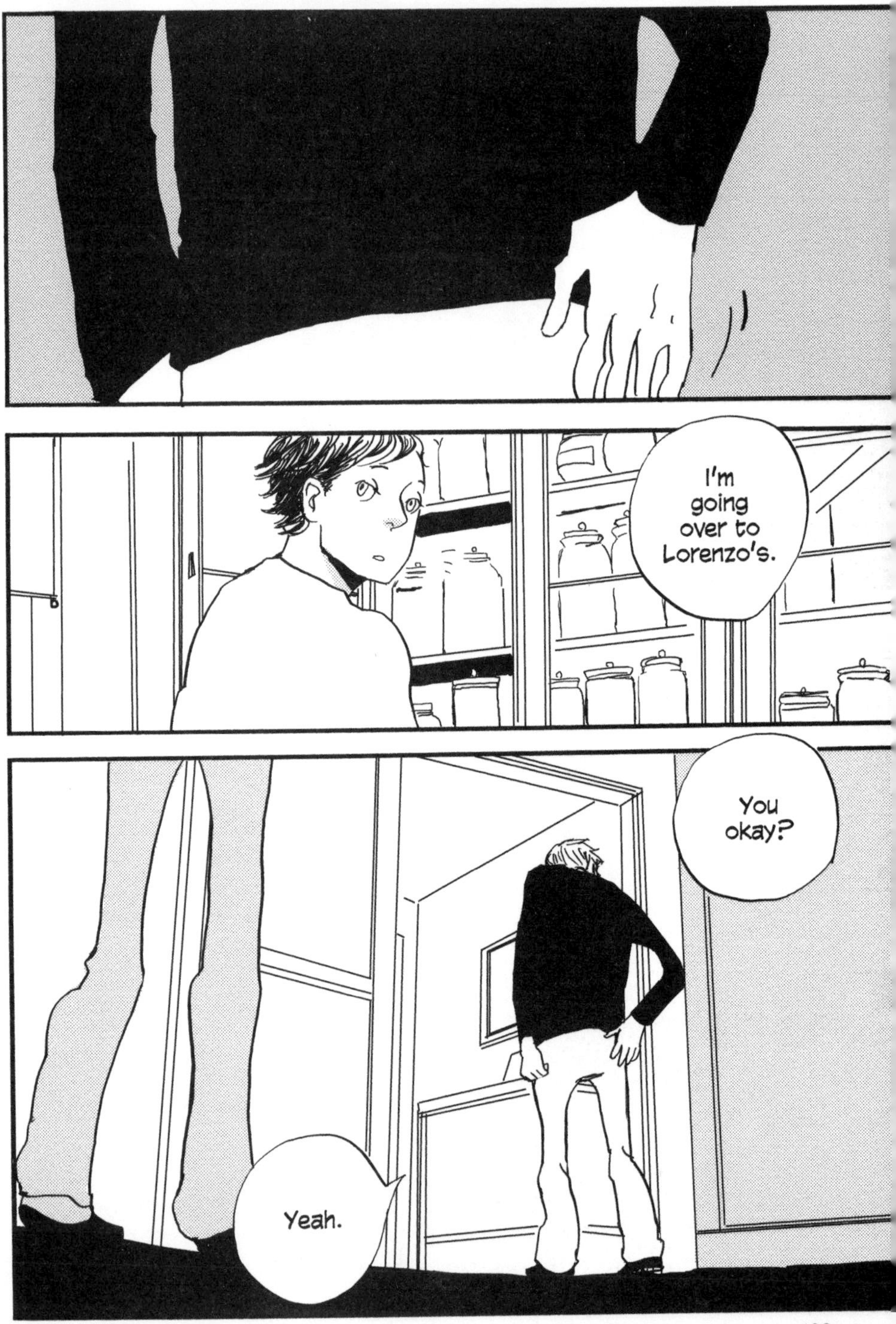
I'm going over to Lorenzo's.
You okay?
Yeah.

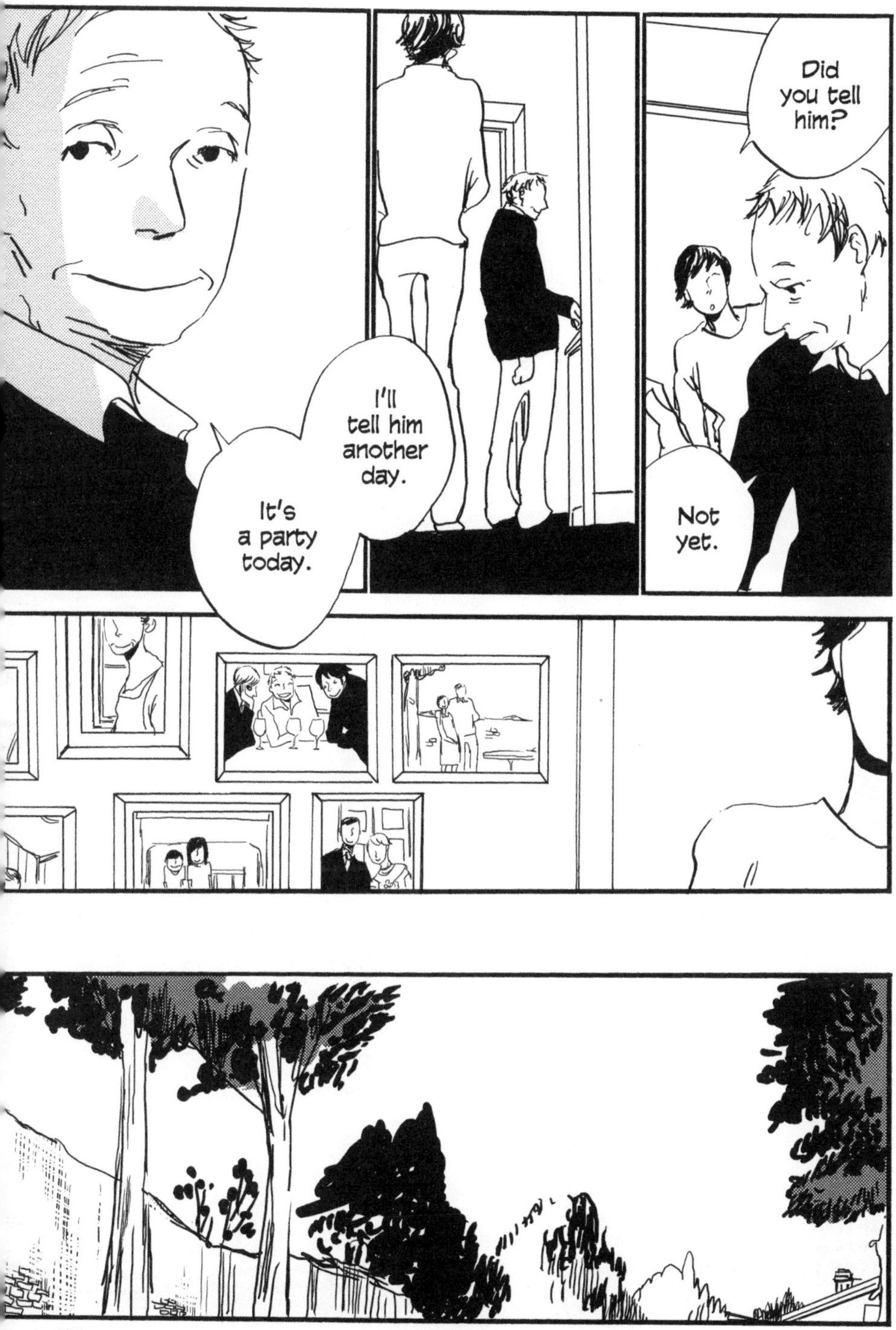
Did you tell him?
Not yet.
I'll tell him another day.
It's a party today.

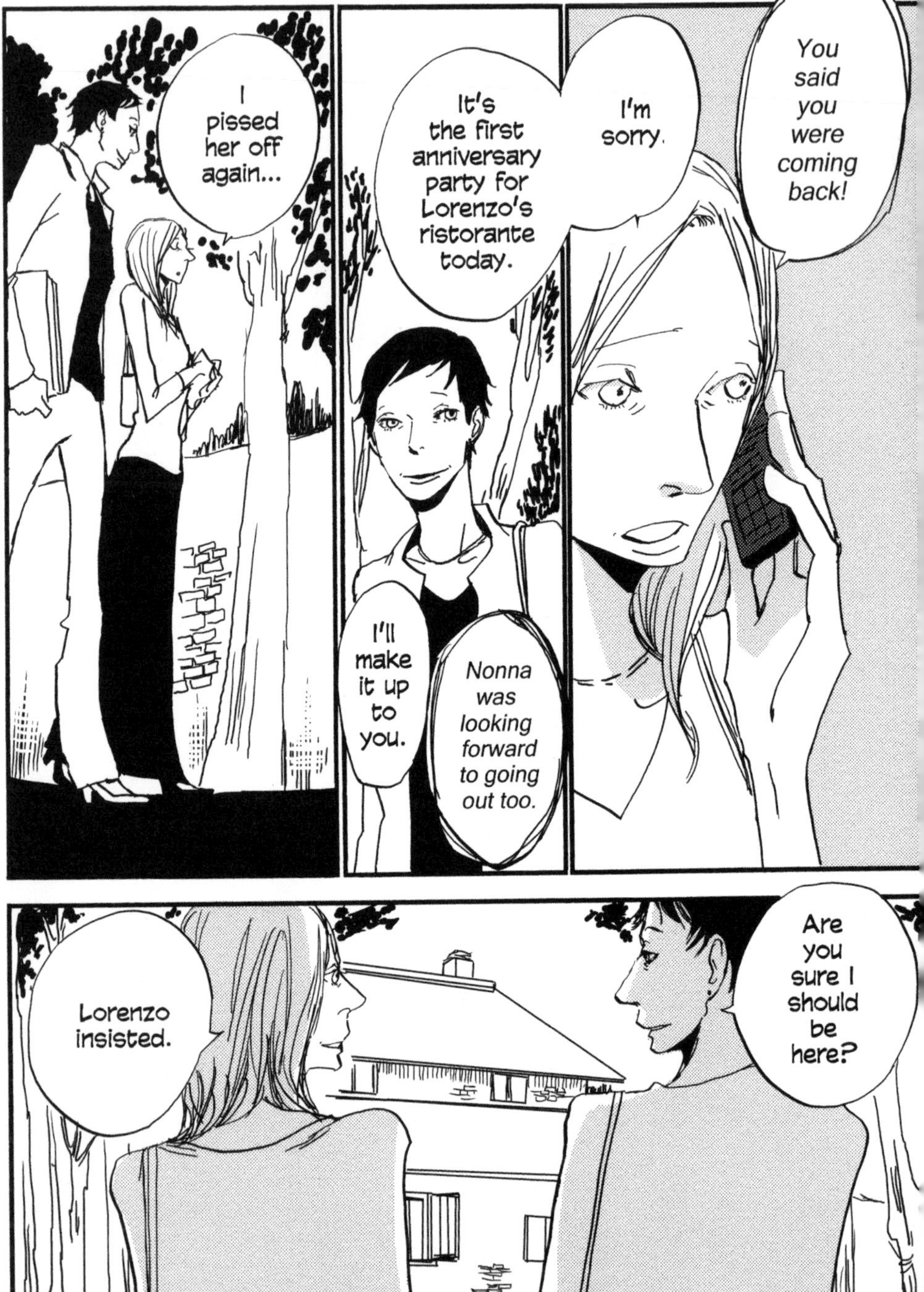
You said you were coming back!
I'm sorry.
It's the first anniversary party for Lorenzo's ristorante today.
Nonna was looking forward to going out too.
I'll make it up to you.
I pissed her off again...
Are you sure I should be here?
Lorenzo insisted.

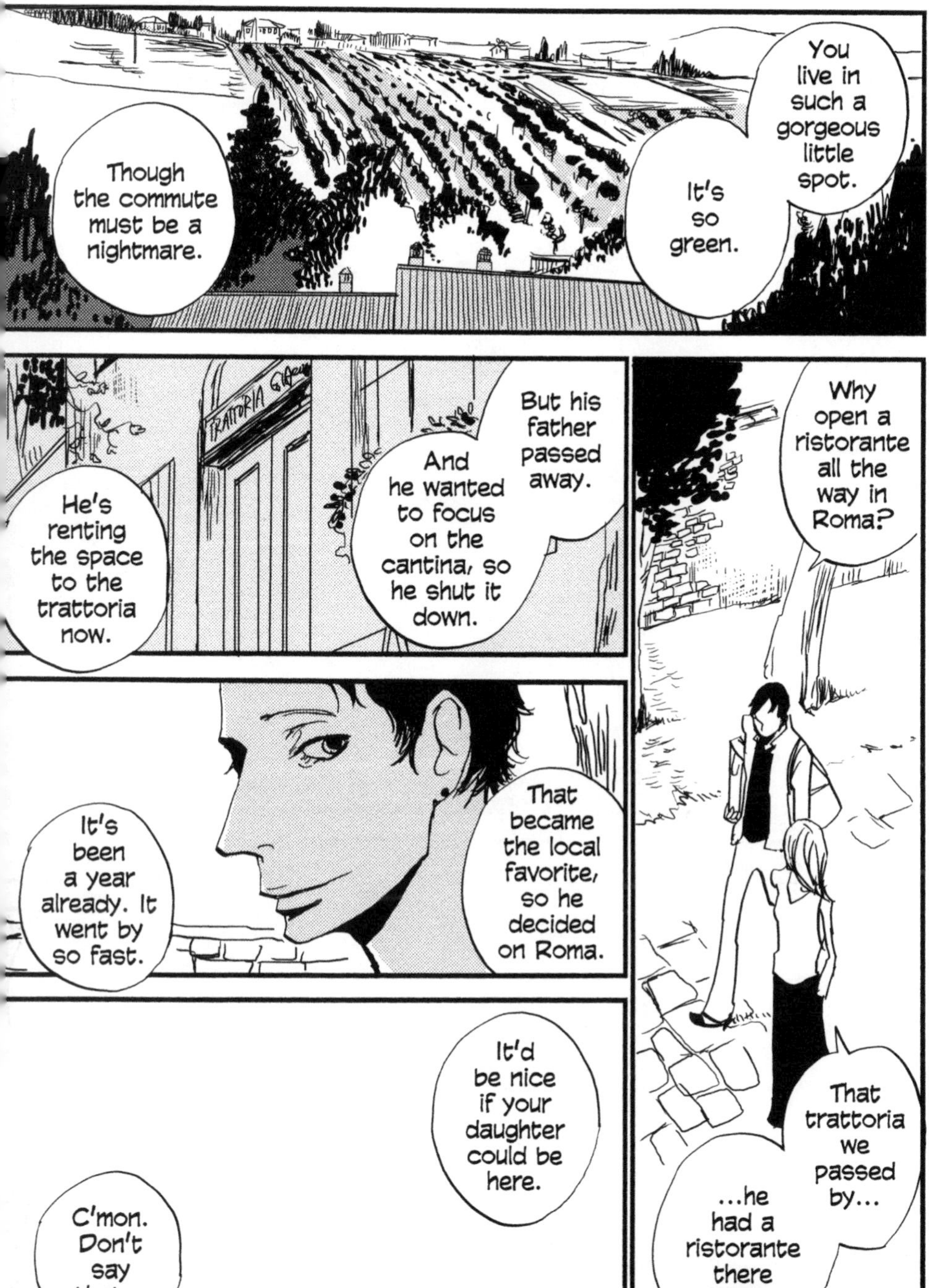
You live in such a gorgeous little spot.
It's so green.
Though the commute must be a nightmare.
Why open a ristorante all the way in Roma?
That trattoria we passed by...
...he had a ristorante there once.
But his father passed away.
And he wanted to focus on the cantina, so he shut it down.
He's renting the space to the trattoria now.
That became the local favorite, so he decided on Roma.
It's been a year already. It went by so fast.
It'd be nice if your daughter could be here.
C'mon. Don't say that...

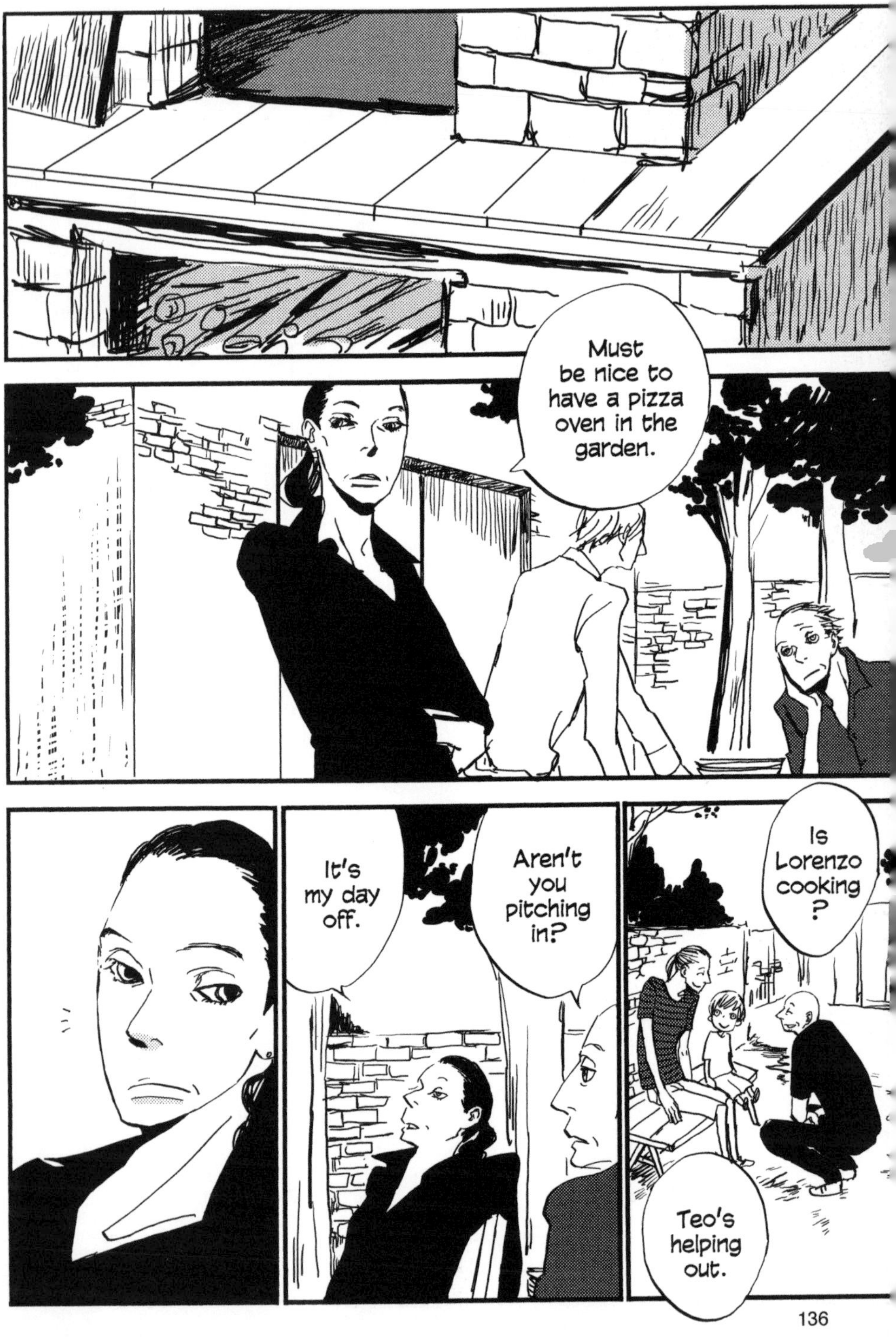
Must be nice to have a pizza oven in the garden.
Is Lorenzo cooking?
Teo's helping out.
Aren't you pitching in?
It's my day off.

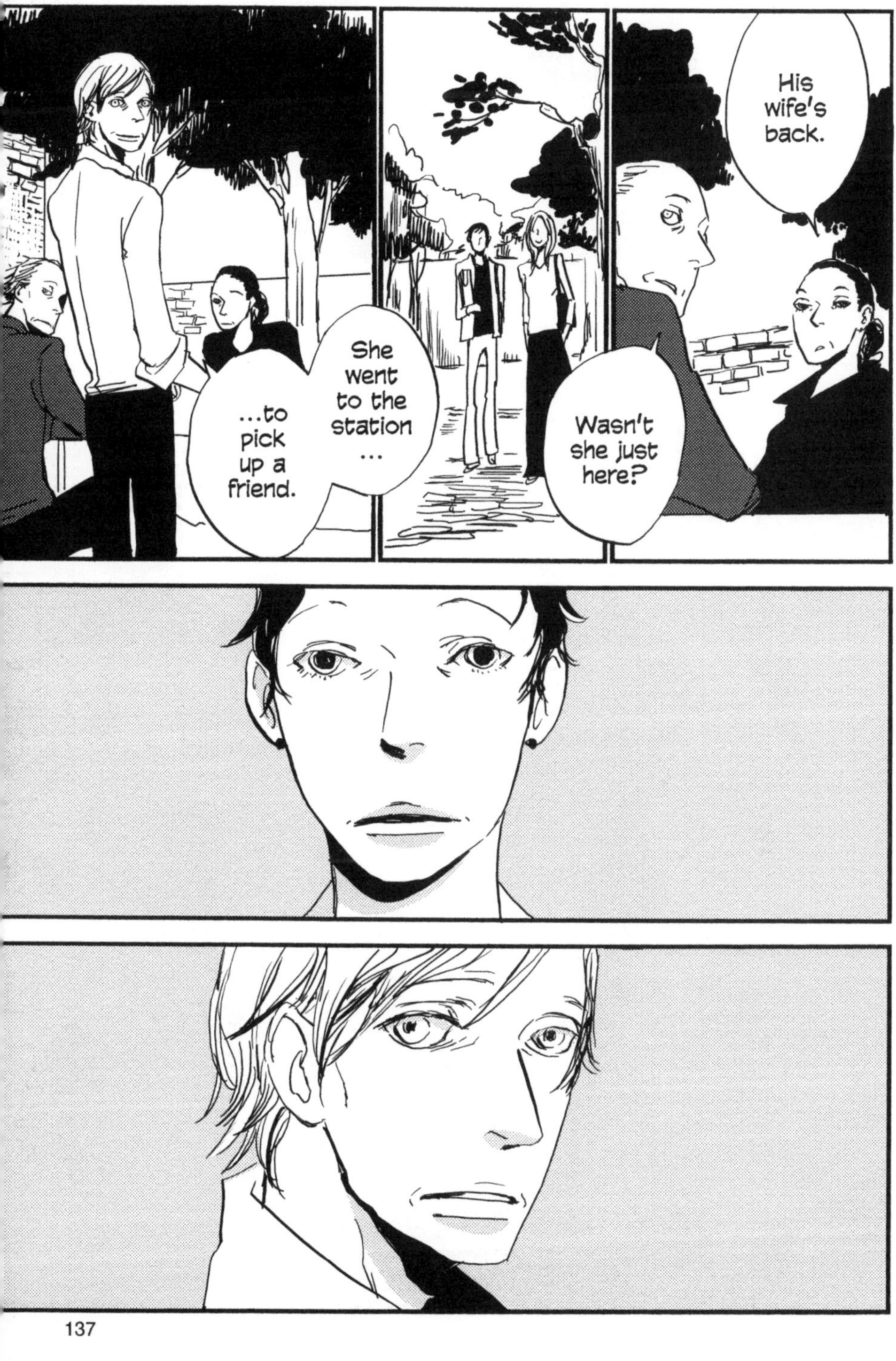
His wife's back.
Wasn't she just here?
She went to the station ...
...to pick up a friend.

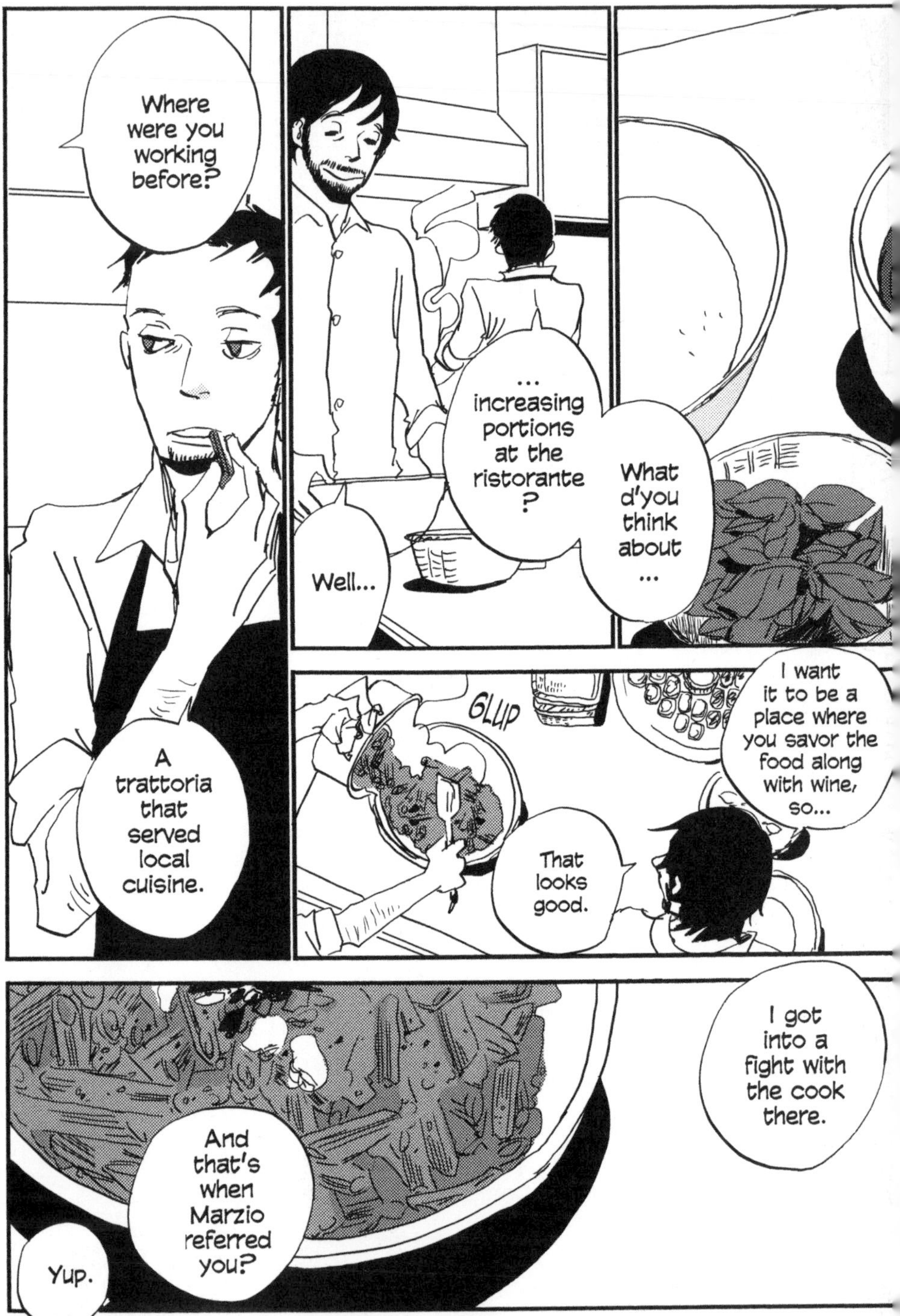
What d'you think about ...
... increasing portions at the ristorante?
Well...
I want it to be a place where you savor the food along with wine, so...
GLUP
That looks good.
Where were you working before?
A trattoria that served local cuisine.
I got into a fight with the cook there.
And that's when Marzio referred you?
Yup.

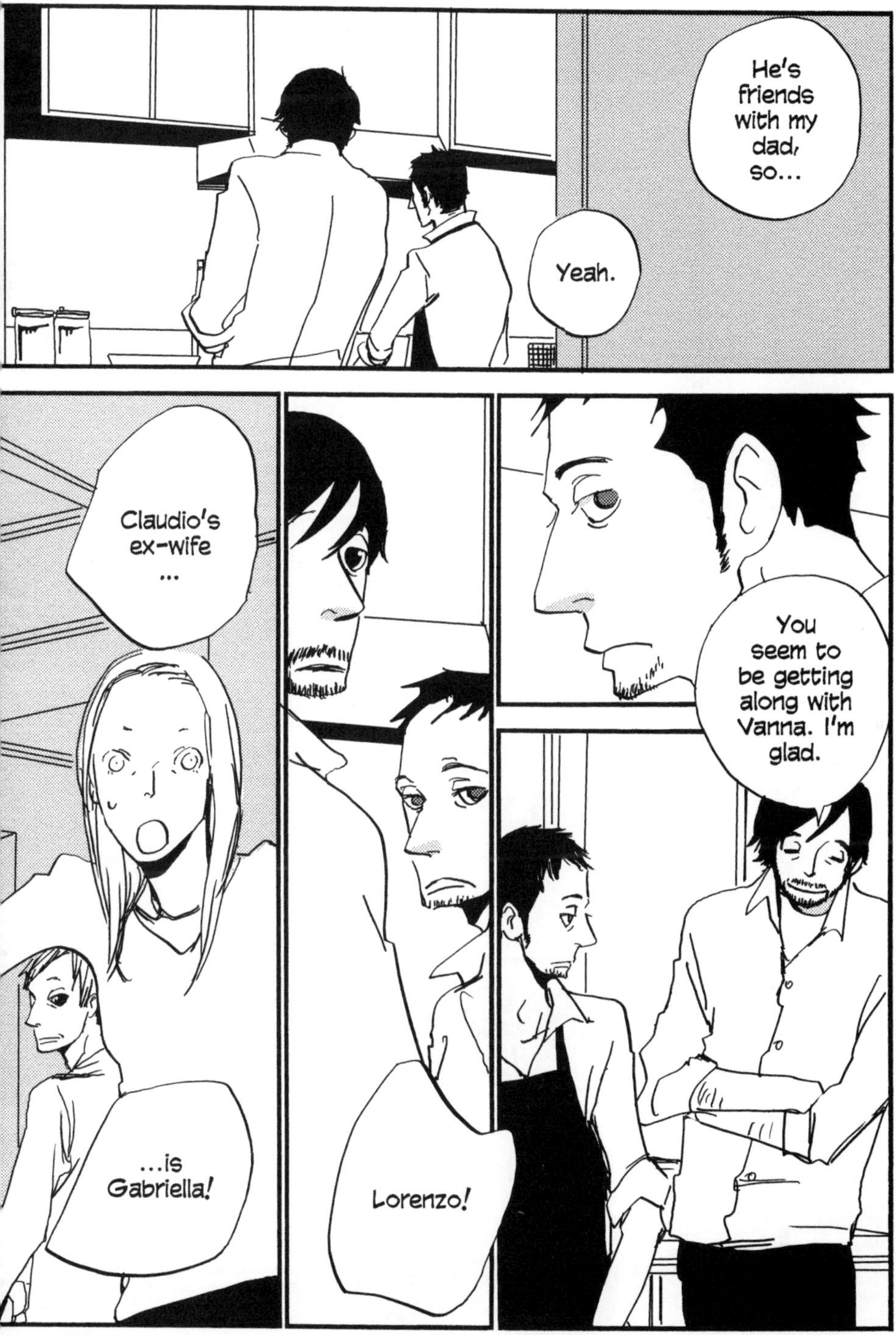
He's friends with my dad, so...
Yeah.
You seem to be getting along with Vanna. I'm glad.
Lorenzo!
Claudio's ex-wife ...
...is Gabriella!

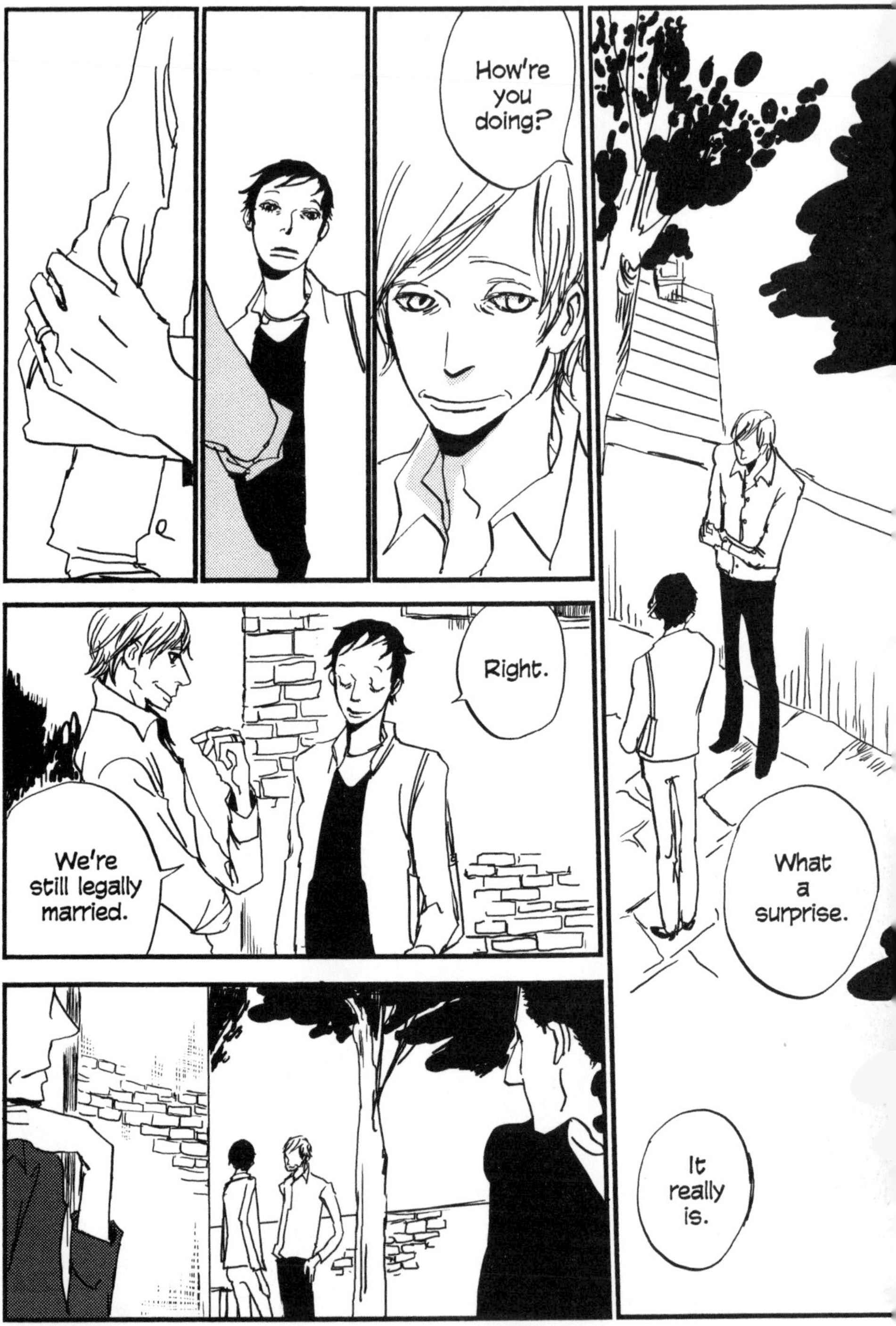
What a surprise.
It really is.
How're you doing?
Right.
We're still legally married.

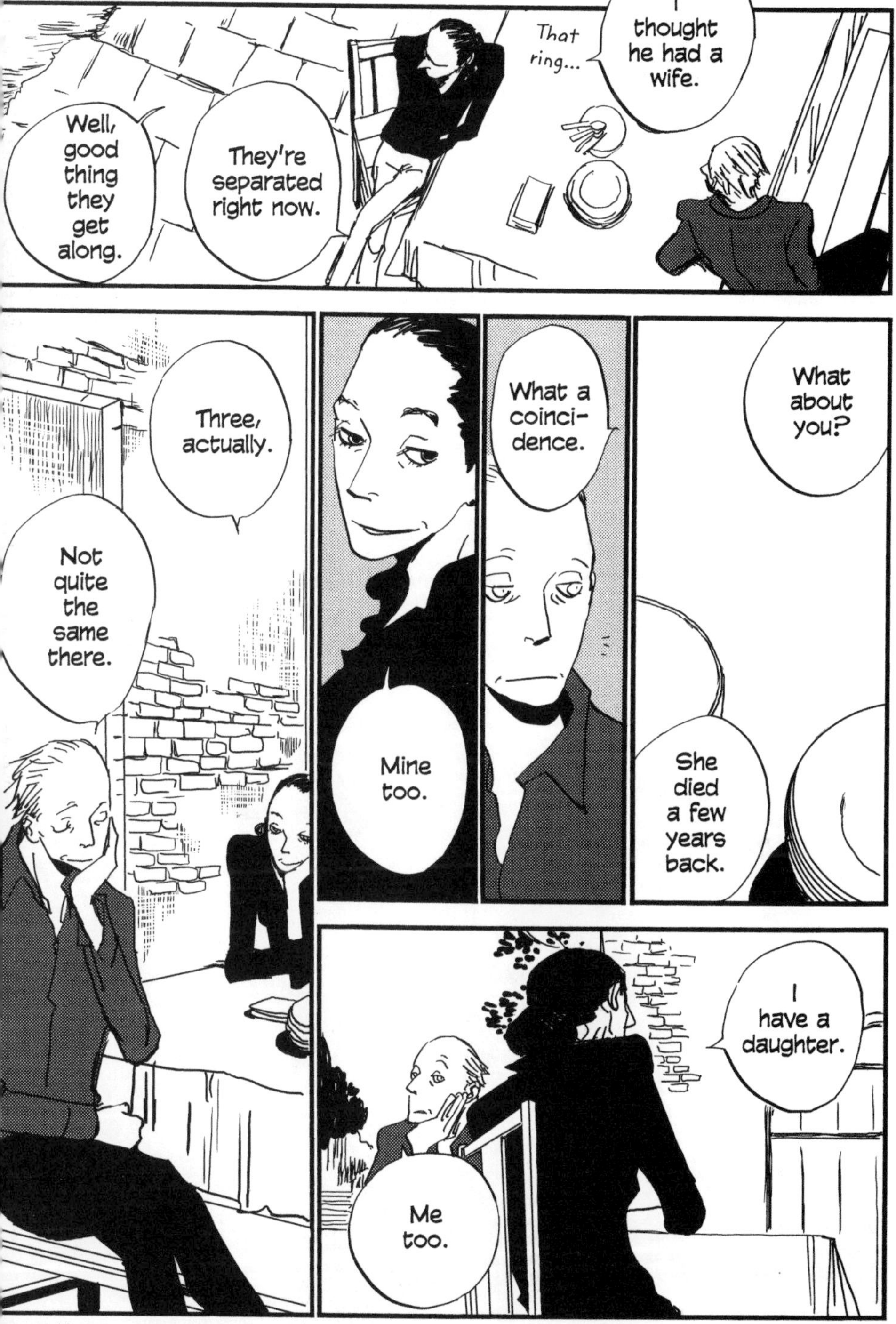
That ring...
I thought he had a wife.
They're separated right now.
Well, good thing they get along.
What about you?
She died a few years back.
What a coinci-dence.
Mine too.
I have a daughter.
Me too.
Three, actually.
Not quite the same there.

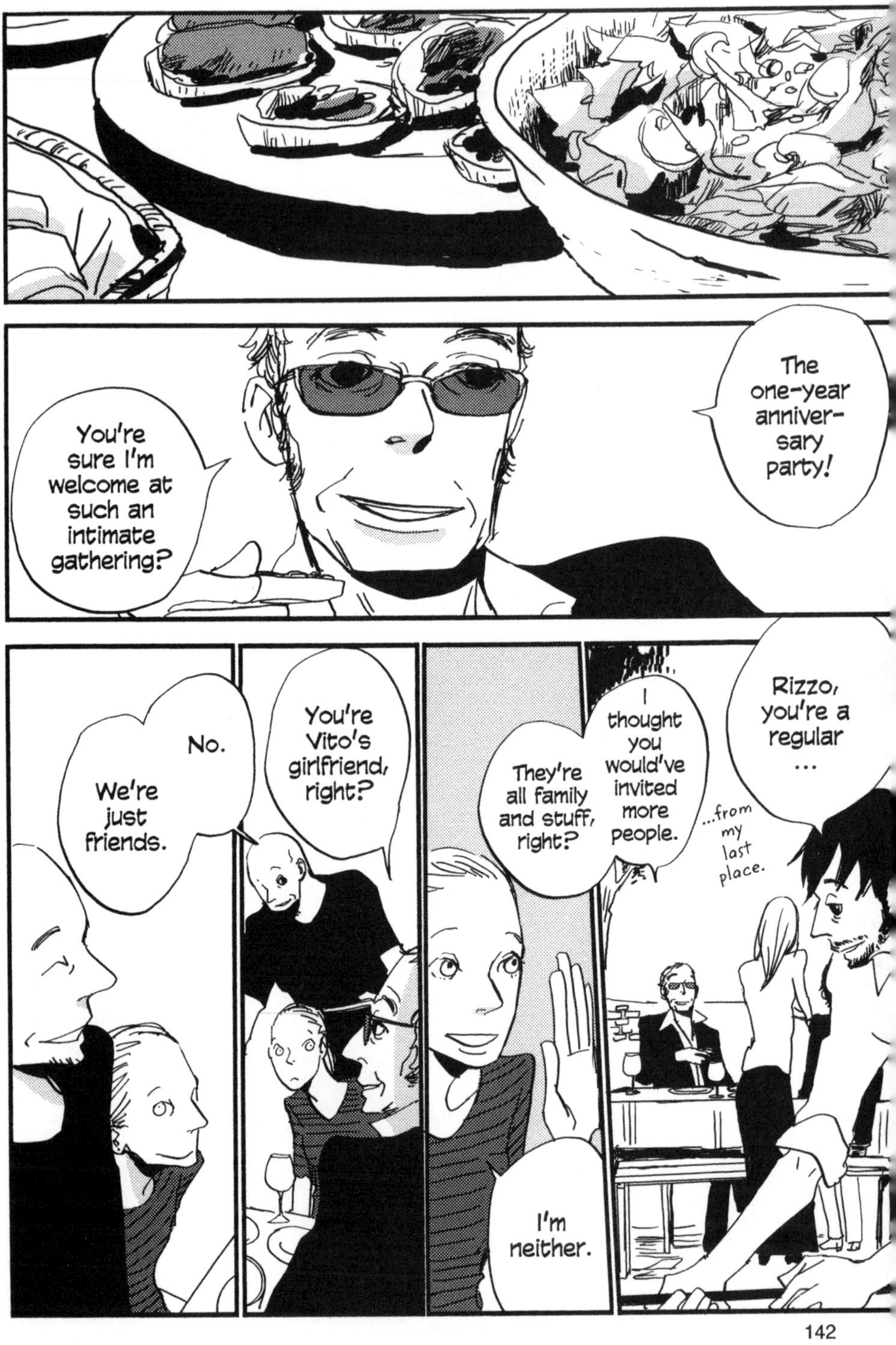
The one-year anniver-sary party!
You're sure I'm welcome at such an intimate gathering?
Rizzo, you're a regular ...
...from my last place.
I thought you would've invited more people.
They're all family and stuff, right?
I'm neither.
You're Vito's girlfriend, right?
No.
We're just friends.

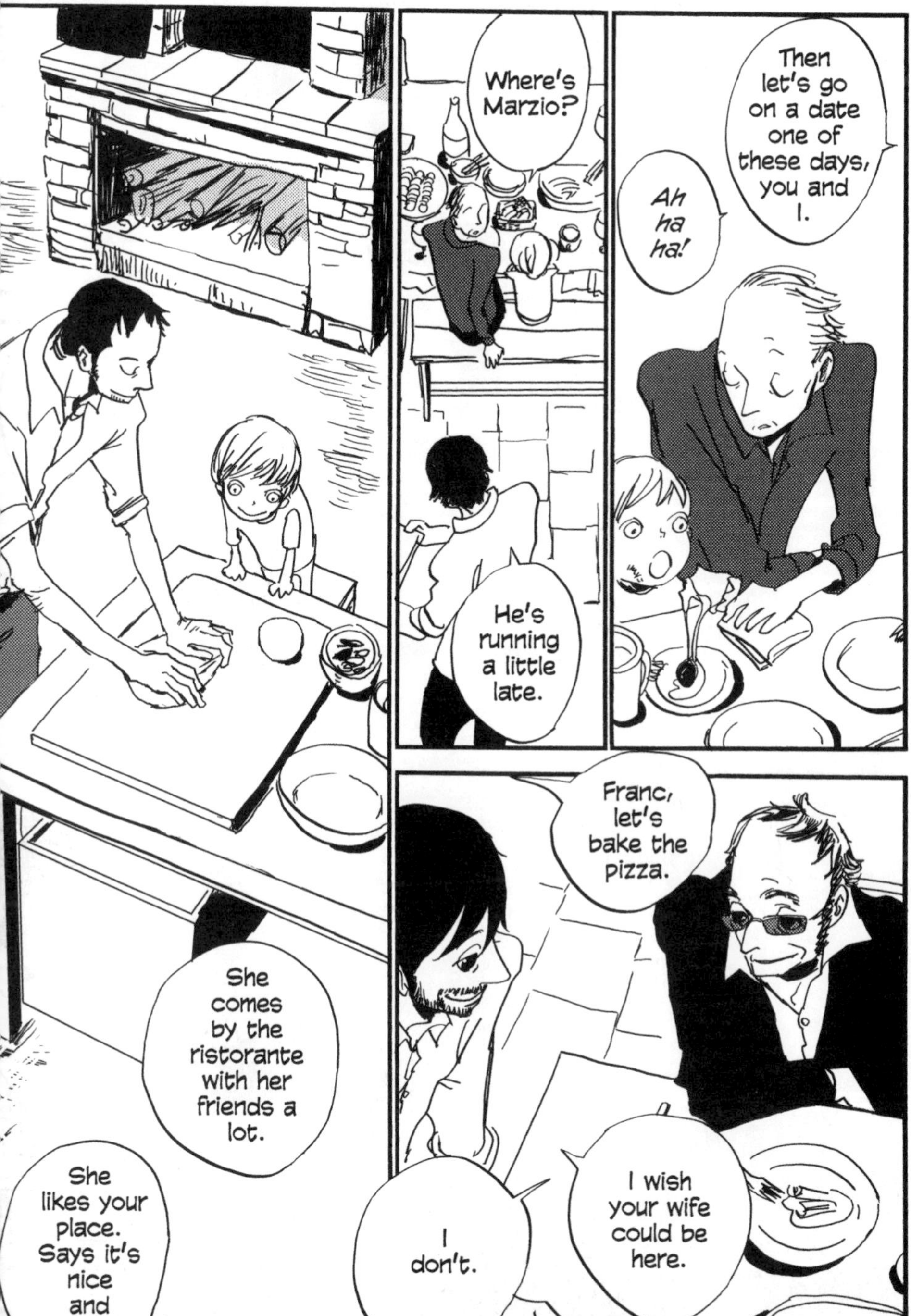
Then let's go on a date one of these days, you and I.
Ah ha ha!
Where's Marzio?
He's running a little late.
Franc, let's bake the pizza.
I wish your wife could be here.
I don't.
She comes by the ristorante with her friends a lot.
She likes your place. Says it's nice and calm.

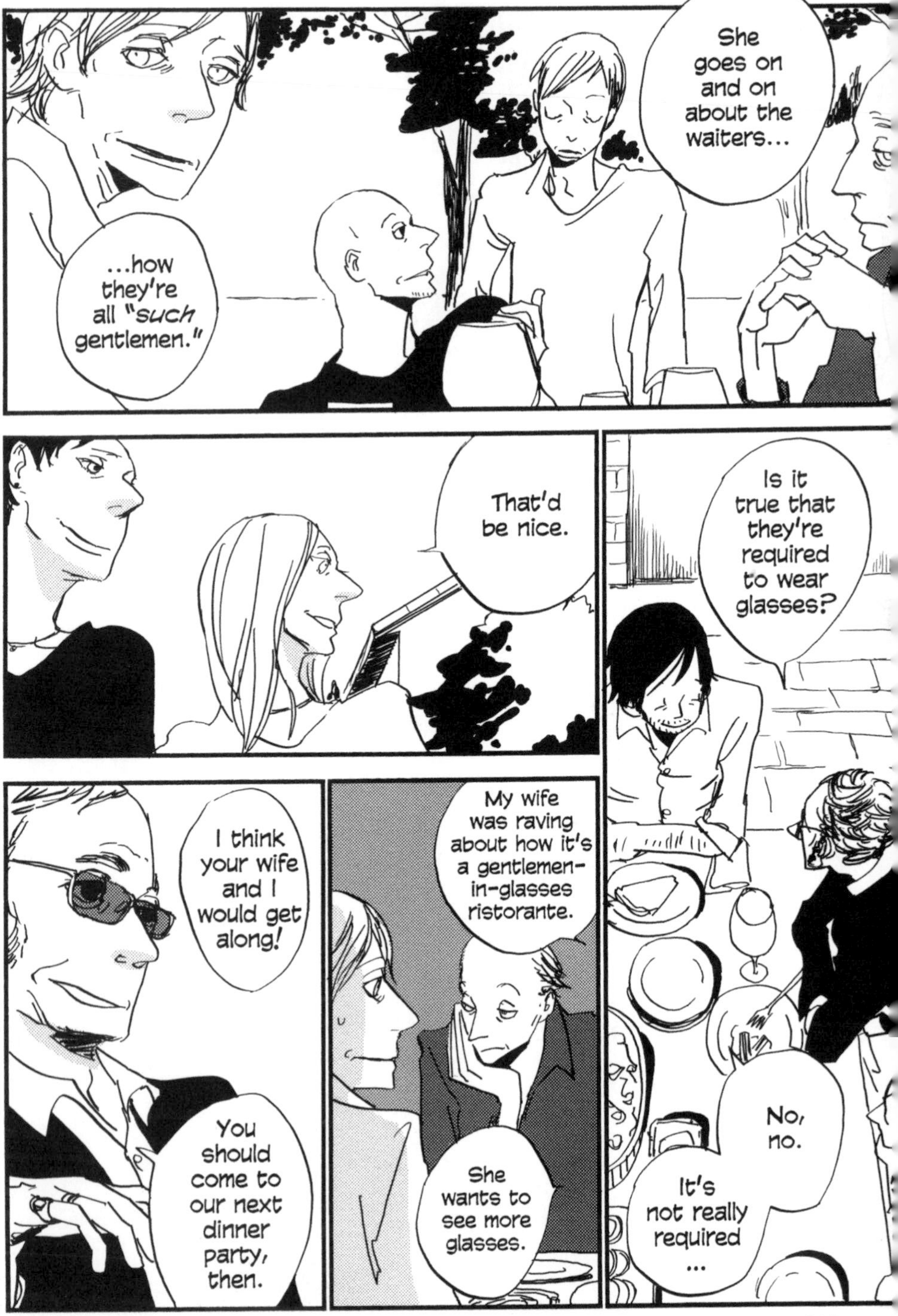

She goes on and on about the waiters...
...how they're all "*such* gentlemen."
Is it true that they're required to wear glasses?
No, no.
It's not really required ...
That'd be nice.
My wife was raving about how it's a gentlemen-in-glasses ristorante.
She wants to see more glasses.
I think your wife and I would get along!
You should come to our next dinner party, then.

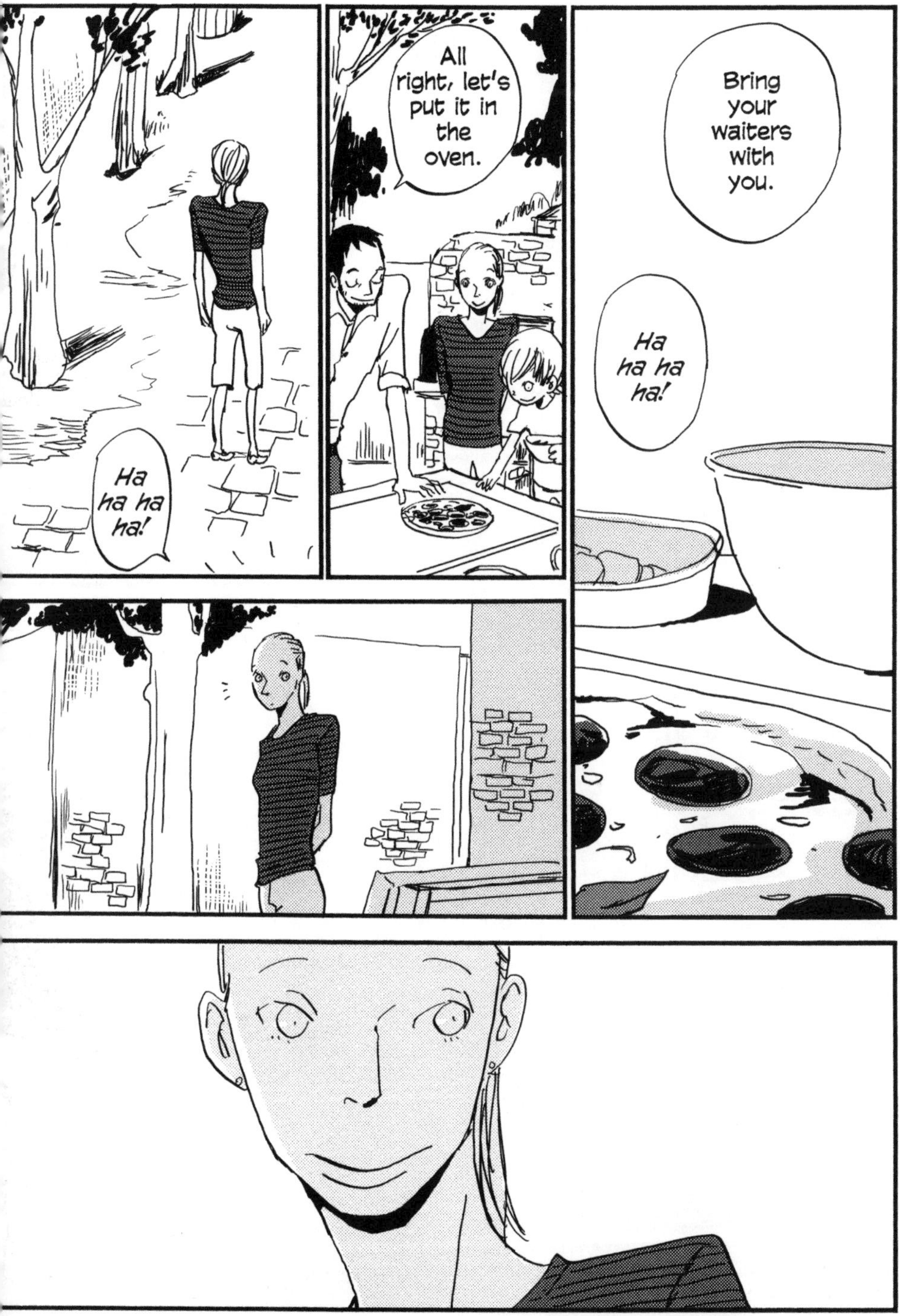
Bring your waiters with you.
Ha ha ha ha!
All right, let's put it in the oven.
Ha ha ha ha!

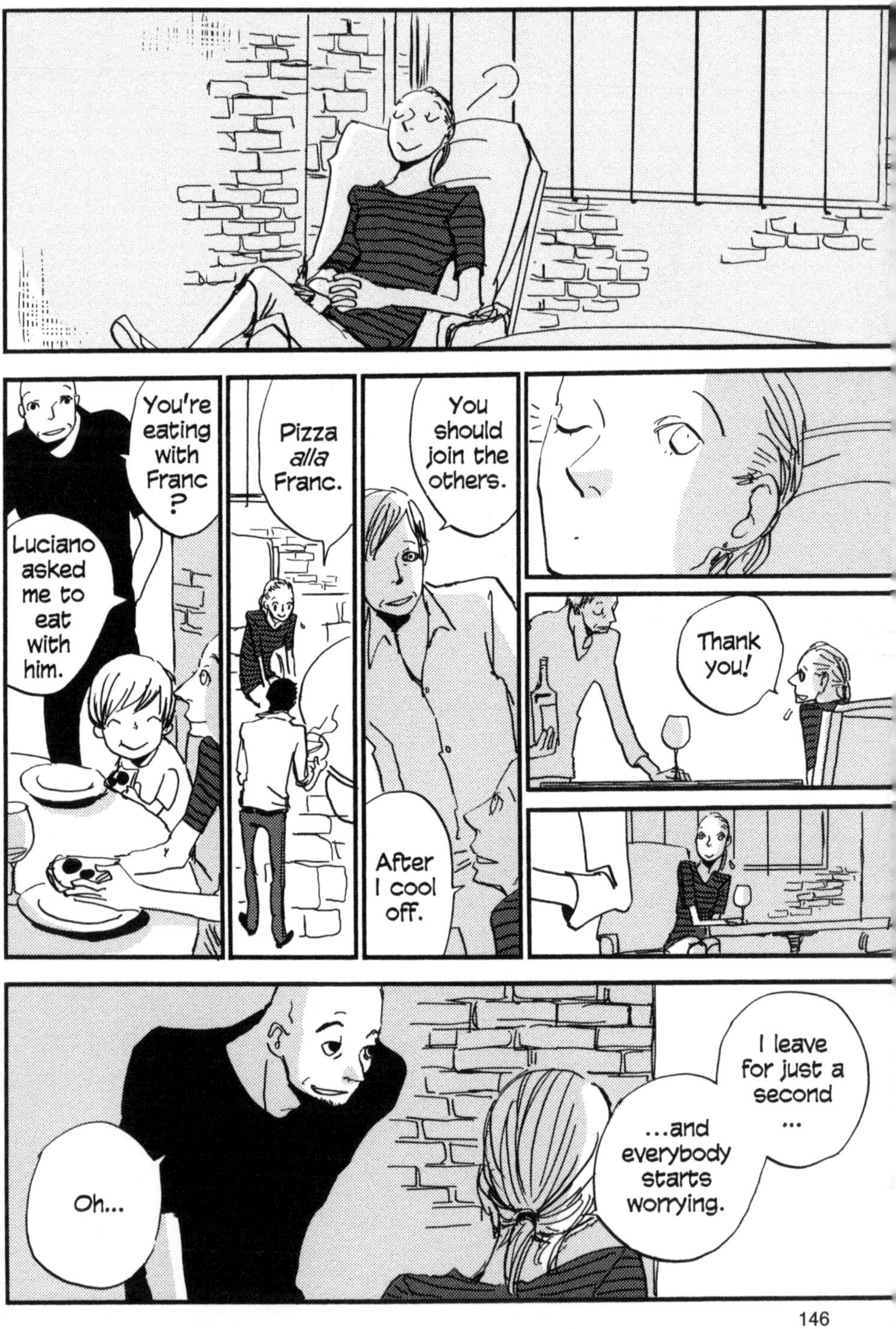
Thank you!
You should join the others.
After I cool off.
Pizza *alla* Franc.
You're eating with Franc?
Luciano asked me to eat with him.
I leave for just a second ...
...and everybody starts worrying.
Oh...

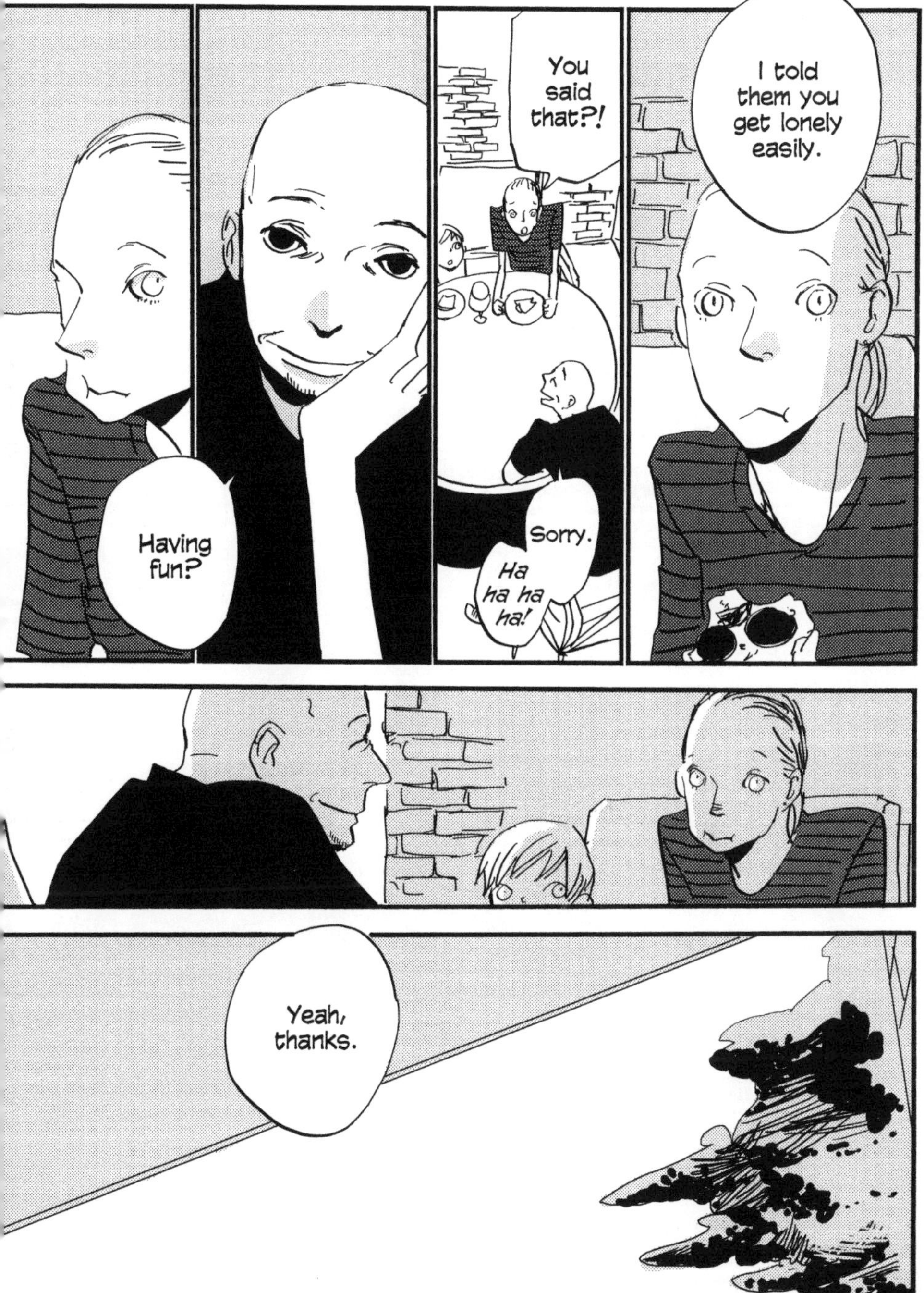
I told them you get lonely easily.
You said that?!
Sorry.
Ha ha ha ha!
Having fun?
Yeah, thanks.

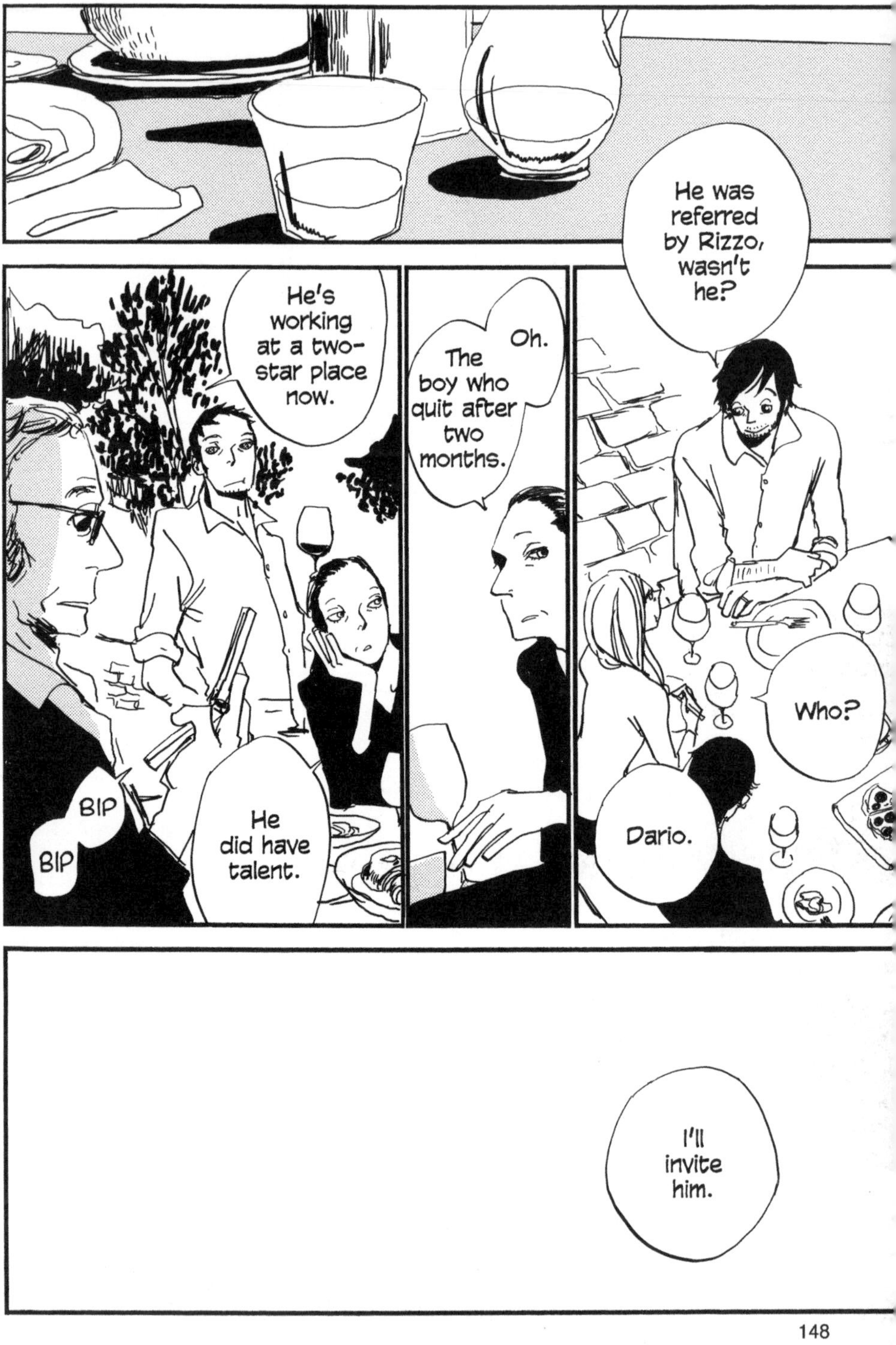
He was referred by Rizzo, wasn't he?
Who?
Dario.
Oh.
The boy who quit after two months.
He's working at a two-star place now.
He did have talent.
BIP
BIP
I'll invite him.

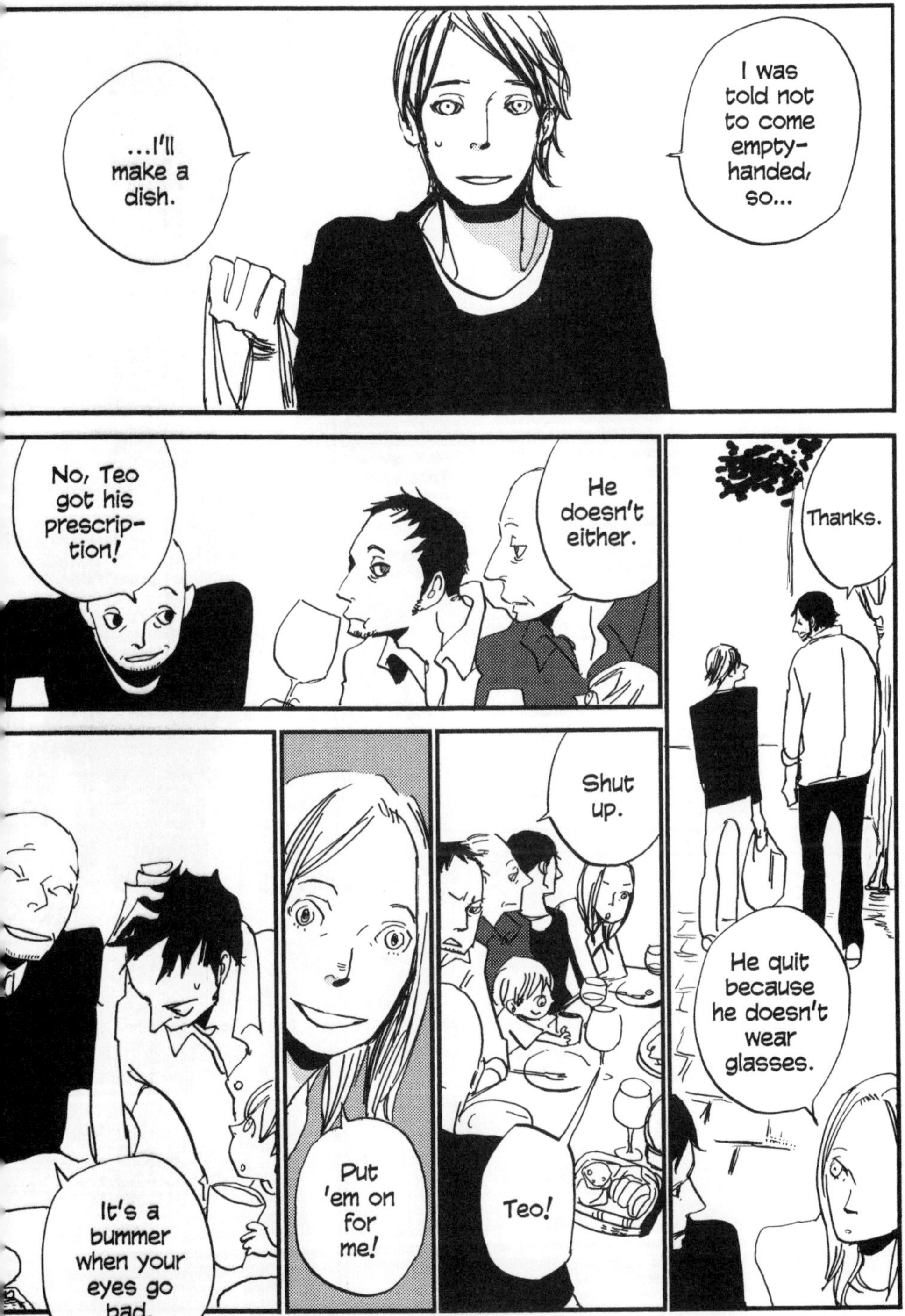
I was told not to come empty-handed, so...
...I'll make a dish.
Thanks.
He quit because he doesn't wear glasses.
He doesn't either.
No, Teo got his prescription!
Shut up.
Teo!
Put 'em on for me!
It's a bummer when your eyes go bad.

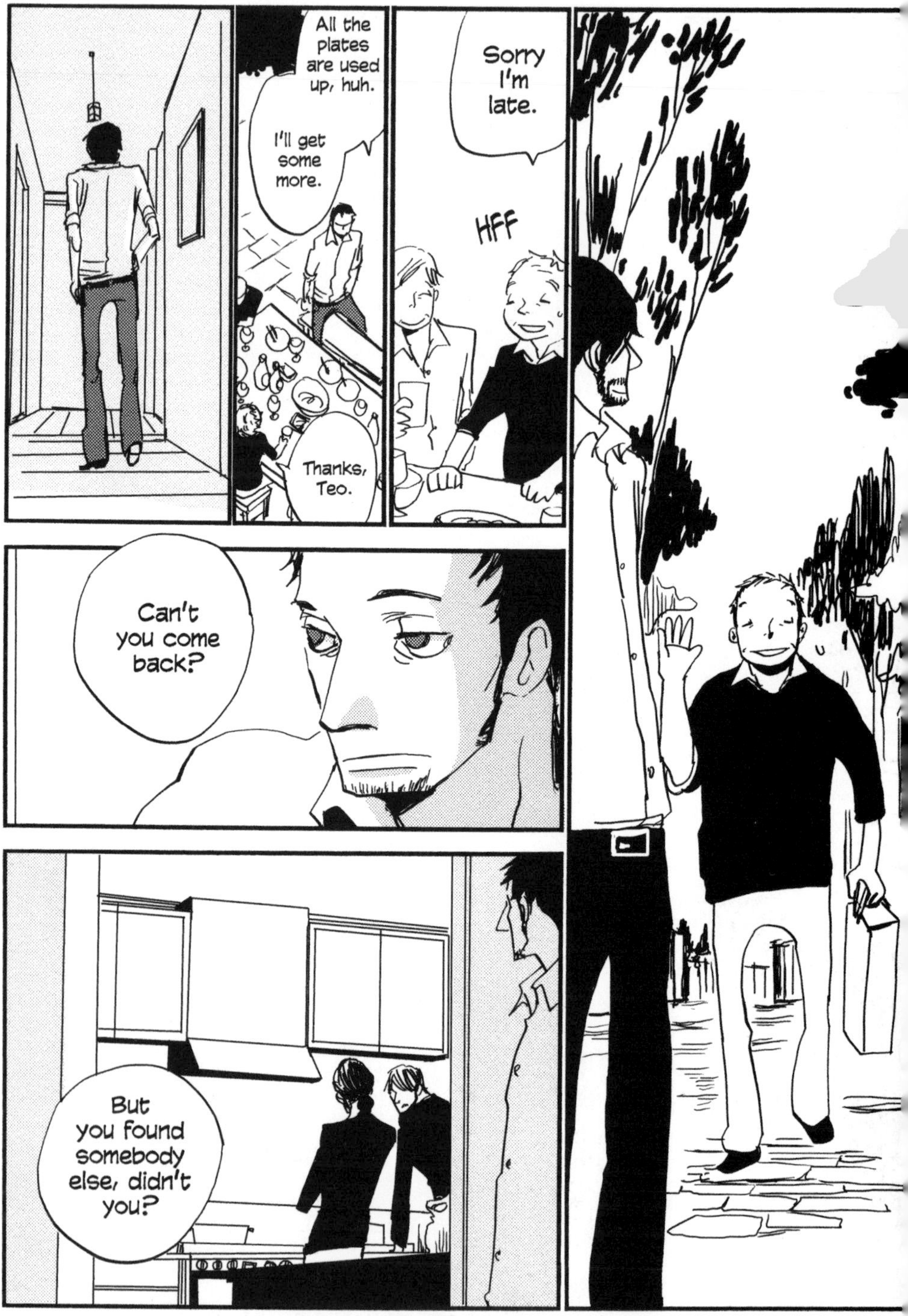
Sorry I'm late.
HFF
All the plates are used up, huh.
I'll get some more.
Thanks, Teo.
Can't you come back?
But you found somebody else, didn't you?

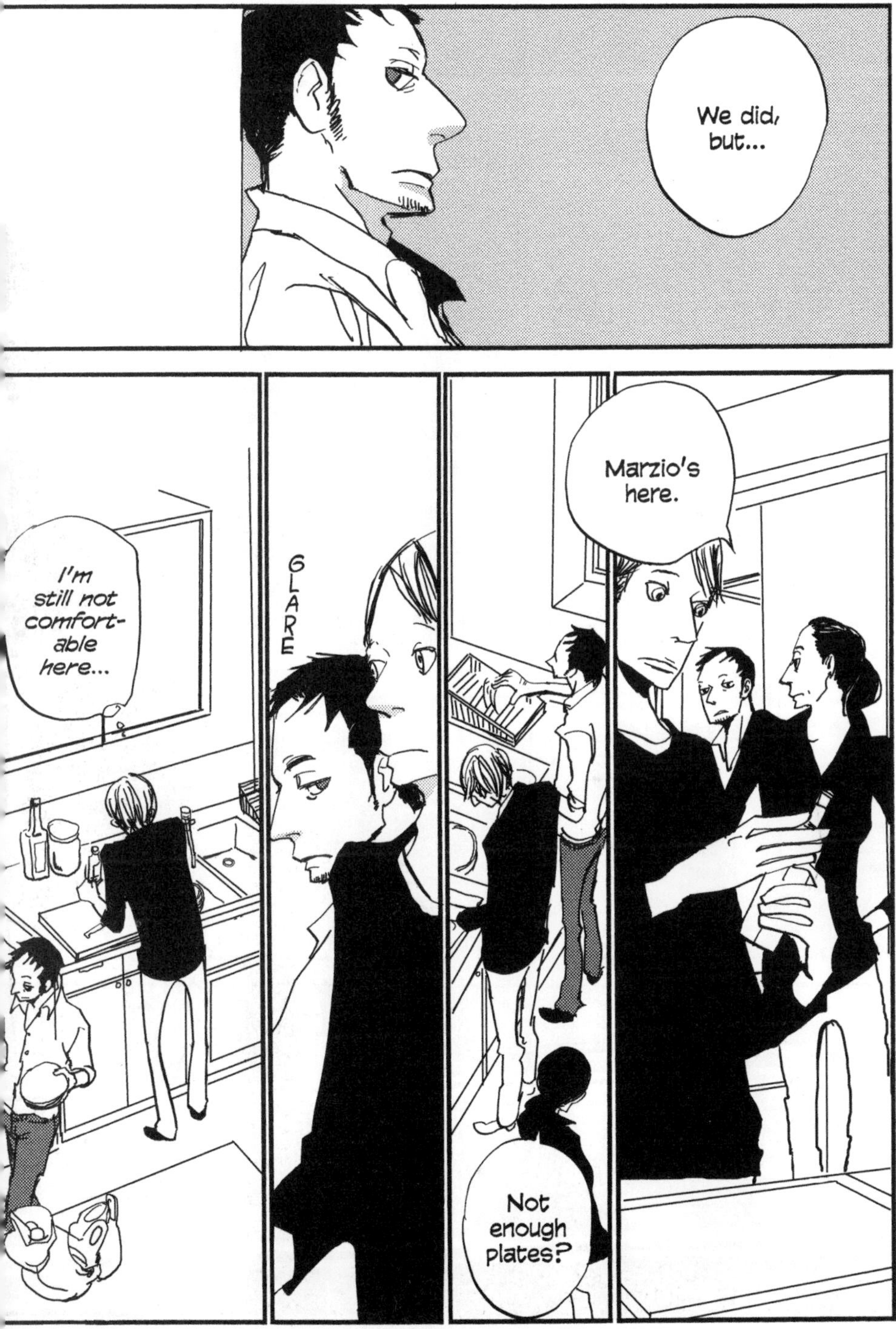
We did, but...
Marzio's here.
Not enough plates?
GLARE
I'm still not comfortable here...

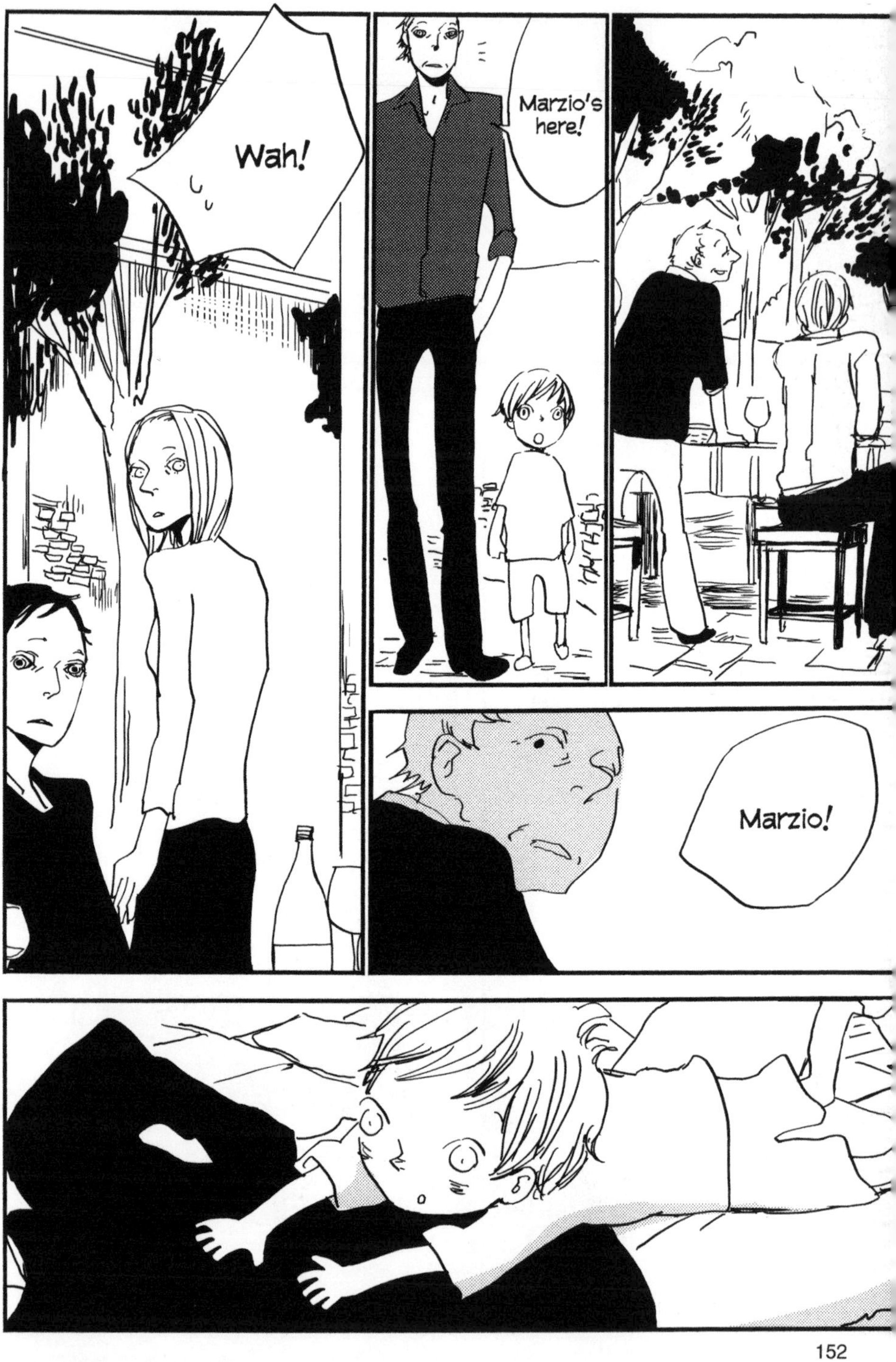
Marzio's here!
Marzio!
Wah!

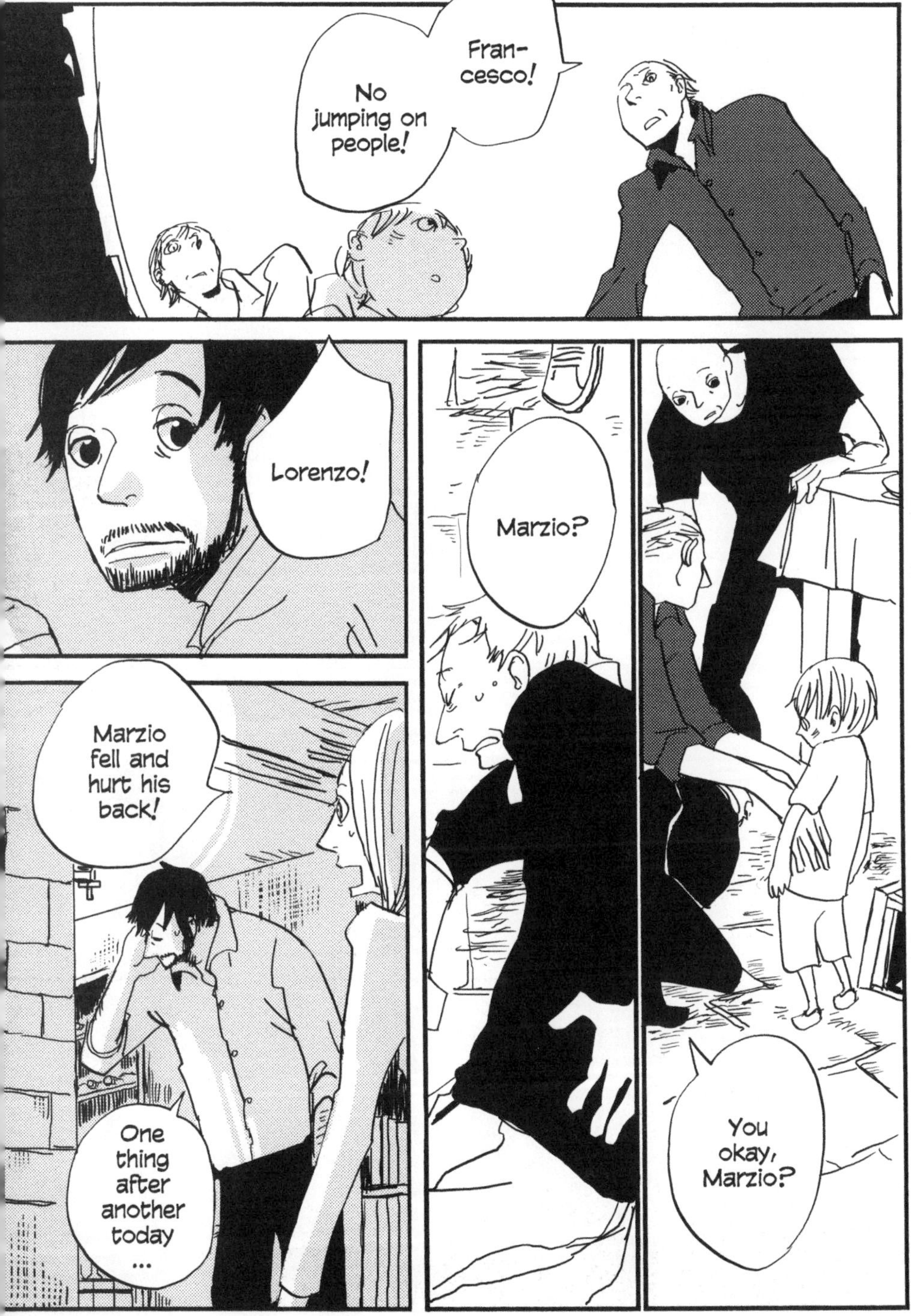
Fran-cesco!
No jumping on people!
You okay, Marzio?
Marzio?
Lorenzo!
Marzio fell and hurt his back!
One thing after another today ...

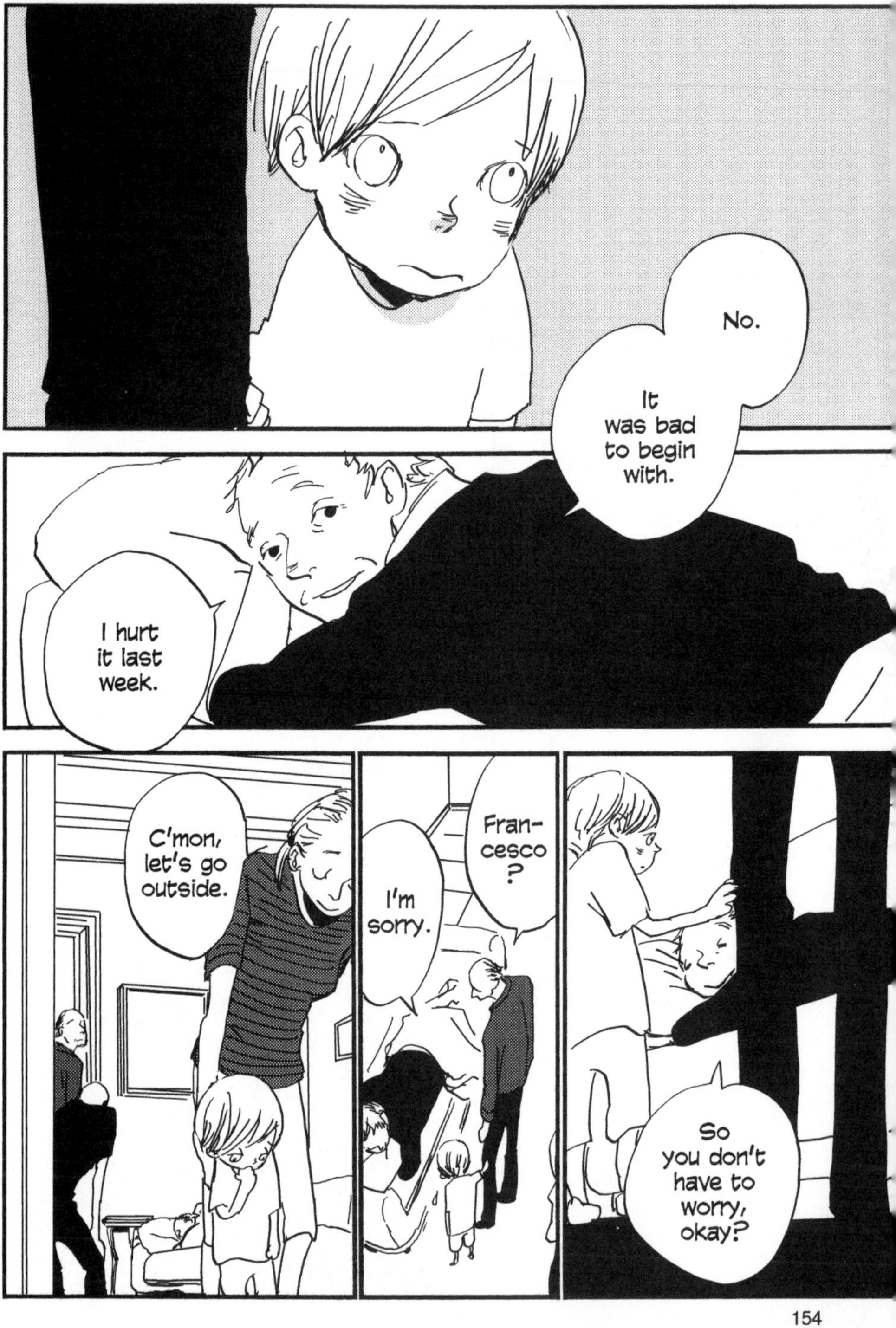
No.
It was bad to begin with.
I hurt it last week.
So you don't have to worry, okay?
Fran-cesco?
I'm sorry.
C'mon, let's go outside.

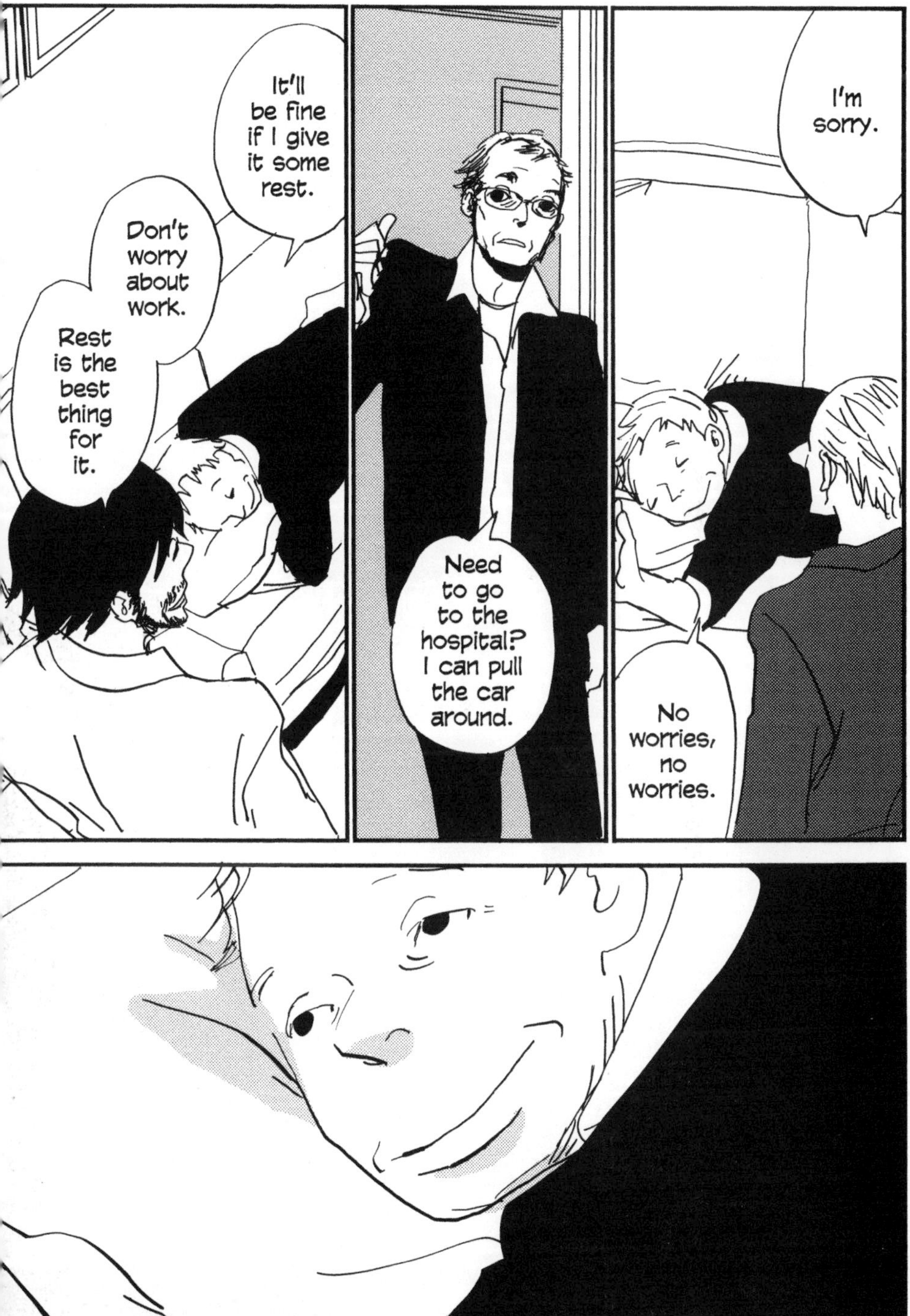
I'm sorry.
No worries, no worries.
Need to go to the hospital? I can pull the car around.
It'll be fine if I give it some rest.
Don't worry about work.
Rest is the best thing for it.

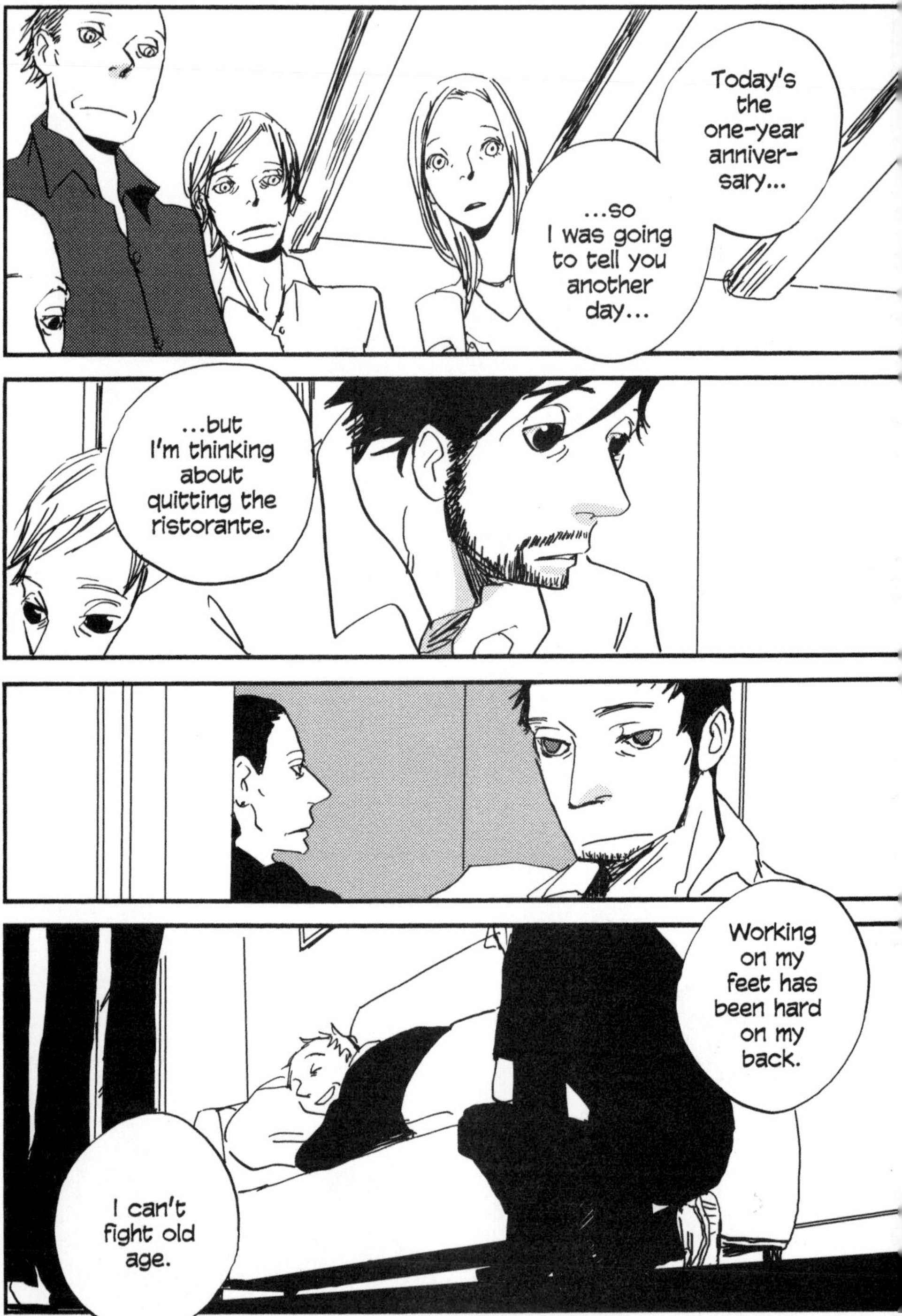
Today's the one-year anniversary...
...so I was going to tell you another day...
...but I'm thinking about quitting the ristorante.
Working on my feet has been hard on my back.
I can't fight old age.

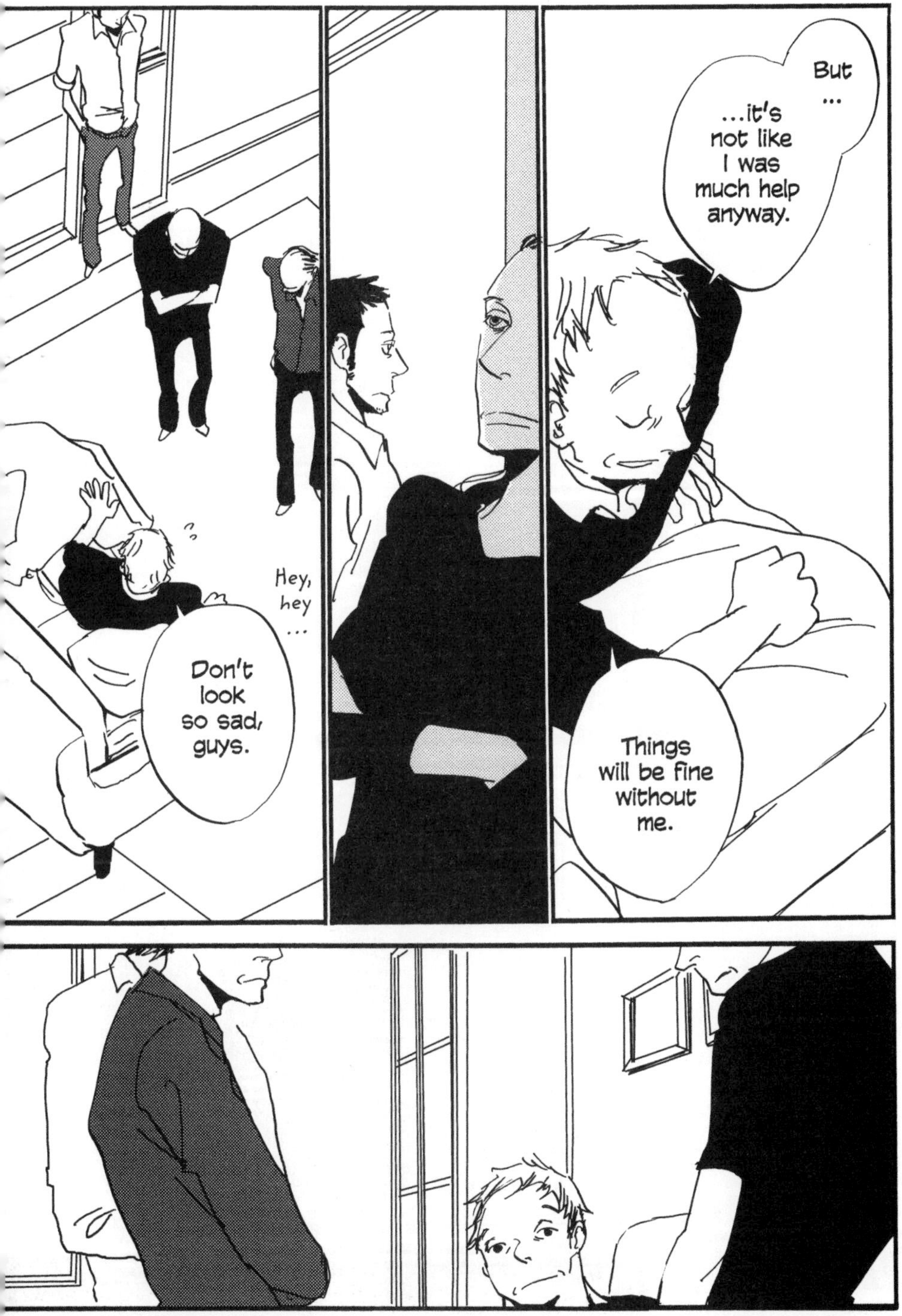
But ...
...it's not like I was much help anyway.
Things will be fine without me.
Hey, hey ...
Don't look so sad, guys.

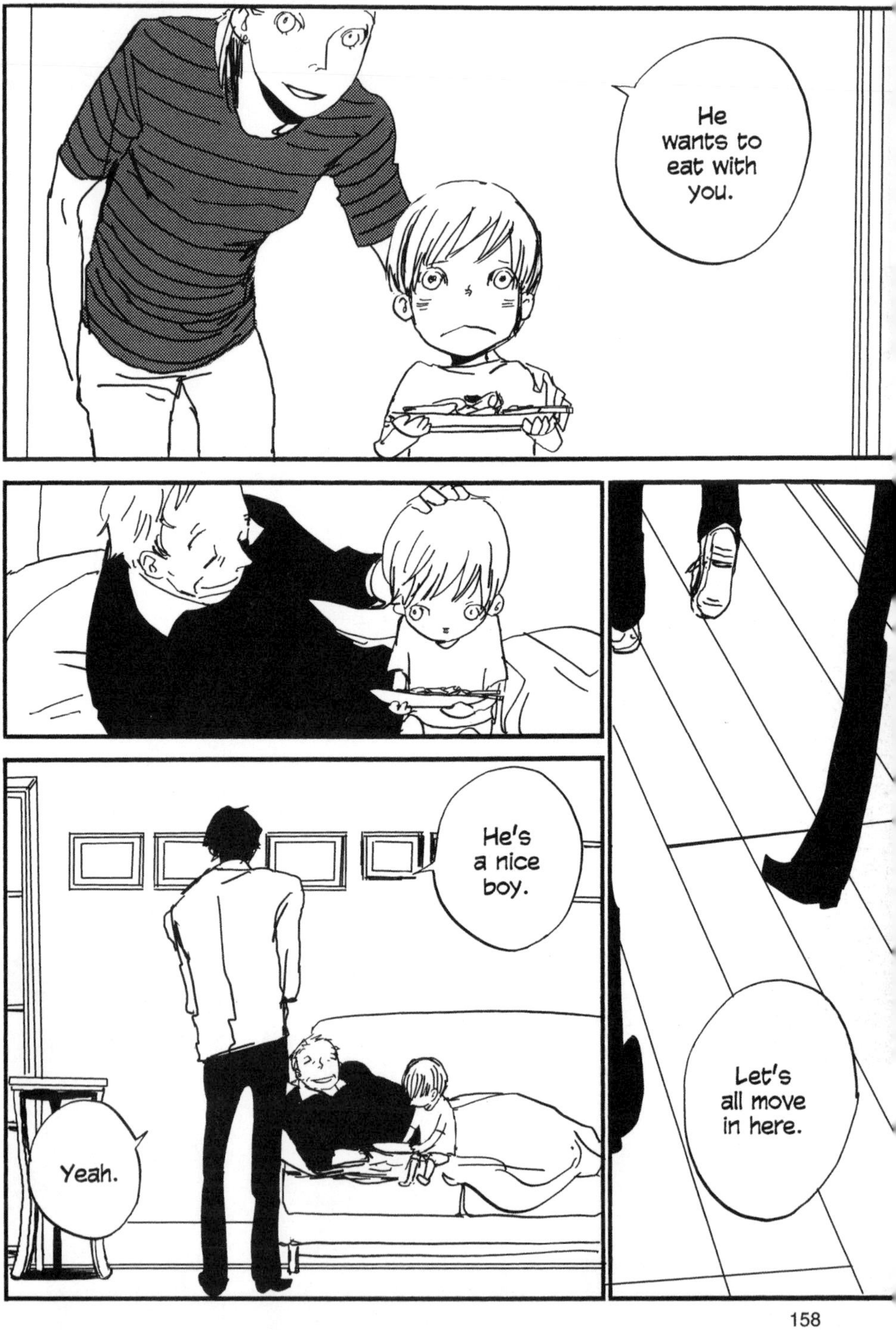
He wants to eat with you.
Let's all move in here.
He's a nice boy.
Yeah.

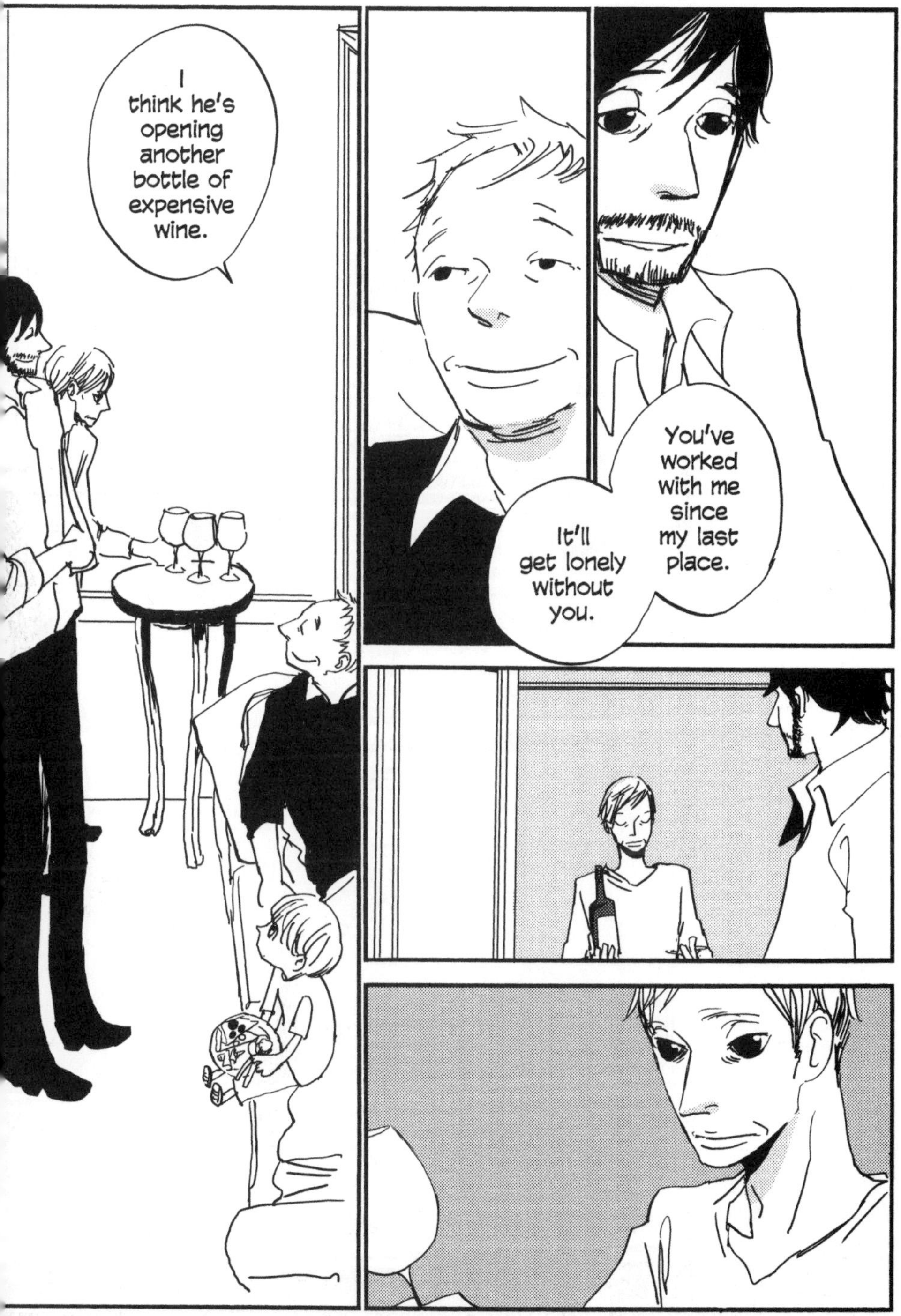
You've worked with me since my last place.
It'll get lonely without you.
I think he's opening another bottle of expensive wine.

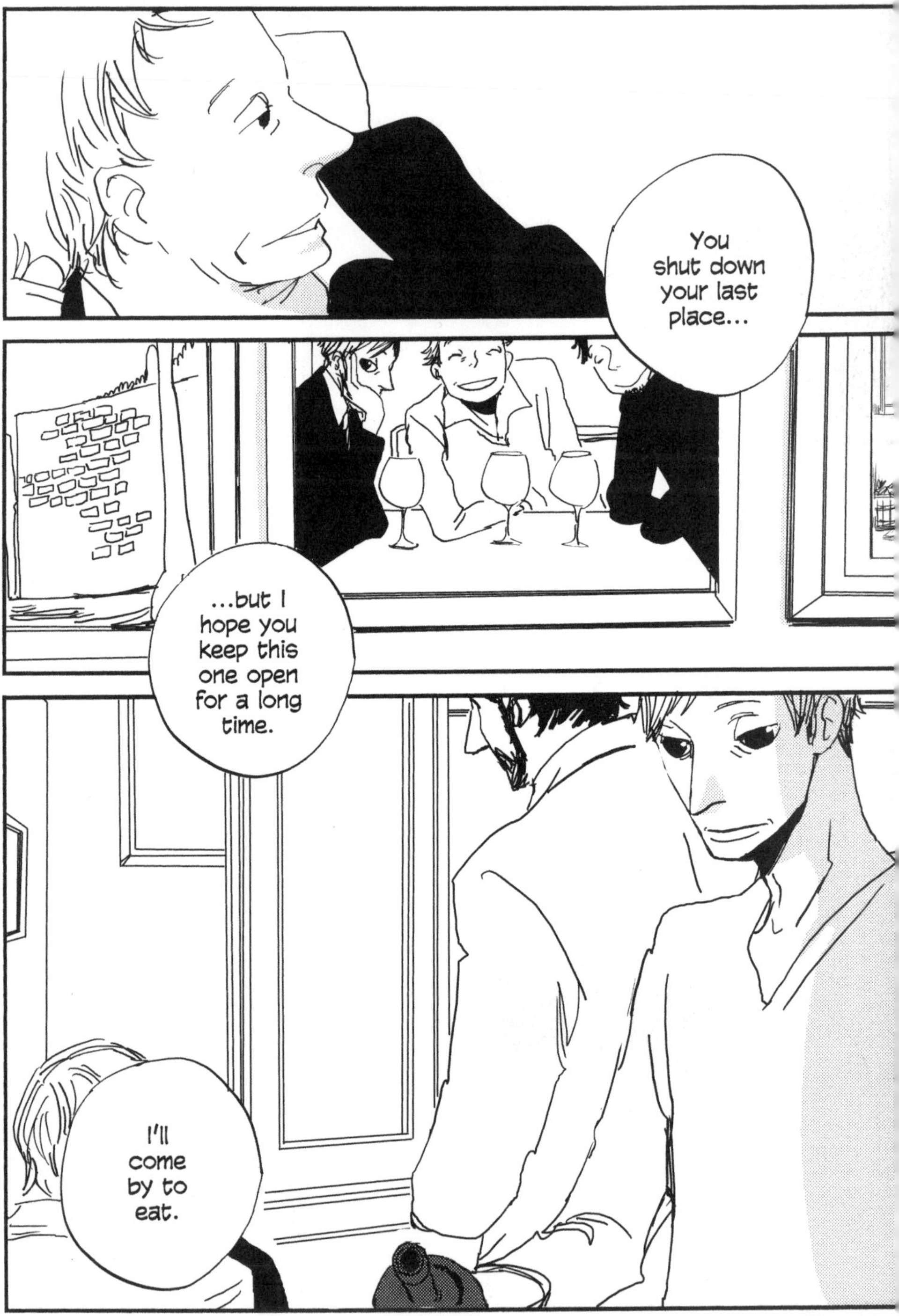
You shut down your last place...
...but I hope you keep this one open for a long time.
I'll come by to eat.

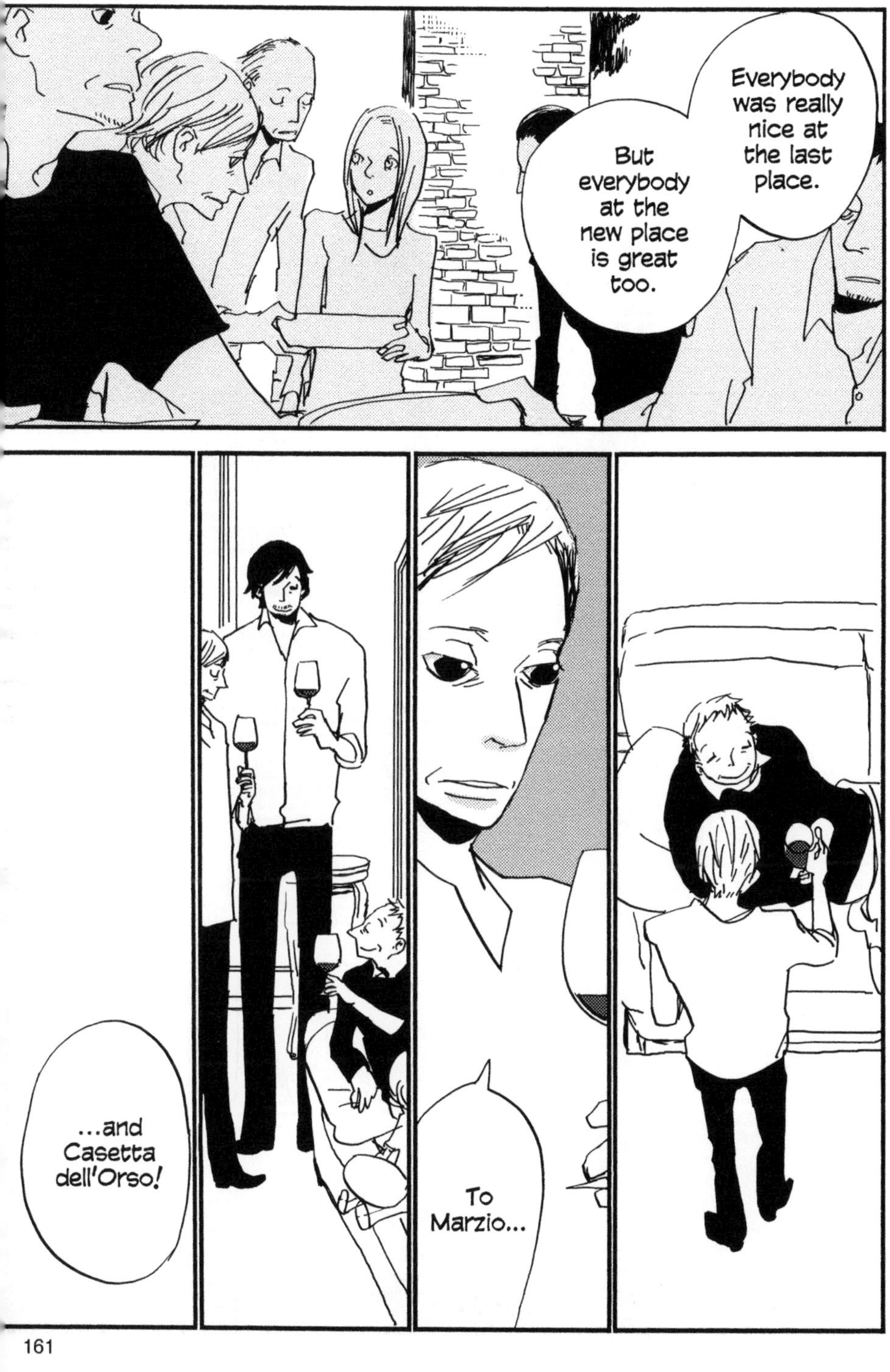
Everybody was really nice at the last place.
But everybody at the new place is great too.
To Marzio...
...and Casetta dell'Orso!

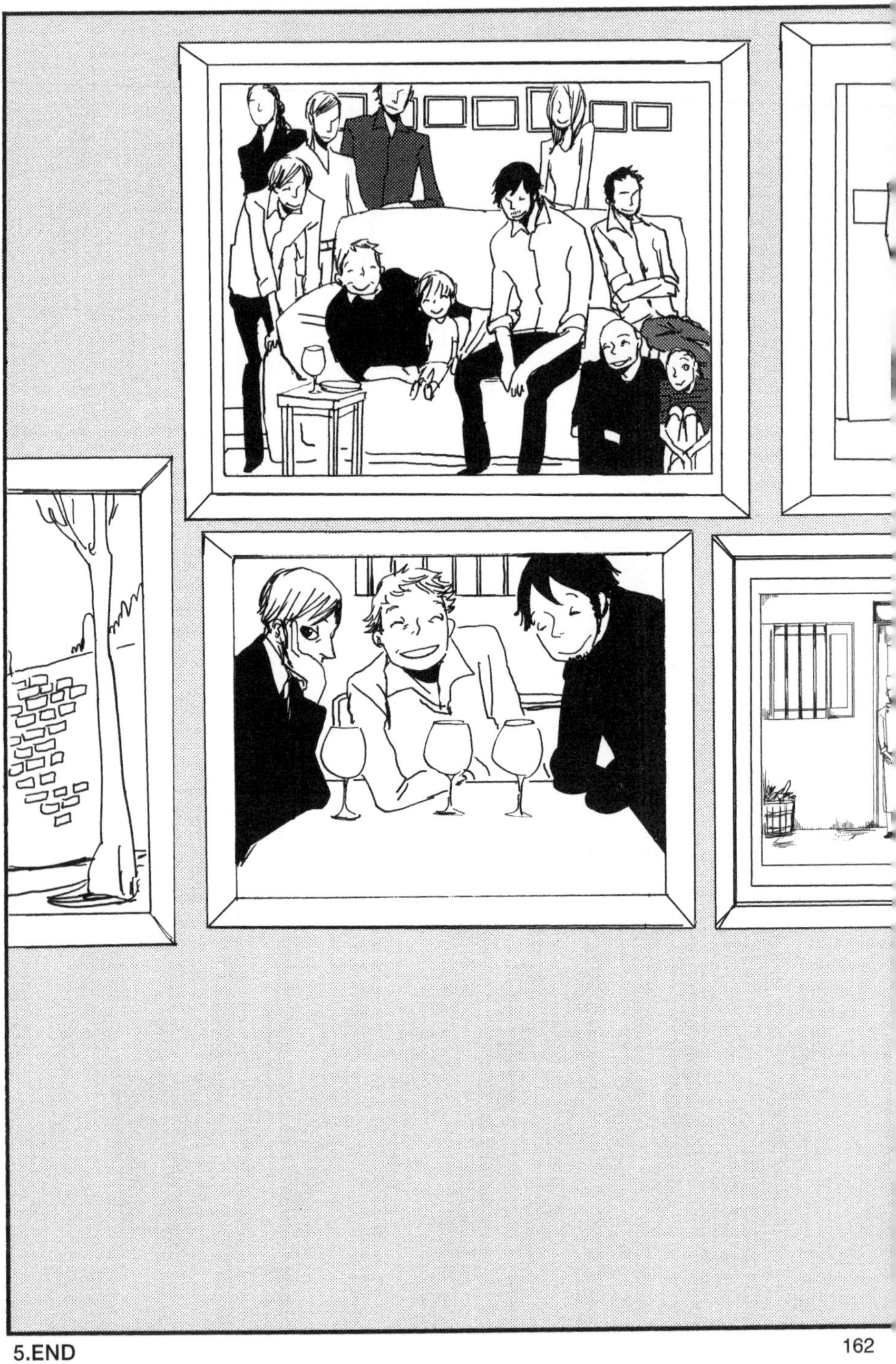

5.END

to be continued···

GENTE

buona serata

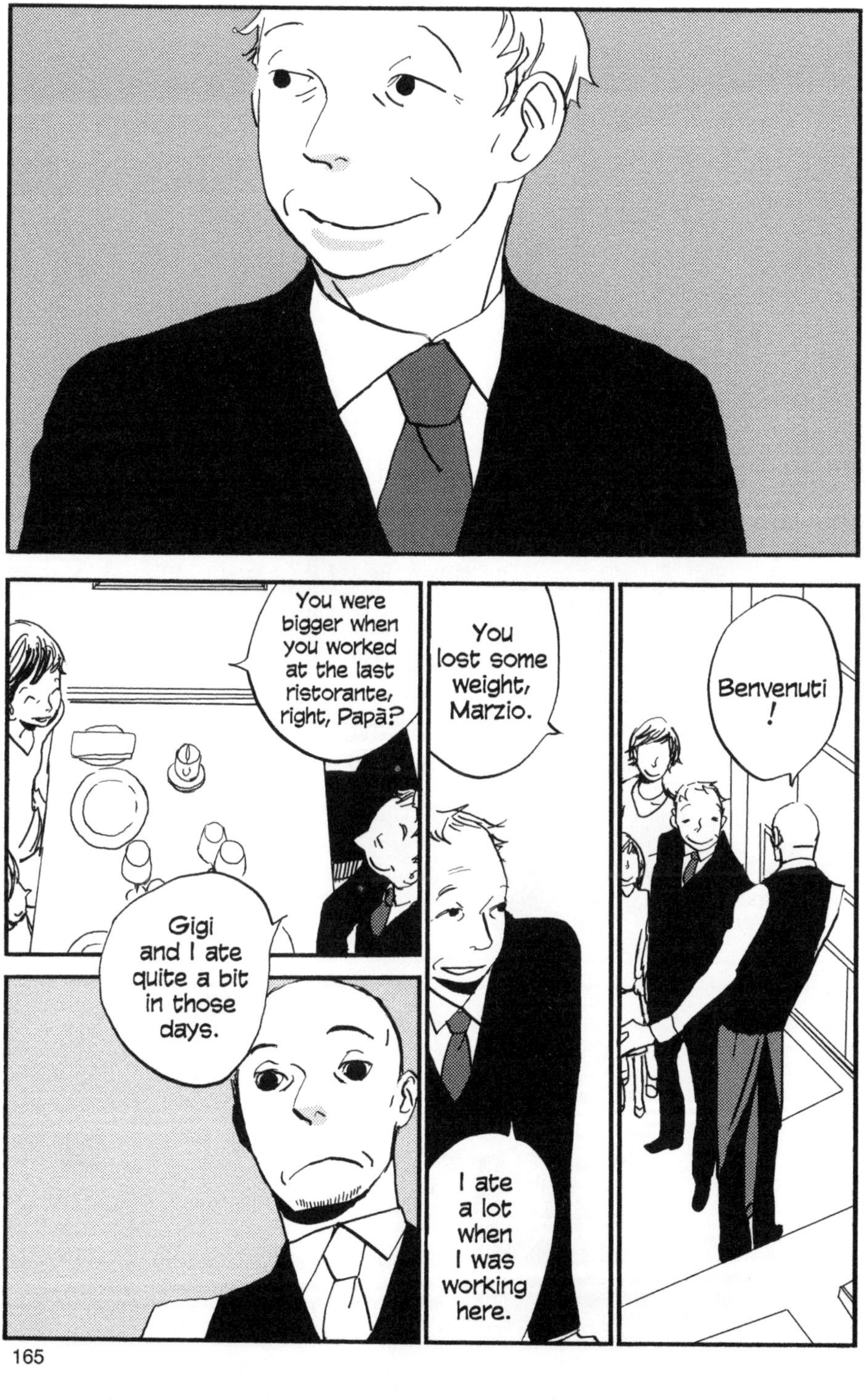
Benvenuti!
You lost some weight, Marzio.
I ate a lot when I was working here.
You were bigger when you worked at the last ristorante, right, Papà?
Gigi and I ate quite a bit in those days.

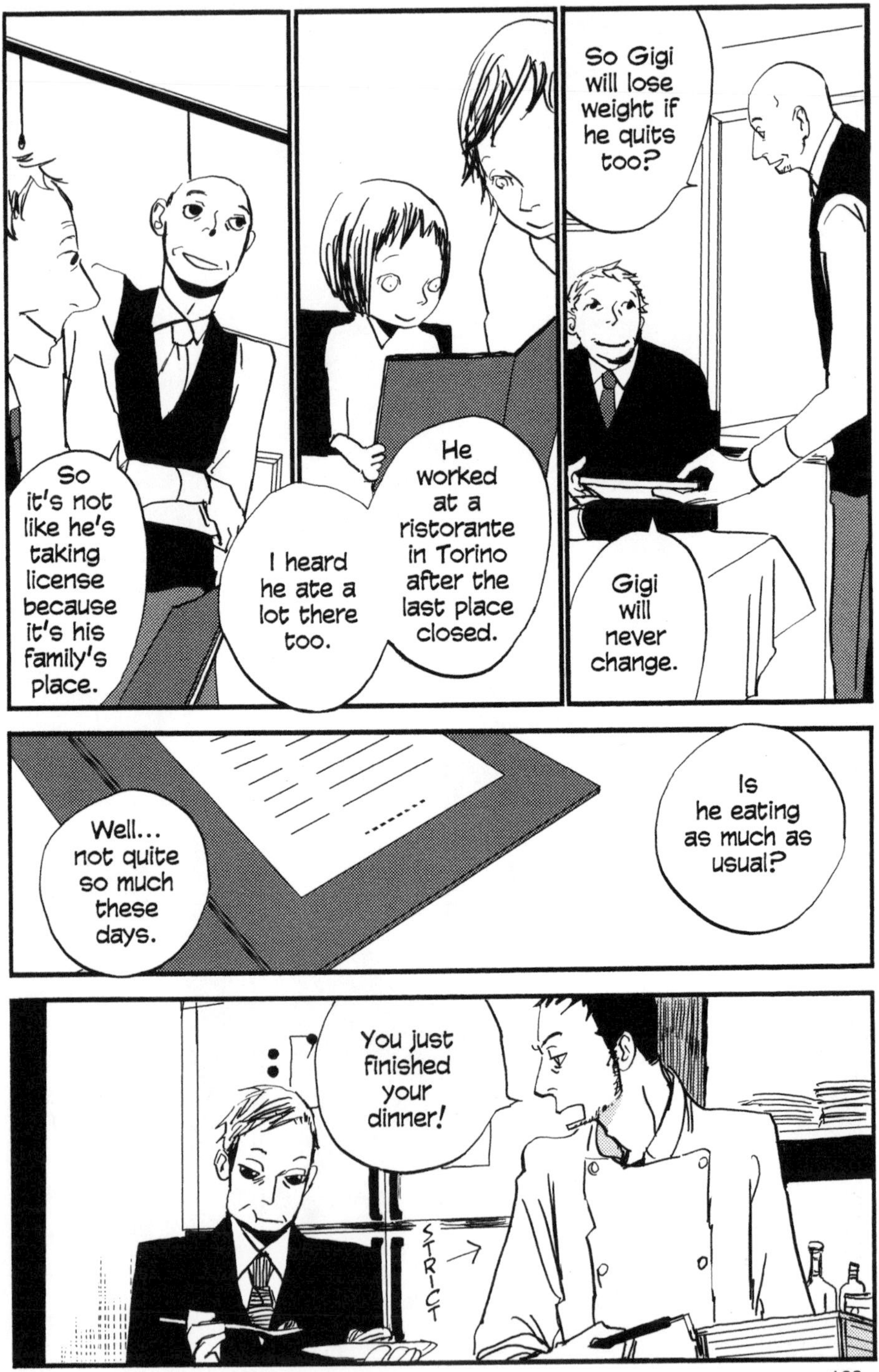
So Gigi will lose weight if he quits too?
Gigi will never change.
He worked at a ristorante in Torino after the last place closed.
I heard he ate a lot there too.
So it's not like he's taking license because it's his family's place.
Is he eating as much as usual?
Well... not quite so much these days.
You just finished your dinner!
STRICT
:

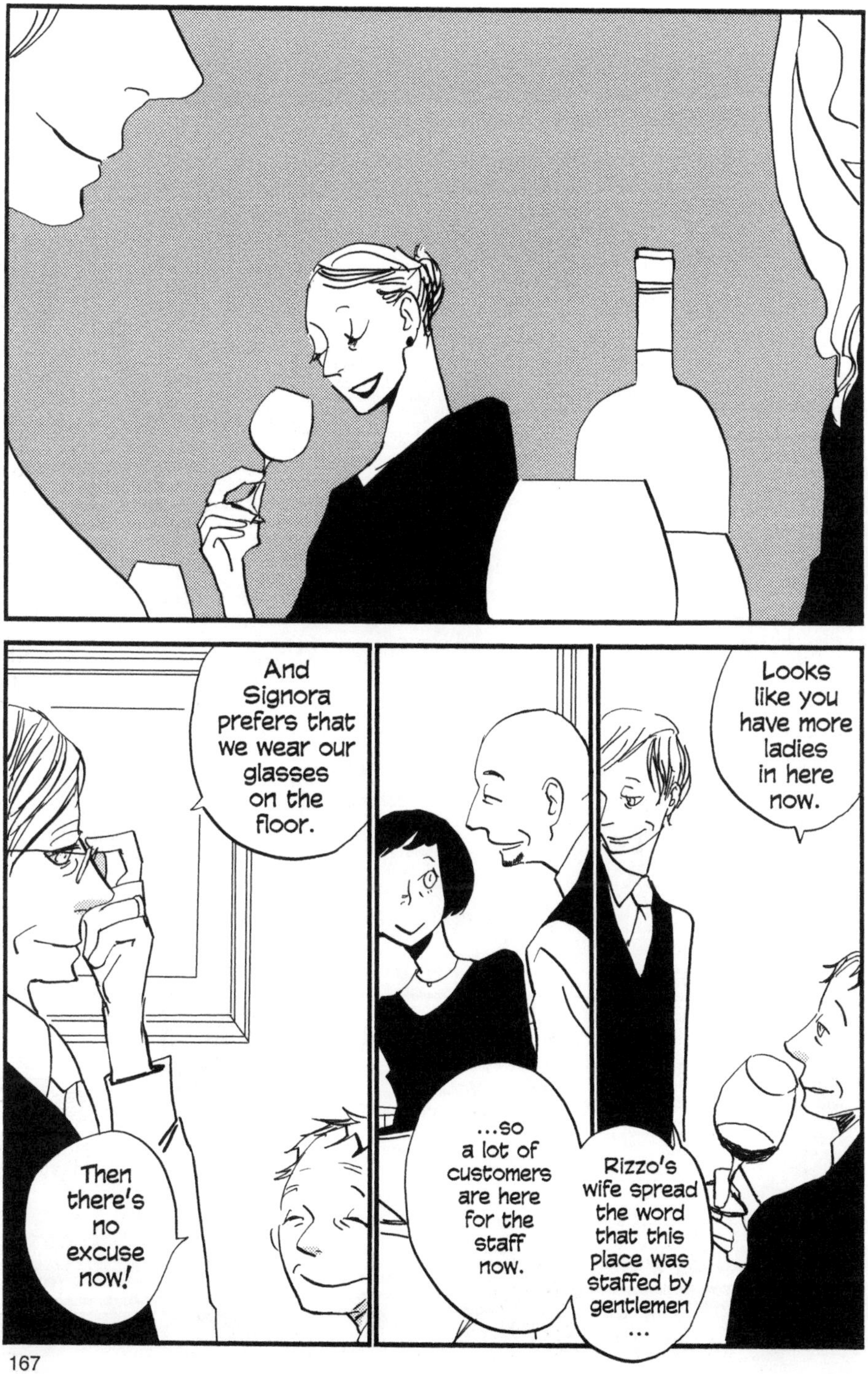
Looks like you have more ladies in here now.
Rizzo's wife spread the word that this place was staffed by gentlemen...
...so a lot of customers are here for the staff now.
And Signora prefers that we wear our glasses on the floor.
Then there's no excuse now!

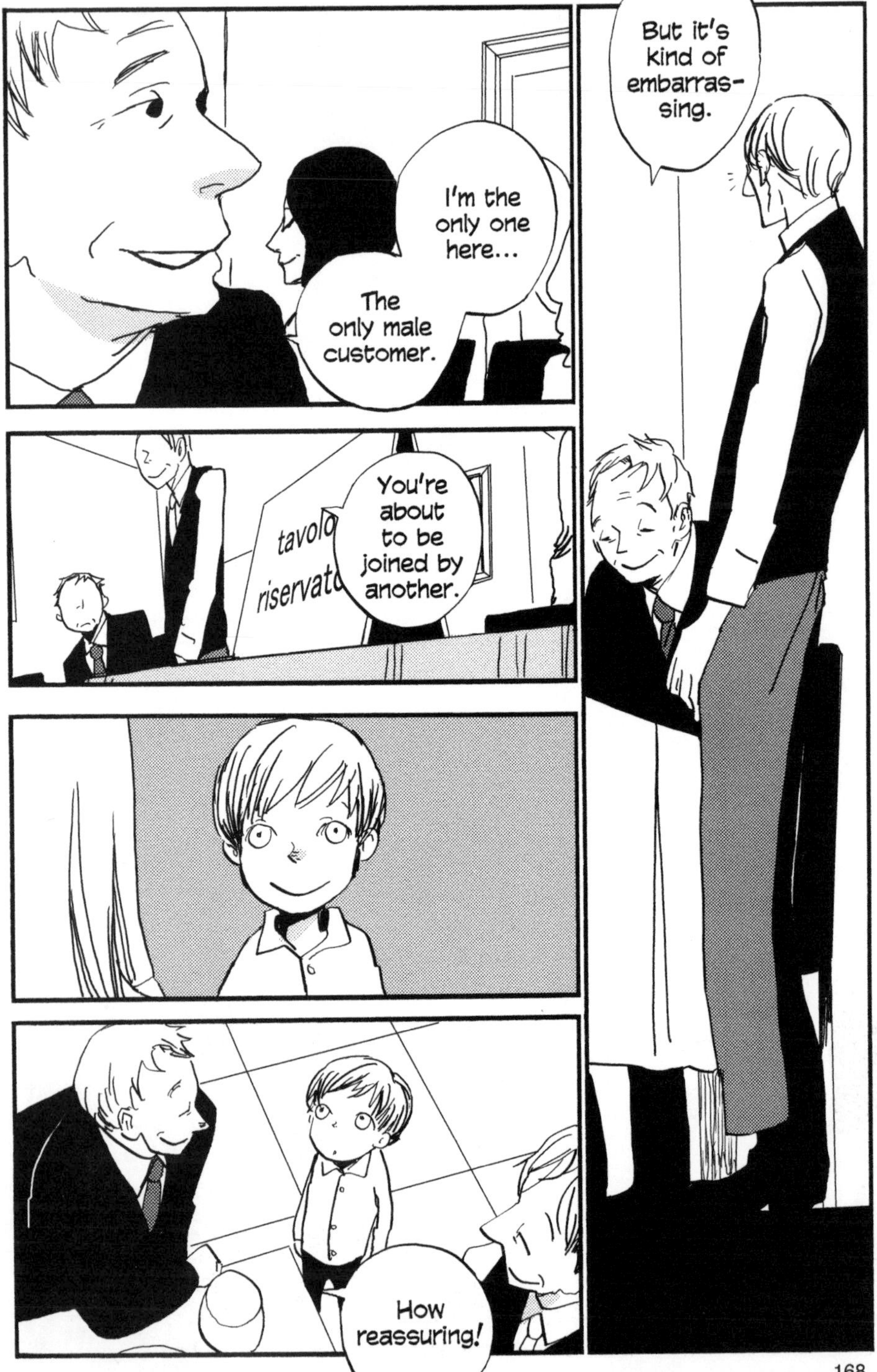
But it's kind of embarras-sing.
I'm the only one here...
The only male customer.
tavolo
riservat
You're about to be joined by another.
How reassuring!

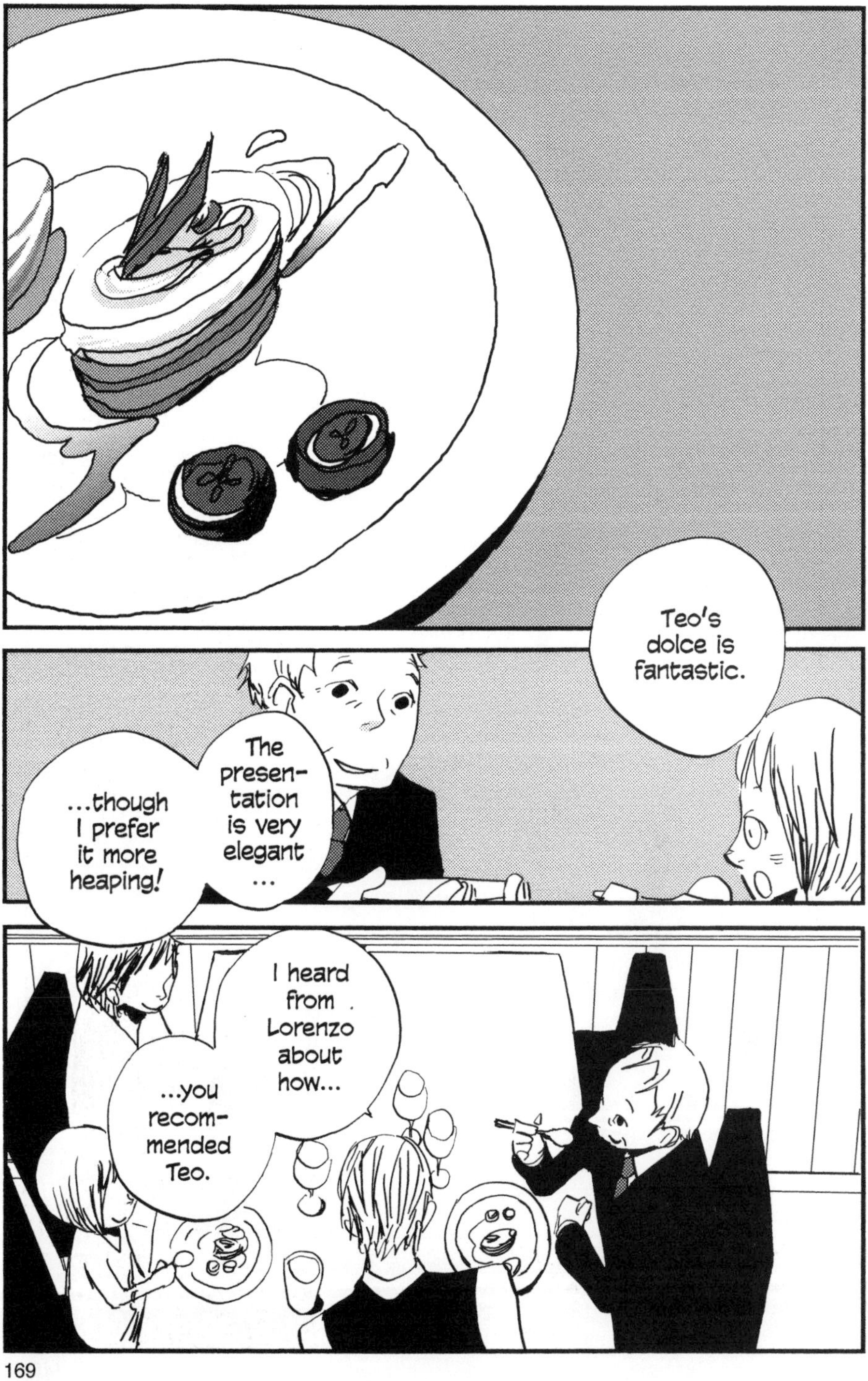
Teo's dolce is fantastic.
The presentation is very elegant...
...though I prefer it more heaping!
I heard from Lorenzo about how...
...you recommended Teo.

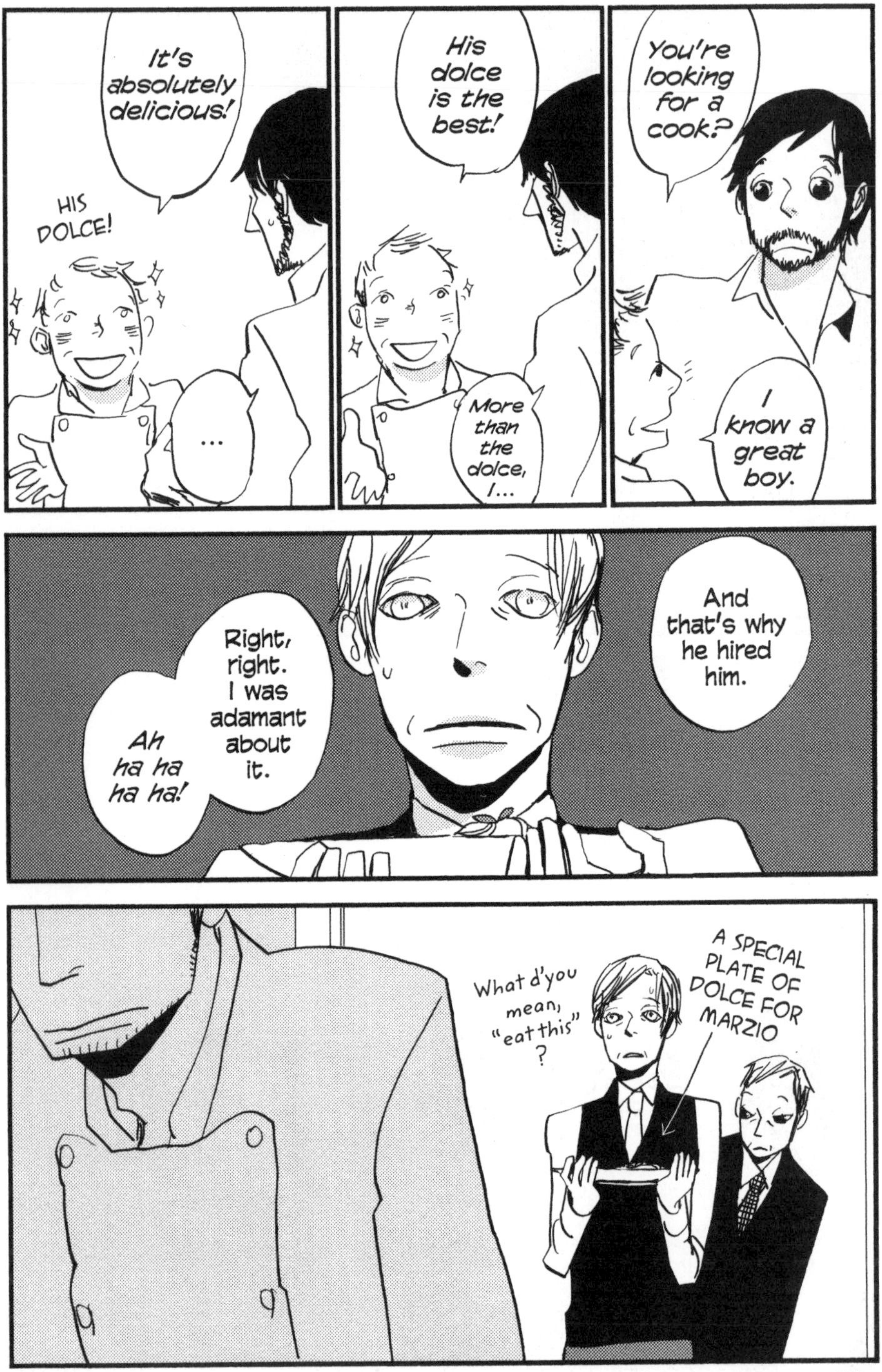
You're looking for a cook?
I know a great boy.
His dolce is the best!
More than the dolce, I...
It's absolutely delicious!
HIS DOLCE!
...
And that's why he hired him.
Right, right. I was adamant about it.
Ah ha ha ha ha!
A SPECIAL PLATE OF DOLCE FOR MARZIO
What d'you mean, "eat this"?

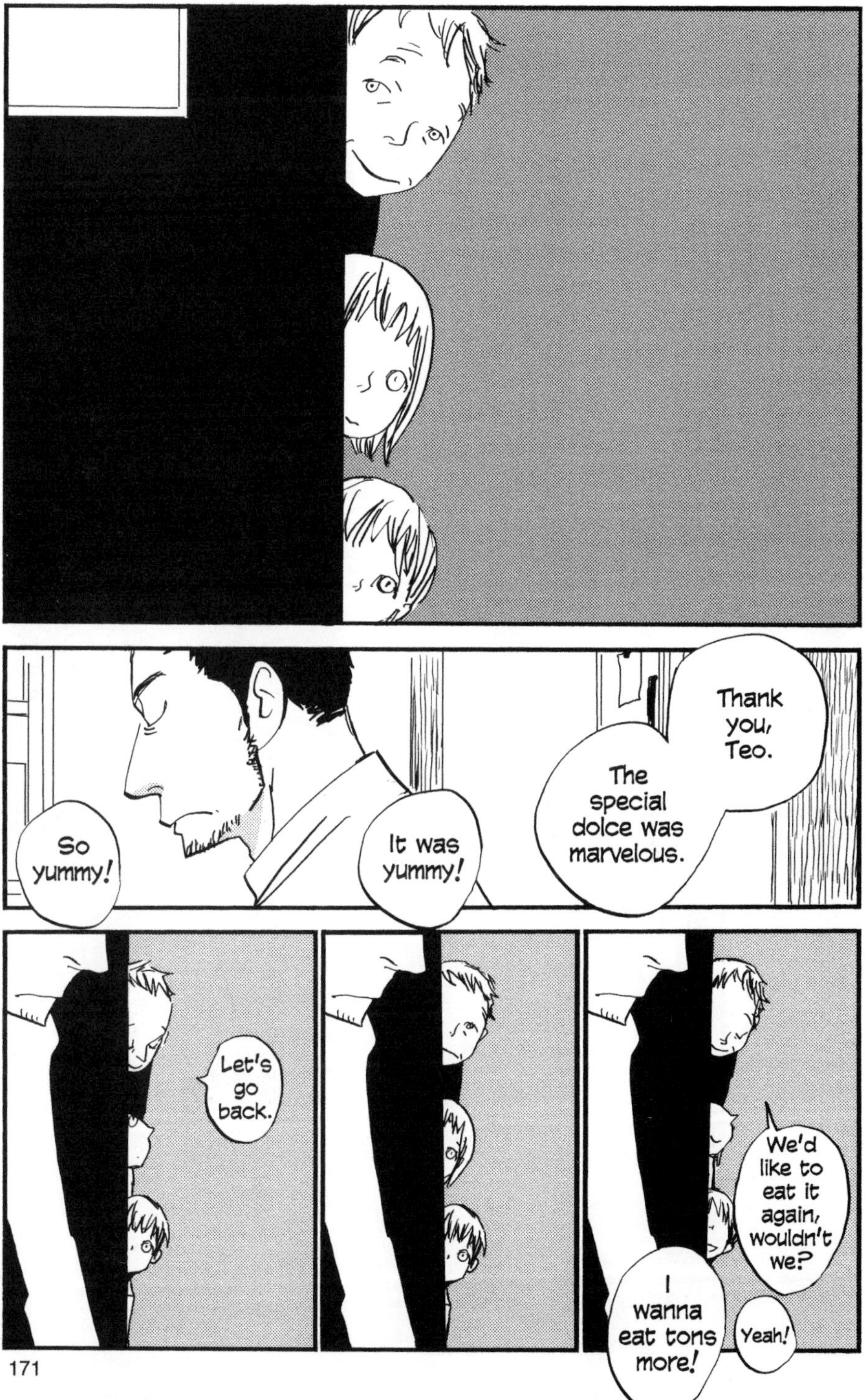
Thank you, Teo.
The special dolce was marvelous.
It was yummy!
So yummy!
We'd like to eat it again, wouldn't we?
Yeah!
I wanna eat tons more!
Let's go back.

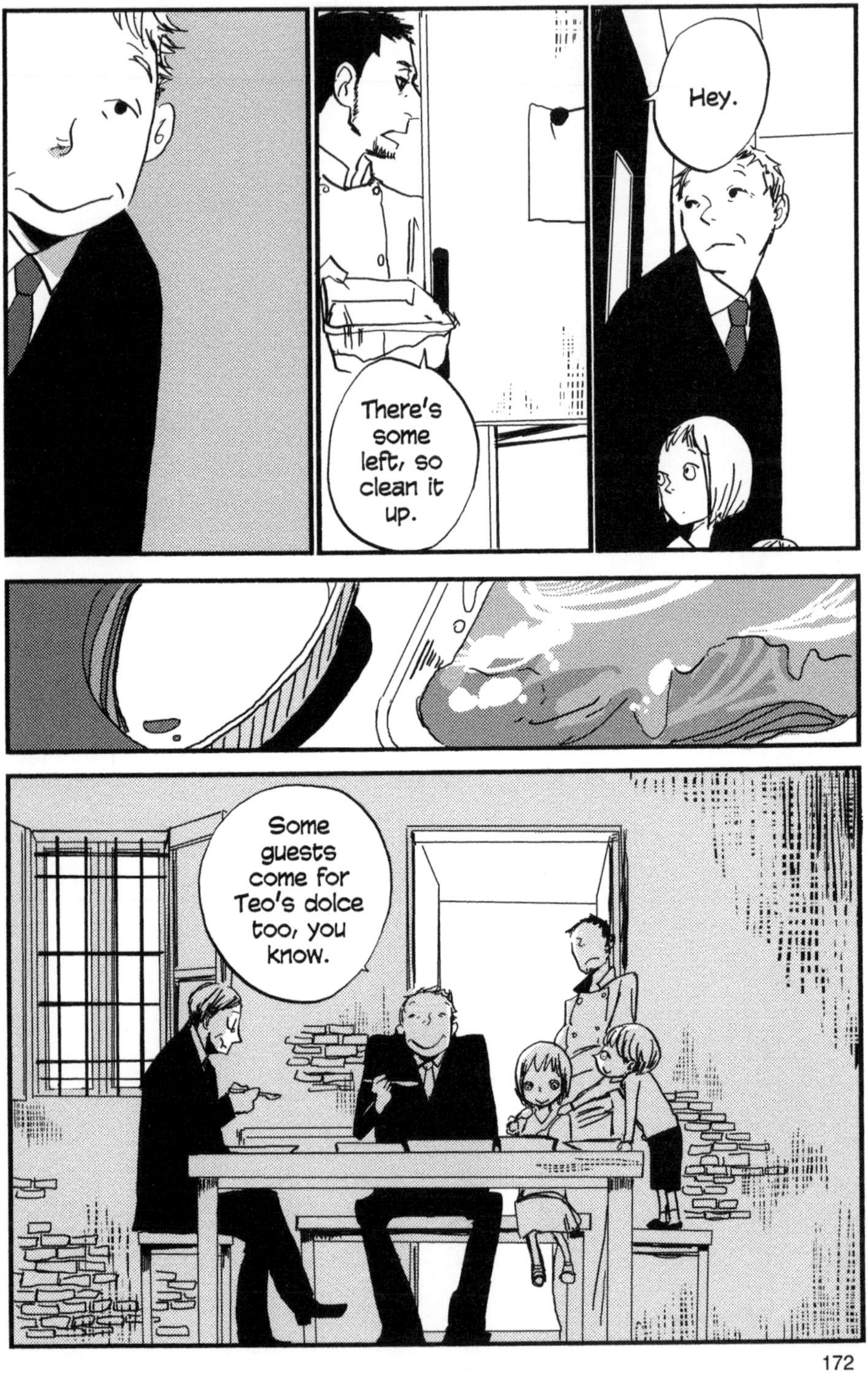
Hey.
There's some left, so clean it up.
Some guests come for Teo's dolce too, you know.

GENTE

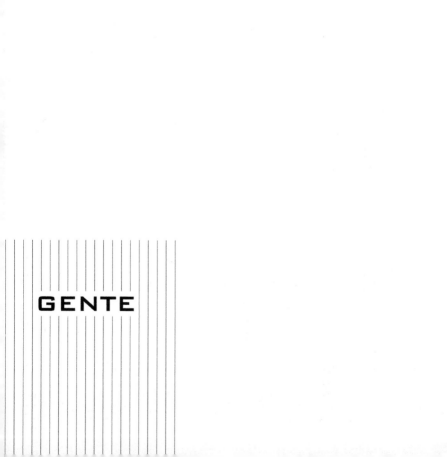

Useful Italian Expressions

aperitivo: a cocktail and/or a small plate before a meal

casetta dell'orso: little house of the bear

cucina: kitchen

benvenuti: welcome (greeting)

bon giorno: good day

buona sera: good evening (greeting)

buona serata: good evening (when taking leave)

barista: bartender

bella donna: beautiful woman

cameriere: waiter

capo cameriere: head waiter

cantina: wine shop

dolce: dessert, or sweet

enoteca: wine bar

nonno: grandpa

nonna: grandma

ristorante: a formal restaurant that focuses on haute cuisine

trattoria: a tavern, less formal than a ristorante

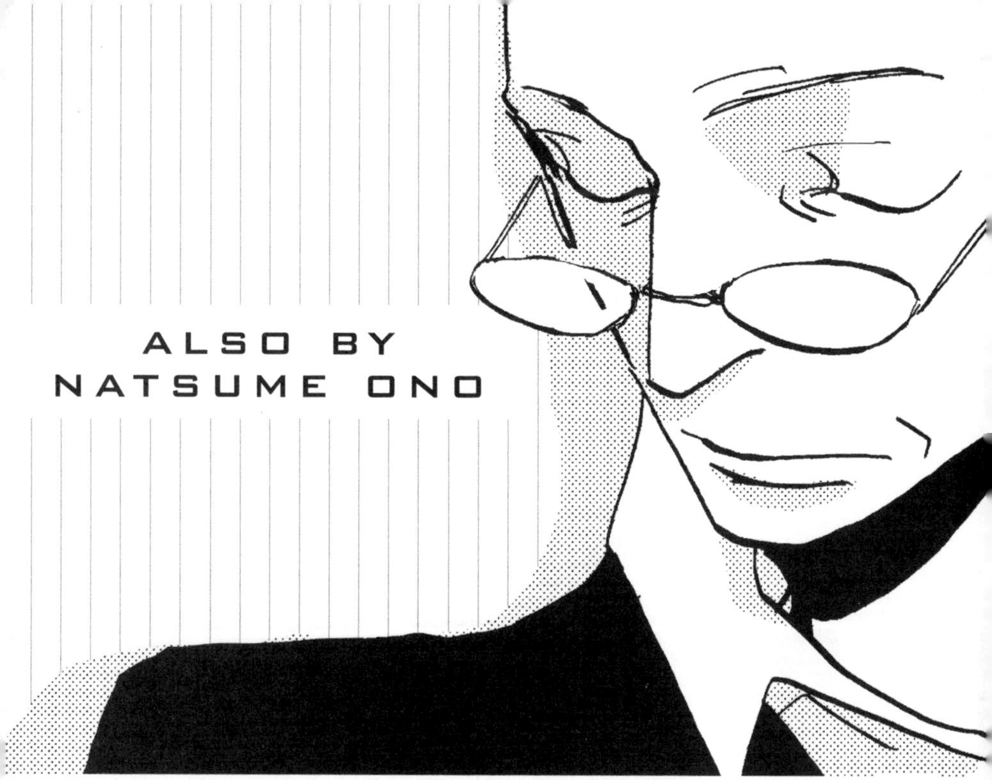

ALSO BY NATSUME ONO

NOW AVAILABLE IN BOOKSTORES

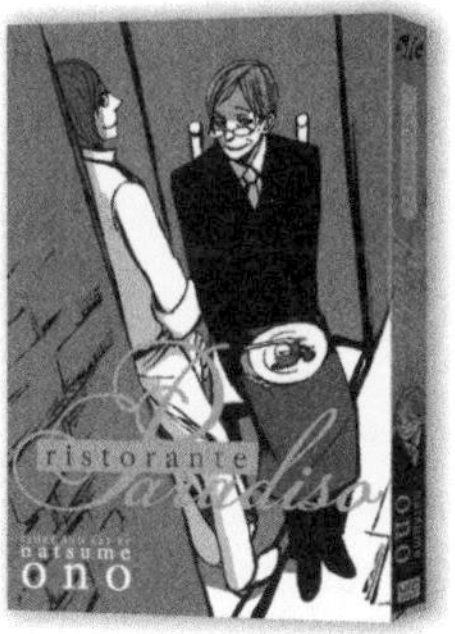

ristorante
Paradiso
natsume
ono

© 2006 NATSUME ONO

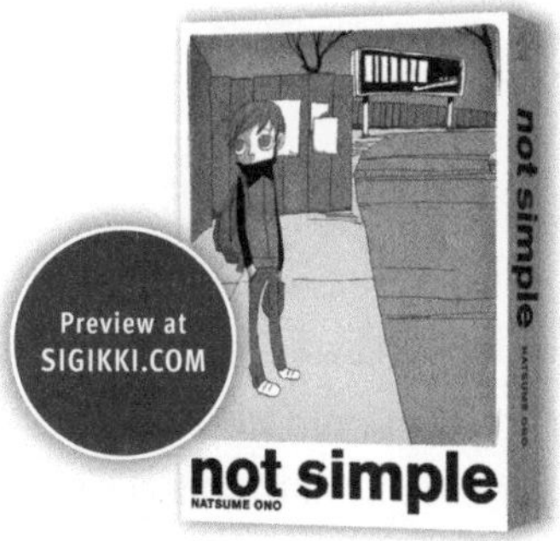

not simple
NATSUME ONO
Preview at
SIGIKKI.COM

© 2006 Natsume ONO/Shogakukan

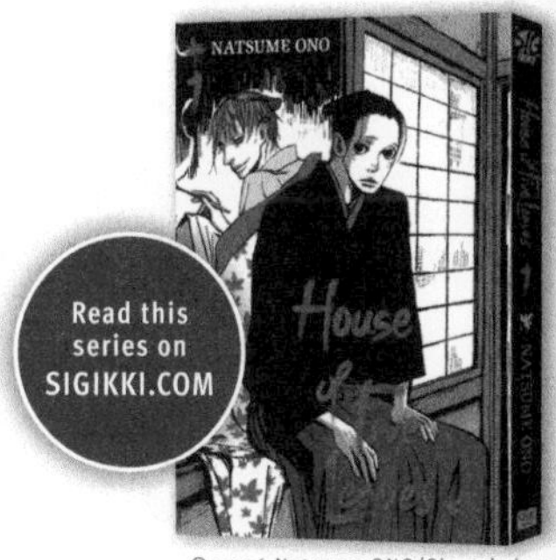

NATSUME ONO
House of Five Leaves
Read this
series on
SIGIKKI.COM

© 2006 Natsume ONO/Shogakukan

Ristorante Paradiso

The story that introduced Casetta dell'Orso, a charming little restaurant in the center of Rome staffed entirely by bespectacled gentlemen. A young woman named Nicoletta arrives one evening to confront her mother, who abandoned her years before. But an overwhelming crush on the restaurant's headwaiter, Claudio, leads Nicoletta down an unexpected path.

not simple

Ian, a young man with a fractured family history, travels from Australia to England to America in the hope of realizing his dreams and reuniting with his beloved sister. His story unfolds backwards through the framing narrative of Jim, a reporter driven to capture Ian's experiences in a novel: *not simple*.

House of Five Leaves

Masterless samurai Akitsu Masanosuke becomes a bodyguard for Yaichi, the charismatic leader of a gang called "Five Leaves." Although disturbed by the gang's sinister activities, Masa begins to suspect that Yaichi's motivations are not what they seem. The deeper he's drawn into the world of the Five Leaves, the more he finds himself fascinated by these mysterious outlaws.

GENTE
THE PEOPLE OF RISTORANTE PARADISO
VOLUME 1

VIZ SIGNATURE EDITION

STORY AND ART BY NATSUME ONO

TRANSLATION · Joe Yamazaki
TOUCH-UP ART & LETTERING · Rina Mapa
COVER DESIGN · Frances O. Liddell
EDITOR · Daniel Gillespie

© 2007 NATSUME ONO
First Published in Japan in 2007 by
OHTA PUBLISHING COMPANY

The stories, characters and incidents mentioned
in this publication are entirely fictional.

Printed in the U.S.A.

Published by VIZ Media, LLC
P.O. Box 77010
San Francisco, CA 94107

10 9 8 7 6 5 4 3 2 1
First printing, August 2010

www.viz.com   www.vizsignature.com

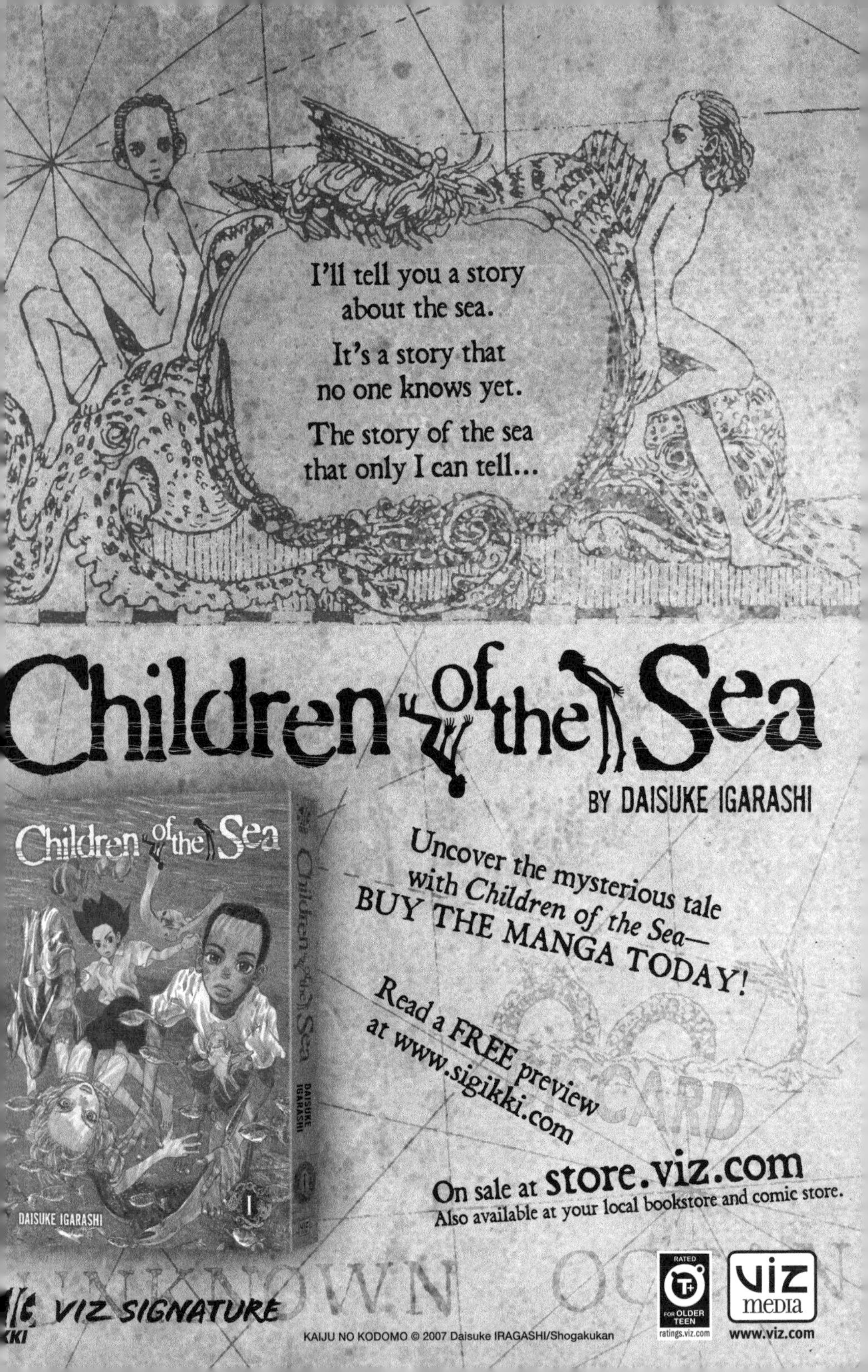
I'll tell you a story about the sea.
It's a story that no one knows yet.
The story of the sea that only I can tell...
Children of the Sea
BY DAISUKE IGARASHI
Children of the Sea
DAISUKE IGARASHI
1
Uncover the mysterious tale with *Children of the Sea*—
BUY THE MANGA TODAY!
Read a FREE preview at www.sigikki.com
On sale at store.viz.com
Also available at your local bookstore and comic store.
VIZ SIGNATURE
KAIJU NO KODOMO © 2007 Daisuke IRAGASHI/Shogakukan
RATED T+ FOR OLDER TEEN
ratings.viz.com
viz media
www.viz.com

THIS IS THE
LAST PAGE OF
THIS BOOK.

Gente reads left to right to preserve
the intended orientation of the art.